"The presentation of embracing diversity is done w with this in regard to presenting the concept. The b concept and keeping it simple and to the point."
—Gayle Fisher, Profes

"I like that the key terms are given at the beginning of the chapter. It helps to know what is important while reading. I also like that the key definitions are put in the margins. It makes it easier for reviewing and studying."
—Joe Hoff, student at University of Wisconsin–LaCrosse

Online Study Center
Prepare for Class

Online Study Center
Improve Your Grade

Online Study Center
ACE the Test

Do you find the marginal callouts useful?

#	Answer		Number of Responses	Percentage
1	Strongly agree		166	38.16%
2	Agree		207	47.59%
3	Somewhat agree		55	12.64%
4	Disagree		7	1.61%
	TOTAL:		**435**	**100.00%**

Mean : 1.777   Mean Percentile : 80.57%   Standard Deviation : 0.723

"It's nice that the book specifically tells you the resources you can use and where you can find them."
—Kristin Chimento, student at Miami University

Do you find the concept checks useful?

#	Answer		Number of Responses	Percentage
1	Strongly agree		117	27.08%
2	Agree		205	47.45%
	Somewhat agree		86	19.91%
	Disagree		24	5.56%
	TOTAL:		**432**	**100.00%**

Mean : 2.039   Mean Percentile : 74.02%   Standard Deviation : 0.831

CONCEPT CHECK 2.1

Do you think some majors or careers might be better suited to one learning style over another? Athletes may be more tactile-kinesthetic, physicians more visual. What about actors or accountants? How will your learning style influence your career choice? What challenges will you face?

"I like the quizzes and that the [text] is short and to the point."
—Fernando Monzon, student at Miami Dade College

Data in barcharts from student survey at San Francisco State University.

STUDENT ACHIEVEMENT SERIES

The Confident Student

Sixth Edition

Carol C. Kanar

Houghton Mifflin Company

Boston　　　New York

To Steve, Always

Vice President, Executive Publisher: *Patricia A. Coryell*
Executive Editor: *Mary Finch*
Sponsoring Editor: *Shani B. Fisher*
Marketing Manager: *Edwin Hill*
Marketing Associate: *Erin Timm*
Editorial Assistant: *Amanda Nietzel*
Senior Project Editor: *Fred Burns*
Editorial Assistant: *Katherine Roz*
Senior Art and Design Coordinator: *Jill Haber*
Cover Design Director: *Tony Saizon*
Senior Photo Editor: *Jennifer Meyer Dare*
Composition Buyer: *Chuck Dutton*
New Title Project Manager: *James Lonergan*

Cover image credit: © Randy Faris/CORBIS

Printed in the U.S.A.

Library of Congress Control Number: **2006931541**

Instructor's examination copy:
    ISBN-10: 0-618-83398-6
    ISBN-13: 978-0-618-83398-6

For orders, use student text ISBNs:
    ISBN-10: 0-618-76643-X
    ISBN-13: 978-0-618-76643-7

2 3 4 5 6 7 8 9—VH—10 09 08 07

brief contents

contents

14 BUILDING CAREER SKILLS 326

preface

▶ A TEAM APPROACH: THE FIRST BOOK BUILT BY PROFESSORS AND STUDENTS, FOR PROFESSORS AND STUDENTS

Over the past two years Houghton Mifflin has conducted research and focus groups with a diverse cross section of professors and students from across the country to create the first textbook that truly reflects what professors and students want and need in an educational product. Everything we have learned has been applied to create and build a brand new educational experience and product model from the ground up for our two very important customer bases. *Student Achievement Series: The Confident Student* is based on extensive professor and student feedback and is designed to meet the teaching needs of today's instructors as well as the learning, study, and assessment goals of today's students. Professors and students have been involved with every key decision regarding this new product development model and learning system—from content structure, to design, to packaging, to the title of the textbook, and even to marketing and messaging. Professors have also played an integral role as content advisors through their reviews, creative ideas, and contributions to this new textbook.

It has long been a Houghton Mifflin tradition and honor to partner closely with professors to gain valuable insights and recommendations during the development process. Partnering equally as closely with students through the entire product development and product launch process has proved also to be extremely gratifying and productive.

▶ WHAT STUDENTS TOLD US

Working closely with students has been both rewarding and enlightening. Their honest and candid feedback and their practical and creative ideas have enabled us to develop an educational learning model like no other on the market today.

Students have told us many things. While price is important to them, they are just as interested in having a textbook that reflects the way they actually learn and study. As with other consumer purchases and decisions they make, they want a textbook that is of true value to them. *Student Achievement Series: The Confident Student* accomplishes both of their primary goals: it provides them with a price-conscious textbook, and it presents the concepts in a way that pleases them.

Today's students are busy individuals. They go to school, they work, some have families, they have a wide variety of interests, and they are involved in many activities. They take their education very seriously. Their main goal is to master the materials so they can perform well in class, get a good grade, graduate, land a good job, and be successful.

Different students learn in different ways: some learn best by reading, some are more visually oriented, and some learn best by doing through practice and assessment. While students learn in different ways, almost all students told us the same things in terms of what they want their textbook to "look like." The ideal textbook for students gets to the point quickly, is easy to understand and read, has fewer and/or shorter chapters, has pedagogical materials designed to reinforce key concepts, has a strong supporting website for quizzing, testing, and assessment of materials, is cost conscious, and provides them with real value for their dollar.

Students want smaller chunks of information versus long sections and paragraphs typical of traditional textbooks. This format provides them with immediate reinforcement and allows them to assess the concepts they have just studied. They like to read materials in bulleted formats that are easier to digest than long sections and paragraphs. They almost always pay special attention to key terms and any materials that are boldfaced or highlighted in the text. In general they spend little time reading or looking at materials that they view as superficial, such as many of the photographs (although they want some photos for visual enhancement) and boxed materials. However, they do want a textbook that is visually interesting, holds their interest, and is designed in an open, friendly, and accessible format. They want integrated web and technology components that focus on quizzing and provide them with an interactive place to go to for help and assessment. They don't want web sites that simply duplicate what is in the textbook or that provide information that is not essential to understanding the text's key concepts.

While students learn and study in a variety of different ways, a number of students told us that they often attend class first to hear their professor lecture and to take notes. Then they go back to read the chapter after (not always before) class. They use their textbook in this fashion to get not only the information they need, but to reinforce what they have learned in class. Students told us that they study primarily by using index or flash cards that highlight key concepts and terms, by reading lecture notes, and by using the supporting book web site for quizzing and testing of key concepts. They also told us that they are far more likely to purchase and use a textbook if their professor actively utilizes the textbook in class and tells them that they need it.

▶ ## Taking What Professors and Students Told Us to Create Student Achievement Series: The Confident Student

Student Achievement Series: The Confident Student provides exactly what students want and need pedagogically in an educational product. While other textbooks on the market include some of these features, the *Student Achievement Series* is the first to incorporate fully all of these cornerstones, as well as introducing innovative new learning methods and study processes to completely fulfill the wishes of today's students. It does this by:

- Presenting information that is concise and to the point

- Organizing more content in bulleted lists or succinct formats

- Highlighting and boldfacing key concepts and information

- Creating a design that is open, user friendly, and interesting for today's students

- Developing a supporting and integrated web component that focuses on assessment of key concepts through quizzing and other means

- Selecting meaningful photos, graphics, and other traditional chapter components that students will not view as superficial

- Creating a product that is easier for students to read and study

- Providing students with a price-conscious product

- Providing students with a product they regard as valuable

When we asked students to compare a chapter from this new learning model versus chapters from other traditional competing textbooks, students overwhelmingly rated this new product model as far superior in terms of providing them with the kind of textbook they want.

▶ PROFESSORS AND STUDENTS: WE COULDN'T HAVE DONE IT WITHOUT YOU

We are very grateful to all of the students across the country who participated in one form or another in helping us create and build the first educational product pedagogically designed specifically for them and their learning and educational goals. Working with these students was an honor, as well as a lot of fun, for all of us at Houghton Mifflin. We sincerely appreciate their honesty, candor, creativeness, and interest in helping us to develop a better learning experience. We also appreciate their willingness to meet with us for lengthy periods of time and to allow us to videotape them and use some of their excellent quotes. We wish them much success as they complete their college education, begin their careers, and go about their daily lives.

Student Participants

Adam Delaney-Winn, Tufts University

Adrienne Rayski, Baruch College

Alison Savery, Tufts University

Aliyah Yusuf, Lehman College

Angelique Cooper, DePaul University

Angie Brewster, Boston College

Barry Greenbaum, Cooper Union

Caitlin Offinger, Amherst College

Catie Connolly, Anna Marie College

Cheng Lee, University of Wisconsin LaCrosse

Christina Fischer, University of Illinois at Chicago

Cyleigh Brez, Miami University

Danielle Gagnon, Boston University

Donna Gonzalez, Florida International University

Durrell Queen, University of NY

Emma Harris, Miami University

Erika Hill, University of Florida

Evan Miller, Parsons School of Design

Fernando Monzon, Miami Dade College

Fritz Kuhnlenz, Boston University

Gabriel Duran, Florida International University

Gerius Brantley, Florida Atlantic University

Giovanni Espinoza, Hunter College

Gregory Toft, Baruch College

Helen Wong, Hunter College

Henry Lopez, Florida International University

Jessie Lynch, Miami University

Joe Barron, Providence College

Joe Hoff, University of Wisconsin LaCrosse

Jordan Simkovi, Northwestern University

Karissa Teekah, Lehman College

Katie Aiken, Miami University

Kevin Ringel, Northwestern University

Kristin Vayda, Miami University

Kristin Chimento, Miami University

Laura Beal, Miami University

Laura Schaffner, Miami University

Lindsey Lambalot, Northeastern University

Maggie Dolehide, Miami University

Marika Michalos, City College of New York

Matt Janko, University of Massachusetts Amherst

Matt Nitka, University of Wisconsin LaCrosse

Matthew Dripps, Miami University

Matthew Konigsberg, Baruch College

Michael Werner, Baruch College

Nichelina Mavros, Fordham University

O'Neil Barrett, Borough of Manhattan Community College

Patrick Thermitus, Bentley College

Paulina Glater, DePaul University

Rachel Hall, Miami University

Rebecca Tolles, Miami University

Rehan Noormohammad, Northeastern Illinois University

Rita Diz, Lehman College

Robert White, DePaul University

Ryan Bis, Boston University

Sam Trzyzewski, Boston University

Sarah Marith, Boston University

Stephanie DiSerio, Miami University

Steven Lippi, Boston College

Tanya Fahrenbach, Benedictine University

Travis Keltner, Boston College

Vanessa Uribe, Florida International University

Veronica Calvo, Keiser College

525 Students in MKTG 431: Principles of Marketing, San Francisco State University

Working with these students
was an honor. . . . We sincerely
appreciate their honesty, candor,
creativeness, and interest in
helping us to develop a better
learning experience.

We are equally as grateful to all of the professors across the country who participated in the development and creation of this new textbook through content reviews, advisory boards, and/or focus group work regarding the new pedagogical learning system. As always, professors provided us with invaluable information, ideas, and suggestions that consistently helped to strengthen our final product. We owe them great thanks and wish them much success in and out of their classrooms.

Professor Participants and Reviewers

Phyllis Ary, Ouachita Baptist University, AR

Susan Bierster, Palm Beach Community College, FL

Ann Fellinger, Pulaski Technical College, AZ

Gayle Fisher, Tallahassee Community College, FL

Carolyn Hart, South Arkansas Community College

Sheryl Hartman, Miami Dade College, FL

Grace Kehrer, Middlesex Community College, NJ

Jeanine C. Long, Ph.D., Southwest Georgia Technical College

Jaseon Outlaw, Arizona State University

Peggy G. Perkins, University of Nevada, Las Vegas

Candace R. Ready, Piedmont Technical College, SC

Rebecca Samberg, Housatonic Community College, CT

Anna E. Shiplee, University of West Florida

Elizabeth Shumway, Lakeland College, WI

Holly Smith, Lake Community College, FL

Rhonda Westerhaus, Pratt Community College, KS

Dr. Richard W. Williams, Northwestern State University, LA

> **As always, professors provided us with invaluable information, ideas, and suggestions that consistently helped to strengthen our final product.**

▶ THE CONFIDENT STUDENT

The Confident Student, Sixth Edition, is informed by my desire to help students gain the confidence that comes from self-knowledge and achievement to meet the challenges of college, life, and work. The vital study skills, critical thinking strategies, self-discovery techniques, and self-management tools that made previous editions of *The Confident Student* successful have been retained with the *Student Achievement Series*. Prominent features include *Awareness Checks, Confidence Builders, Computer Confidence, Critical Thinking, Your Reflections,* and *Thinking Ahead About Career*, along with themed exercises that address learning styles, collaboration, and computer/Internet applications that have transitioned to the new edition with updates. The *Online Study Center* supplements the sixth edition in a more streamlined web site. As those who have used previous editions have learned, students who use *The Confident Student* will find in this book all the strategies they need to become confident, successful, lifelong learners.

New to the Sixth Edition

The new *Student Achievement Series* design and concept for *The Confident Student* is the most exciting feature of the Sixth Edition. As the first Student Success textbook in Houghton Mifflin's Student Achievement Series, the Sixth Edition has special design elements that promote active reading and learning. The special design elements include the chapter opening photograph that reflects a central concept or chapter theme, with clearly stated objectives, a chapter outline, and list of key terms. Section headings are color coded to the objectives they address. Key terms and definitions are called out in the margins. Icons designate exercises by type and direct students to the Online Study Center where they can find additional learning resources. These textual aids promote student interaction with the text and enhance instructional delivery as well, by serving as reference points for both students and instructors.

A more intentional focus on the theme of confidence is evident in every chapter, beginning in Chapter 1 with Figure 1.1: Are You a Confident Student? This figure lists and defines fourteen traits of confident students. The second page of each chapter begins with a statement that addresses a trait for students to reflect on as they read about and apply chapter concepts.

Awareness Checks in several chapters have been recast in a Likert-type format to provide students and instructors with more information on the attitudes and skills they address.

Concept Check is a new feature that tests students' ability to apply chapter concepts to real-world situations. Each Concept Check is called out in the margin beside the chapter section that explains the concept addressed.

The Chapter Review has been moved to the end of each chapter, where it more logically follows as the summary feature. In the previous edition, the number of Chapter Review items varied, but now each review has ten items for consistency and ease of scoring.

Problem Solving has been moved from Chapter 4 to Chapter 3. This move serves two purposes: Problem solving is more clearly addressed as a critical thinking skill in Chapter 3. Chapter 4 now focuses exclusively on goal setting with more expanded coverage of the relationship between goals and values and how to make action plans for setting and reaching goals.

A new Chapter 10 combines concentration and memory, with emphasis on their role in processing information. A new introduction makes the connection between concentration and memory as part of an information-processing system that is enhanced by the use of active learning strategies. Also new are Awareness Check 16 and the critical thinking exercise.

Chapter 14 Building Career Skills has been updated with the latest Department of Labor projections for 2004–2014. The chapter also has a new introduction, new coverage on majors and careers, revised Awareness Checks, and a new Computer Confidence on researching careers online.

Computer Confidence in Chapters 1, 6, and 15 has been revised to reflect new technological developments and concerns about the use of technology.

The Online Study Center is a centralized new web site that absorbs the former student textbook web site and contains resources that have been revised for the Sixth Edition.

> **FEATURES RETAINED FROM THE FIFTH EDITION**

The Confident Student, Sixth Edition, continues to be a highly visual student-centered text with a strong academic base. The new Student Achievement Series design enhances these qualities. In addition, the text's signature features that promote active learning have been retained.

Awareness Checks in every chapter are brief checklists or assessment questionnaires that orient students to a chapter concept or discussion topic. Many of the Awareness Checks have been recast in a Likert-type format, followed by a brief explanation that helps students assess their attitudes, skills, and prior knowledge.

Confidence Builders in every chapter address learning strategies, attitudes, and career skills. Their purpose is to broaden students' understanding and build confidence by extending the discussion of chapter topics into related areas of interest or research. Students are encouraged to pursue these topics further by doing online searches using keywords that are provided.

Computer Confidence is a feature that provides students with an opportunity to build confidence using technology in school and beyond. Computer Confidence has been updated to reflect new trends and concerns about its use.

Critical Thinking exercises enhance the text's pedagogical foundation. Critical Thinking has a new format that improves its accessibility. Through this feature, students learn to integrate critical thinking naturally into their approach to studying and interacting in the classroom as they are asked to question, more fully process, and consider different viewpoints surrounding the issues and concepts presented in the chapter.

Your Reflections is a journaling activity that poses several questions for students to think about and respond to in writing. The Reflections provide an excellent opportunity for students to assess their progress, reflect on what they are learning, and plan ways to apply their new skills. The Reflections can also be used as a personal log, or as a springboard to discussion.

Exercises in every chapter, designated by icons, address learning styles, collaborative activities, and computer/Internet applications. Many of the exercises in the text and online have been revised and some are new. Internet exercises are available by accessing the Online Study Center at college.hmco. com/pic/KanarTCS6e.

> **AN EFFECTIVE TEACHING AND LEARNING PACKAGE**

FOR INSTRUCTORS

The Instructor's Resource Manual that accompanies *The Confident Student* contains an answer key for the exercises and chapter-by-chapter suggestions for using the text. Also included are sample course syllabi, a brief bibliography, a set of reproducible masters for overhead transparencies, and handouts to use as supplementary materials. Collaborative activities by Candy Ready of

Piedmont Technical College, the section on integrating SCANS workplace competencies with course objectives, and information on portfolio assessment in student success courses have been retained from the Fifth Edition. You can find the Instructor's Resource Manual, PowerPoint slides, as well as materials you may have previously used on the HM ClassPrep CD-Rom by visiting the **Online Teaching Center**, at college.hmco.com/pic/KanarTCS6e.

A new **Eduspace Course Cartridge** allows flexible, efficient, and creative ways to present learning materials and online interactions. This online course management system, powered by Blackboard, was created specifically for *The Confident Student*. With this new content students can dig deeper into the assessments, journal entries, and exercises. This resource provides first-year students with their first experience of online college courses. Eduspace content includes: practice exercises, journal prompts, homework and testing resources, collaborative exercise tools, vocabulary flashcards, discussion boards, and articles.

The Confident Student Eduspace course also includes the interactive Video Skillbuilders. These online exercises combine video clips featuring discussions with students, instructors, and experts, with articles and activities designed to give students a fully engaging learning experience. Topics include: time management, critical thinking, test taking, note taking, and health and wellness.

Instructors may also make use of an electronic gradebook, receive papers from students enrolled in the course via the Internet, and track student use of the communication and collaboration functions.

College Survival Consulting Services provide you with consultation and training for the design, implementation, and presentation of student success and first-year course. Through Team Up programs, our experienced consultants can provide help to you and your colleagues in establishing or improving your student success program. We offer assistance in course design, instructor training, teaching strategies, annual conferences, and much more. Call your College Survival Consultant today at 1-800-528-8323 or visit us online in the Online Teaching Center.

The HM Assessment and Portfolio Builder Etoken provides your students with online access to a personal assessment tool that assists them in preparing for lifelong learning. Students build a portfolio by responding to questions about their skills, attitudes, values, and behaviors in three key life areas: **Personal Growth, Career Growth,** and **Community Growth**. Each of these modules asks students to provide supporting evidence for questions where they rate themselves as highly proficient—great practice for critical thinking skills, as well as creating a résumé or preparing for interviews. An **Accomplishments Report** summarizes the results of their responses. The HMAPB also provides access to Houghton Mifflin's web-based **Career Resource Center**, which includes tips, exercises, articles, and ideas to help students succeed on their journey from college to career.

The **Houghton Mifflin Success Planner** is an 18-month, week-at-a-glance academic planner available as a package with this text. The Success Planners assists students in managing time both on and off campus, and includes additional reading about key learning strategies and life skills for success in college and beyond.

Package your textbook with one of our assessment tools, including the Retention Management System™ College Student Inventory (from Noel-Levitz). The CSI is an early-alert, early-intervention program that identifies students with tendencies that contribute to dropping out of school. Students can participate in an integrated, campus-wide program. Houghton Mifflin Company offers you three assessment options that evaluate students on 19 different scales: Form A (194 questions), Form B (100 questions), or an online etoken (that provides access to either Form). Advisors are sent three interpretive reports: The Student's Report, the Advisor/Counselor Report, and The College Summary and Planning Report.

The **Myers-Briggs Type Indicator® (MBTI®) Instrument*** is the most widely used personality inventory in history—and it is available for packaging with *The Confident Student*. The standard Form M self-scorable instrument contains 93 items that determine preferences on four scales: Extraversion-Introversion, Sensing-Intuition, Thinking-Feeling, and Judging-Perceiving. Talk to your sales rep about completing our qualifications form for administering the MBTI on your campus.

Videos to support your course are available to adopters of this textbook. **The Interviewing Process: Strategies for Making the Right Impression** (ISBN: 0-618-37982-7) takes students through the interviewing process from start to finish, with strategies to be successful in a job search with simulated interview scenarios. **Money and Finances** (0-618-38255-0) discusses strategies to help students develop the skills of good money management, including the pitfalls of credit-card spending and a discussion of financial aid. Contact your sales representative, or call Faculty Services at 1-800-733-1717 to get a copy of these videos for your classroom.

FOR STUDENTS

The Online Study Center includes a Skill Builder Library where students can read articles and do exercises to improve proficiency in math, writing, science, vocabulary, and research skills. This feature also includes the Confidence Builder Web Search where students can investigate the concepts from the textbook in online search exercises.

Students can use the Interactive Skill Finder to help determine their confidence index: a measure of what they already know about the skills covered in the textbook and what needs improving. This web site also includes the following articles and exercises: Remembering Cultural Differences, Internal/External Distractors, Textbook Exercises, Flashcards, ACE Practice Tests, Additional Exercises for Review, Locus of Control quizzes, and Glossary.

 ACKNOWLEDGMENTS

First of all, I thank my husband, Stephen P. Kanar, for being the person he is and for steadfastly providing the encouragement and support I needed to complete the Sixth Edition.

* *MBTI and Myers-Briggs Type Indicator are registered trademarks of Consulting Psychologists Press, Inc.*

A book is the product of many people's efforts. I am indebted to everyone at Houghton Mifflin who contributed to the development and production of the Sixth Edition, and I especially want to thank these people: Pat Coryell and Mary Finch, I am grateful for your enthusiastic support throughout several editions of *The Confident Student*. Shani Fisher, your wide range of knowledge on a variety of topics continues to amaze and inspire me. Thank you for sharing. To Amanda Nietzel who saw this book through to its completion, thank you. To Fred Burns who has worked with me over the years and who managed the production of *The Confident Student*, again I say "Thanks for a job well done." Kudos to Jill Haber, Chuck Dutton, and Katherine Roz for your work on the production of this book. Thank you, Vickie Putman for your work in securing permissions. My appreciation goes to Judith Krimski and Karen Lindsay for the superb new design and art work that enhances the Sixth Edition. To Edwin Hill and Evelyn Yang, I express my thanks for your contributions to the success of the Sixth Edition. I also want to remember Andrew Sylvester whose influence is reflected this edition. Thank you all.

To the reviewers (listed earlier) who read my manuscript and provided me with many fine suggestions for developing the new Student Achievement Series edition, you have my thanks.

Finally, I remain deeply grateful to the many students whose hopes and achievements inspire each new edition of this book. Wherever you are, I wish you the fulfillment of your dreams.

I would invite your feedback on this book. Tell me what works and what doesn't work for you. I would be grateful for any suggestions you have that will help me to improve the text. The most efficient way to reach me is through e-mail at collegesurvival@hmco.com.

CCK

To the Student

Student Achievement Series: The Confident Student, Sixth Edition, is designed to help you define your goals and develop the thinking skills, learning strategies, and personal qualities essential to academic and career success. This book includes thorough discussions, illustrations, easy-to-understand suggestions, and special design elements that will help you become a confident student and lifelong learner.

How to Use this Book

Begin with the Skill Finder on pages xxiv–xxxii, which precede Chapter 1. Use it to get an idea of what the book covers, to discover which learning strategies you need to develop or improve, and to find out which chapters may be the most useful to you. In addition, try these suggestions to get the most you can out of *The Confident Student.*

1. Look at the chapter-opening photograph and read the objectives. Glance over the chapter outline and list of key terms. Based on your examination of these features, what questions come to mind? This pre-reading activity will help you assess your prior knowledge about the chapter's topic and will prepare you for maximum learning.

2. Read each chapter one section at a time. If you have questions, write them in the margin or in a notebook so you can bring them up in class discussion.

3. Pay special attention to the photographs, figures, and other visual elements that may clarify and expand your understanding of chapter concepts.

4. Complete the Awareness Checks. Do the chapter exercises and try out the suggestions in the Confidence Builders, Computer Confidence boxes, and Critical Thinking boxes to reinforce your grasp of each new strategy or skill.

5. To relate what you are learning to real-world situations in life and work, complete Thinking Ahead About Career. Access the Career Resource Center to further explore articles and exercises related to your success after college.

6. Do the Concept Checks in each chapter.

7. For personal assessment of what you have learned and how it may affect your life, complete Your Reflections at the end of each chapter.

8. To round out your understanding of a chapter, complete the Chapter Review.

9. Finally, talk over the chapter with a friend or with members of a study group. Discussing a chapter is an excellent way to review it and fill in any gaps in your understanding.

Skill Finder

This questionnaire will help you determine your *confidence index:* a measure of what you already know about the skills covered in this book and which skills need developing or improving. Read each statement. How confident are you that you possess the skill or knowledge that the statement describes? Check the column that best expresses your level of confidence: *Very Confident, Fairly Confident, Not Very Confident,* or *Not Confident.* Give yourself 3 points for a check in the *Very Confident* column, 2 points for a check in the *Fairly Confident* column, 1 point for a check in the *Not Very Confident* column, and no points for a check in the *Not Confident* column. Add your points and write your score in the space labeled *Section Total.* When you have completed your Skill Finder, transfer your section totals to Table 1 on page xxxi, add them, and write your score in the space labeled *Grand Total.* Use your section totals and grand total from Table 1 to help you find your confidence index for each section (Table 2, p. xxxii) and your overall confidence index (Table 3, p. xxxii). A more detailed explanation of how to calculate and interpret your confidence index follows at the end of the Skill Finder.

You will notice an asterisk following some of the statements in the Skill Finder. The asterisk identifies the statement as an essential workplace skill. Access the Career Resource Center and visit *The Confident Student* web site for links to online articles that address the identified skills.

Words in italics identify some of the key terms explained in each chapter. *The Online Study Center* web site has online flash cards to help you remember these key words. You can also print out a list of the key terms and their definitions.

Online Study Center

The complete Skill Finder is also available in an interactive format. Log on to the web site at college.hmco.com/pic/KanarTCS6e.

Very Confident	Fairly Confident	Not Very Confident	Not Confident	
3	**2**	**1**	**0**	**Success is a matter of choice, not chance.**
☐	■	☐	■	1. I know the difference between elective courses and required courses.
☐	■	☐	■	2. I have a *mentor* I can turn to for advice.
☐	■	☐	■	3. I have a college catalog, and I know what kinds of information it contains.
☐	■	☐	■	4. I know what services my college offers to help students financially, academically, and in other ways.
☐	■	☐	■	5. I have an academic support group.
☐	■	☐	■	6. I use email and am aware of its benefits.*
☐	■	☐	■	7. I am flexible and able to adapt to change.*
☐	■	☐	■	8. I am comfortable in a culturally diverse environment.*
☐	■	☐	■	9. I am able to manage my finances.
☐	■	☐	■	10. I know the advantages and disadvantages of using credit cards.

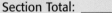

Section Total: _____

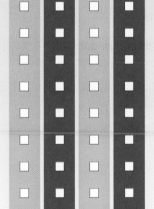

				Motivation and learning are connected.
☐	■	☐	■	11. I know what my basic skill strengths and weaknesses are.
☐	■	☐	■	12. I know what my *learning style* is and how to use it to my advantage.
☐	■	☐	■	13. I adapt easily to others' teaching and learning styles.
☐	■	☐	■	14. I understand how motivation and learning are connected.
☐	■	☐	■	15. I am aware that people may have *multiple intelligences*.
☐	■	☐	■	16. I know what *critical thinking* is, and I am able to think critically.*
☐	■	☐	■	17. I take personal responsibility for my learning and its outcomes.*
☐	■	☐	■	18. I know where and how I learn best, and I try to create those conditions for myself.
☐	■	☐	■	19. I am usually able to manage my own feelings and behavior.
☐	■	☐	■	20. I am aware that there are different ways to learn and that it is up to me to choose appropriate strategies.

Section Total: _____

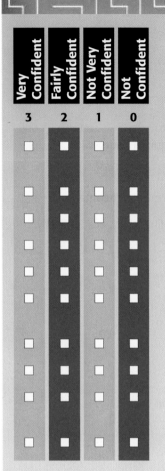

Very Confident	Fairly Confident	Not Very Confident	Not Confident	
3	**2**	**1**	**0**	**Thinking critically and reading are lifelong learning skills.**
☐	☐	☐	☐	21. Before reading or listening to lectures, I first examine my own *assumptions* about the topic.
☐	☐	☐	☐	22. I know how to predict test questions from reading and lectures.
☐	☐	☐	☐	23. I am able to determine an author's or speaker's purpose.
☐	☐	☐	☐	24. I am able to find my own purpose for reading and studying.
☐	☐	☐	☐	25. I am able to use *creative thinking* to meet many challenges.*
☐	☐	☐	☐	26. I know how to evaluate what I am learning for its *reliability, objectivity*, and *usefulness*.
☐	☐	☐	☐	27. I am an *active reader* rather than a *passive reader*.*
☐	☐	☐	☐	28. I know how to find main ideas, identify supporting details, and make inferences.
☐	☐	☐	☐	29. I am able to calculate my reading rate so that I can manage my reading and study time more effectively.
☐	☐	☐	☐	30. I use a textbook marking system.

Section Total: _____

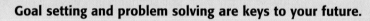

Goal setting and problem solving are keys to your future.

Very Confident	Fairly Confident	Not Very Confident	Not Confident	
☐	☐	☐	☐	31. I know the difference between a *short-term goal* and a *long-term goal*.
☐	☐	☐	☐	32. Setting goals is an important part of my planning.*
☐	☐	☐	☐	33. When things get difficult, I am not inclined to give up.
☐	☐	☐	☐	34. I usually do not have trouble making decisions.*
☐	☐	☐	☐	35. I know why I am in college.
☐	☐	☐	☐	36. I am able to tell when a goal is a realistic one.
☐	☐	☐	☐	37. I have a *positive attitude* toward others, myself, and the future.*
☐	☐	☐	☐	38. I am aware of different types (categories) of goals.
☐	☐	☐	☐	39. When I have a problem, I am able to identify its causes.
☐	☐	☐	☐	40. I solve problems through planning rather than by relying on time or chance to take care of them.*

Section Total: _____

Very Confident	Fairly Confident	Not Very Confident	Not Confident	
3	**2**	**1**	**0**	**Listening and note taking are cornerstones of classroom success.**
□	■	□	■	41. Most people would describe me as a good listener.*
□	■	□	■	42. I know the difference between *active listening* and *passive listening*.
□	■	□	■	43. I am not usually distracted when I am listening to a lecture.
□	■	□	■	44. I recognize the *signal words* that are clues to a speaker's important ideas.
□	■	□	■	45. I have a note-taking system that usually gives me good results.
□	■	□	■	46. I consider myself to be an effective speaker or presenter.*
□	■	□	■	47. I know how to use a computer to organize my notes.
□	■	□	■	48. My interpersonal skills make it easy for me to participate in group activities.*
□	■	□	■	49. I am almost always prepared for class.
□	■	□	■	50. I use my course *syllabus* to keep up with assignments.

Section Total: _____

Very Confident	Fairly Confident	Not Very Confident	Not Confident	
□	■	□	■	**Time management is essential to college, life, and career success.**
□	■	□	■	51. I realize that time is a resource I must use efficiently and wisely.*
□	■	□	■	52. I usually have no trouble finding time for studying.
□	■	□	■	53. I almost always arrive on time for classes.
□	■	□	■	54. I hand in projects and assignments on time.
□	■	□	■	55. I rarely miss class for any reason.
□	■	□	■	56. I am aware of different types of schedules and how they can help me manage my time.
□	■	□	■	57. As a student athlete, or the friend of one, I know the challenges athletes face and how they can manage their time more effectively.
□	■	□	■	58. I know what causes *procrastination* and how to avoid it.
□	■	□	■	59. I know how to use a computer to improve my time management.
□	■	□	■	60. I understand the connection between time management and study environment.

Section Total: _____

Very Confident	Fairly Confident	Not Very Confident	Not Confident	
3	**2**	**1**	**0**	**Choose success by managing your health and well-being.**
☐	☐	☐	☐	61. I maintain a *balanced diet*.
☐	☐	☐	☐	62. I exercise regularly to keep fit.
☐	☐	☐	☐	63. I have learned ways to reduce stress.
☐	☐	☐	☐	64. I know what *Internet addiction* is and how to avoid it.
☐	☐	☐	☐	65. Through self-management, I am able to control my emotions.*
☐	☐	☐	☐	66. I am sociable and make friends easily.*
☐	☐	☐	☐	67. I do not abuse alcohol or other harmful substances.
☐	☐	☐	☐	68. Overall, my self-esteem is high.*
☐	☐	☐	☐	69. I can accept the need for change.
☐	☐	☐	☐	70. I deal responsibly with sexual situations and relationships.

Section Total: _____

				To be successful, know how to find, organize, and study information.
☐	☐	☐	☐	71. I am able to tell what is important in a textbook chapter.
☐	☐	☐	☐	72. I know how to use the common parts of textbooks and chapters.
☐	☐	☐	☐	73. I have my own reading–study system, such as *SQ3R*, that I use consistently.
☐	☐	☐	☐	74. I have no trouble maintaining interest in what I read.
☐	☐	☐	☐	75. I use mapping and diagramming techniques to organize information.
☐	☐	☐	☐	76. I know the purpose of graphics, and I know how to read and interpret them.
☐	☐	☐	☐	77. I have a system for learning new words and terms.
☐	☐	☐	☐	78. I use different strategies for learning different types of information.
☐	☐	☐	☐	79. I know how to *survey* web sites to find the resources I need.
☐	☐	☐	☐	80. I know how to use a computer for outlining or charting information.*

Section Total: _____

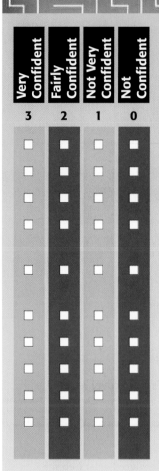

Very Confident	Fairly Confident	Not Very Confident	Not Confident	
3	**2**	**1**	**0**	**Concentration, learning, and memory are linked.**
☐	☐	☐	☐	81. I am able to control both *internal distractions* and *external distractions.**
☐	☐	☐	☐	82. I know how to find or create a study environment for maximum concentration.
☐	☐	☐	☐	83. I understand how having a study system improves concentration.
☐	☐	☐	☐	84. I know how attitude, time management, and goal setting affect my ability to concentrate.*
☐	☐	☐	☐	85. Neither the instructor's style nor the subject matter affect my ability to concentrate.
☐	☐	☐	☐	86. I understand how the mind processes information.
☐	☐	☐	☐	87. I know how *sensory memory, short-term memory*, and *long-term memory* differ.
☐	☐	☐	☐	88. I know why I forget and that I can improve my ability to remember.
☐	☐	☐	☐	89. I understand the connection between learning and memory.
☐	☐	☐	☐	90. I have learned a variety of memory-enhancing techniques, and I use them successfully.

Section Total: _____

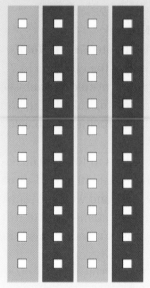

				Being well-prepared for tests will reduce anxiety and ensure success.
☐	☐	☐	☐	91. When it comes to tests, I know what, when, and how to study.
☐	☐	☐	☐	92. I am almost always well prepared for a test.
☐	☐	☐	☐	93. I know when it is appropriate to use guessing strategies.
☐	☐	☐	☐	94. I am able to control my feelings and attention during tests.
☐	☐	☐	☐	95. I review my errors and learn from my mistakes.
☐	☐	☐	☐	96. I am good at taking several different types of tests.
☐	☐	☐	☐	97. I know what *test anxiety* is.
☐	☐	☐	☐	98. I know the common causes of test anxiety and how to eliminate them.
☐	☐	☐	☐	99. I understand how *positive self-talk* can help me.
☐	☐	☐	☐	100. I use my self-management skills to help me prepare for tests.*

Section Total: _____

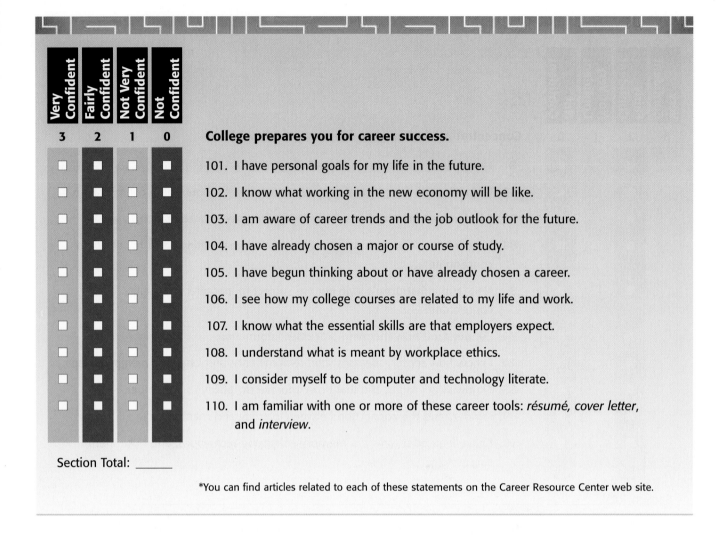

Very Confident	Fairly Confident	Not Very Confident	Not Confident	
3	**2**	**1**	**0**	**College prepares you for career success.**
☐	☐	☐	☐	101. I have personal goals for my life in the future.
☐	☐	☐	☐	102. I know what working in the new economy will be like.
☐	☐	☐	☐	103. I am aware of career trends and the job outlook for the future.
☐	☐	☐	☐	104. I have already chosen a major or course of study.
☐	☐	☐	☐	105. I have begun thinking about or have already chosen a career.
☐	☐	☐	☐	106. I see how my college courses are related to my life and work.
☐	☐	☐	☐	107. I know what the essential skills are that employers expect.
☐	☐	☐	☐	108. I understand what is meant by workplace ethics.
☐	☐	☐	☐	109. I consider myself to be computer and technology literate.
☐	☐	☐	☐	110. I am familiar with one or more of these career tools: *résumé, cover letter,* and *interview*.

Section Total: _____

*You can find articles related to each of these statements on the Career Resource Center web site.

Online Study Center

INTERPRETING YOUR SCORE AND CONFIDENCE INDEX

Now that you have completed the Skill Finder, transfer your *Section Totals* to Table 1, page xxxi. This Score and Correlation Chart lists the chapters in *The Confident Student*, Sixth Edition, that address the skills covered in each section. There are no right or wrong answers. The reasons for calculating your score are to find out which skills need developing or improving and to calculate your Confidence Index.

Your Confidence Index (CI) is a number on a scale from 1 to 10 based on how confident you are about your skills as identified by this questionnaire. Use your CI to help you determine which skills you already possess and which skills you need to develop. For example, take your section total for statements 1–10 from Table 1. This number will be somewhere between 0 and 30. Suppose your section total is 24. Find this number in the column labeled *Score Ranges* on Table 2. Read across to the second column where you will see a CI of 8. This high CI means that you already possess some background for the skills covered in Chapter 1. However, suppose your CI for section 1 is below 5. A CI in the lower ranges may indicate a lack of confidence or some unfamiliarity with the skills covered in Chapter 1. In the first case, you can build on your background to take your skills to a higher level. In the second case, you can use your new self-knowledge as motivation for developing new skills. Finding your CI for each section of the Skill Finder will give you a brief overview of the skills covered in *The Confident Student*, Sixth Edition, and will show you where you are in your skill development.

Calculate your overall CI by taking your grand total from Table 1 and using it to find your score range on Table 3. For example, if your grand total is 270, locate this number in the *Score Ranges* column and read across to find your CI of 8. An overall CI of 8 means that you may already possess a number of essential skills which you can develop to even higher levels.

Whatever your Confidence Index, this book will help you build the skills you need to be successful in college and your career. Complete the Skill Finder again at the end of the course to see how much your CI has improved.

TABLE 1

SCORE AND CORRELATION CHART

STATEMENTS BY NUMBER	YOUR TOTAL POINTS PER SECTION	(CHAPTER WHERE SKILLS ARE COVERED)
1–10		Choosing Success in College (1)
11–20		Motivating Yourself to Learn (2)
21–30		Thinking Critically and Creatively (3) and Becoming an Active Reader (13)
31–40		Thinking Critically and Creatively (3) and Setting Goals (4)
41–50		Sharpening Your Classroom Skills (5)
51–60		Making the Most of Your Time (6)
61–70		Maintaining Your Health and Well-Being (7)
71–80		Creating Your Study System (8) and Organizing Information for Study (9)
81–90		Controlling Your Concentration and Improving Learning and Memory (10)
91–100		Preparing for Tests (11) and Reducing Test Anxiety (12)
101–110		Building Career Skills (14)
Grand Total		

TABLE 2

YOUR CONFIDENCE INDEX PER SECTION

SCORE RANGES	CONFIDENCE INDEX
29–30	10
26–28	9
23–25	8
20–22	7
17–19	6
14–16	5
11–13	4
8–10	3
5–7	2
2–4	1
0–1	−1

TABLE 3

YOUR OVERALL CONFIDENCE INDEX

SCORE RANGES	CONFIDENCE INDEX
330	10
297–329	9
264–296	8
231–263	7
198–230	6
165–197	5
132–164	4
99–131	3
66–98	2
33–65	1
0–32	−1

The Confident Student

Becoming a confident student

Let a vision of your future inspire you to achieve your dreams.

Success does not happen by chance: It is the result of honest self-assessment, goal setting, and planning for the future.

Everyone benefits from the kind of support that a network of faculty, advisors, mentors, and helpful others can provide.

Learning to cooperate with others through understanding and acceptance is an important part of your college experience.

active learning, two traits that will make your college experience a successful one.

▶ CHOOSE SUCCESS AND PLAN FOR IT
Use Self-Assessment to Build Confidence
Define Your Goals
Think Ahead to a Major or Career

▶ FORM AN ACADEMIC SUPPORT GROUP
Faculty
Advisors and Counselors
Mentors
Extend Your Support Group

▶ EMBRACE DIVERSITY
Your Diverse Campus
Diverse Students, Needs, and Services
Adult Learners
Students with Disabilities

Non-Native Speakers of English
Students with Diverse Sexual Orientations

▶ BE AN ACTIVE LEARNER
Know Where to Find Help
Inform Yourself
Get Involved
Ask Questions with Confidence
Special Challenges for Commuters

▶ CHOOSE FINANCIAL SUCCESS
Set Financial Goals
Follow a Budget
Live Within Your Means
Be Credit Card Wise

▶ *Manage your finances successfully by setting goals, following a budget, living within your means, and using credit wisely.*

▶ *Active learning is your key to academic success. Active learners take initiative to find help, get involved, and ask questions.*

Resources include time, money, space, materials, people—anything that helps you to complete a task.

Technology in the workplace consists of appropriate tools for specific tasks, their management, and their use.

Interpersonal skills valued in the workplace include teamwork, teaching and leadership abilities, and working cooperatively with others from diverse backgrounds.

W hat is it like to begin a new term in college, or to take on a new job, free from self-doubt and certain that you will succeed? How does it feel to enter a class on the first day, believing that good grades are within your reach? What if you had the confidence in your skills to tackle any assignment, knowing you would succeed? The fact is that you, or anyone, can achieve this level of confidence.

Confidence comes from accomplishment, one successfully completed task at a time. Success is not a chance occurrence but is the result of your choices and actions. You can choose your future by using your college's **resources** and **technology,** by developing **interpersonal skills,** and by adopting the learning strategies that will help you accomplish your academic and career goals.

Chapter 1 is your challenge to become a confident student. Take Awareness Check 1 on page 4 to get started.

KEY TERMS

self-assessment, *p. 5*
goal, *p. 5*
major, *p. 6*
support group, *p. 7*
mentor, *p. 8*
diversity, *p. 12*
active learner, *p. 16*
budget, *p. 23*

SCANS TERMS

resources, *p. 3*
technology, *p. 3*
interpersonal skills, *p. 3*

AWARENESS CHECK 1

Are You Ready for Success?

A	B	C

Check *definitely true* (column A, 3 points), *somewhat true* (column B, 2 points), or *not at all true* (column C, 1 point) to explain how each statement applies to you.

1. I already think of myself as a confident student.

2. I have selected a major, and I have a career goal in mind.

3. I know what an academic support group is, and I use one.

4. I use email and other technology to enhance learning and study.

5. I embrace diversity and respect others' values that differ from my own.

6. I know what services my college offers and where to find them.

7. I am well informed on campus, local, and world events.

8. I have and use my college catalog and other campus publications.

9. I do not hesitate to ask questions in class or to find out what I need to know.

10. I have a budget and am able to manage my finances and credit card use.

A score of 25–30 means you are on your way toward achieving academic success. A score of 15–24 shows some skill strengths and some weaknesses. If your total is 1–14, your confidence will grow as you develop skills and achieve success. Whatever your score, the Skill Finder preceding this chapter or online will help you determine your confidence index as related to the skills covered in The Confident Student.

CHOOSE SUCCESS AND PLAN FOR IT

▶ *Success does not happen by chance: It is the result of honest self-assessment, goal setting, and planning for the future.*

College is about the future. Graduation is not just a time marker that ends several years of study. For first-time college students, graduation is the beginning of a lifetime of challenges that will require additional learning and the development of new skills. For adult learners, graduation is a chance to start over, taking life in a new direction. College also exposes everyone to people from many different backgrounds and cultures, providing a safe environment where all students can interact freely and develop the interpersonal and communication skills essential to a successful life.

What makes college such a positive experience is its insistence that you can leave old habits and unproductive behaviors behind and develop new strategies to help you achieve your academic, career, and life goals. Plan now for future success by taking three steps: Use self-assessment to build confidence, define your goals, and think ahead to a major and career.

Use Self-Assessment to Build Confidence

A **self-assessment** is an evaluation of your skills, abilities, experience, values, or other traits or qualities. When you self-assess, you do a mental test or check of your behavior or accomplishments. The *Skill Finder* printed on the eight pages preceding this chapter or online is a self-assessment you can take to determine what you already know about the skills covered in *The Confident Student*. The *Awareness Checks* in every chapter are self-assessment tools that help you determine what you already know about chapter concepts.

Many students enter college feeling insecure because of past failures or difficulties. As a result, they may tend to underestimate the worth of the knowledge and experience that they have accumulated. For example, not only your academic skills but also jobs you've held, places you've lived or traveled, your interests, your talents, and even your military experience are the background you bring to college. Your background provides the framework on which to build new skills and integrate new knowledge. Make your background work for you by continually trying to relate what you are learning to what you already know. Any connection you can make to prior knowledge will serve as a confidence builder.

You can develop the personal traits that confident students share. Figure 1.1 on page 6 lists fourteen traits of confident students, and each chapter of this book focuses on one or more of the traits.

Self-assessment is the process of testing, checking, or evaluating your behavior and accomplishments.

CONCEPT CHECK 1.1

Do you have a trait or quality that is not listed in Figure 1.1? If so, what is your trait, and how does it build your confidence?

Define Your Goals

A **goal** is a desired outcome that you will work to achieve. Goals can be personal, academic, or career related. Some students say, "I don't like to set goals because I prefer to be spontaneous." Unfortunately, if you do not set goals, your life may move along according to whim—often someone else's. If you want to stay in charge of your life, set goals, make plans to achieve them, and follow through. A goal is an objective. The plan you make for reaching that goal is a commitment. Commitments give our lives meaning. A goal will keep you focused on the future and will build your confidence by helping you to maintain a positive outlook. Throughout the text, and especially in Chapter 4, *Setting Goals*, we will discuss goal setting in greater detail.

Goal means outcome or objective, a desired end that you will work to achieve.

FIGURE 1.1

ARE YOU A CONFIDENT STUDENT?

TRAITS OF CONFIDENT STUDENTS	DESCRIPTIONS OF THE TRAITS
FLEXIBLE	You have an open mind, adapt well to change, and are eager to try new strategies.
SELF-MOTIVATED	You know what you want and will strive to accomplish your goals.
AN INDEPENDANT THINKER	You think for yourself, using strategies that enable you to meet challenges analytically and creatively
ENTHUSIASTIC	You have a positive attitude, are optimistic, hopeful, and energetic.
RESPONSIBLE	You own your actions, accept the consequences, and don't make excuses.
SELF-MANAGED	You have the self-discipline to prioritize tasks and meet obligations.
EMOTIONALLY INTELLIGENT	You control your impulses rather than allowing your feelings to control you.
STUDIOUS	You know where, when, how, and what to study; and you use a study system.
COMMITTED	You have pledged your time and effort to succeed and will do what is necessary to improve your performance.
AN ACTIVE LEARNER	You use learning strategies and memory techniques to keep your mind active and focused.
PERSISTENT	You never give up. You remain focused on your goals despite setbacks.
ASSERTIVE	You have the strength to face challenges and take intellectual risks.
SKILLED	You know your strengths and weaknesses, and you work hard to develop new skills.
FUTURE ORIENTED	You set goals, make plans for achieving them, and you follow through on your plans.

Think Ahead to a Major or Career

Major refers to an academic discipline, field of study, or certification program such as English, nursing, or electrical engineering.

There is no better way to begin setting goals than to choose a **major,** or field of study. Once you have chosen a major, you can begin to set long-term and short-term goals that will help you complete your program and earn a degree. Of course, you might say, "I'm not ready to select a major," and perhaps you need time to become adjusted to college life before making this decision. On the other hand, you might already have a major or career goal in mind. In either case, now is the time to think about your future—where you want to live, how much money you will need to support the life you want, and the career choices that will generate your desired level of income.

Selecting a major gives purpose to your college experience and keeps you focused on the future. To help you think ahead to a major or career, visit your college's career center, where you can explore your options. A career counselor can suggest surveys or assessments you can take to find out which jobs or careers are best for you, based on your interests and skills. In Chapters 4 and 14, you will find more detailed information about major selection and career goals.

FORM AN ACADEMIC SUPPORT GROUP

▶ *Everyone benefits from the kind of support that a network of faculty, advisors, mentors, and helpful others can provide.*

In a community of learners the primary function of each faculty member, administrator, employee, and department is *to help you reach your goals*. Everyone in your college community hopes that you will succeed. Therefore, your college is rich in resources that can guide your progress. For example, people are an important resource. If you have not already done so, form a **support group:** a network of people to whom you can turn for advice, answers to questions, or a boost in confidence.

Support group refers to a network of people you can rely on for advice and help.

Faculty

Your instructors are in the best position to advise you concerning all matters related to their classes. If you are having difficulty in a course, for example, don't postpone getting help or hope that your problem will go away. Make an appointment with your instructor as soon as possible.

Find an instructor with whom you are especially comfortable and turn to this person when you need advice. If your instructor is unable to answer one of your questions or to suggest ways to solve a problem, he or she can direct you to another person or office where help is available.

Advisors and Counselors

Academic advisors and career counselors are professionals who address students' academic and personal needs such as choosing a major, selecting courses, preparing course schedules, or finding help for a special problem like test anxiety.

Counselors and advisors know your college's rules and requirements. They may provide special services to students having unique needs such as international students, adult learners, minority students, students with disabilities, and transfer students. Because department names and professional titles differ from campus to campus, check your catalog, campus directory, or web site to learn where the services you need are provided.

Your instructors want you to succeed in their courses. They can answer questions about classroom topics, assignments, and tests, and they can give you sound advice about where to seek extra help if you need it.

Mentors

Mentor refers to a person who acts as an ally, taking a personal interest in you.

A **mentor** is an ally, a friend, someone who takes a personal and professional interest in you. On many college campuses today, instructors may serve as mentors to students. Mentors may offer tips on how to study, take tests, and reduce stress. They may also help students plan their schedules for the following term.

The relationship between student and mentor serves several purposes. It gives the student a contact person on campus to turn to for advice, for help in solving a problem, or for specific suggestions on how to meet course requirements. Mentors and instructors often work together to help students achieve their goals.

Many students complain that the close relationships that they enjoyed with faculty in high school are not available in college. Mentoring programs may be one way to fill the gap. Such programs may operate differently from campus to campus, but the goal of any mentoring program is the same: to help students choose success. To find out whether there is a mentoring program on your campus, call the admissions office.

Extend Your Support Group

Each subject area department, such as English or math, may have special requirements that pertain only to that discipline. Department heads can answer your questions about requirements, course offerings, and the availability of sections. They can also direct you to an instructor's office or mailbox, and they can provide instructors' office phone numbers or email addresses.

Other helpful people include your resident advisor if you live on campus, your coach if you are an athlete, or your club and organization sponsors. All these people share your interests and can help you form networks with others as you engage in campus life.

Don't underestimate the value of making friends with other students. Find a contact person in each class with whom you can exchange personal information in case one of you is absent. Your new friends may become your partners in a study group or the people you rely on when you need a ride or other favor.

Your academic support group might include an advisor, an instructor, a department head or secretary, a coach or club sponsor, and a friend in each class. Their role is a supporting one. They are available when you need them because in a community of learners, you are not alone.

COMPUTER CONFIDENCE

Using Technology to Build Communication Skills

The communication skills of reading and writing are among those that employers value most highly. College is a great place to hone your communication skills not only through classroom participation but also through the use of email, course management systems, and the Internet.

Email has several advantages other than the obvious ones of saving money on long-distance phone calls and the fact that you can send and receive messages any time:

- Share notes and materials with classmates, update group members with whom you are working on projects, and keep each other informed about meeting times and deadlines.

- Share ideas with students on other campuses; collaborate on research projects and other activities.

- Communicate regularly with your instructor to ask questions, set up appointments, or explain an absence.

- Communicate with researchers in your field of interest, seek career information, or submit a résumé or job application online.

- Practice your writing skills as you plan what to say in your messages and experiment with ways to organize your ideas.

- Hone your email skills for the workplace, where sending and receiving messages online are major means of interoffice communication.

Even if you don't have a computer, you probably can get access to one in your college library, residence hall, or computer center. Most colleges allow students to set up email accounts through the campus computer system, and some may charge a fee. To find on-campus addresses, check your campus email directory, web page, or campus-wide information system (CWIS) if these are available. For off-campus addresses, use an Internet search engine such as Netfind.

Many instructors use course management systems that allow students to submit work online for grading and to participate in other online activities. Some campuses provide online testing services, entire courses, or online components of conventional courses. For example, your writing course may be taught in a computer lab where you learn to plan, organize, and write papers online. Writing online, whether for messaging or submitting course material, calls for effective communication skills. Try these six tips to communicate more effectively:

Tips for Effective Online Communication

1. To make a good impression on instructors and employers, choose an email address that identifies you but is neither cute nor offensive. The best choice is your name. Some variations include your full name, your first initial plus last name, and your last name followed by your first initial. Reserve names like Funnygirl@blot.com or Fastmax@planet.net for casual communications with your friends.

2. Keep your messages brief and to the point. Keep papers and assignments on topic. Messages that are too long or wordy waste time—both yours and the reader's. Papers and responses to assignments that ramble or contain tired expressions detract from your development of the topic.

3. Be aware of your reader and adjust your tone accordingly. Is your message business or personal? Your tone will be more casual for a personal message than for a business communication and more formal when writing to an instructor than when writing to a friend.

4. Observe rules of *online etiquette* (polite communication). Because online writing is spontaneous—messages and responses can be transmitted instantly—you may have a tendency to write without thinking, which can result in miscommunication. Think before you write, and choose words carefully. Do not put anything in writing that you would not say in person. When in doubt, wait a while before sending a message so that you can review it and make changes as needed. Browse the Web for articles on rules for writing online. Try the search phrases *online etiquette* or *email etiquette*.

5. For email, stick to simple typing. Avoid using features like different fonts. These may not translate well and could cause confusion. For assignments and other online course activities, follow the guidelines your instructor suggests.

6. Check messages regularly and answer in a timely fashion. Especially if you are communicating with an instructor, or taking a course online, you wouldn't want to miss an essential piece of information or a deadline.

EXERCISE 1.1 COMPUTER APPLICATION

THE FOLLOWING EXERCISE WILL GIVE you practice communicating online. If you have a computer, you do not have to complete the first item.

1. **Do you have access to computers on campus? If so, find out how to open an account and get an email address. Then briefly explain the process involved and where you had to go to set up your account.**

   _____

   _____

2. **Write your email address on the following line:**

   _____

   _____

3. **List the names and addresses of an instructor and the students with whom you regularly communicate, and briefly explain the reason for your messaging.**

   _____

   _____

4. **What writing activities other than email do you conduct online?**

   _____

   _____

5. **Visit a web site that addresses online etiquette. Then explain one new rule that you learned. Try the search phrase _email etiquette_ or ask your instructor for suggestions.**

   _____

   _____

EXERCISE 1.2 COMPUTER APPLICATION

WHAT COURSE ARE YOU TAKING this term that may give you the most difficulty? To build confidence in yourself and in your ability to pass this course, establish a good relationship with the instructor. Then you will feel comfortable asking questions in class or making an office visit to get help with an assignment. As a start, introduce yourself to the instructor via email. Write a brief message that includes the following items, and take notes on the lines provided. End your message by thanking the instructor for his or her time.

1. **Your name, course, and section number:**

   _____

   _____

2. **Your major or career goal:**

   _____

   _____

3. **Why you are taking the course, and what you hope to get out of it:**

   _____

   _____

4. **Why you think the course may be difficult for you:**

   _____

   _____

EXERCISE 1.3 COMPUTER APPLICATION

HAVING A SUPPORT GROUP TO turn to when you need information, the answer to a question, help with a problem, or a boost in confidence makes adjusting to college easier. Write the names, addresses, and phone numbers of several people in your support group on the following chart. Post the chart in a handy place. If you need space for more support group members, go to the Online Study Center to download additional copies of the chart.

My Support Group

	Phone number	Address/office	Email address
Family members			
1.			
2.			
Instructors			
1.			
2.			
Classmates			
1.			
2.			
Advisor, coach, or other person			
1.			
2.			

EMBRACE DIVERSITY

▶ *Learning to cooperate with others through understanding and acceptance is an important part of your college experience.*

The composition of the U.S. population is undergoing rapid change. In 1996, the Census Bureau had projected that by 2020 minority groups collectively would make up 33 percent of the population, a projection that underestimated the rate of growth by about twenty years. We can assume that the minority population will continue to grow, becoming an even larger percentage of the total over the next decade. Because you will live and work in an increasingly diverse society, it is

Online Study Center
Prepare for Class
Remembering
Cultural Differences

important that you take the opportunity college provides to break down barriers that divide people.

Your Diverse Campus

Diversity means variety and refers to the racial, ethnic, cultural, and other differences among people.

Diversity means variety, pure and simple. Diversity on campus—and in society at large—refers to the variety of races, ethnic groups, cultures, religions, sexual orientations, nationalities, and other conditions and perspectives that are represented. Colleges have responded to student diversity by offering services and opportunities to meet a variety of needs. Moreover, diversity has many benefits. Exposure to different customs and ways of thinking challenges your ideas and broadens your worldview. Because your campus is a small slice of the larger society, it provides you with an opportunity to hone your interpersonal skills and to develop intercultural communication skills that will prepare you for a career in an increasingly diverse workplace.

Creating a learning environment where all are treated with respect and where all are free to pursue their educational goals is everyone's responsibility. Do your part by being open to ideas and customs that may differ from your own. If you harbor any stereotypical thinking that prevents cross-cultural communication, now is the time to let it go. Look around you at your classmates and instructors. They are people—first.

Embrace diversity by reaching out to others in a spirit of friendship and community. Make all students feel welcome, just as you want to be welcomed. Accept others' differences, listen without being critical, and establish friendships based on shared interests and values. As you form your support group, think of others' differences not as barriers to communication but as bridges to understanding. Let your support group ring with the harmony of different voices.

CONCEPT CHECK 1.2

How do you respond to diversity? Try making an effort to meet someone new in each class. What are your similarities and differences? What can you learn from each other?

Diverse Students, Needs, and Services

Your college probably offers a number of programs, services, and interest groups that serve the needs of a diverse student population. On some campuses, women's groups, international student organizations, lesbians' and gay men's coalitions, and religion-based student associations provide a place to socialize and conduct special-interest activities.

Although socializing with others like yourself is important, it is equally important to reach out to those who differ. Getting involved in extracurricular activities can help you find new friends who share your interests. Joining a group that appeals to students interested in an art such as dance, drama, or music or interested in a career such as engineering or teaching can serve as a starting point for getting involved in campus life.

Service learning provides another way to get involved. This teaching method integrates classroom activities with community service. If service learning is not an option on your campus, you can still get involved in organizations like Habitat for Humanity, or you can work as a hospital volunteer. Your participation in student government, campus organizations, or community service activities can provide opportunities for you to interact with others from diverse backgrounds.

Adult Learners

Adult students, twenty-five and older, make up a significant number of the student body on any campus. Many have stories like this woman's:

I am twenty-seven and a divorced mother of two children. I'm continuing my education because I want a better life for my family. I have to work part-time, keep up with my studies, and make time for my kids—all of which is much harder than I ever thought it could be. At night I'm so tired that I'm barely able to get dinner on the table. After helping my boys with their homework and getting them into bed, I'm often too exhausted to study. Time management is my biggest problem. At times I've felt like giving up, especially at first because I felt out of place among all the younger students. But I've made friends and am now in a study group that is helping me become more organized. We meet at my house, which is good for me.

Adult learners are welcomed on campuses today for several important reasons. First of all, adult learners bring with them knowledge and skills that enrich the college experience for everyone. Second, most people change jobs or careers two or more times during their lives and seek additional skills or training. Moreover, learning does not end at graduation—it is a lifelong process. Despite such current positive views about adult learners, these students often enter college feeling out of place, wondering whether they will be able to catch up and keep up. Adult learners have jobs and families and may feel pressured as they add course requirements to their already full calendars. Embracing diversity means learning from each other's unique experiences and remembering that all students, no matter what their ages, face similar problems of adjustment in college.

Students with Disabilities

Disabilities are of two types: physical disabilities and learning disabilities. Physical disabilities are more apparent and include such things as blindness or paralysis. Learning disabilities are not so easy to recognize and may hinder students' speaking, listening, writing, thinking, or other academic skills. Though their skills may be lacking, their intelligence is not. Most students with learning disabilities have developed coping strategies but still may need help with taking notes or getting to and from class, or they may require extra test-taking or writing time—services that all colleges provide. If you have a disability, take the initiative to find out where these services and others like them are available and make your requests known. Instructors may not know what you need unless you ask for it. Offer students with disabilities the same friendship and support that you would offer anyone else. When goals and interests are shared in an environment of respect, then disabilities pose no barriers to success.

Non-Native Speakers of English

Even on a campus that embraces diversity, the temptation may be great for non-native speakers of English to restrict their interaction with others to those who speak their own language. Many of these students go home to families that also do not speak English. The time that they spend in class may be the only opportunity that non-native speakers of English have to use English. It is crucial for these students to make friends with and to interact with native speakers. Therefore, if you are a non-native speaker of English, seek opportunities to practice your English skills. Participate in class discussions. Join clubs or organizations in which you will meet native speakers who share your interests.

If you are a native speaker of English, reach out to the non-native speakers in your classes. Invite them to join a study group after class or take the initiative to collaborate with them in group activities within class.

Students with Diverse Sexual Orientations

Many heterosexuals react negatively toward gays and lesbians because of learned stereotypes that act as barriers to communication and obscure the truth. For one thing, you cannot determine a person's sexual orientation based on his or her outward appearance. Within the lesbian and gay community, as in any community, a variety of values, behaviors, and personality traits are represented. Finally, gay and lesbian students, like most students, just want to make friends, pursue their educational goals, find meaningful work after college, and build lasting relationships. The LGBTA (Lesbian, Gay, Bisexual, and Transsexual Alliance) is active on some campuses and provides a meeting place for students with diverse sexual orientations.

Any student can choose success. No matter what your age or background is, and no matter what your academic performance has been, college offers a new beginning. Every chapter in this book contains strategies that will help you build the confidence and skills needed to achieve your goals.

C R I T I C A L

T H I N K I N G

Exercise Overview

What is your college doing to embrace diversity? This exercise will help you determine what policies and programs your college has in place to address the needs of a diverse student population.

Exercise Background

Today's campus is more diverse than ever. The percentage of the campus population that each racial, ethnic, or other group comprises varies with both the college and the region of the country in which it is located. How a college responds to diversity can affect a student's comfort level and academic success either positively or negatively.

Exercise Task

Research and answer the following questions by finding relevant printed materials, by interviewing the appropriate people on campus, or by browsing your college's web site. Your instructor or a librarian can suggest resources and ways to begin your search. Share your answers orally or in writing as your instructor directs.

1. Assess the diversity on your campus. What ethnic, racial, international, or other kinds of groups are represented? What percentage of the students, faculty, administration, and staff does each group comprise?

2. What courses that address diversity issues are offered?

3. Is diversity mentioned in your college's mission statement? If so, how?

4. What college policies or procedures are designed to meet the needs of a diverse student population?

5. To what extent does your college promote interaction among students from diverse backgrounds?

6. Do you find any discrepancies between your college's policy on diversity and actual practice? If so, explain the discrepancies.

7. Based on the facts you have found, what conclusions can you draw about your college's commitment to diversity? For example, how does diversity benefit your campus? Do all students feel welcome? What, if anything, should be done to improve relations among the diverse groups on your campus?

Present your answers orally or in writing as your instructor directs.

CONFIDENCE BUILDER

How Flexible Are You?

Flexibility is one of the traits of a confident student. Learning to be flexible in your daily activities prepares you to meet life's greater challenges.

Do you hold on to cherished opinions, even in the face of conflicting evidence? Do your first impressions of people remain largely unchanged, even after you get to know them? How do you handle broken relationships, changes in plans, or personal and financial setbacks? If you have difficulty adapting to change, then much of your life—whether at college, at work, or at home—is probably filled with stress. Change, according to many experts, is one of life's greatest sources of stress. People who are inflexible in their beliefs, attitudes, and plans set themselves up for disappointment, discomfort, and distress.

The way to adapt to change is to be flexible. Flexibility is a trait employers often cite as being a valuable personal skill, and it is one you can develop. What are some of the situations at college that call for flexibility? You painstakingly make out a schedule—only to find out that one of your courses is closed. Your roommate is a day person; you are a night person. You spend hours studying for a test, you are motivated and ready to perform, and then your instructor postpones the exam until next week. How can you adapt to day-to-day changes such as these that can make your life miserable if you let them? How can you become more flexible? The following three tips may help.

Watch your attitude. Remember that you are not perfect, and neither is anyone else. Life does not always proceed according to schedule. It isn't the end of the world if things don't go as planned. Learn to shrug instead of vent. Make room in your schedule for unplanned circumstances.

Have a contingency plan. You can't plan for all emergencies or temporary setbacks, but you *can* anticipate some changes. For example, have alternatives in mind when you select courses. Expect that in any situation in which two people live together, conflicts will arise. Remind yourself to stay calm, talk things over, and be willing to compromise. Whenever you make a schedule, set a goal, or plan for a future event, try to build into your plans some alternatives in case things don't work out.

Keep an open mind. Change has its good points. Change keeps you from getting in a rut. Change also opens up possibilities you may not have previously had a reason to consider. Above all, successfully adapting to change helps you grow and makes it easier for you to accept the next change that comes along.

College is a great place to loosen up rigid ways of thinking and behaving in order to become a more flexible person. The challenges that a college education offers, the diverse learning community, and the opportunity to expand your mind will enable you to meet the even greater challenges in your life that lie ahead.

To learn more about the value of flexibility, do an online search using these keywords as a starting point: *flexibility, adapting to change, stress,* and *change.*

BE AN ACTIVE LEARNER

> *Active learning is your key to academic success. Active learners take the initiative to find help, get involved, and ask questions.*

Some students sit passively in a lecture or class discussion, letting their minds wander, not taking notes, and never asking questions. Later, they wonder why they can't remember what the lecture or discussion was about. The key to getting more out of class, and out of your college experience as a whole, is your active engagement in the process. An **active learner** is one who gets involved by taking notes, asking questions, participating in discussions, and joining clubs and organizations—someone who pays attention and knows what is going on in class and on campus. Your active involvement makes you a better informed and more confident student.

All of the strategies explained in the chapters of this book promote active learning. This section explains several things that you can do right now to become an active learner: Know where to find help, inform yourself, get involved, and ask questions with confidence.

Active learner, opposite of passive learner, refers to a person who is both aware of and involved in the process of learning.

Know Where to Find Help

It is up to you to seek the help you need, when you need it. For example, if you have a learning disability or a health problem that needs special attention, you should inform your instructors so that they can help you get whatever assistance you might require.

Your campus offers a variety of resources to help you succeed. Though every college is different, you can probably find on your campus the offices and services listed in Figure 1.2. Check your college catalog, campus directory, or web site for specific listings.

FIGURE 1.2

KNOW YOUR WAY AROUND CAMPUS

OFFICES/CENTERS	SERVICES THEY PROVIDE
Registrar's Office	Records grades, issues transcripts, answers questions about graduation requirements, credits, and other related matters
Career Center	Offers career counseling, career-related interest and skill assessment, job placement services, recruitment programs
Academic Advising and Counseling Office	Provides academic advising and counseling, help with course selection, planning, and scheduling
Financial Aid Office	Handles loan and scholarship applications, work/study grants, campus employment, fees, fines, and payments
Library/Media Center	Provides print and online resources and other media and technology for students' and instructors' use
Tutorial Center	Trains and provides student tutors in a variety of subjects and may or may not charge fees
Learning Lab/Center	Offers materials and programs for independent or course-related work in skill development
Student Health Services	May provide limited or emergency health care or refer students to appropriate agencies

Inform Yourself

One way to become an active learner is to read your college's publications. Most colleges publish a catalog, newspaper, or student bulletin, and these contain a wealth of information that can keep you informed and involved in campus life.

The *college catalog* lists important dates, deadlines, fee payment schedules, and course offerings by discipline. Your *college newspaper* contains information of interest to the college community along with articles that report on local, national, and world events from a student's perspective. Your student government association may sponsor a *student bulletin* that informs you of campus activities or a *student handbook* that summarizes college policies and regulations in plain language. Bulletin boards and kiosks may display flyers advertising various services and upcoming events. By regularly checking your college's publications, you will become more knowledgeable about your campus and its culture.

As an active learner, also pay attention to what is going on in the surrounding community and the world. Keep informed by regularly reading a newspaper and other periodicals. Television news and web sites are additional sources of information. Make a point of getting your news from a variety of different sources so that you are exposed to a wide range of opinions. Keeping up with current events helps you build background, adding to your knowledge framework.

EXERCISE 1.4

USE YOUR COLLEGE CATALOG (online or hard copy) to find the answers to the following questions, noting the page number where you found each answer. *Hint:* Use the contents and index to help you find the topics each question covers.

1. **How many credits are required for graduation?**

   _____

2. **What degrees are offered?**

   _____

3. **What GPA must you maintain in order to avoid being placed on probation?**

   _____

4. **Does your college offer a grade of I (incomplete)?**

   _____

5. **What happens if you don't make up an incomplete grade?**

   _____

6. **Is class attendance required? Is there an attendance policy stated in the catalog?**

   _____

7. **What are the degrees held and colleges attended by one of your instructors?**

   _____

8. **Where do you go to get a campus parking permit?**

   _____

9. **What courses are all students required to take?**

   _____

10. **On what dates are final exams given?**

    _____

11. **When does the next registration period begin?**

    _____

12. **What are the number and title of a reading course offered?**

    _____

13. **How many math courses are all students required to take?**

    _____

14. **What are two clubs or organizations you can join?**

    _____

15. **What is the college president's name?**

    _____

Get Involved

Active learning takes place in a social setting as well as an academic one. One of the important outcomes of a college education is that it provides opportunities for you to work cooperatively and interact socially with a diverse group of people. Through interaction with others, you may find new interests and develop communication skills and relationships that will help you build an impressive résumé. However, this will happen only if you take the initiative to participate in campus activities, events, and organizations.

A word about *Greek organizations*: As do all other organizations, fraternities and sororities have advantages and disadvantages. They can be strong support groups where you can develop social skills, lasting friendships, and a network of people who can help you make a smooth transition from college to career. On the negative side, Greek organizations can be both exclusive and expensive. Some may have a reputation for excessive drinking and socializing that undermines their members' academic success. Some may require you to participate in activities and events that leave little time for study, and this negative aspect may also apply to many other types of organizations.

Active learning takes active involvement. Therefore, if you are a *commuter*, you have some special challenges. Because you do not live on campus, it may be less convenient for you to participate in campus events and organizations, and this may limit your opportunities for social interaction. To get involved, try to schedule classes so that you have some free time on campus to participate in an organization or study group. Arrange with other commuters to share transportation to and from extracurricular activities. Because most of your interaction with students and instructors will take place in class, make the most of it by volunteering for projects, answering questions, and participating in class and small group discussions.

Ask Questions with Confidence

Questioning is the hallmark of active learning. By asking questions, you can clear up any misunderstandings you may have about the information presented in class and assigned readings. Unfortunately, most students hesitate to ask questions for many reasons. Some students fear that others will think they are trying to impress the instructor. Others fear that their questions may make them seem uninformed. Still others may be shy and will hold back, hoping that another student will ask their question. All these fears betray a lack of confidence. To overcome your fear of asking questions, remember that your goal is to learn, and learning requires action. In addition to asking questions in classes and lectures, you can contact your instructor through email and during office hours. Also knowing *how* to ask questions will give you the confidence to speak out. Try the following tips. Four key words, all beginning with *T*, will help you remember them:

▼ **Topic:** Your question should directly relate to the lecture or the topic under discussion. Avoid asking questions that were answered in your assigned reading or in a previous class or lecture. The best way to insure that your questions are on topic is to attend class regularly and read assigned material.

▼ **Tone:** Ask your question in a respectful tone of voice. This is not the time for sarcasm or inappropriate remarks. A serious question merits a serious answer.

▼ **Timing:** No one likes to be interrupted. Wait for a pause in the lecture or discussion to ask your question. Also, observe your instructor's teaching style. Some instructors prefer you to hold your questions until the end of the lecture while others may not mind if you ask questions along the way.

▼ **Trust:** Look at the person to whom you are directing the question, and listen attentively to the answer, using appropriate body language such as eye contact or a nod of the head to show understanding. This is *the posture of engagement*, and it helps establish trust between you and those to whom you are speaking.

EXERCISE 1.5

TAKE A WALKING TOUR OF your campus. Your college may not have all of the places listed here, but find as many of them as you can and write down their building and office or room numbers. If an office on the following list is not on your campus, write *none* in the space provided. Post this list in a handy place.

Important Campus Locations

Registrar's office _____

Student health service _____

Career center _____

Advisors' offices _____

Athletic director's office _____

Learning labs and centers _____

Financial aid office _____

English or other department office _____

Library _____

Tutorial center _____

Computer center _____

Veterans office _____

Office of Diversity _____

Housing office _____

Campus security _____

EXERCISE 1.6 COLLABORATIVE ACTIVITY

APPLY WHAT YOU HAVE LEARNED about the places to find help on campus. Discuss and answer the following questions, doing any research that may be needed. Resources to consider include your college catalog and your college's web site. Working in a group or with a partner, follow the guidelines for successful collaboration that appear on the inside back cover. Write your evaluation on your own paper or download the Collaborative Exercise Form from the Online Study Center.

1. **Adult Learners**

   a. **What special services or programs exist on your campus for adult learners?**

   _____

   b. **Where is the service or program offered (office or other location)?**

   _____

   c. **Give the name of a contact person to ask for information.**

   _____

2. **Women**

   a. **What special services or programs exist on your campus for women?**

   _____

   b. **Where is the service or program offered (office or other location)?**

   _____

   c. **Give the name of a contact person to ask for information.**

   _____

3. **Students with Disabilities**

   a. **What special services or programs exist on your campus for the learning disabled and physically disabled?**

   _____

b. Where is the service or program offered (office or other location)?

_____

c. Give the name of a contact person to ask for information.

_____

4. **Does your campus provide help for students who need to reduce stress? Where is the service offered, and who is a person to contact for information?**

_____

5. **Does your campus provide help for students who need a tutor? Where is the service offered, and who is a person to contact for information?**

_____

Group Evaluation:

Evaluate your discussion. Did everyone contribute? Did you accomplish your task successfully? What additional questions do you have about places on campus to go for help? How will you find answers to your questions?

FIGURE 1.3

GUIDELINES FOR GROUP DISCUSSION

Each chapter contains a collaborative exercise—an activity intended for partners or a small group. Exercise 1.6 in this chapter is an example. Successful collaboration requires teamwork. Ideally, every member has a role, and everyone participates fully. Before beginning an exercise, decide which members will perform the following roles. Also be aware that some activities may require different roles and responsibilities from those described here. Your instructor may have additional guidelines as well.

ROLES	RESPONSIBILITIES
Leader	The leader makes sure everyone understands the assignment's _purpose_ (what you are expected to learn) and _task_ (what you are expected to do). The leader keeps the discussion on target and settles conflicts. Although everyone's responsibility is to stay on task and avoid rambling or socializing, the leader is in charge.
Recorder	Everyone takes notes. The recorder compiles the notes into a final report to present to the whole class, but everyone should be prepared to share in the discussion.
Researcher	The researcher manages whatever resources are needed—textbook, handouts, dictionary, or other materials—and refers to them for answering questions or resolving arguments about facts.
Timekeeper	The timekeeper makes sure the group starts and ends on time, emails or calls group members to remind them of meeting times, follows the discussion, and helps the leader keep things moving so that the task gets completed on time.

A small group is a good place to develop the interpersonal skills that employers expect. Courtesy, professionalism, and respect for others' opinions are hallmarks of successful group interaction. Monopolizing the discussion, interrupting, making personal remarks, and socializing are unproductive behaviors that you should avoid.

Most campuses have kiosks and bulletin boards for posting important academic and social events. You can easily check for new listings on your way to and from classes.

Special Challenges for Commuters

If you commute to college, you may be at a disadvantage in one respect. It may be less convenient for you to become involved in activities and events than it would be if you lived on or near campus. However, there are ways for you to take a more active part in campus life. Consider your interests. What are your career aspirations? Is there an activity that you would like to try but have not had an opportunity to pursue? Many clubs and organizations on your campus would be happy to have you as a member. If you join one of these groups, you will meet people who share your interests, and you may learn even more about an activity you already enjoy. You may also meet people with whom you can share transportation to and from campus activities and events. Your catalog and student handbook contain a list of campus organizations. You could also drop by your student government office and introduce yourself. Someone there can tell you about the many activities and upcoming events in which you can take part. Forming a study group that meets on campus or scheduling some on-campus study time is another way to remain on campus and stay involved.

CHOOSE FINANCIAL SUCCESS

▶ *Manage your finances successfully by setting goals, following a budget, living within your means, and using credit wisely.*

If you ask college students what they want out of college, many will be quick to tell you that they want "a better job" or "a high-paying career." They have other goals, to be sure, but financial success is a top priority. Therefore, it is important to understand that financial success begins now, not sometime in the future. How you manage your money today lays the foundation for successful money management tomorrow—not only in your personal life but also in the workplace, where you might be responsible for making decisions about purchases and expenditures and for allocating funds.

Are you in debt, always running a little short of cash, or do you follow a budget? Are you satisfied with your current financial situation, or would you like to keep better track of your earning, spending, and saving? This section explains a few basic principles that will help you improve the way you manage your money:

▼ Set financial goals.

▼ Follow a budget.

▼ Live within your means.

▼ Be credit card wise.

Set Financial Goals

Most financially successful people know how much they make, account for every dollar they spend, and follow a long-term plan for saving and investing in their future. Think of financial success as a pyramid where the foundation rests on a regular income. Each level of the pyramid is a stage in planning and money management that leads to successful achievement at the top, as illustrated in Figure 1.4 on page 24.

Where are you on the pyramid? What are your long-term and short-term financial goals? Do you have a regular income or savings? Do you budget and manage your money as well as you could? Right now you may be thinking only about how you are going to finance your education for the next four years. But you are probably also looking ahead to your career and the life you want to lead, the kind of home you want to own, and the things you want to have. For example, financing an education is a long-term goal that you can reach by determining what your earnings are, how much your education will cost, and how you will budget or supplement your income to meet expenses on a monthly basis year-in and year-out. You may have to take out a student loan, or you may already have a scholarship that pays for part of your education. The levels of the pyramid in Figure 1.4 represent money management experience, so no matter what level you are on, making a budget, or sticking to one you have already made, can help you reach your goals.

Follow a Budget

A **budget** is a plan for spending and saving money based on earnings. A budget has two purposes: (1) to help you live within your means, and (2) to help you keep track of where your money goes so that you can find ways to cut costs and increase your savings. Your first step in making a budget is to determine the source and amount of your income (money in) and your expenses (money out). The chart near the bottom of page 24 lists typical sources of college students' income and expenses:

Budget refers to a summary of earnings and expenditures—your plan for spending and saving.

FINANCIAL SUCCESS PYRAMID

FIGURE 1.4

Success

Investing

Handling loans
and debt

Managing expenses

Setting goals and budgeting

Establishing credit base

Earning income

Money In	Money Out
work	tuition
spouse's income	books
parents' support	housing
scholarship	car payment
loan	food
savings	utilities and phone
investments	insurance
other sources	gas
	clothing
	entertainment
	personal items
	household expenses
	other expenses

The second step in making a budget is to determine which of your expenses are fixed or fluid. *Fixed* expenses recur over time and don't change. Rent, car payments, tuition, and insurance premiums are examples of fixed expenses. *Fluid* expenses may change from month to month both as to type and amount. Food, phone, utilities, entertainment, and clothing are examples of fluid expenses. Although fixed expenses are beyond your control, you do have some control over fluid expenses. For example, you can't make your landlord lower the rent, but you can cut your utility and food costs by using energy-saving methods and fixing your own meals. Suppose your expenses are greater than your source of income. You must find ways to cut expenses. Ideally, a realistic budget should pay your expenses and leave money for savings. Through saving and investing you can build wealth. In college, your savings may be small and investments may be nonexistent. But as you gain career or work experience, your income will increase, providing the means to save and invest—if you manage your growing income wisely.

Figure 1.5 shows an example of one student's monthly budget. Rick Morales, a college student, has a monthly income of $1,295. His budget does not include expenses for tuition and books, which are covered by a scholarship. Rick's income is based on his earnings over several summers, a part-time job, plus a supplement from his parents. He has both a checking account and a savings account. Rick usually keeps his expenses under $1,295. In October, he spent a total of $1,245 and deposited $50 in his savings account. Rick looks for ways to save money. He shares an apartment to reduce his rent and associated costs, rides his bicycle to cut car expenses, and eats most meals at home to save on food costs. By putting money aside each month, he is building a safety net to cover unexpected expenses.

RICK'S BUDGET FOR OCTOBER   FIGURE 1.5

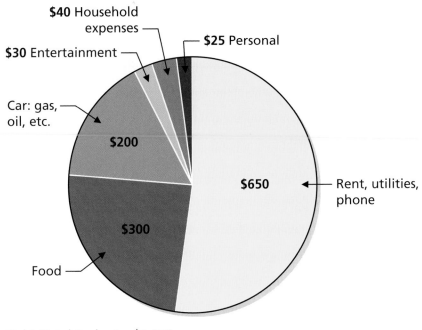

$40 Household expenses

$30 Entertainment

$25 Personal

Car: gas, oil, etc.

$200

$650 — Rent, utilities, phone

$300

Food

Rick's Total Budget = $1,245

EXERCISE 1.7

PART 1. Make a money-in, money-out list of your income sources, expenses, and amounts for one month on the following chart.

MONEY IN		MONEY OUT	
Source	**Amount**	**Expense**	**Amount**
_____	_____	_____	_____
_____	_____	_____	_____
_____	_____	_____	_____
_____	_____	_____	_____
_____	_____	_____	_____
_____	_____	_____	_____
_____	_____	_____	_____
_____	_____	_____	_____
_____	_____	_____	_____

PART 2. Based on your income and expenses, make a monthly budget that you can follow. Your budget can be in the form of a pie chart like Rick's budget in Figure 1.4, a simple list, table, or any way that you want to present it. Be creative. As a final step, write a short paragraph explaining how you can reduce expenses.

_____

_____

_____

_____

Live within Your Means

Self-management and personal responsibility are the keys to living within your means. Unfortunately, advertising and the availability of credit cards make spending seem attractive and affordable. Resist the temptation to buy clothes or personal items that you don't need or to finance big-ticket items that you can do without. In addition, try these ten money-saving tips:

1. Don't use shopping as a form of entertainment.

2. Don't buy on impulse. Think about purchases based on need rather than desire.

3. Carry cash with you, and leave credit cards at home. If you have to pay cash, you will be less tempted to buy things you don't need.

4. Reduce energy costs by turning the heat down and the air conditioner up. Don't leave lights burning in an empty room. Take quick

showers, and don't leave the water running while brushing your teeth. Fill the bathtub only half way. Use the energy-saving setting on appliances.

5. Cut food costs by eating in, clipping coupons, looking for bargains, and using leftovers.

6. Be creative in finding ways to make extra money. For example, offer to house sit, baby sit, or do odd jobs for pay.

7. Use public transportation, ride a bicycle, or walk wherever you can.

8. If you must drive, shop around for the lowest gas prices.

9. You probably have clothes that you don't wear. Instead of letting them hang in the closet, offer to exchange them with someone in your size. Both of you will have the benefit of a "new" outfit without the cost.

10. For entertainment, search the college or local paper for free concerts, events, and local points of interest such as museums and parks.

No matter how deprived postponing gratification may make you feel, the reward that comes from taking control of your life and spending habits more than makes up for not having everything you want now. In addition, by constantly looking for ways to cut costs, you are building valuable experience for creative money management in the workplace.

Be Credit Card Wise

The first credit cards, such as Diners Club and Carte Blanche, were available mainly to businesspeople on expense accounts. Major credit cards were introduced to the general public in the 1960s, ushering in an era of unforeseen spending and debt that has steadily increased. Economist Alan Greenspan cites credit card debt and misuse as a source of many Americans' financial troubles today.

Used wisely, credit cards have several advantages. Buying on credit and paying off your balance on time, every time, is one way to establish a good credit rating. A positive credit history indicates that you are a responsible person, a distinction that can be an asset when you are applying for a loan or a job. Credit cards are convenient and a source of ready cash for emergencies—two advantages that quickly become disadvantages when credit cards are abused.

Credit card companies market to college students, luring them with incredible offers and gifts that often come with a stiff price of annual fees, high interest rates, late fees, and other penalties lurking in the fine print. But the greatest disadvantage is that having a credit card encourages you to spend more than you should. Before you know it, you are living beyond your means and mounting a burden of debt that will be hard to reduce before it ruins your credit rating.

Follow these tips for using credit cards wisely and see Figure 1.6 Choosing a Credit Card: Issues and Questions on page 28.

1. Have no more than two credit cards, and preferably only one. The more cards you have, the more you are likely to spend. Do not be tempted by credit card applications that come in the mail. Tear them up and throw them away.

2. Use your card in moderation and save it for emergencies. Charge airline tickets and hotel rooms so that you don't have to carry a large amount of cash when traveling.

CONCEPT CHECK 1.3

How many cards do you have, and what kinds of items do you charge with them? Do you keep a running balance, or do you pay in full each month? Is there anything you would like to do differently, and why?

FIGURE 1.6

CHOOSING A CREDIT CARD: ISSUES AND QUESTIONS

ISSUES	QUESTIONS
INTEREST RATE	What is the finance charge if I carry a balance?
MINIMUM PAYMENT	What is the minimum I can pay each month? When is it due?
ANNUAL FEE	Is there an annual fee, and how much is it?
LATE FEES AND OTHER PENALTIES	What is the late fee? What other penalties apply?
GRACE PERIOD	Is there a grace period? (If you do not pay the full balance, finance charges may begin immediately, or there may be a grace period of a few days in which no finance charges are assessed.)

3. Do not charge more than you can pay off each month, and pay the full amount on time to avoid finance charges.

4. If you do carry a balance, keep it low, pay more than the minimum each month to reduce interest, and avoid late payment fees. If possible, do not make any additional charges until the balance is paid off.

5. Reduce the need for a credit card by establishing a checking account. When you write a check and note the expenditure in your check register, subtracting it from your balance, it is much easier to see where your money goes.

If you do get into financial trouble, deal with it immediately. The longer you wait, the worse it will get. You want to avoid having your account turned over to a collection agency. Instead, ask creditors for help in developing a payment plan. Also, seek counseling. A reliable source is the National Foundation for Credit Counseling (NFCC), or ask a trusted family member or college financial aid officer for suggestions.

Financial success does not happen by chance; it is the result of good choices. Using proven money management skills such as setting goals, budgeting, living within your means, and using credit cards wisely will start you on your way to the top of the financial pyramid.

Thinking ahead about Career

Purpose and Instructions

A workplace focus in Chapter 1 is on building interpersonal skills by forming a support group, embracing diversity, and gathering information from available resources. Use the knowledge you have gained from this chapter to solve work-related problems such as the one explained in the following case study. Read the case study on your own or with a partner and then answer the case questions.

Case Study

You have completed your degree program and have been hired for the career of your dreams. The company you work for is in a town far away from your family, friends, and the campus that has been your home for the past several years. You are eager to make a good impression, you have several innovative ideas that you hope to put into practice, and you have confidence in your skills. Although you have made a few new friends at work, you are still feeling the stress of finding yourself alone in a new town at a new job. You know it is just a matter of time until you feel at home in your new environment, but you wish there were something you could do in the meantime.

Case Questions

1. **Define the problem as you see it.**

   _____

   _____

2. **This chapter's strategies include form a support group, embrace diversity, know where to find help, inform yourself, and get involved. Which one of these strategies might be the most helpful solution to your problem? Why?**

   _____

   _____

3. **Explain how you would use the strategy selected for number 2 to solve the problem. For example, if you choose *form a support group*, how would you do it? Who would be the members?**

   _____

   _____

4. **Access the Career Resource Center and read the article entitled "Coworker Relationships" in the *Professionalism and Corporate Cultures* section of *Skills for Your Future*. Based on this article, what else have you learned that could be helpful in this situation?**

   _____

   _____

Your *Reflections*

To *reflect* means to think seriously. Your reflections are your carefully considered thoughts; for example, you might reflect on something you value or hope to accomplish. Near the end of each chapter, you will have an opportunity to reflect on what you have learned and how you will apply the information. Your reflections can help you set goals, focus your actions, and monitor your progress.

For your first reflection, consider what you have learned from this chapter about becoming a confident student. Use the following questions to stimulate your thinking; then write your reflections. Incorporate in your writing specific information from the chapter.

- Would you describe yourself as *flexible?* Why or why not?

- Which of the active learning strategies explained in Chapter 1 do you already use?

- Figure 1.1, on page 6, lists the traits of confident students. Which traits do you possess?

- What is one skill or attitude explained in this chapter that you would like to develop, and what can you begin doing today to make that happen?

Chapter review

ATTITUDES TO DEVELOP

- belief in yourself
- viewing the future positively
- respect for others' differences
- willingness to ask questions

SKILLS TO PRACTICE

- Using technology for communication
- interacting cooperatively with others
- active learning strategies
- managing your finances

CONCEPTS TO UNDERSTAND

self-assessment	diversity	involved	inform	goals
accomplishment	flexible	support	timing	major

Confidence comes from (1) _____. Confident students are (2) _____, or open-minded, and they know that success is a matter of choice, not chance. Chapter 1 explains three strategies that will help you choose success, plan your future, and gain self-confidence: Use (3) _____ to build confidence; define your (4) _____; think ahead to a (5) _____ or career.

Choose success by forming an academic (6)_____ group made up of people with whom you can network and to whom you can turn for help or advice.

Choose success by embracing (7) _____. Reach out to others, respect their differences, and seek common ground. Expect to learn something from everyone you meet, and do your part to make all students feel welcome.

Choose success by becoming an active learner. For example, become familiar with your campus and its services, and know where to find help. Read campus, local, and national publications to (8)_____ yourself. Whether you live on campus or commute to college, get (9)_____ in campus life and organizations. Participate in class and do not hesitate to ask questions. Good questions have four characteristics: *topic, tone,* (10) _____, and *trust*.

When you choose to be successful, you take your life and your future in your own hands. Follow your choices with appropriate action for maximum learning, and you will become a confident student.

To access additional review exercises, go to **college.hmco.com/pic/KanarTCS6e.**

Online Study Center
Review Exercise
ACE Self-Test

Online Study Center

Prepare for Class, Improve Your Grade, and ACE the Test. This chapter's *Student Achievement* resources include

Chapter exercises/forms	Review exercise	Confidence Builder Web search
Remembering cultural differences	ACE Self-Test	

To access these learning and study tools, go to **college.hmco.com/pic/KanarTCS6e.**

Look as far up as you can see. Then reach a little higher.

Explain the different ways people learn; identify your own learning style and explain how self-motivation ensures success.

Describe yourself as a learner: What do you do well, and what skills would you like to develop?

▶ *Define* critical thinking *and explain the role that it plays in learning; also, identify some learning strategies that make studying more efficient and productive.*

▶ *Identify the learning styles of instructors, classmates, and coworkers and explain how being flexible can help you accomplish your goals.*

Motivation is the incentive or desire that prompts you to act. For example, a desire for love, companionship, and a family motivates your search for a life partner. A desire for a certain level of income motivates your career choice. Wanting to help others is the incentive for volunteering your services. Why have you come to college? What do you want most out of life? What kind of work would you like to do in the future? Answer those questions, and you will find your incentives to study, learn, and succeed.

In other words, the motivation to learn lies within you—it is your responsibility. First, decide what you want. Then become a self-starter, one who is not afraid to ask questions and who takes the initiative to set goals and put

KEY TERMS
learning style, *p. 37*
visual learners, *p. 38*
auditory learners, *p. 38*
tactile/kinesthetic learners, *p. 38*
locus of control, *p. 44*
internal locus of control, *p. 44*
external locus of control, *p. 44*

SCANS TERMS
personal responsibility, *p. 34*
basic skills, *p. 34*

plans into action. Being self-motivated means that you take **personal responsibility** for your life and its outcomes. Personal responsibility is a quality that employers and others value and respect.

To help you get motivated and stay motivated, this chapter explains four keys to success in college: Assess your strengths and weaknesses, discover and use your learning style, adapt to others' styles, and develop critical thinking and learning strategies. Use these keys to unlock your learning process, free the confident student within you, and open doors in the workplace.

Personal responsibility is a quality of people who take initiative and accept the consequences of their actions.

ASSESS YOUR STRENGTHS AND WEAKNESSES

▶ *Describe yourself as a learner: What do you do well, and what skills would you like to develop?*

Basic skills include reading, writing, and math, among others.

The first of this chapter's keys to success in college is a realistic assessment of your strengths and weaknesses in the **basic skills** of reading, writing, and math. Today, computer skills are also essential. If you do not know what your strengths and weaknesses are in those areas, you may overestimate your skills and take courses for which you are unprepared. Or you may underestimate the value of your experiences outside of college, which can make up for some skill deficiencies. For example, you may have gained knowledge and abilities from reading, working, traveling, or serving in the military that you can apply to your college courses. Knowing what you can and cannot do, and making decisions based on that knowledge, will help you make responsible course selections.

Form a study group with students who have different strengths.

Your self-assessment should take into consideration the advice you have received from helpful people at your college. Your academic advisors and instructors are eager for you to be successful. That is why they have invested so much time in testing you, advising you, and perhaps requiring you to take a skill-development course in reading, writing, math, or computer literacy. They also know that a strong foundation in these basic skills is a career asset.

Self-assessment is a key to success in the workplace as well as in college. When confronted with any new learning situation, ask yourself questions such as "What do I already know?" "What skills do I have that I can use?" "What personal qualities apply?" "What additional knowledge, skills, or qualities do I need?" Your answers will provide the self-knowledge you need to make good choices.

For an informal assessment of your strengths and weaknesses in the basic skills, complete Awareness Check 2.

AWARENESS CHECK 2

What Are Your Strengths/Weaknesses in Basic Skills?

A	B	C	
			Check *definitely true* (column A), *somewhat true* (column B), or *not at all true* (column C) to explain how each statement applies to you.
☐	☐	☐	1. I can read college textbook assignments without difficulty.
☐	☐	☐	2. I can distinguish between main ideas and details.
☐	☐	☐	3. I can determine an author's purpose.
☐	☐	☐	4. I know how to write a well-organized essay.
☐	☐	☐	5. My sentences are clear in meaning and error free.
☐	☐	☐	6. I have an extensive vocabulary and good spelling skills.
☐	☐	☐	7. I can add, subtract, multiply, and divide with few or no errors.
☐	☐	☐	8. I can easily understand concepts presented in algebra or geometry courses.
☐	☐	☐	9. I am computer wise and Internet savvy.
☐	☐	☐	10. Assessment tests place my basic skills at college level or beyond.

If you answered definitely true *to all ten statements, you may already have a solid foundation in the basic skills, making it easy for you to acquire new knowledge. If you answered* somewhat true *or* not at all true *no more than three times, your strengths should enable you to overcome your weaknesses. More than three* somewhat true *or* not at all true *answers may suggest basic skill development as a top priority. An advisor can help you select appropriate courses. Basic, or academic, skills are one kind of "intelligence" and the one most often addressed in college courses. However, there are other kinds of intelligence, as this chapter explains. The more you learn about the ways that you learn, the more control you will have over what you learn, and the more confident you will grow.*

Howard Gardner's Multiple Intelligences Theory

Those who study intelligence are divided between two camps: Some believe intelligence is a single ability measured by IQ tests, and others think intelligence is multifaceted. Howard Gardner, a professor at Harvard University's Graduate School of Education, belongs to the second camp. Author of *Frames of Mind* (1983) and *Multiple Intelligences: The Theory in Practice* (1993), Gardner argues that we have seven intelligences. In 1996, Gardner added an eighth intelligence to his theory: *naturalistic*. Everyone possesses these intelligences to some degree, but some people may show greater strength in one or more areas. Gardner also believes that we can encourage the development of our intelligences and that we can learn to use them to our advantage.

- **Linguistic** intelligence is characterized by skill with words and a sensitivity to their meanings, sounds, and functions. If your linguistic intelligence is high, you probably learn best by reading.

- **Logical-Mathematical** intelligence is characterized by skill with numbers, scientific ability, and formal reasoning. If your logical-mathematical intelligence is high, you probably learn best by taking a problem-solving approach to learning. Outlining or making charts and graphs may be good study techniques for you.

- **Bodily-Kinesthetic** intelligence enables people to use their bodies skillfully and in goal-oriented ways such as playing a sport or dancing. If your bodily intelligence is high, you may be able to learn more effectively by combining studying with some physical activity.

- **Musical** intelligence is characterized by the ability to find meaning in music and other rhythmical sounds and to reproduce them either vocally or with an instrument. If your musical intelligence is high, you may want to choose a career in music or engage in leisure activities that allow you to pursue your musical interests. Although studying to music is a distraction for some, you may find that it aids your concentration.

- **Spatial** intelligence is characterized by the ability to perceive the world accurately and to mentally reorganize or reinterpret those perceptions. For example, an artist perceives accurately what a bowl of fruit looks like—the colors and sizes of the fruit and how the fruit is arranged. However, the artist's painting of the bowl of fruit is a new interpretation—the artist's mental image of the bowl of fruit—and this image may distort the sizes or change the colors of the fruit. If your spatial intelligence is high, you may learn best by finding ways to visualize or restructure the material that you want to learn.

- **Interpersonal** intelligence is characterized by the ability to read people's moods and intentions and to understand their motives. Empathy is another characteristic of interpersonal intelligence. *Empathy* is the ability to identify with another person's feelings. People who have a high degree of interpersonal intelligence may be said to have "good people skills." If your interpersonal intelligence is high, you may learn best by collaborating with others on projects or by participating in a study group.

- **Intrapersonal** intelligence is characterized by self-knowledge: the ability to read your own emotions, to understand what motivates you, and to use that understanding to shape your behavior. If your intrapersonal intelligence is high, you should be able to make use of all your other intelligences to find the best study methods that will work for you.

- **Naturalistic** intelligence is the ability to perceive the world from an environmental perspective: feeling, sensing, and relating to your environment through its natural features and rhythms. For example, people living in remote cultures become skilled at coping with nature, navigating without maps, and surviving in a hostile climate. For others, this intelligence may reveal itself in curiosity about nature, love of the outdoors, or special ability in the natural sciences.

In his more recent work, Gardner explores the possibility of additional intelligences but acknowledges that further study is needed before he feels comfortable about defining and adding another type of intelligence to his list.

Gardner's theory of multiple intelligences (MI) is widely accepted among educators. However, opinions about the theory's usefulness differ. Some psychologists and educators praise Gardner for raising public awareness about the many facets of intellectual ability. But others are concerned because the theory has never been formally tested and because Gardner's naturalistic intelligence, unlike his original seven, does not seem to be an independent category. Instead, it may be a special application of one or more other intelligences. In any case, it is well to remember that most employers place great value on verbal and math skills, believing that they are stronger predictors of success at work. The practical value of Gardner's theory may be that it encourages students to discover and use all of their talents and intellectual capacities to create success in college and in life.

To learn more about Gardner's research and its applications, do an online search using these keywords: *learning styles, multiple intelligences, Howard Gardner.*

DISCOVER AND USE YOUR LEARNING STYLE

▶ *Explain the different ways that people learn, identify your own learning style, and explain how self-motivation ensures success.*

Discovering and using your learning style is the second key to success in college. Like everything else about you, your learning style is uniquely your own, different from anyone else's. Your **learning style** is your characteristic and preferred way of learning. Another way to look at learning style is to think of it as the conditions under which you find it easiest and most pleasant to learn and to work. For example, suppose you buy a new piece of software. What would be the easiest, quickest, and most pleasant way for you to learn how to use it? Would you read the manual, follow the instructions on a tutorial disk, ask a friend who knows how to use it, or sign up for a course? None of these ways is the *best* way to learn how to use new software, but one of these ways, or a combination of them, may be the best way for *you* to learn.

Your learning style has many components. We will discuss four of them:

1. Your five senses
2. Your body's reactions
3. Your preferred learning environment
4. Your level of motivation

Online Study Center
Confidence Builder
Web Search

Learning style is a preferred way of learning, but you can also adapt your study methods to take advantage of other learning styles as well.

EXERCISE 2.1   LEARNING STYLE

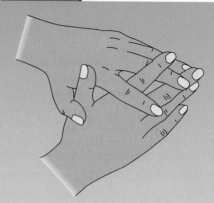

TRY THIS EXPERIMENT FOR A vivid example of the way your learning style affects you.

1. **Fold your hands.**

2. **Look at which thumb and fingers are on top. Are they your left or right?**

3. **Now fold your hands again so that the other thumb and fingers are on top. Does this position feel comfortable to you?**

4. **Fold your hands your preferred way and notice any difference in feeling.**

Folding your hands is something you do automatically, and because you always do it your preferred way, you feel comfortable. But when you fold your hands differently, you have to think about what you are doing. You feel uncomfortable because that position is not natural for you. Your learning style is automatic in a similar way. When you are in a classroom environment that matches your learning style, everything feels right. But if the environment does not match your style, you may feel out of place, uncomfortable, and unable to do your best. To combat feelings of discomfort in a classroom environment, understand your learning style. Find ways to adapt your style to fit the environment, and you will be successful. Adapting your style is like learning to live with the wrong thumb on top. At first, it may feel a little strange, but with practice the difference will not be noticeable.

Your Five Senses

Visual learners prefer to learn by reading or watching.

Auditory learners like to learn by listening.

Tactile/kinesthetic learners learn best by hands-on or motor activity.

Is your learning style primarily visual, auditory, or tactile? **Visual learners** prefer to learn by reading or watching. **Auditory learners** like to learn by listening. **Tactile/kinesthetic learners** learn by doing, by touching or manipulating objects, or by using their hands. Figure 2.1 provides examples of each learning style and shows how learning style preferences affect how you go about completing a task such as learning how to use new software or assembling a child's toy. As you read the chart, remember that it illustrates *preferences:* what each type of learner feels most comfortable doing. The most successful learners are those who take control of the learning situation by adapting to different modes of instruction and by using a combination of learning methods.

Though everyone can learn to adapt to different learning styles, most people have difficulty at first when asked to do something that seems unnatural to them. Imagine the frustration of a visual learner whose instructor gives a lecture without any visual aids. You may have felt a similar frustration in classrooms when the instructor presented material in a sensory mode other than your preferred one. For example, if you are a student who dislikes lecture courses, loses concentration, or has trouble following ideas, maybe you're not an auditory learner. To be successful in a lecture class, you may need to develop strategies that will help you adapt to auditory modes of instruction. For one thing, you could concentrate on developing good note-taking skills and listening techniques as explained in Chapter 5. To fill in gaps in your notes, compare them with those of someone in the class who does have a strong auditory preference and who is good at taking notes.

Because instructors' teaching styles and methods differ, you must be flexible enough to adapt to whatever instructional mode is being used. Figure 2.2 illustrates some common teaching methods, the learning style preferences they appeal to, and some adaptive strategies for you to try. To determine your sensory preferences, complete Awareness Check 3 on page 40.

FIGURE 2.1

LEARNING STYLE PREFERENCES

LEARNING PREFERENCE	DEFINITION	LEARNING TO USE NEW SOFTWARE	ASSEMBLING A CHILD'S TOY
Visual	Prefers visual sense. Must *see* to understand. Learns best by reading and watching.	Looks at diagrams. Reads a manual. Watches someone demonstrate the process.	Tries to duplicate picture on the box. Reads instructions silently while assembling toy.
Auditory	Prefers auditory sense. Must *hear* to understand. Learns best by listening to an explanation.	Attends a class or workshop to hear explanation. Listens to someone read the instructions.	Reads instructions aloud while working. Asks someone to read each step.
Tactile/Kinesthetic	Prefers tactile sense. Learns best by engaging in hands-on or physical/ motor activity.	Uses trial-and-error. Combines learning with physical/motor activity.	May ignore the instructions or resort to them only when trial-and-error method fails.

FIGURE 2.2

ADAPTING LEARNING STYLE TO TEACHING METHOD

TEACHING METHODS	LEARNING STYLE/ SENSORY PREFERENCE	ADAPTIVE STRATEGIES TO TRY
Lecture/class discussion	Auditory	Take notes (tactile and visual). Watch for visual cues such as gestures and facial expressions that emphasize important points (visual). Pay attention to visual aids or information written on chalkboard (visual).
Videotaped presentations Use of visual aids	Visual	Listen to instructor's explanations or comments and copy them into your notes (auditory and tactile). Summarize presentation in your notes and read summary aloud to review (auditory and tactile).
Hands-on or motor activity	Tactile/Kinesthetic	Summarize the activity in your notes to read later (auditory and visual). Listen to any explanation that accompanies the activity (auditory).

AWARENESS CHECK 3

What Are Your Sensory Preferences?

Check all of the statements that seem true of you.

☐ 1. I learn best by reading on my own.

☐ 2. I get the best results from listening to lectures.

☐ 3. I enjoy courses where there is some physical activity involved.

☐ 4. I can learn how to do something by watching a demonstration of how it's done.

☐ 5. Class discussions are helpful to me.

☐ 6. I like to type and to use computers.

☐ 7. Illustrations, charts, and diagrams improve my understanding.

☐ 8. I'd rather listen to the instructor's explanation than do the assigned reading.

☐ 9. I get more out of labs than lectures because of the hands-on approach.

☐ 10. How-to manuals and printed directions are helpful to me.

☐ 11. I like to use audiocassette tapes of lessons and exercises.

☐ 12. I'd rather work with machines and equipment than listen to or read explanations.

☐ 13. I can learn to do something if someone shows me how.

☐ 14. I can follow directions best when someone reads them to me.

☐ 15. It's not enough to show me; I have to do it myself.

Statements 1, 4, 7, 10, and 13 are characteristic of visual learners. Statements 2, 5, 8, 11, and 14 are characteristic of auditory learners. Statements 3, 6, 9, 12, and 15 are characteristic of tactile learners. If your checks are spread evenly among two or more categories, you may be equally comfortable using one or more of your sensory modes. But remember that this Awareness Check is only an informal survey. For a formal assessment of your learning style, see an academic or career development counselor, who may be able to give you one of several well-known tests.

Your Body's Reactions

When you are in a classroom or study area, lighting, temperature, and the comfort of the furniture may or may not affect your ability to pay attention or to get your work done. If your body does react strongly to these and other influences such as hunger, tiredness, or mild illness, then you may lose concentration. You should take care of these physiological needs before attempting to do anything that demands your full attention. Determining your physiological preferences and building your schedule accordingly is one way to use your learning style to create the conditions under which you will stay most alert.

Like most people, you probably have a peak time of day when you are most alert and energetic. Throughout the day your concentration, attention, and energy levels fluctuate. In the morning you might be alert and ready for anything, but by afternoon you might feel sapped of energy. If you are a morning person, then it would make sense to schedule your classes in the morning if you can. But if you are alert and concentrate better in the late afternoon or at night, then schedule as many of your courses as possible in the evening hours. If you anticipate that a certain course will be difficult, make every effort to schedule it at your peak time of day. Then plan to do as much of your studying as possible at this time of day.

If you learn to accept what you cannot change, then you can adapt to situations that don't meet your preferences, knowing that you will have to try harder to pay attention and remain on task. Although you have limited control over your classroom environment, you can set up your study environment to reflect your preferences. See Chapter 10 for a detailed discussion and suggestions. Awareness Check 4 will help you understand how your body's reactions might affect your ability to learn.

AWARENESS CHECK 4

How Does Your Body React?

Check the statements that best describe you.

1. I feel most alert in the morning hours.

2. I don't "come alive" until afternoon or early evening.

3. I am definitely a night person.

4. I concentrate and work best in a brightly lighted room.

5. Bright light distracts me; I prefer natural or nonglare lighting.

6. Overhead lighting is never right; I need an adjustable lamp.

7. The temperature in a classroom does not usually affect my concentration.

8. I can't work or concentrate in a room that is too hot or too cold.

9. I usually get chills when sitting next to a fan, air conditioner, or open window.

10. If my chair or desk in class is uncomfortable, I am usually able to ignore it and concentrate.

11. If my chair is not the right height, my back or neck aches.

12. If I feel a little ill or headachy, I can't think about anything else.

13. I can ignore feelings of hunger or tiredness long enough to keep my attention on my work.

14. Mild feelings of illness usually don't distract me from my work.

Your answers to the Awareness Check indicate the following about your body's reactions: the time of day when you are most alert (items 1–3), your lighting preferences (items 4–6), your temperature preferences (items 7–9), your comfort in relation to furnishings in your classroom (items 10–11), the extent to which hunger, tiredness, and illness affect your ability to concentrate in class (items 12–14).

EXERCISE 2.2   LEARNING STYLE

ANSWER THE FOLLOWING QUESTIONS ABOUT your best class and your worst class—*best* meaning the class in which your performance has been most successful and *worst* meaning the class in which your performance has been the least successful. Compare your body's reactions to each classroom environment (questions 1–6). Then determine to what extent your body's reactions affect your learning in each class and what you can do to adapt more effectively (questions 7–8).

1. **What time does the class meet, and are you most alert at this time?**

   best class _____

   worst class _____

2. **Is the temperature in the classroom generally comfortable for you?**

   best class _____

   worst class _____

3. **What type of lighting is available in the classroom, and do you find the lighting acceptable?**

   best class _____

   worst class _____

4. **Are you generally rested or tired when you go to class?**

   best class _____

   worst class _____

5. **Have you eaten recently before class, or do you become hungry during class?**

   best class _____

   worst class _____

6. **Would you describe the seating arrangement and the furniture in the classroom as comfortable or uncomfortable?**

   best class _____

   worst class _____

7. **What relationship do you see between your body's reactions and your performances in your best and worst class?**

   _____

   _____

8. **What can you do to improve your performance in your worst class? What can you do to make your worst class seem more like your best class?**

   _____

   _____

Your Preferred Learning Environment

A learning environment is much more than the place where your class meets. The way the class is structured is also an important part of the learning environment. In what kind of learning environment are you most comfortable? Do you like a traditional classroom, where desks are arranged in rows and the instructor directs activities? Or are you more comfortable in a looser arrangement, where instructor and students sit together in a circle, for example, or where small groups of students sit together at tables?

Perhaps you are a self-directed student who prefers to work alone in a self-paced class or lab. Or you may need a lot of direction and supervision while you learn. You may be a student who learns more from the instructor's lectures and comments than from class discussions. Or you may be a student who doesn't get much out of class unless you have opportunities to share ideas with others in group activities. The following comments illustrate three learning environment preferences. Do you recognize yourself in one of these comments, or do you have yet another preference?

1. **Carol:** The instructors are the ones I've paid my money to hear; they're the experts. I resent it when class time is taken up answering questions that are covered in the reading assignments.

2. **Andy:** I hate this class. All the instructor does is lecture. I learn more from class discussions and listening to different people's opinions.

3. **Grant:** I don't like it when I have to adjust my pace to the rest of the class. I'd rather work independently so I can progress at my own rate, taking as much time as I need.

Carol likes a traditional, teacher-centered classroom. Andy prefers a student-centered environment. Grant, who likes to work alone, prefers individualized instruction.

Most of the time you will have to adapt to whatever learning environment is available. However, understanding your preferences will enable you to select the kind of classes in which you are most comfortable, if you have a choice. Advisors and other students are good sources of information about the type of learning environment a specific course or instructor provides.

EXERCISE 2.3   LEARNING STYLE

Exercise Purpose

Learning style preferences can influence, but not necessarily determine, how well you will do in a course. Knowing how you learn can help you create a study environment and materials that work best for you. This exercise will help you find out more about your learning preferences.

Exercise Background

As you have learned from taking Awareness Checks 3 and 4, self-assessment is the key to discovering your learning style. These short, informal tests provide a brief example of the kinds of questions asked and behaviors surveyed on more extensive formal and informal inventories. Tests like the following help you identify personality traits or preferences that may influence your life interests and career choices as well as the ways that you learn, interact with others, make decisions, and solve problems.

- Meyers-Briggs Type Indicator (MBTI)

- Kolb Learning Style Inventory

- Hogan/Champagne Personal Style Inventory

- Keirsey Temperament Sorter

One or more of these tests may be available to you through your college's career center or counseling department.

Exercise Task

1. Take a learning styles inventory such as those listed previously. Your instructor may suggest one or may direct you to an office on campus where such testing is done. If you prefer, you can also search the Internet for an informal inventory. Many are available free of charge. Try the search phrases *learning styles, learning styles inventories,* and *learning styles and testing.* See also college.hmco.com/pic/KanarTCS6e for suggested sites.

2. Compare your results on whatever inventory you take with your results from Awareness Checks 3 and 4. What is your learning style? What do your results suggest that you do to improve your learning and studying?

3. Write a paragraph in which you explain the results of your search and assessment and be prepared to share it in class.

Your Level of Motivation

Locus of control refers to the source of motivation: internal (self) or external (other).

Your motivation and your attitude—positive or negative—toward college, work, instructors, and your abilities may depend on your **locus of control**. J. B. Rotter, a psychologist, first explained the concept in 1954 as part of his social learning theory. *Locus* means place. Your locus of control is where you place responsibility for control over your life. Do you believe that you are in charge? If so, then you may have an *internal* locus of control. Do you believe that others more powerful than you are in control of what happens to you? If so, then you may have an *external* locus of control.

What does locus of control mean to you as a student, and how can it affect your motivation? To find out, complete Awareness Check 5; then read the explanation that follows.

Your Locus of Control

Internal locus of control means self-motivation, taking responsibility for your actions and their consequences.

Students who have an **internal locus of control** can see a direct connection between their efforts and their grades. These students tend to be self-motivated, positive thinkers. They believe they can do whatever they set out to accomplish. They are not afraid of change. They welcome challenges. When they make a mistake, they can usually trace it to something they did wrong or something they did not understand. These students don't believe in luck or fate. They are in control of their lives. When things go wrong, they try to figure out what they can do to make things right again.

External locus of control means others control your motivation, and you see little or no connection between your actions and their consequences.

Students who have an **external locus of control** see little or no connection between their efforts and their grades. They may believe that teachers award grades on the basis of personal feelings or that their grades result from good or bad

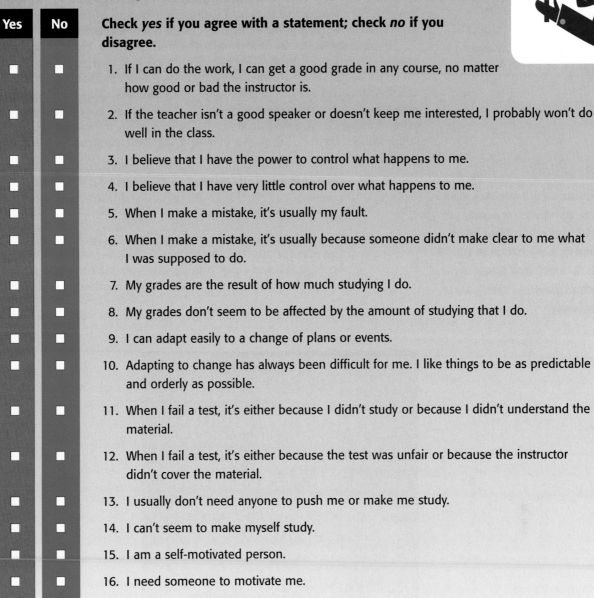

AWARENESS CHECK 5

What Is Your Locus of Control?

Yes	No	
☐	☐	**Check *yes* if you agree with a statement; check *no* if you disagree.**
☐	☐	1. If I can do the work, I can get a good grade in any course, no matter how good or bad the instructor is.
☐	☐	2. If the teacher isn't a good speaker or doesn't keep me interested, I probably won't do well in the class.
☐	☐	3. I believe that I have the power to control what happens to me.
☐	☐	4. I believe that I have very little control over what happens to me.
☐	☐	5. When I make a mistake, it's usually my fault.
☐	☐	6. When I make a mistake, it's usually because someone didn't make clear to me what I was supposed to do.
☐	☐	7. My grades are the result of how much studying I do.
☐	☐	8. My grades don't seem to be affected by the amount of studying that I do.
☐	☐	9. I can adapt easily to a change of plans or events.
☐	☐	10. Adapting to change has always been difficult for me. I like things to be as predictable and orderly as possible.
☐	☐	11. When I fail a test, it's either because I didn't study or because I didn't understand the material.
☐	☐	12. When I fail a test, it's either because the test was unfair or because the instructor didn't cover the material.
☐	☐	13. I usually don't need anyone to push me or make me study.
☐	☐	14. I can't seem to make myself study.
☐	☐	15. I am a self-motivated person.
☐	☐	16. I need someone to motivate me.

Look at your answers in both columns. If you checked mostly odd-numbered items in the yes *column and mostly even-numbered items in the* no *column, then you may have an internal locus of control. If you checked mostly even-numbered items in the* yes *column and odd-numbered items in the* no *column, then you may have an external locus of control. Based on the text descriptions of students who have an internal or external locus of control, which one most accurately describes you?*

luck. These students tend to be negative thinkers who need someone to motivate them and give them a push to succeed. They believe that many of the things they want in life are out of reach or that other people are holding them back. They may be afraid of change and may prefer to follow familiar routines. When they make mistakes, they blame others for being unfair or for not giving them the right information. They believe that they have little control over their lives. When something goes wrong, they may believe that they can do nothing about it.

Research shows that locus of control affects achievement. The more internal your locus of control, the greater your chances for success in college. Thinking positively about yourself and your abilities, accepting responsibility for motivating yourself, and doing what is necessary to succeed will produce results not only in college but also in your job or career and in your personal life. If you already have an internal locus of control, recognize it for the asset that it is. Use your ability to motivate yourself to stay in control and on track. Everyone can benefit from becoming more self-motivated.

Online Study Center
Locus of Control

1. **Become a positive thinker.** Earlier in this chapter, you assessed your strengths and weaknesses. Focus on your strengths. Remind yourself of all the things you do well and take action to overcome your weaknesses.

2. **Take responsibility for motivating yourself.** Realize that only you can make yourself study. When you study as you should, congratulate yourself and enjoy your good grades. When you don't study, accept the consequences and don't blame others.

CONCEPT CHECK 2.2

Listen carefully to a friend talk about a course, an instructor, or a grade. Can you tell whether your friend has an internal locus of control or an external locus of control? What specific words or actions reveal your friend's source of motivation?

One aspect of an internal locus of control is a willingness to adapt to the learning environment.

3. **Accept the fact that success results from effort.** If you are not getting where you want to go, then apply yourself with more determination and be persistent. The greater your effort and persistence, the more likely you are to get what you want.

4. **Start listening to yourself talk.** Eliminate the nameless "they" from your vocabulary. "*They* made me do it," "*They* keep me from succeeding," and "If only *they* had told me" are comments externally motivated students make when things go wrong. By replacing *they* with *I* in your vocabulary, you are taking control of your life.

EXERCISE 2.4   COLLABORATIVE ACTIVITY

DISCUSS THE FOLLOWING SITUATIONS WITH your group members. Follow the guidelines for successful collaboration that appear on the inside back cover. Determine whether each of the following situations is one that you can control, and be able to explain why or why not. Write your evaluation on your own paper or download the Collaborative Exercise Form from the Online Study Center. Share your work with the rest of the class. Then evaluate your work.

1. **You arrive late for class because:**
   Your alarm didn't go off.
   Your ride didn't come.
   You had to work late the night before.
   You had car trouble.

2. **Studying is difficult for you because:**
   There are too many distractions at home.
   You have a family to take care of.
   The textbooks are difficult or boring.
   You don't know what to study.

3. **You never seem to have enough time because:**
   People are always interrupting you.
   Your instructors assign too much outside work.
   You have too many things to do.
   You often procrastinate.

4. **You often leave homework undone because:**
   You are too tired to do it.
   You can't seem to turn down your friends' offers to socialize.
   You get stuck or don't understand how to do the assignment.
   You put work or family obligations first.

Group Evaluation:

Evaluate your discussion. Did everyone contribute? Did you accomplish your task succesfully? What additional questions do you have about locus of control? How will you find answers to your questions?

Online Study Center   *www.college.hmco.com/pic/KanarTCS6e*

C R I T I C A L

T H I N K I N G

Exercise Overview

Claire Weinstein and her colleagues at the University of Texas have developed *strategic learning,* a method for teaching students how to learn. The method involves choosing appropriate strategies for each learning task. For example, listening attentively and taking good notes are appropriate strategies for listening to lectures. This exercise will help you understand and try out strategic learning.

Exercise Background

According to Weinstein and her colleagues, strategic learning has three components: *Skill, will,* and *self-regulation. Skill* means know your strengths and weaknesses, determining what a learning task requires and choosing a task-appropriate strategy. *Will* is the desire to learn and the self-motivation to do what is required. Will involves commitment, a positive attitude, and the avoidance of self-sabotaging thoughts and actions. *Self-regulation* means taking personal responsibility for learning and accepting the outcomes of your actions. Only you are in control of your time, motivation, concentration, and stress. If your grades are not what they should be, then, as a self-regulated student, you must determine what went wrong and choose alternative learning strategies. The strategic learning method helps students manage their learning and deal with the consequences.

Exercise Task

To think critically about skill, will, and self-regulation, first be sure that you understand the concepts as previously stated. Then try to make connections between these concepts and this chapter's four keys to success in college. Write your answers to the following questions.

1. When you assess your strengths and weaknesses, are you employing skill, will, or self-regulation?
2. How does will affect motivation?
3. How is self-regulation involved in learning style?
4. What roles do skill, will, and self-regulation play in developing good study skills or habits?
5. What do you need to be successful in an algebra course? (*Hint:* as a prerequisite for taking algebra, you need basic math skills. What other skills do you need? How do will and self-regulation fit in?)

Source: Claire Ellen Weinstein, Gary Hanson, Lorrie Powdril, Linda Roska, Doug Dierking, Jenefer Jusman, and Erin McCann, "The Design and Evaluation of a Course in Strategic Learning," *National Association for Developmental Education, Selected Conference Papers,* Vol. 3 (Denver, CO, 1997).

The internal and external loci of control represent extremes of behavior. Your locus of control is your index of personal responsibility. The more internal you are, the more you believe that you are in control of your life. The more external you are, the more you believe that someone or something outside yourself is controlling the circumstances that affect your life. In other words, the degree to which you *believe* you can control what happens to you largely determines the amount of control you *actually* have.

ADAPT TO OTHERS' STYLES

▶ *Identify the learning styles of instructors, classmates, and coworkers and explain how being flexible can help you accomplish your goals.*

Everyone has a learning style. In your college's diverse learning community, it is important to acknowledge and accept the different ways in which instructors teach and students learn. Adapting to others' styles is the third key to your success.

When working collaboratively with classmates or when speaking in front of a class, acknowledge others' styles. For example, a person who prefers to work alone may have to be encouraged to participate with group members. Similarly, if you are planning to give an oral presentation, supplement it with visual aids to appeal to the visual learners in class.

You probably won't find it difficult to adapt to your classmates' styles. Many of them are your friends, but you should make an effort to get along with all of your classmates since you will be working with them throughout the term.

The greatest challenge lies in adapting to your instructors' teaching styles. Just as you have a learning style, your instructors have teaching styles. An instructor's teaching style determines, to some extent, the instructional methods he or she prefers to use. Although educational researchers define a number of teaching styles, we will consider only two basic types: *independent* and *interactive*. Each of these styles represents an extreme of behavior. However, many instructors' styles fall somewhere between these extremes. For example, an instructor may use *mixed modes:* a combination of teaching methods such as lecturing, collaborative activities, and group discussion.

The instructor whose style is *independent* is usually formal and businesslike with students and places more importance on individual effort than on group effort. This instructor expects students to assume responsibility for learning, to work independently, and to seek help when needed. Lecturing is the preferred teaching method of this instructor, who will often call on students rather than ask for volunteers. Students often feel competitive in this instructor's class. If you feel most comfortable in lecture courses and like working independently, then you may do your best work with an instructor whose style is independent.

On the other hand, the instructor whose style is *interactive* is usually informal with students and places more importance on group effort than on individual effort. The interactive instructor guides students step by step through tasks and anticipates their needs. Small group activities and large group discussions are this instructor's preferred teaching methods. Rather than call on students, he or she will usually ask for volunteers. Students often feel cooperative in this instructor's class. If you feel more comfortable in classes where students do most of the talking, and if you would rather work with others than by yourself, then you may be able to do your best work with an instructor whose teaching style is interactive.

EXERCISE 2.5 COLLABORATIVE ACTIVITY

GET TOGETHER WITH A CLASSMATE who is taking one or more of your courses. Analyze the instructor's teaching style by completing the checklist that follows. Fill in the name of the course; then check each phrase that describes the instructor. If you analyze more than one instructor's style, complete a checklist for each one. To download an additional checklist, go to http://collegesurvival.college.hmco.com/students. Then compare your checklist with your partner's. Do your results agree?

Teaching Style Checklist

Course: _____

☐ 1. **Formal, businesslike attitude**

☐ 2. **Informal, casual attitude**

☐ 3. **Encourages competition among students**

☐ 4. **Encourages cooperation among students**

☐ 5. **Lectures most of the time**

☐ 6. **Holds class discussions most of the time**

☐ 7. **Stresses importance of individual effort**

☐ 8. **Stresses importance of group effort**

☐ 9. **Often uses visual aids**

☐ 10. **Rarely uses visual aids**

☐ 11. **Calls on students**

☐ 12. **Asks for volunteers**

☐ 13. **Expects students to ask for help**

☐ 14. **Guides students step by step**

☐ 15. **Mainly sticks to facts**

☐ 16. **Often shares personal experiences**

☐ 17. **"Tells" what to do, gives directions**

☐ 18. **"Shows" what to do, gives directions**

If you checked mostly odd-numbered items, your instructor's teaching style is independent. If you checked mostly even-numbered items, your instructor's teaching style is interactive. If you checked some even- and some odd-numbered items, your instructor's style may combine modes from both the independent and interactive styles.

If you do not like or do not get along with one of your instructors, you may be reacting negatively to a teaching style that conflicts with your learning style. However, don't let personal feelings keep you from being successful in the course. Instead, focus on what you *can* do to meet the instructor's requirements and make an extra effort to adapt to his or her teaching style. By making this effort, you may find that your relationship with your instructor will improve dramatically.

In an ideal situation, advisors would match students with instructors who have similar styles. But in the real world, you may not always get the courses and instructors that you want. Also, you may not know in advance what an instructor's teaching style is. A good rule of thumb to remember when dealing with instructors is that it is *your* responsibility to adapt to their styles, not the other way around. By learning to adapt to your instructors' styles now, you are preparing for the future. Throughout your career, you will encounter employers, coworkers, and others whose styles differ from yours, and you will be expected to work effectively with all of them.

DEVELOP CRITICAL THINKING AND LEARNING STRATEGIES

▶ *Define* critical thinking *and explain the role it plays in learning. Also, identify some learning strategies that make studying more efficient and productive.*

Read the following student comments about studying and learning. Do any of them sound like statements you have made? Can you think of another one? Add it to the list in the space provided.

Student A: "My academic skills are OK, but I still don't make the grades I want."

Student B: "I study a lot, but I often study the wrong things."

Student C: "I usually get the main idea but forget the details."

Student D: "I never seem to have enough time for studying."

Student E: "I've found several Internet sources on my research topic, but I don't know how good they are."

Your comment about studying and learning: _____

_____

These statements illustrate common problems that students encounter as they attend classes and study. You can solve these problems by learning to think critically and study efficiently. However, you may have to work hard to overcome your difficulties and may need to devote some time to skills development.

Developing critical thinking and learning strategies is your fourth key to success in college. Knowing how to study helps you apply your knowledge and use your skills so that you can be successful in your courses. For example, if you learn how to listen effectively and take good notes, then you will be able to follow lectures and to record essential information for study and review. If you learn how to manage your time, then you will be able to keep up with assignments and meet deadlines. If you learn how to prepare for and take tests, then you will be able to make the grades you want. If you learn how to evaluate what you read, on the Internet and elsewhere, then you will be able to select appropriate sources when researching a topic.

Learning styles, critical thinking, and learning strategies overlap. *Thinking critically* is the means by which you make sense of the world around you. The learning activities that college students must do require critical thinking. For example, you must be able to make decisions, solve problems, reason logically, use your creativity, and know how to use appropriate learning strategies. Developing critical thinking skills will also make you more employable in the future. Those who can think critically and who know how to gather and use information will get the best jobs and will advance more rapidly in their careers than those who don't.

Studying is a kind of concentrated thinking that, at its best, involves more than one of your senses. For example, when you read and underline a textbook chapter, you are using your visual and tactile senses. Studying is easier and more efficient when you use what you know about your learning style to create the conditions in which your concentration will be greatest. Figure 2.3 on page 52 shows how critical thinking and learning strategies work together to help you complete typical tasks that your instructors might ask you to do. Chapters 5 and 6

Online Study Center
Review Exercise
ACE Self-Test

and Chapters 8–14 focus on the specific learning strategies that can help you become a more confident, skilled student.

Chapter 3 provides a more detailed explanation of critical thinking and how to develop and use your critical thinking skills. The fact is that you have already been using critical thinking for many everyday tasks. For example, choosing courses and making this semester's or quarter's schedule required you to *make decisions:* What courses should I take? At what times should I schedule them? If a course you had wanted to take was filled or if your work hours conflicted with the class hours, those situations required you to use your *problem-solving* skills. Two exercises in each chapter, Critical Thinking and Thinking Ahead About Career, ask you to apply skills or knowledge that you have gained from the chapter to practical situations that you might encounter either in college, at work, or in your personal life. In other words, when you use what you already know to find out what you don't know, you are thinking critically.

FIGURE 2.3

USING CRITICAL THINKING AND LEARNING STRATEGIES

CRITICAL THINKING	TASKS TO DO	LEARNING STRATEGIES NEEDED/USED
Making decisions	Decide when to study. Decide what's important. Select courses. Decide what to study.	Set up a schedule. Read for main idea, details, key terms. Know requirements; use resources. Review notes, old tests, assignments.
Solving problems	Solve math problems. Avoid procrastination. Reduce test anxiety.	Record problems and solutions on note cards. Make and follow a schedule. Practice relaxation techniques.
Reasoning	Write a speech. Follow an author's ideas. Compare theories.	Make an outline. Look for patterns of organization. Make a chart or information map.
Knowing how to learn	Learn from reading. Learn from listening.	Locate, understand, interpret information. Use listening and note-taking skills.
Thinking creatively	Compose an original piece of work. Develop a project.	Keep an "idea" journal. Combine ideas in unique ways.

Thinking ahead about Career

Purpose and Instructions

A workplace focus in Chapter 2 is on taking personal responsibility for your success through self-motivation and self-management. You can use the knowledge you have gained from this chapter to solve work-related problems such as the one explained in the following case study. Read the case study on your own or with a partner and then answer the case questions.

Case Study

Jan graduated from college five years ago. She is an insurance agent for a large company, and she thinks by now she should have been promoted. She has applied for a management position whenever one has become available, but she is always passed over. Jan doesn't understand why. She has sold as many policies as her coworkers have, more than some, and she is good at what she does.

Now and then, of course, she does get angry with customers, but it's always their fault. Either they don't read their policies, or they don't listen to her explanations. She can't help it if they don't understand what their coverage is. Jan also argues with her supervisor. She can't understand why the supervisor expects her to be on time every day. Some mornings she's just tired, and sometimes she is "unavoidably detained." She thinks that the supervisor's demands are unrealistic.

As far as her coworkers are concerned, Jan can't be bothered. She's too busy to take part in office social activities, and she's too financially strapped to participate in the various charity drives that her coworkers organize. At her last evaluation, Jan's supervisor told her that her people skills needed improving. "You're not being fair," Jan said.

When a management position recently became vacant, and Jan's application was again denied, she blamed it on bad luck.

Case Questions

1. What position does Jan want?

   _____

2. What problems with customers, coworkers, and her supervisor are keeping Jan from reaching her goal?

   _____

3. What is Jan's locus of control, and how is it affecting her behavior?

   _____

4. Access the Career Resource Center and read the article entitled "Personal Responsibility at Work" in the *Self-Responsibility and Self-Motivation* section of *Skills for Your Future*. Based on this article, what can Jan do to change her behavior and improve her chances of getting ahead in her career?

   _____

   _____

Your *Reflections*

Reflect on what you have learned from this chapter about self-motivation. Let this reflection be a profile of yourself as a learner. Monitor your progress by revisiting your profile throughout the term, making changes as you gain new skills. Use the following questions to stimulate your thinking, and include in your profile specific information from the chapter.

- What have you learned from this chapter's Awareness Checks about your basic skills, learning style, and locus of control?

- What do Gardner's MI theory and Weinstein's strategic learning method say about you?

- How do you rate yourself on the critical thinking skills and learning strategies listed in Figure 2.3?

- Your profile is a self-assessment. How will you use the information you have gained from it?

Chapter review

To review the chapter, reflect on the following confidence-building attitudes and skills. Complete **Concepts to Understand** by filling in the blanks with words or terms from the list provided. Then practice your new skills at every opportunity.

ATTITUDES TO DEVELOP
- self-motivation
- personal responsibility
- willingness to adapt

SKILLS TO PRACTICE
- self-assessment
- critical thinking
- acknowledging and adapting learning styles

CONCEPTS TO UNDERSTAND

| learning | senses | strategies | adapt | decisions |
| problems | reactions | internal | academic | critical |

Strategies for becoming a confident, successful student include making use of the four keys to success in college discussed in this chapter.

Assessing your (1) _____ strengths and weaknesses is the most important key. Being realistic about what you are able to do will help you select the right courses.

Discovering and using your (2) _____ style is another important key to your success. Use your five (3) _____ to help you take in information accurately and remember what you learn. Let your body's (4) _____ tell you when you are most alert; then try to plan your schedule accordingly. Know which learning environment you prefer but be willing to adapt to others. Increase your level of motivation by developing an (5) _____ locus of control.

The third key is your willingness to (6) _____ to others' styles. No matter how much an instructor's style or your classmates' styles differ from your own, it is still *your* responsibility to meet course requirements. Make whatever adjustments are needed for you to achieve success and to establish good relations with classmates and instructors.

A fourth key to success in college is to develop (7) _____ thinking and learning (8) _____. Making (9) _____ and solving (10) _____ are just two of the critical thinking skills involved in studying. All the important strategies you will need to develop or improve—such as how to take notes, listen effectively, and prepare for and take tests—are covered in this book.

To access additional review exercises, go to **college.hmco.com/pic/KanarTCS6e.**

Online Study Center
Review Exercise
ACE Self-Test

Online Study Center

Prepare for Class, Improve Your Grade, and ACE the Test. This chapter's *Student Achievement* resources include

| Chapter exercises/forms | Review exercise | Confidence Builder Web search |
| Article: *Locus of Control* | ACE Self-Test | |

To access these learning and study tools, go to **college.hmco.com/pic/KanarTCS6e.**

3

Thinking critically and creatively

The critical thinker asks, "What?" and "How?" The creative thinker asks, "Why?" and "What if?" These questions are a starting point for considering any subject.

▶ *Recognize the ideas and beliefs that you and others take for granted, the knowledge and experience that shape opinions.*

▶ *Predict a successful learning outcome by setting a goal, having a purpose, and choosing an appropriate strategy.*

▶ *Know how to find the underlying meaning in stated information.*

▶ EXAMINE ASSUMPTIONS

▶ PREDICT OUTCOMES

Set Goals for Learning
Use Purpose-Guided Study

▶ MAKE INFERENCES

Read and Listen for Purpose, Ideas, and Meaning
Recognize Organizational Patterns
Integrate New Information with Prior Knowledge
Define New or Unfamiliar Terms

▶ EVALUATE INFORMATION AND SOURCES

Reliability
Objectivity
Usefulness

▶ THINK THROUGH DECISIONS AND PROBLEMS

Apply the COPE Strategy

▶ *Use the COPE strategy for making decisions and for thinking through problems to find workable solutions.*

▶ *Determine whether an informational source is credible by applying standards of evaluation such as reliability, objectivity, and usefulness.*

Critical thinking is logical, analytical, self-reflective, conscious, and purposeful reasoning.

Creative thinking has some of the qualities of critical thinking but is also inventive and original.

What is **critical thinking?** Broadly defined, it is *the process of constructing and evaluating meaning.* Specifically, critical thinking is *logical*, or *analytical*, reasoning that helps you make sense of the information you receive from any source. Critical thinking is also the process of *self-reflection*, whereby you examine your actions and their consequences. Critical thinking is both *conscious* and *purposeful:* You know that you are doing it, and you know why.

Creative thinking is *inventive* and *original* thinking. Creative thinking often operates outside the bounds of logic, seeking new forms of expression. Like critical thinking, creative thinking is self-reflective, conscious, and purposeful. Critical thinking helps you analyze a topic in depth to find shades of meaning. Creative thinking helps you apply what you have learned in new

critical thinking, *p. 57*
creative thinking, *p. 57*
assumption, *p. 59*
prediction, *p. 61*
inference, *p. 64*
purpose, *p. 66*
central idea, *p. 66*
supporting details, *p. 66*
evaluate, *p. 69*
reliability, *p. 70*
objectivity, *p. 71*
options, *p. 75*
challenge, *p. 75*

Thinking skills are among the essential skills that employers value. Thinking skills include decision-making and problem-solving abilities.

SCANS TERM

thinking skills, *p. 58*

contexts. For example, the ideas you gather from several sources of information might inspire you to write a poem, paint a picture, or produce an original essay. Critical and creative thinking are a necessary part of making decisions, solving problems, and other important tasks.

This chapter begins with four strategies for thinking critically and creatively: Examine *assumptions*, *predict* outcomes, make *inferences*, and *evaluate* information and sources. Take the first letter of each italicized word to make the acronym A PIE—a memory aid that will help you recall these strategies. The chapter ends with COPE, a problem-solving process that exercises your **thinking skills** to meet academic and career challenges.

AWARENESS CHECK 6

Are You a Critical and Creative Thinker?

Choose one of the following as your response to each statement: *always* (4 points), *usually* (3 points), *occasionally* (2 points), *rarely* (1 point). Write your number of points in the box beside each statement. When you are finished, add your score.

Points

1. I use a strategy for predicting what assignments or lectures will cover.
2. I have a purpose and a goal in mind before I begin to study.
3. I can think both logically (inside the box) and creatively (outside the box).
4. I can identify my own and others' assumptions—what we take for granted.
5. I have some strongly held opinions, but I am open to other viewpoints.
6. I understand what is stated and what is meant in lectures and printed materials.
7. I am able to integrate new information with what I already know.
8. I take time to define new or unfamiliar terms as part of my study routine.
9. I know how to evaluate the worth of print and online sources.
10. I use strategies for making decisions and solving problems.

Total

Add your score. If your total is 35–40, your critical and creative thinking skills are already helping you to meet your academic and life challenges. If your total is 25–34, you have some thinking skill strengths on which to build new skills. If your total is 10–19, you have much to gain by developing your thinking skills. Whatever your level of skill, this chapter will help you become a more critical and creative thinker.

EXAMINE ASSUMPTIONS

▶ *Recognize the ideas and beliefs that you and others take for granted, the knowledge and experience that shape opinions.*

An **assumption** is an idea or belief taken for granted. Assumptions are based on what we know or have experienced. Everyone has certain assumptions about family, education, government—any aspect of one's life or world—and people's assumptions differ. For example, most people agree that some sort of health care reform is needed. Those who favor nationalized health care subsidized by government funding assume that under such a system costs for services would be lower, and more people would be able to afford health care as a result. Those opposed to nationalized health care assume that lower costs would mean lower payments for services, which would result in a decline in the quality of service. They may also assume that their taxes would be increased to pay for the program. What do those on either side of this issue stand to gain or lose? What evidence supports their assumptions? Are there other points of view?

These are the kinds of questions critical thinkers ask. To think critically, examine your assumptions—and others' assumptions—to determine what is known, believed, or taken for granted about the topic or issue at hand. Keep an open mind and be willing to change your assumptions based on new evidence or experiences. Before you read anything or listen to a lecture, examine your assumptions by asking yourself, "What do I already know about the topic?" and "What opinions have I already formed?"

Assumptions can be compelling. Your beliefs, the ideas you take for granted, shape your thoughts and actions. Figure 3.1 illustrates how examining your assumptions extends to several skill areas and activities.

> An *assumption* is an idea or belief taken for granted based on knowledge or experience.

EXAMINE ASSUMPTIONS: HOW YOU CAN USE THIS CRITICAL THINKING STRATEGY

FIGURE 3.1

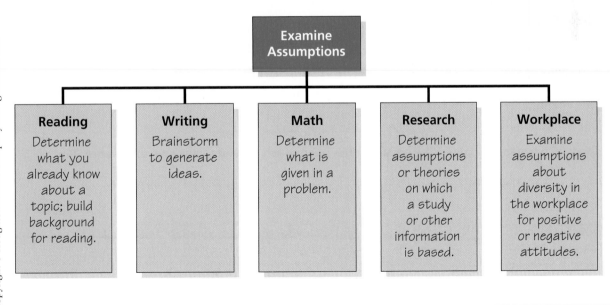

Reading	Writing	Math	Research	Workplace
Determine what you already know about a topic; build background for reading.	Brainstorm to generate ideas.	Determine what is given in a problem.	Determine assumptions or theories on which a study or other information is based.	Examine assumptions about diversity in the workplace for positive or negative attitudes.

IT IS IMPORTANT TO RECOGNIZE and analyze the assumptions that you bring to everyday interactions with people as well as to the subjects you study.

To examine some of your assumptions about other people, look at the group in the following photograph, and then answer the questions.

1. **Who are these people? What assumptions can you make based on their clothing or on other details in the photograph?**

    _____

    _____

2. **Where are they, and what do they seem to be doing? What details in the photograph help you make your assumptions?**

    _____

    _____

3. **Based on their expressions, what do these people seem to be thinking or feeling?**

    _____

    _____

4. **How do your assumptions about the people in the photograph relate to your own experiences?**

    _____

    _____

5. **Has your learning style either helped or interfered with your ability to complete this exercise? Explain your answer.**

    _____

    _____

PREDICT OUTCOMES

▶ *Predict a successful learning outcome by setting a goal, having a purpose, and choosing an appropriate strategy.*

A **prediction** is a decision made beforehand about the outcome of an event. Predictions are based on assumptions. Because you believe that certain things are true, you expect or believe that certain things will happen. If you believe, for example, that you are good at math, then you can predict that you will do well in a math course. If you have a favorite author who has just published a new book, you can predict that you will probably like it. Your prediction is based on the assumption that the new book will be similar to others by this author that you have read and enjoyed.

Predictions are often the result of asking yourself questions and looking for answers. When you wake up in the morning, you may wonder, "What will the weather be like today? What should I wear?" You look out the window at a sunny, cloudless sky. You step outside, and it is breezy and cool enough for a sweater. You remember that yesterday's weather started out cool, but by noon the temperature had risen to eighty degrees. Predicting that today's weather will be the same, you dress in layers so that you can remove some of your clothing as the temperature warms. By lunchtime, however, clouds have begun to form. Friends tell you that rain has been forecast. You run out to your car to grab an umbrella from the trunk. In doing so, you have acted on the prediction that it will rain. Based on new information—the clouds and your friends' comments—you now think rain is a likely occurrence.

Before listening to a lecture, reading an assignment, or taking a test, predict outcomes by asking and answering questions such as these: "What am I expected to learn?" "What should I study and how?" Figure 3.2 illustrates how making predictions extends to several skill areas and activities.

Prediction refers to a decision made in advance or the anticipation of an outcome.

PREDICT OUTCOMES: HOW YOU CAN USE THIS CRITICAL THINKING STRATEGY

FIGURE 3.2

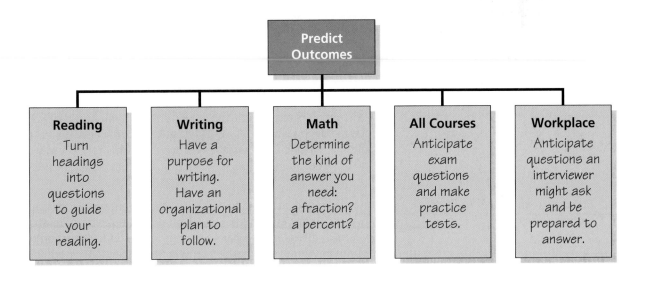

Set Goals for Learning

Before you begin reading an assignment or studying for a test, set goals. Decide how much you will read in one sitting or what to study for a test. Choose an appropriate strategy for completing your task, and set aside time to do it. The thoroughness of your studying, the amount of time you put into it, and the degree of understanding you have about the material should enable you to predict the grade you will get. With practice, your goals will become more reasonable and your predictions more accurate. Use your successes and failures on previous assignments or tests to guide your goal setting. For example, if you can't remember what you read because you did not underline or make notes, then start using those strategies. If you repeatedly miss a certain kind of problem or question on a test, talk to your instructor. Find out why you are missing these items and what you can do to improve your performance. Then set a new goal to reach the outcome you want.

Use Purpose-Guided Study

Whether listening to a lecture or reading an assignment, asking "Why am I doing this?" and "What do I need to learn?" will help you discover a guiding purpose for the activity. Purpose-guided study will improve your ability to predict outcomes. For example, use a lecture's topic or title and the speaker's cues to establish a purpose for listening and to help you predict what comes next. The title or topic may also suggest the speaker's main idea. Watch for cues such as facial expressions, gestures, notes on a blackboard or screen, and visual aids. Numbers (*first, second*) or phrases (*most important, for example*) alert you to important ideas and concepts. Make it your purpose to listen and watch for these cues and let them guide your note taking.

Use these tips to read textbook chapters with a purpose: Read the title and headings because they reveal the author's hidden outline of the central idea and

FIGURE 3.3

PURPOSES AND STRATEGIES FOR INFORMATIONAL READING

PURPOSE	STRATEGY	WHEN TO USE
Reading for central ideas and major details	Read carefully at normal speed; slow down for difficult parts; pay attention to headings; ask guide questions.	The first time you read a chapter
Reading to find facts and other details	Scan-read for dates, names, places, lists of steps, or other factual matter. (*Scan* means to glance rapidly over a page, looking for specific information or the answer to a question.)	To look for an answer to a question missed on a test; to look for information you know will be on a test; to look for answers to questions covering a chapter; to verify information in your notes; to survey and review chapters
Reading to analyze difficult or complex passages	Read slowly; pay attention to every word; break sentences into parts and express the parts in your own words; summarize difficult passages.	To read a sentence or passage that you don't understand; to analyze a complex or difficult section that you want to understand more fully; to read literature, especially poetry

most important supporting evidence. Turn each heading into a question that you will try to answer as you read each section. For example, if a section heading is *How to Compare Credit Card Offers,* then you could ask, "What are the offers and conditions?" and "What steps should I follow to compare them?" As you read the section, underline or take notes on the information that answers your questions.

Figure 3.3 lists three main purposes for reading informational material, such as that found in textbook chapters, and three strategies best suited to each purpose.

The first purpose and strategy will help you understand how the author constructed the arguments or discussions in the text. Reading with the second purpose in mind will help you make predictions and discover the author's intent. The third purpose and strategy will help you read complex or technical material as well as literature.

EXERCISE 3.2 · COLLABORATIVE ACTIVITY

APPLY WHAT YOU HAVE LEARNED so far about predicting outcomes by completing this exercise with group members. Follow the guidelines for group discussion that appear on the inside back cover.

Select Chapter 1 or 2 of *The Confident Student*. Think critically about the chapter to anticipate and predict what questions might appear on a test. Each group member may have different assumptions about what is important. By sharing your information gathered from notes and other sources, you should be able to determine the kinds of questions your instructor might ask. Based on your discussion, write three test questions that address what your group decides are some important chapter concepts. Your questions can be true/false, multiple-choice, short answer, or essay. Then share your questions in a class discussion.

CONFIDENCE BUILDER

Thinking Creatively

Creative thinking is a skill you can develop.

How does creative thinking differ from critical thinking? The tool of the critical thinker is *analysis*. The tool of the creative thinker is *invention*. Analysis is the process of logical reasoning. When you think through the steps of a process or consider all sides of an issue or argument, you are using analysis. When you come up with a solution to a problem, or when you use what you know to discover what you don't know, you are using invention.

Critical thinking and creative thinking work together. The COPE problem-solving strategy, explained later in this chapter, provides a good example. The COPE strategy defines a problem as a *challenge*, which is a positive way of looking at a difficult situation. Your first step is an analytical one: to clearly identify your challenge. Suppose you have gained 10 pounds. Your challenge is "I need to find a weight-loss program I can live with." To add a creative thinking step, ask yourself, "What is in conflict with the result I want?" You might say, "My conflicts are that I hate diets, and I don't have time for exercise." Now you have a clue that will help you work through COPE's second step, considering your *options*. Since any effective weight-loss program involves a combination of diet and exercise, you must choose from among the possible options one that will help you overcome your conflicts. Analysis helps you determine what the options are. Invention helps you arrive at a *plan*, the third step of COPE. Your plan will be one that you create that combines a diet you can live with and an exercise program you can follow in the time you have available.

The last step of COPE, *evaluate*, works by both analysis and invention. Suppose that after five weeks, you have lost only two pounds. Now you must analyze what has happened. Did you stick to your diet? Did you make time for exercise? What has gone wrong? More importantly, what can you do about it? Again, thinking creatively about your challenge will help you discover ways to modify your weight-loss plan and to get back on track.

No matter what your challenge, a valuable question to ask that starts the creative thinking process is "What if?" This question takes you beyond what you know to imagine what could be. For example, what if you could avoid procrastination? What if you could fight your distractions and control your concentration? What if you took charge of your learning by designing your own study system that incorporated strategies known to increase comprehension and improve retention? Imagine what you could achieve.

By using a combination of critical and creative thinking, you can meet any challenge. Invention and analysis are your tools.

To learn more about creative thinking, do an online search using these keywords as a starting point: *creativity, thinking creatively, creative thinking.*

Online Study Center
Confidence Builder
Web Search

MAKE INFERENCES

> *Know how to find the underlying meaning in stated information.*

Much of what you learn in college courses comes from reading textbooks and listening to lectures. Reading and listening are active processes that require concentration and critical thinking. To fully engage your mind, read or listen for two levels of meaning. The *literal level* consists of stated information. The *implied level* is the suggested meaning—the unstated ideas or a viewpoint that you get by making inferences from what is stated. An **inference** is an informed guess about an author's or speaker's meaning. Some of your inferences will be more informed than others and will be based on the prior knowledge or experience that you bring to the topic and on how well you understand the stated information. Figure 3.4 shows how making inferences extends to many skill areas and activities. Now read the following poem and make some inferences about the author's meaning.

Inference means an informed guess or conclusion drawn from stated information, based on prior knowledge and experience.

On Reading a Favorite Poem
Carol Kanar

Deep in the Maine woods,
On a starless September night,
Lights flicker, then go out.
Miles from any incandescence,
I sit in a thicket of fear,
Black, thorough,
And mourn the sudden loss of sight
As if it were not temporary.
The mind adjusts, takes its measure
Of eternity.
My book lies open in the dark;
I read by lights I cannot see.

MAKE INFERENCES: HOW YOU CAN USE THIS CRITICAL THINKING STRATEGY

FIGURE 3.4

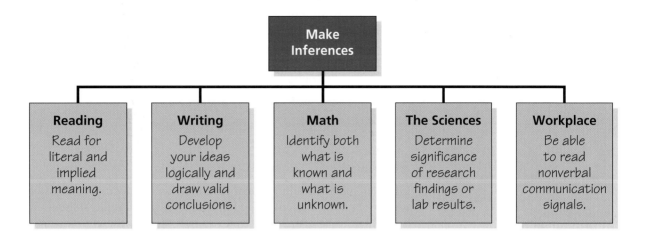

On a literal level, the author states facts of time, place, and event. Something happens on a September evening in the Maine woods that causes the lights to go out. On an implied level, what inferences can you make from these facts and the other stated information in the poem? Because the night is "starless," you can infer that it is cloudy, perhaps even stormy. A downed utility line could explain why the lights go out. "Deep in the Maine woods" may suggest that the poem's speaker is isolated, far from neighbors or a town. What experience do you bring to the poem? Have you ever been in the woods on a starless night? Have you ever spent time in Maine during September when frontal storms pass through and power outages are common? Why does the author mention the "loss of sight" and "eternity"? What do these ideas suggest to you? A poem's literal and implied meaning can support more than one interpretation.

Your experience not only affects the inferences you make from poetry but also influences how you read textbooks. If you have some prior knowledge about a subject, understanding may come easier. New material and unfamiliar concepts make greater demands on you as a reader. Reading on two levels of meaning will help you think critically about your assignments and make good inferences. At the literal level, pay attention to what an author *says:* the main idea and supporting details. At the implied level, determine what an author *means* by reading between the lines and making inferences about the significance of the information or ways to apply it. For example, when you read a chapter in an algebra textbook, determine what rules or steps are involved in solving a certain kind of problem. Then practice applying the rules and steps to similar kinds of problems in the chapter. When you read a chapter in a psychology textbook, read about experiments on two levels. At the literal level, determine who conducted the experiment, why, what data were collected, and what happened. At the critical level, determine the experiment's significance. What did it prove, and why is it an important piece of research?

Making inferences also applies to situations outside of your studies. If you have children, you have learned to tell whether your child has a harmless cold, has a bad case of the flu, or is pretending to be sick. Cold and flu symptoms are similar, but with the flu they are more pronounced and last longer. A child may have a fever with either a cold or the flu, but if the child is faking, there is no fever. Mothers and fathers are good at making inferences about the severity and meaning of their children's symptoms based on their experiences. No matter what the situation, the more facts you have and the more experience you have had in similar situations, the more valid your inferences will be.

The following four steps will help you process information on two levels so that you can make meaningful inferences about what you learn.

1. Read and listen for purpose, ideas, and meaning.

2. Recognize organizational patterns.

3. Integrate new information with prior knowledge.

4. Define new or unfamiliar terms.

Read and Listen for Purpose, Ideas, and Meaning

Whether you are reading a textbook or an online document or listening to a lecture, your goal is to identify the important ideas and understand their meaning. In a nutshell, these are the strategies to use: Identify the author's or speaker's purpose, find the central idea, and read or listen for the examples and other details that support the central idea.

Purpose means aim or goal.

A **purpose** is an aim or a goal—what you are expected to learn, understand, or be able to do. A purpose statement usually comes early in a lecture, near the beginning of a textbook chapter, or in the first few paragraphs of an article. But even if the purpose is not stated, you can infer it from the title and introduction. Suppose you are assigned to read "Chemical Reactions," a chapter in your chemistry textbook. The introduction states, "This chapter explains the main types of chemical reactions." From the title and this sentence, you can infer that the author wants you to know everything about chemical reactions: what a chemical reaction is, what the main types of chemical reactions are, and why they are important. Use this information to guide your reading by looking for a definition of *chemical reaction* and the names and properties of the main types. An author's or speaker's purpose guides the choice of examples and other details. By determining a purpose for reading or listening, you are on your way toward finding the most important ideas.

Central idea (also called the *main idea*) refers to an author's or speaker's stated or implied viewpoint on a topic.

Supporting details consist of facts, reasons, examples, or other stated information that supports a central idea.

Many students say, "I can't tell which ideas are the most important in a lecture or a textbook chapter." The ideas that you need to identify are the central idea and the details that support it. The **central idea,** or main idea, is the author's or speaker's opinion about a topic. The **supporting details** are the examples, facts, reasons, or other stated information on which the author's opinion is based. In other words, the central idea tells you *what* a lecture or chapter is about. The details answer the questions *why, how, when, where,* and *what if?* Suppose you are listening to a lecture on reducing test anxiety. After a brief introduction, the speaker says, "Because test anxiety is a learned response, you can unlearn it by identifying and overcoming its causes." If you correctly identify this statement as the central idea, then you can ask yourself several questions that will help you listen for the details: How is text anxiety "learned"? What causes test anxiety? How can you overcome it?

In some printed materials the central idea may be unstated, or implied. However, you can infer the central idea from the title, the introduction, or the first few paragraphs and the last paragraph. Taken together, these parts of an article or chapter contain key details that will help you figure out what the central idea is. Chapters 8 and 13 explain in more detail how to read and study from textbooks and other printed materials. Chapter 5 explains strategies for listening to lectures and taking notes on the important ideas.

EXERCISE 3.3   COLLABORATIVE ACTIVITY

APPLY WHAT YOU HAVE LEARNED so far about making inferences by completing this exercise with group members. Follow the guidelines for group discussion that appear on the inside back cover. Read the following paragraph and determine whether you can make the inferences that follow it. Discuss each inference, arrive at a consensus, and then check *yes* or *no* for each statement. Finally, evaluate your work.

> Susan is not doing well in her composition course. She missed the first two days of class because she was dropping and adding other courses. She missed the introduction to the course and the instructor's description of the course requirements. Her instructor gave her a syllabus, but she didn't read it. As a result, she was not prepared for the first grammar test, and she earned a D on it. She decided that the instructor was too demanding, and she tried to get into another section. Unfortunately, the drop-add period was over. Susan's advisor convinced her to stay in the course and suggested that she make an appointment with the instructor to see what she can do to catch up. The advisor believes that if Susan begins right now to take a serious interest in the course, do the assignments, and keep up with the syllabus, she can still do well in the course because it is early in the semester.

YES NO

☐   ☐   **1. Susan will fail the course.**

☐   ☐   **2. The instructor is too demanding.**

☐   ☐   **3. If Susan had read the syllabus, she might have known that a test was scheduled.**

☐   ☐   **4. The instructor may be willing to let Susan make up what she missed on the first two days of class.**

☐   ☐   **5. It is important to attend the first few days of class.**

Group Evaluation:

Evaluate your discussion. Did everyone contribute? Did you accomplish your task successfully? What additional questions do you have about making inferences from facts? How will you find answers to your questions? Write your evaluation on your own paper, or download the group exercise form from the Online Study Center at college.hmco.com/pic/KanarTCS6e.

Recognize Organizational Patterns

Common organizational patterns link a central idea and details. If you can spot the pattern early in a chapter or lecture, you can use it as a guide to predict what will follow. Key words may suggest how ideas are organized. For example, if the author's or speaker's main idea is that memory is a three-stage process, then the key words *three-stage process* should alert you to the **process** pattern of organization. Read or listen for the explanation of each stage and how it works.

You can learn to recognize six other common organizational patterns that help you follow an author's or speaker's ideas:

1. If two things are being compared, the pattern is **comparison and contrast**. Read or listen for similarities and differences.

2. If an author or speaker explains *why* something happens, the pattern is **cause and effect**. Read or listen for reasons and results.

3. If an author or speaker groups items into categories, the pattern is **classification**. Determine the number of categories and identify the characteristics of each category.

4. If an author or speaker supports a main idea by giving examples, the pattern is **example**. Read or listen for key introductory phrases such as *for example* and *for instance.*

5. If an author's or speaker's details follow a certain order, the pattern is **sequence**. Read or listen for numbers in a sequence or for events that are explained according to time periods. A sequence is often part of a process, especially when the stages of a process occur in a certain order or at specific times. Processes explain *how* things happen. Sequences explain *when* things happen.

6. If an author or speaker provides an extended meaning of a word or a concept, the pattern is **definition**. Read or listen for words and phrases such as *the meaning is, can be defined as,* and *to define.*

An author or speaker who brings together more than one organizational pattern in a single explanation is using **mixed patterns**. For example, someone might use classification to describe the kinds of students who attend a certain college and then use comparison and contrast to describe the similarities and differences among them. Identifying organizational patterns requires slow and careful reading. Similarly, careful listening may help you identify key words that can serve as clues to a speaker's pattern.

Integrate New Information with Prior Knowledge

As you learn new information, you will quickly forget it unless you integrate it with prior knowledge. This is why making inferences is so important. Try to understand the significance of each new skill or concept you learn. Determine how you will use the information; then put your knowledge into action. For example, in a writing class you learn to develop an essay by stating your central idea and supporting it with specific details and examples. Why not use that skill to write papers for your other courses or to develop a speech, which also benefits from a clearly stated central idea and well-chosen examples? Using skills in new contexts expands your knowledge base.

No matter what you learn in a course, find ways to apply your knowledge. Determine how new information is testing your assumptions and challenging your beliefs. One goal of learning is to make positive changes in your life. Self-reflect regularly to examine how your college experience is changing you.

Define New or Unfamiliar Terms

Most academic disciplines use special terminology to describe theories, concepts, and principles. You may have encountered the terms *id, ego,* and *superego* in a psychology course; *photosynthesis* in a biology course; and *integer, binomial,* and *polynomial* in a math course. In order to understand the information presented in each course, make an effort to learn the meaning of the key terms related to each discipline. Use your dictionary and textbook glossaries. While reading or listening to a lecture, keep a separate note pad or 3″ × 5″ cards handy for listing unfamiliar words that you can look up later.

The best way to develop your vocabulary is by reading. The more you read, the more you are exposed to new words and ideas that will increase your store of knowledge.

CONCEPT CHECK 3.1

What is one skill you have learned in your student success course that you can apply at work or in your other courses? Why is this skill important, and what will it help you accomplish?

EXERCISE 3.4

THE FOLLOWING STATEMENTS MIGHT BEGIN sections of a textbook chapter or an article. Read each statement to predict the author's organizational pattern. Write the letter of your answer in the space provided.

A. cause and effect   C. sequence   E. classification   G. process

B. example   D. comparison and contrast   F. definition

1. _____ A computer is an information-processing system that, in some ways, works much like your brain.

2. _____ Numbering consecutive pages in a document is easy if you follow these steps.

3. _____ A computer has five major units: input, control, storage, retrieval, and output.

4. _____ Computer-managed inventory control systems have proven beneficial to small businesses for a number of reasons.

5. _____ In the following section, we will examine two data-processing programs and their advantages and disadvantages.

6. _____ The ability to move sentences and paragraphs around is but one example of the features of a word processor that make writing easier.

7. _____ People who have never used computers can be grouped into three general categories: those who are afraid learning will be time-consuming and difficult, those who resist learning for personal or other reasons, and those who want to learn but have neither the means nor the opportunity to do so.

8. _____ What does it mean to be *computer literate*?

9. _____ The next section traces the development of the computer from a crude piece of equipment that was little more than a calculator to the complex information processor it has become.

10. _____ Learning how to use a word-processing program can be easy if you follow these steps.

EVALUATE INFORMATION AND SOURCES

▶ *Determine whether an informational source is credible by applying standards of evaluation such as reliability, objectivity, and usefulness.*

To **evaluate** means to determine worth or value. To evaluate also means *to judge*, that is, to make decisions about whether something is right or wrong, good or bad, fair or unfair. If you decide to withdraw from a course, you must evaluate that decision on the basis of whether doing so will be good or bad for you. On the one hand, withdrawing from a course may have a negative effect on your grade point average. But a positive effect might be that it would leave you more time to devote to your remaining courses. Evaluating your progress in a course means checking yourself for improvement. What skills have you mastered since the beginning of the term, and what effect has the application of these skills had on your grades?

Evaluate means to determine worth or value, to make judgments.

Making evaluations is a critical thinking strategy you use in other areas of your life besides college. Deciding whether to take a job, quit a job, marry, divorce, or buy a home all depend on making judgments about these important decisions. At work, you may be asked to judge which machines, tools, or procedures produce the desired outcomes.

An evaluation is a *measurement* of worth. "How much will this help or hurt me?" and "How important is this to me?" are questions you can ask when making evaluations. To make evaluations, you need a standard to go by. To evaluate the worth of continuing a relationship that has proved unsatisfying, your standards might be the expectations you have for a good relationship. To evaluate the purchase of a car, your standards might include the car's safety, dependability, and affordability. There are many criteria, or standards, by which you can make sound evaluations. As a college student, you can evaluate what you learn by applying three basic standards: *reliability, objectivity,* and *usefulness*. Figure 3.5 shows how making evaluations extends to several skill areas and activities.

Reliability

Reliability means dependability, credibility, and trustworthiness.

To evaluate a source for **reliability,** determine its credibility and trustworthiness by finding answers to three questions:

▼ Who says so?

▼ What are his or her credentials?

▼ How does he or she know?

EVALUATE INFORMATION AND SOURCES: HOW YOU CAN USE THIS CRITICAL THINKING STRATEGY

FIGURE 3.5

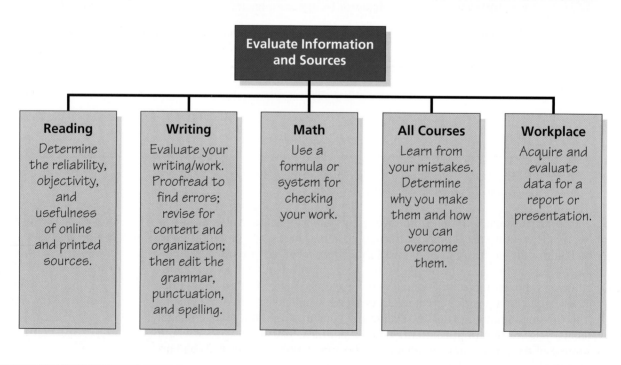

Evaluate Information and Sources

Reading	**Writing**	**Math**	**All Courses**	**Workplace**
Determine the reliability, objectivity, and usefulness of online and printed sources.	Evaluate your writing/work. Proofread to find errors; revise for content and organization; then edit the grammar, punctuation, and spelling.	Use a formula or system for checking your work.	Learn from your mistakes. Determine why you make them and how you can overcome them.	Acquire and evaluate data for a report or presentation.

As you read, research, and listen to lectures, remember that primary sources are more reliable than secondary sources. A *primary source* is a firsthand or direct source of information. A *secondary source* is an interpretation of a primary source. For example, if the President of the United States addresses the nation on television, the text of his speech is a primary source. If a newscaster summarizes what the President said, the summary is a secondary source. A newspaper account of the President's speech is also a secondary source unless the newspaper reprints the entire text of the speech. Have you ever listened to a newscaster's summary of a speech and wondered whether the newscaster heard the same speech you heard? A secondary source is only as reliable as the person who interprets the primary source.

When you are researching a topic, you may have difficulty determining whether a source is primary or secondary. Look at the bibliographies at the ends of books and articles. If the same titles and authors appear over and over again, chances are good that they represent either primary sources or reliable secondary sources of information. If you are just beginning to do research, your instructor or a librarian can help you select sources and evaluate their reliability.

Another way to evaluate reliability is to check an author's background or credentials. If you are researching a scientific topic such as global warming, a research scientist with a PhD who is on the faculty at a major university will be a more reliable source than a concerned political activist who writes letters on the subject to the local newspaper. Instructors try to select textbooks that are reliable sources of information, written by experts who may be instructors themselves. A textbook's title page may list the author's college affiliation.

Objectivity

To evaluate a written or oral presentation for **objectivity,** determine how even-handed, unemotional, and free from bias it is by asking and answering three questions:

Objectivity means even-handedness, expressing opinions that are unclouded by emotion or bias.

▼ What is the author's or speaker's purpose?

▼ Are all sides of the issue presented or acknowledged?

▼ Is the language free of slanted or manipulative words and phrases?

If an author's or speaker's purpose is to inform, then you should expect factual details and reasoned opinions. You should also expect fair treatment of differing viewpoints and language that is free of words and phrases designed to provoke emotional reactions that could cloud your judgment. Although most authors and commentators—including textbook authors and college lecturers—would probably say that they are objective, some may have a motive, viewpoint, or bias that influences their choice of words or examples.

An author or speaker who has something to gain by a change in readers' beliefs or behaviors will not be as objective as one who has nothing to gain. Those whose purpose is to persuade may write forcefully in favor of one viewpoint. If they try to persuade fairly, they will acknowledge other viewpoints. Those who attempt to persuade unfairly are likely to distort facts, leave out facts, state opinions as if they were facts, and use manipulative language. Usually they have something to gain by appealing to your emotions or changing your beliefs or behavior. Advertisers want your money. The proponents of various interest groups want your support. Politicians want your vote. Where self-interest is high, objectivity is low.

Can you spot the manipulative language in these two examples?

▼ An animal rights activist says, "We must stop the needless torture of animals in medical experiments that serve only to provide researchers on college campuses with lucrative grants."

▶ A medical researcher says, "No one in our profession sets out to torture animals in painful experiments, but some pain and even death may be necessary if, through these experiments, we can effect cures that will prevent the loss of human life."

In the first example, the activist tries to manipulate your feelings by suggesting that research is an excuse to get grant money, that animals in experiments are always tortured, and that the experiments are needless. In the second example, the researcher denies that anyone in his or her profession would deliberately cause an animal pain. At the same time, the researcher suggests that some animal pain or death is acceptable if it will save human lives. In this example, the researcher manipulates your thinking so that you must make a choice: your life or an animal's life.

Manipulative language is characterized by simple arguments that seek to explain complex issues. Read the next two examples.

PASSAGE A

It is becoming impossible to find good candidates willing to run for public office. A politician's life is an open book. The would-be candidate for office must dodge photographers and news reporters lurking in the bushes around his house, eavesdropping on his conversations in restaurants, and spying on him through binoculars when he thinks he has escaped from their prying eyes. If a person has ever taken a drink, smoked a marijuana cigarette, had a meaningless affair, or cheated on an exam, his chances of winning an election are compromised. The press has gone too far. Everyone, even a political candidate, is entitled to a private life.

PASSAGE B

As soon as someone runs for election, it is understood that she gives up her right to privacy. Indeed, the U.S. Constitution guarantees no one a right to privacy. We the public have a right to know what to expect from those who seek office. Cheating on one's husband or on an exam is not the issue. The real issue is whether we can trust a person who has a history of dishonesty or poor judgment. We want our elected officials to be responsible people. Therefore, the press performs a valuable public service by exposing candidates' indiscretions.

Both passages oversimplify the issues their proponents raise. Both authors manipulate your thinking by appealing to your emotions instead of to your reasoning. The author of the first passage blames the press for making people afraid to run for office. The author of the second passage praises the press for exposing the weaknesses of potential candidates. The first author wants you to identify with the candidate whose privacy has been violated. The second author appeals to your right as a citizen to know as much as you can about a candidate. Are members of the press scandalmongers or public servants? Neither passage offers convincing evidence to support its author's viewpoint.

Usefulness

To evaluate the usefulness of what you are learning, consider what you have already gained from it. Has it improved your understanding of the subject? Have you gained a skill or knowledge you can use now or in the future? Can you relate the knowledge or skill to your course objectives? Has the information made you more interested in the topic it covers? If you answered *no* to all of these questions, then try to figure out what is missing and what you might need to learn next. Figure 3.6, on page 73, lists additional tips for evaluating online sources.

EXERCISE 3.5

IDENTIFY WORDS OR PHRASES IN passages A and B on page 72 that appeal to readers' emotions and manipulate their feelings.

Passage A: _____

_____

_____

_____

_____

_____

Passage B: _____

_____

_____

_____

_____

_____

FIGURE 3.6

TIPS FOR EVALUATING ONLINE SOURCES

STANDARDS TO APPLY	QUESTIONS TO ASK
AUTHORITY	Who is the author, editor, host, or web master? What are the source's credentials? (author's degrees, publications) What bias is revealed? (affiliations with known groups/companies)
COVERAGE	Is coverage thorough, detailed? Is the information specific? Is it balanced, presenting more than one side or argument?
DOMAINS	What is the address (URL)? Is it affiliated, unaffiliated, or unrestricted? (affiliated: *.edu, .gov;* unaffiliated: *.net;* unrestricted: *.info*) *Caution:* Affiliated sites tend to be trustworthy, but others may be questionable.
CURRENCY	When was the information last updated (posting date)? Is it updated regularly?
LINKS	Is the site linked to other sites? Can the site be accessed from a variety of other sites (an indication of usefulness)? Are the links of the same quality as the site?
DOCUMENTATION and STYLE	Is the information on a site attributed to a source? How much information comes from primary or secondary sources? (Primary sources are more reliable.) Is the style appropriate; free of slang, jargon, and errors?

Exercise Overview

In addition to reading words, we also "read" expressions, gestures, and other visual cues in photographs and artwork for their meaning. This exercise will give you practice in reading and making inferences from advertising material that combines both print and visual elements.

Exercise Background

Companies spend millions each year on magazine advertising. Obviously, the ads are effective, or companies wouldn't be willing to pay the high price of running an ad in a widely read publication such as *Time*, *Newsweek*, or *People*. Advertisers have much to gain by researching and appealing to the market for their products and services. Why do some ads appeal to you more than others? Thinking critically about the ads you read will make you a more informed consumer.

Exercise Task

Working on your own or with a partner, examine the Samsung TV ad that has appeared in several high-circulation magazines. Then answer the following questions.

1. To whom does the ad appeal?

2. What consumer need does the ad address?

3. Who are some of Samsung's competitors?

4. The ad shows a young man holding a big-screen TV. Compare the man's clothing with that of the people depicted on the TV screen. What inferences can you make from your comparison?

5. Check the meaning of "elegance" in your dictionary. Apart from the dictionary definition, what images or ideas do you associate with elegance?

6. In your opinion, what do most consumers want in a TV?

7. Read the ad copy, paying particular attention to the words "imagine" and "elegance." Based on your reading and on your answers to questions 4, 5, and 6, what do you think is the advertiser's message?

8. Is your reaction to the ad as a whole positive or negative? Why?

9. If you were in the market for a new TV, would you consider buying the Samsung model pictured in the ad? Why or why not?

10. In your opinion, is the ad effective? Explain your answer.

EXERCISE 3.6　　COMPUTER APPLICATION

LOOKING AHEAD TO THE FOLLOWING chapters of *The Confident Student*, choose one topic that you would like to pursue further such as time management, concentration, memory—anything that interests you. Research your topic on the Internet. Find two different web sites that deal with this topic and explain which one seems most useful based on the tips for evaluating online sources in Figure 3.6, p. 73. Be prepared to discuss in class the topic you chose, a brief summary of the information found on the web sites you selected, and your evaluation of the web sites.

THINK THROUGH DECISIONS AND PROBLEMS

> ▶ *Use the COPE strategy for making decisions and for
> thinking through problems to find workable solutions.*

Decision making and problem solving are two critical thinking skills that you will use now and throughout your life. Decision making and problem solving are linked. Both require you to consider several **options** or alternatives before making a choice or taking an action. Some people have trouble making decisions either because they see too many options, or they don't know what the options are. Decision by indecision may result. Think of a problem as a **challenge**—a call to action that

Options are choices, alternatives.

Challenge means "call to action."

requires the full use of your abilities and resources. You might say, "If I do nothing, everything will work out." Unfortunately, problems don't go away. Without your intervention, they will become more difficult to solve. Face decisions and problems squarely, and you will soon be back on track and moving toward your goals.

As a college student, you will make one of your most important decisions when you choose a major. Your major determines your course selection and your career path. Some students enter college knowing exactly what they want to do. Others prefer to take a few introductory courses before deciding on a major. In the first case, keep an open mind so that you don't limit your opportunities. In the second case, don't wait too long to make a decision. Choosing a major puts you in control of your future. You can set goals for completing your education based on the requirements of your major, and you can begin to seriously consider career options.

How do you go about making this important decision? A good place to begin is with your interests and your accomplishments so far. What subjects appeal to you? What skills do you have? In what courses have you always done your best work? What do you like to do in your leisure time? Answering these questions may help you pinpoint some possible majors or careers that might be a good fit for you. Check your college catalog for a list of majors. Go through the list and check off the ones that appeal to you. Then carefully consider the majors you have checked, and try to narrow the list to one or two majors to explore in depth. The next section explains a problem-solving method that you can apply to major selection and other challenges. For more information on choosing majors, see also Chapters 4 and 14.

Apply the COPE Strategy

To think through a problem to a solution requires a consistent method, or strategy. For example, scientists follow protocols to conduct lab experiments. Physicians rule out serious conditions first when diagnosing an illness. The COPE strategy illustrated in Figure 3.7 and explained in this section is a series of steps that you can follow to solve academic, personal, and work-related problems. COPE stands for Challenge, Option, Plan, Evaluation.

THE COPE STRATEGY

FIGURE 3.7

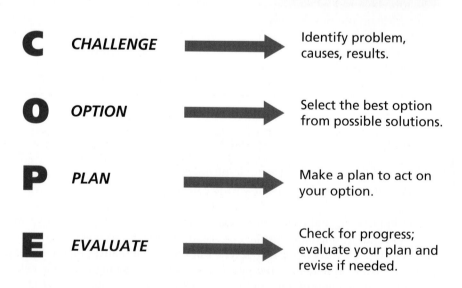

C *CHALLENGE* ⟶ Identify problem, causes, results.

O *OPTION* ⟶ Select the best option from possible solutions.

P *PLAN* ⟶ Make a plan to act on your option.

E *EVALUATE* ⟶ Check for progress; evaluate your plan and revise if needed.

STEP 1 — Identify your **challenge**, or problem.

Some people view a problem as an obstacle or a setback. This is negative thinking. To approach a problem in a more positive way, think of it as a challenge—difficult but solvable. State your challenge in writing. Seeing it in print will make it real for you. Answer the following questions in your statement:

▼ What is the problem?

▼ How is it hurting you?

▼ What do you want to do?

   Suppose you don't have a major. You may not see this as a problem yet, but it can have some negative consequences, as Chris explains:

Not having a major makes me feel as if I have no direction, no basis on which to select courses. I worry that I am wasting my time and money. As a result, I am losing focus, and my grades are beginning to suffer. I have several interests and career ideas and would like to choose a major and begin making plans for my future, but I don't know where to begin.

The following example is a challenge statement that Chris wrote as a response to Step 1 of COPE. The three parts of the statement are identified in parentheses:

I have not chosen a major (the problem), *and this is causing me to lose focus and my grades to suffer* (how it hurts). *I want to learn more about possible majors and find one that is a good fit for me* (what you want).

STEP 2 — Select as a solution the best **option** from those possible.

Most problems can be solved in a number of ways. Some alternatives may be better than others. When faced with a challenge, it helps first to determine what the alternatives are, to note next the advantages and disadvantages of each, and then to choose the best option. Keep in mind that the solution you choose may not work. Be ready to try your next best option if necessary. It may help to list your options along with their advantages and disadvantages. Reread the challenge statement following Step 1. By thinking about the problem and talking about it with others, Chris identified several options for learning more about majors and careers. As a response to Step 2 of COPE, this student made the chart shown on page 78.

   All three options have value. Like Chris, you might decide to begin your search by going to the career center first. A survey of your interests and values is a good starting point for choosing a major. Chances are good that you will be happiest and most successful taking courses and pursuing a career in a field that allows you to do what you enjoy doing. Remember that it is more important to choose a major that interests you than to select one that will lead to a specific career. The fact is that most majors, apart from the specialized skills that they teach, also teach you general skills such as thinking critically and using technology that you can apply to a wide variety of jobs and careers. Also, some on-the-job training is a fact of life, no matter what career you choose. What most employers are looking for is someone who has strong communication skills, who knows how to learn, and who is flexible, confident, and willing to work hard to succeed.

Option	Advantage	Disadvantage
Talk to recent grads. Tell them I'm in the process of selecting a major and ask their advice.	Their recent college experience and workplace knowledge may give me some ideas.	I don't know any recent grads. However, I may be able to access some through an alumni database.
Choose a major that appeals to me and research its career possibilities on the Web.	My college web site and those of other colleges and businesses may provide many search opportunities.	Some sites are better than others, and I could waste time searching sites that don't tell me what I need to know. I'll ask an advisor or librarian to suggest some good sites.
Visit the college career center or a career counselor and take some interest surveys.	Career counseling and testing can narrow my search to majors that are appropriate for me.	I will need to set aside time and make appointments for the services, but it will be worth the effort.

STEP 3 Write an action **plan** and follow it to meet your challenge.

Suppose that, like Chris, you want to find a major that is a good fit for you. Your plan should address two questions: "What actions will I take?" and "How much time should I allow for my plan to work?" Setting a time limit keeps you from wasting time in the long run. If you are not making progress toward your goal within a reasonable length of time, then you either need to set a new goal or make a new plan. Writing your action plan is the commitment you will make to solve your problem or to meet your challenge.

Suppose you decide to talk to a recent graduate about your search for a major. To set a time limit for completing the task, you make an appointment with the grad. Then, as your response to Step 3 of COPE, you write the following list of questions to ask as your action plan.

▼ What field did you major in, and what influenced your choice?

▼ How did you get your current job or position?

▼ If I want a career in your field, does it matter what my major is?

▼ What skills are essential for success in your job?

▼ What personal qualities do employers in your field expect?

EXERCISE 3.7

CHOOSING A MAJOR REQUIRES A balance between critical and creative thinking. This exercise will help you do both.

To think critically, or analytically, start with a list of majors offered at your college. To find a list of majors, check your college catalog or web site. Check the ones that interest you most. Make a list of those majors and add to the list any others that you might want to consider. Think about each one, gradually narrowing your list to three choices. Now select one major as your *trial major,* and write it on the following line:

_____

To think creatively, you are going to use your intuition. This will help you avoid information overload, the feeling of helplessness that comes from having too many options to consider. Close your eyes and visualize yourself doing something that you really enjoy. What courses would let you pursue that interest? What job or career can you think of that would allow you to do what you enjoy most? What major immediately comes to mind? This is your *dream major.* Write it on the following line:

_____

Are your trial major and your dream major the same? If so, this will be your *tentative major.* If your trial major and dream major are different, select the one that appeals to you most, and that will be your tentative major. Your choice will remain tentative until you are certain that it is right for you. Until then, continue to explore your options because you can always change your mind.

After asking these questions at your interview, are you any closer to making a decision about a major? If not, write another action plan and continue your research. Periodically, you need to evaluate the progress you are making, which is Step 4 of COPE.

STEP 4 **Evaluate** your plan by asking questions to assess your progress.

Remember that many problems we encounter have developed over time; therefore, it will take time to solve them. If you have clearly defined your goal, or the solution you want, and have made a plan to achieve it within a reasonable length of time, then you can evaluate your progress by asking questions like these:

▼ Is my plan working?

▼ How close am I to reaching a solution?

▼ What am I doing that is helping or not helping?

▼ What more can I do?

If you are having trouble answering these questions, then you may need to make a new plan or redefine your goal.

Suppose your efforts to find a major that suits you have worked. You have made a selection, so that challenge has been met. Now you can begin to pursue your major by setting long-term and short-term goals as explained in Chapter 4. On the other hand, if you were not successful in choosing a major, continue exploring options until you succeed.

EXERCISE 3.8   LEARNING STYLE

MARIE IS A POOR PROBLEM SOLVER. Read about her problem and think about what she should do to become a successful problem solver.

I have a big problem this term: my French class. I'm flunking, and I don't know why. I've stopped going to class because it was depressing me to sit there feeling stupid. Now I can forget about how much I hate it, and I can sleep late on Friday mornings, too. I'm angry at the college for having so many requirements for students to fulfill. I'm disgusted at my French instructor, who refuses to speak any English in class. How can I learn if I can't understand what's going on? I passed Spanish in high school, so I know this problem is not mine. It must be their crazy new method of teaching languages. Maybe I should take beginning Spanish again. At least I know I could pass!

1. **What is Marie's problem?**

   _____

   _____

2. **Is Marie self-motivated (internal locus of control) or other-motivated (external locus of control)?**

   _____

   _____

3. **What new behaviors could Marie adopt to help her solve her problem?**

   _____

   _____

4. **Write a short action plan for Marie to follow this week.**

   _____

   _____

Thinking ahead about Career

A workplace focus in Chapter 3 is on building thinking skills as a foundation for analytical and creative problem-solving throughout life. Use the knowledge you have gained from this chapter to solve work-related problems such as the one explained in the following case study. Read the case study on your own or with a partner, and then answer the case questions.

Case Study

Isaac teaches composition at a community college. Like many of his colleagues, he reads 125 papers every two weeks, spending about 20 minutes on each one. He marks grammar errors and notes handbook pages for student reference, writes suggestions for improving content and organization, and assigns grades. Isaac wants to reduce his time per paper by several minutes but feels he cannot leave out any step of his grading process. The writing center at Isaac's college will provide a student reader to assist Isaac. Student readers have passed composition with an A and have scored in the 90th percentile on a standardized test of grammar and mechanics; however, they cannot be responsible for assigning grades. Can you come up with a plan to save Isaac some time without compromising either his grading process or the writing center's policy?

Case Questions

1. **What is Isaac's problem?**

   _____

   _____

2. **What solution does he want?**

   _____

   _____

3. **How has the writing center offered to help and under what condition?**

   _____

   _____

4. **Access the Career Resource Center and read the article entitled "Problem Solving" in the *Critical Thinking and Problem Solving* section of *The Bridge*. Based on this article, how would you approach solving Isaac's problem?**

   _____

   _____

Your *Reflections*

Reflect on what you have learned from this chapter about thinking critically and creatively. Use the following questions to stimulate your thinking; then write your reflections. Include in your writing specific information from the chapter.

- Based on your answers to Awareness Check 6, are you a critical and creative thinker? Why or why not?

- Reflecting on the acronym A PIE and on the critical thinking strategies that the letters stand for, how do you plan to use one of the strategies in your courses or at work?

- Have you selected a major? How will the COPE strategy help you choose one or explore in depth the one you have chosen?

- What is one skill or attitude explained in this chapter that you would like to develop, and what can you begin doing today to make that happen?

Chapter review

To review the chapter, reflect on the following confidence-building attitudes and skills. Complete **Concepts to Understand** by filling in the blanks with words or terms from the list provided. Then practice your new skills at every opportunity.

ATTITUDES TO DEVELOP
- self-reflection
- self-reliance
- self-confidence

SKILLS TO PRACTICE
- active reading and listening
- thinking critically and creatively
- decision making and problem solving

CONCEPTS TO UNDERSTAND

objectivity	inferences	usefulness	choice	plan
assumptions	reliability	evaluate	predict	option

Critical thinking is a logical, analytical, self-reflective, conscious, and purposeful process. Creative thinking is an inventive process. This chapter explains how you can think critically and creatively and offers tips for making decisions and solving problems.

Follow these steps to think critically: Examine your own and others' (1) _____ to determine what you take for granted, and be willing to change your opinions in light of new evidence. (2) _____ outcomes by setting goals for learning and by using purpose-guided study. Reading or listening on two levels, literal and critical, will help you make (3) _____ from what you learn. To evaluate information and sources, apply three standards: (4) _____ , (5) _____ , and (6) _____ .

A decision is a (7) _____ among alternatives. Decision making and problem solving are linked. Decisions are part of the problem-solving process. COPE, a four-step process explained in this chapter, can help you solve problems by first stating your challenge, then choosing the best (8) _____ among those possible, and making an action (9) _____ . After a reasonable length of time, (10) _____ your plan to see if it is working, and make changes as needed.

To access additional review exercises, go to
college.hmco.com/pic/KanarTCS6e.

Online Study Center
Review Exercise
ACE Self-Test

Online Study Center

Prepare for Class, Improve Your Grade, and ACE the Test. This chapter's *Student Achievement* resources include

Chapter exercises/forms	Review exercise	Confidence Builder Web search
ACE Self-Test		

To access these learning and study tools, go to **college.hmco.com/pic/KanarTCS6e.**

Setting goals

Your values and your accomplishments are a reflection
of who you are.

> *Determine what is important to you,
> and set goals that reflect your values.*

> *Identify different types of goals, and know
> how to set goals that will help you achieve
> academic and career success.*

▶ **DEFINE YOUR VALUES**

▶ **DIFFERENTIATE BETWEEN LONG-TERM AND SHORT-TERM GOALS**

▶ **SET REACHABLE GOALS**

▶ **WRITE YOUR ACTION PLAN**

▶ *Make a commitment to reach your goals by writing and following an action plan.*

▶ *Learn the six characteristics of reachable goals that will make your dreams attainable.*

Values are the underlying principles or ideals that influence opinions and behavior.

What do you want from college? What would you like to be doing five years from now? What grade do you want on your next test, and how will you ensure your success? These questions address goals, or outcomes. Goals have a direct relationship to your **values,** the principles or ideals that you think are important. Values shape your opinions and influence your behavior. For example, if you value learning and achievement, then you can't go to class whenever you feel like it, look over your notes the night before a test, avoid choosing a major until making a decision becomes critical, and still hope to succeed. Success is a matter of desire, intention, and effort. Successful people set goals and work to achieve them.

"But I don't like to set goals," you say; "I'd rather be spontaneous and let things happen." Goals put you in control of your life. Without goals, you leave yourself open to people or circumstances that will manage your life in ways you might not like. Setting goals not only helps you get what you want but also makes

KEY TERMS

values, *p. 85*
long-term goals, *p. 90*
short-term goals, *p. 90*
action plan, *p. 96*

Self-management is one of several personal qualities that are essential to career success.

SCANS TERM

self-management, *p. 86*

you practice **self-management**—a personal quality that employers value. This chapter will help you define your values and set attainable goals.

DEFINE YOUR VALUES

Determine what is important to you, and set goals that reflect your values.

What is important to you? How you answer this question is a direct reflection of your values. Similarly, what you want out of college also reflects your values. Values are intangibles like *a good life, a satisfying relationship,* or *a rewarding career.* Your values influence your goals and shape your actions. What do you value? Why are you in college? Awareness Check 7 will help you think critically about your values.

Here are some other reasons for attending college that you may or may not have considered. In the courses you take, you will be exposed to new ideas, beliefs, and ways of looking at the world. At times, you will be excited by what you are learning; at other times, you will be frustrated by opinions and values that challenge your own. A college education can help you develop a flexible and open mind, sharpen your ability to think, and enrich your life. Best of all, you may discover in yourself talents, skills, and interests that you did not know you possessed.

Most students are in college because they seek the skills and knowledge that will make them employable. Although some enter college with a career in mind, many are undecided. Some students, like Ellen, change their minds. Ellen had always wanted to be a nurse, even though she knew little about what the job entailed. After completing her required courses, she was accepted into her college's nursing program. Ellen's math and science skills were strong, and she enjoyed taking her anatomy and physiology course as well as the other courses in her program. But when one of her courses required her to spend time in a local hospital tending to the needs of the sick, she realized immediately that nursing was not what she wanted to do for the rest of her life. She was suited neither to working in a hospital environment nor to the stress that accompanies a career in nursing. At first, Ellen was at a loss. She had invested her time and money in a career that she no longer wanted to pursue. To change her major could add a year or more to her graduation time; nevertheless, that is what she decided to do. Ellen is now the financial manager of an electronics corporation. She can't imagine having a more rewarding career, and she believes that changing her major from nursing to marketing was the right decision for her.

Ellen's story illustrates how personal, academic, and career goals can overlap. Ellen's career goal was to become a nurse. Her academic goal was to complete her degree in nursing. Ellen had hoped to find satisfaction in her work, so her personal goal was to have a career doing something she liked. At the time she thought she would enjoy being a nurse. As she learned more about her chosen career, however, Ellen's personal goal of job satisfaction was not being met. This led to her decision to change her career goal. She decided that she wanted a management-level position within a large corporation. As a result, her academic goals changed as well. Her new goals were to change her major to marketing and to complete the courses required for her degree.

What about values and ethics? Did they play a role in Ellen's goal setting? *Values* include your judgments about what is right and wrong. They are your standards of

AWARENESS CHECK 7

What Are Your Reasons for Attending College?

Check the reasons for attending college that match your own.

☐ 1. I want to earn a degree, but I haven't yet chosen a major.

☐ 2. My friends are in college, and I want to be with them.

☐ 3. My parents want me to get a college education.

☐ 4. I want to prepare myself for an interesting career.

☐ 5. I have an athletic scholarship, veteran's benefits, or some other source of funding.

☐ 6. I want to make a lot of money.

☐ 7. I want to improve my skills so that I can change jobs or careers.

☐ 8. I want to broaden my knowledge.

☐ 9. I wasn't able to go to college when I was younger; now I want that experience.

☐ 10. Improving my education will help me advance to a higher-level position at work.

A goal should be something that you desire and that you will be motivated enough to reach. Your answers to the Awareness Check provide the key for understanding how your reasons for attending college can motivate you to reach your goals. If you checked only item 2 or item 3, for example, then you may have difficulty motivating yourself to do well because your reasons for attending college are based more on others' expectations than on your own. You need to decide what you want out of college. If you checked only item 7 or item 10, then you have a more specific goal in mind and are probably already working to accomplish it. You may need to find additional motivation only if you encounter a set-back. If you checked only item 1 or item 4, then you have a practical reason for being in college, but you have not chosen a career or major. As soon as you do that, course selection will be easier because you will be motivated by a clearer sense of direction. If you checked only item 6, then you may have set an unrealistic goal. A college education, though it does prepare you for a career, does not guarantee that you will make lots of money. Motivation is easier to find when your goals are realistic, and you believe you can achieve them.

Perhaps you checked several items. Checks beside items 7, 8, 9, and 10, for example, could mean that you are seeking a college education to broaden your understanding and to provide access to a better job. If you checked items 1, 4, and 5, then you may be a student who wants a degree and has the funding to get it, but you are still exploring the possibilities of what you might do with your education. A visit to your college's career center might help you decide on a major or set a career goal that will keep you motivated.

Through service learning you can practice setting and reaching goals while helping others to reach theirs.

FIGURE 4.1

CORE ETHICAL VALUES

Trustworthiness	Be honest and reliable. Don't deceive, cheat, or betray a trust. Be loyal to family, friends, and country. Strive to do what is right.
Respect	Be courteous, considerate, and polite. Show respect for others' differences. Don't threaten or abuse others. Settle disputes peacefully.
Responsibility	Be self-disciplined and self-controlled. Think before you act, and accept the consequences of your behavior. Have high expectations for yourself, do your best, and be persistent.
Fairness	Treat everyone fairly. Listen to others and keep an open mind. Neither make nor accept excuses for bad behavior, and don't take advantage of others.
Caring	Kindness, sharing, compassion, and empathy should be hallmarks of your character. Be gracious, forgiving, and willing to help those in need.
Citizenship	Stay informed and get involved. Take part in community affairs and service learning projects. Obey laws, follow the rules, and show respect for authority. Vote.

Adapted for *The Confident Student* from the Character Counts! Coalition's "Six Pillars of Character" with permission of the Josephson Institute of Ethics, 2006, www.charactercounts.org.

behavior, and they include reliability, respect, responsibility, fairness, caring, and citizenship. *Ethics,* on the other hand, are community standards of behavior. Cheating in college is unethical because the college community expects students to earn their grades. Making personal calls at work or taking office supplies to use at home are unethical practices because someone else has to pay for the calls and the supplies. Employers expect you not to steal from them. Would it have been ethical for Ellen to pursue a nursing career, feeling as she did? No, because the medical community expects its workers to be dedicated. How could Ellen be dedicated to a job she didn't like? Ellen's values shaped her decision to change majors. She did not want to pursue a career in which she might not be able to live up to her employer's and patients' expectations.

Personal values and ethical choices are not only an important part of goal setting; they also influence every aspect of your life. They make up what is called "character." Character is an asset in college, at work, and in all your relations with others. Figure 4.1 lists values that build character. You can build your character by incorporating these values into your life and by considering them as you set goals.

EXERCISE 4.1

Purpose:

This exercise will help you clarify your values in four major areas.

Background:

What are your core values? What values shape your choices and decisions? For example, in *The Working Life,* Joanna Ciulla identifies four values that influence job selection: high salary, security, meaningful work, and time off. These values are specific, but the values listed in Figure 4.1 are more abstract, which is why each one is followed by an explanation. We form our values while growing up, and we continue to refine them throughout life. Family, education, religious training, and other influences shape our values.

Task:

For each of the influences listed next, answer the following questions, using your own paper for the exercise.

- **Family**

- **Education**

- **A major event**

- **A person whom you admire**

1. **What is the influence, and how has it affected your life?**

2. **What lesson did you learn, or what understanding did you reach?**

3. **What value grew out of this influence?**

4. **Why is this value important to you?**

5. **What is another major influence in your life, and what value has it shaped?**

DIFFERENTIATE BETWEEN LONG-TERM AND SHORT-TERM GOALS

> *Identify different types of goals, and know how to set goals that will help you achieve academic and career success.*

A goal is an outcome, an objective, a desired result. Goal setting is an active step that you take toward managing your life. Without goals, you are the victim of chance, a person to whom things happen rather than one who makes things happen. A goal can be any outcome you want, but the more specific it is, the better, and if you write it down, you own it.

If your goal is vague, or unclear, you run the risk of not being able to determine what actions to take. As a result, you will have difficulty writing an action plan. State your goal as an action or a result that can be measured. It may be helpful to identify your goal as personal, academic, or career/work related. Figure 4.2 lists types of goals followed by specific goal statements. Some goals take longer to reach than others. Completing one goal may conclude one of several steps that bring you closer to accomplishing a more far-reaching outcome. When you state a goal or write an action plan, differentiate between your long-term goals and your short-term goals.

Long-term and *short-term* as applied to goal setting are time markers. For example, graduation from college can be viewed as a **long-term goal** because it will take years to accomplish. Choosing a major or program of study, completing each course, and meeting all other graduation requirements are tasks of shorter duration and can be viewed as the **short-term goals** that will bring you nearer to graduation. Because long-term and short-term are relative ideas, it is more pragmatic to think of outcomes and the steps required to reach them. For example, if graduation from college is the outcome (long-term goal), then the completion of each class is a step (short-term goal) toward graduation. If earning a 3.5 grade-point average this semester or quarter is the outcome (long-term goal), then completing each assignment or test with a grade of 3.0 or better is a step (short-term goal) toward the final grade you want. Graduation from college, a long-term goal,

Long-term goals can take from several years to a lifetime to achieve. These goals represent major life outcomes.

Short-term goals are the intermediate steps between setting a long-term goal and achieving it. *Long-term* and *short-term* are relative ideas whose meanings may change depending on the context in which they are used.

FIGURE 4.2

THREE TYPES OF GOALS	
GOAL TYPE	**GOAL STATEMENT**
PERSONAL	• I will lose ten pounds over the next four months. • I will improve my fitness by exercising for twenty minutes at least three days a week this term. • To develop a more positive attitude about studying, I will practice countering negative thoughts with positive ones before tackling an assignment.
ACADEMIC	• I will choose a major by the end of this term. • I will study two hours for every hour spent in class. • I will review my notes for each class every day.
CAREER/ WORK RELATED	• I will find out where and when a job fair is being held in my area and make plans to go. • I will visit the college career center and take an interest inventory within the next two weeks. • I will begin keeping a record of my accomplishments so that I can build my résumé.

could itself be viewed as a short-term goal when seen in relation to a total life plan from first job to starting a family, planning for your kids' college education, and retiring. In other words, each goal you set should have a realistic time frame. Break down each goal into a longer-term outcome to be reached and the shorter-term steps you will take to get there. Figure 4.3 lists long-term and short-term goals and shows their relative relationship.

FIGURE 4.3

LONG-TERM AND SHORT-TERM GOALS

LONG-TERM GOALS	SHORT-TERM GOALS
Graduate from college	I will choose a major in the first year of college. I will complete my required courses first. I will keep track of deadlines and pay fees on time.
Complete my algebra course with an A	I will find a study partner and set up a study schedule within the first two weeks of class. I will take notes in class and review my notes after class. I will do all the problems in a chapter, assigned or not.
Get my financial affairs in order	I will prepare a monthly budget this week. I will pay all bills as soon as they come in. I will use my credit card only for emergencies, and I will not carry a balance.

EXERCISE 4.2

BY SETTING GOALS, YOU CAN manage your life instead of letting life manage you. This exercise will help you think through a desired outcome and break it down into long-term and short-term goals. If you need more space, write your responses on a sheet of paper.

1. **What is one thing in your life that you want very much?**

   _____

2. **What values underlie this desire?**

   _____

3. **Write a long-term goal statement that incorporates your answer to question 1. See Figures 4.2 and 4.3 for examples of goal statements.**

   _____

4. **Break down your long-term goal into three (or more) short-term goals and write your goal statements.**

   _____

   _____

   _____

EXERCISE 4.3

THIS EXERCISE WILL HELP YOU with major selection. If you already have a major, write it in the appropriate space. If you are undecided, select a tentative or working major.

1. **What is your major/tentative major?**

   _____

2. **Search your college web site and catalog for information on your major and briefly summarize the requirements for completion and the amount of time it will take.**

   _____

   _____

3. **Completing the requirements for your major is your long-term goal. Now list three short-term goals to achieve as you work toward the long-term goal.**

   _____

   _____

   _____

4. **What personal value is reflected in your choice of a major?**

   _____

SET REACHABLE GOALS

▶ *Learn the six characteristics of reachable goals that will make your dreams attainable.*

A goal should be reachable—an outcome that you can reasonably expect to achieve. A realistic assessment of your strengths and weaknesses, your level of motivation, and your values will help you set goals that are attainable. Figure 4.4 lists the six characteristics of reachable goals that are explained in this section.

A reachable goal is realistic. It is based on your abilities, interests, needs, and desires. For example, when choosing a career goal, you should consider your skills and interests. If you dislike math and dread balancing your checkbook every month, then accounting may not be a realistic career goal for you. If you like to write, have always done well in English courses, and enjoy working with others to make reports and presentations, then a career as a technical writer might be a realistic goal for you. Your college may have a career center or provide career counseling that will help you evaluate your interests so that you can consider the jobs, professions, or public services best suited to your abilities and preferences. Career counseling can help you determine your chances for employment in specific fields. You might learn that jobs are scarce in a field you have been considering. Or you might discover a new field of interest that offers many employment opportunities.

A reachable goal is believable and possible. You must believe that you *can* reach your goal and that it is possible to reach it within a reasonable length of time. Suppose you want to buy a computer. After doing some comparison shopping, you find that the price is more than you expected, and you decide to wait. You set a goal to save the money. Knowing how much money you need and how much you can

SIX CHARACTERISTICS OF REACHABLE GOALS

FIGURE 4.4

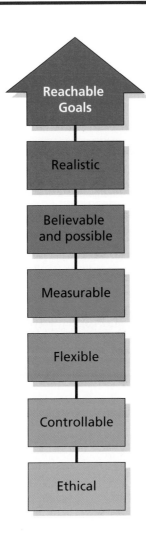

Reachable Goals

Realistic

Believable and possible

Measurable

Flexible

Controllable

Ethical

afford to set aside each month, you determine that it will take five months to save the money. Each month you deposit the amount you have designated. Your goal is believable because you can afford the extra savings. Your goal is possible because you think five months is a reasonable amount of time. Your long-term goal is to save enough money to make your purchase. Each deposit you make represents the achievement of a short-term goal needed to reach the long-term goal.

A reachable goal is measurable. Establish a time frame and a foreseeable outcome. For example, if your goal is "to make a lot of money," decide how you are going to do it, when you are going to do it, and how much is "a lot." Have a foreseeable outcome at the end of which you can say, "I have reached my goal." If you set a goal to graduate from college four years from now, determine which courses to take and plan your schedule so that you can earn a sufficient number of credits each semester or quarter.

A reachable goal is flexible. Rarely do you set a goal and follow it through to completion without any problems. In working toward your college degree, for example, you may fail or withdraw from one or more courses, or you may change majors and lose credits that you have to make up. These are temporary setbacks that may interrupt your progress but need not keep you from reaching your goal. Reassess your action plan. Then revise it, or make a new plan. Although it may take you longer to reach your goal, it is time well spent if you are doing what you want to do.

A reachable goal is controllable. Take charge. Set goals you can control and determine your own time frame for completing them. No one can, or should, set goals for you. Suppose you need to study for an important exam, and you know from past experience that you need at least three days to prepare yourself. Your study partner says, "We can ace this test with a four-hour study session the night before." That strategy may work for her, but will it work for you? If your goal is to

EXERCISE 4.4

ANALYZE ONE OF YOUR PERSONAL, academic, or work-related goals in terms of the six characteristics of reachable goals.

1. **Write your goal statement.**

    _____

    _____

2. **Which of your skills and interests make this a *realistic* goal for you?**

    _____

    _____

3. **What makes your goal *believable* and *possible?***

    _____

    _____

4. **Is your goal *measurable?* For example, how long will it take you to reach your goal? What check-points will you build into your plan?**

    _____

    _____

5. **What makes your goal *flexible?* What will you do if you experience a setback?**

    _____

    _____

6. **Is your goal *controllable?* Can you manage time limits and conditions? Explain your answer.**

    _____

    _____

7. **Is your goal *ethical?* Explain how.**

    _____

    _____

make a good grade, set up your own study schedule and stick to it. You are the best person to determine how much time you will need to prepare for a test.

A reachable goal is ethical. It is fair to all concerned. The steps you take to reach your goal should not in any way cause you to violate rules, take advantage of others, or compromise your values. Suppose you are enrolled in a reading class that requires you to spend at least two hours a week in a learning lab practicing the skills you have learned in class. The reading class is required as a prerequisite for a composition course that is also required. You have set a short-term goal of completing the course with a grade no lower than B. On your way to the lab, a friend says, "Let's cut today. We work on our own in there anyway. If we sign in and leave, no one will know." You know this is probably true because the lab is monitored by a technician who sends a copy of the sign-in sheet to the instructor.

What are the ethics involved in this situation? If you cut the class, you are engaging in unethical conduct for three reasons. First, you are breaking a rule. Second, you are taking advantage of your instructor by signing in and leading him or her to believe that you were present. Third, if honesty is one of your values, then you are compromising it. On the practical side, cutting lab doesn't help you reach your goal. Avoiding practice time prevents your mastery of the skills and may lead to a poor grade. Is it possible to engage in unethical behavior and still reach your goals? In the short term, maybe. But in the long run, unethical conduct catches up with you. Since ethical behavior improves your chances of reaching your goals, it makes sense to say that a reachable goal is also an ethical one.

> **CONCEPT CHECK 4.1**
>
> Think of an academic, personal, or career goal that you have always wanted to achieve. Is your goal reachable? Does it meet all six characteristics? If not, what can you do to make the goal more attainable? Should you select a more realistic goal?

CONFIDENCE BUILDER

How to Develop a Positive Attitude

Changing your attitude is the first step toward solving many problems you will face in college. A negative attitude may be a habit you have developed, a characteristic response to problem solving that has prevented you from being successful in the past. Negative attitudes also affect self-esteem, destroying your confidence and creating an illusion of helplessness. But positive attitudes build confidence and self-esteem, enabling you to take control and find the motivation to do the work necessary to achieve your goals.

As Shakespeare said. "There is nothing good nor bad but thinking makes it so." Choosing to regard a problem as a challenge casts it in a positive light, focusing your attention on the actions you can take to find solutions. Here are five more steps that you can take to develop a more positive attitude.

Visualize yourself being successful. Once you have set a goal, picture in your mind what you will have or will be able to do once you reach it. Keep that picture in your mind whenever you feel negative or are concerned about mastering a skill. For example, some golf instructors advocate using visualization during practice. Golfers picture themselves making a perfect swing, then repeat the process during a game.

Control your inner voice. You talk silently to yourself all the time. If your self-talk is mainly negative and derogatory, you are programming yourself for failure. Listen for those times during studying or test taking when you say to yourself, "I can't do this," or "I'm no good at this" and counteract those negative thoughts with positive ones: "I *can* do this; I just need to practice more," or "I am better at this than I used to be, and I will keep improving."

Reward yourself for doing well. When you know you have done your best or when you have accomplished a short-term goal that will help you reach a long-term goal, treat yourself to a movie, a new paperback novel, or lunch with a good friend. Be sparing with these rewards and save them for when you really deserve them. What you choose as a reward doesn't matter as long as it acts as a positive reinforcement for good behavior.

Be a positive listener and speaker. If you have trouble screening your own words for negative remarks that you need to change into positive ones, listen carefully to others. When a friend says, "I'm not going to pass algebra," explore this problem with him or her. Ask your friend to think of possible solutions. Make positive suggestions such as "Why don't you get a tutor to help you with the concepts you don't understand?" Being a positive listener and speaker may help you to think more positively about your own challenges as well.

Be persistent. *Persistence* means continuing in spite of obstacles. Do not give up at the first setback or sign of failure. Keep trying to reach your goals. Be optimistic, seek help, and try again. Persistence will pay off, and the confidence you feel will be the reward for your effort.

To learn more about the effect of a positive attitude, do an online search using these keywords as a starting point: *work-related attitudes, positive attitude, positive thinking.*

Online Study Center
Confidence Builder
Web Search

Action plan refers to a written plan that establishes a time frame and lists steps for accomplishing a goal.

WRITE YOUR ACTION PLAN

▶ *Make a commitment to reach your goals by writing and following an action plan.*

A goal is the first link in a chain of events that are connected by cause and effect. For example, you may have already selected a major and are now two or three terms into your program. This semester you have some health problems and get behind in one of your required courses. Though you try to make up the work, you have missed too many classes and are unable to catch up. As a result, your grade suffers. However, you do not regard this as a setback from which you cannot recover. Instead, you write an **action plan** that includes a schedule for next term, allowing you to carry a lighter work load and leaving some free time between classes for studying on campus. This schedule should result in a high grade-point average that will offset the previous term's poor performance. Writing an action plan is the same as making a commitment. Your plan commits you to a course of action that should meet with success—if you follow the plan. In any plan, some setbacks are bound to occur. Confident students take these in stride and revise their action plans to overcome difficulties and get back on track.

Suppose your goal in an algebra course is to pass with a grade of A or B. From reading the course syllabus, you learn that homework counts for 25 percent of the grade, unit tests count for 50 percent, and the final exam counts for 25 percent. A missed assignment lowers your homework grade by several points. The homework grade is an easy 25 percent to make because there are proofs in algebra that you can use before handing in your work to determine whether your answers are correct. Unit tests are more difficult, but your instructor will allow you to drop your lowest test score before averaging the grade. Also, you are allowed to retake one more unit test in addition to the one that you drop. The final exam is very important because 25 percent of the grade can make or break your average. What is your action plan for reaching the goal of earning an A in the course? An action plan lists short-term goals, or steps, that will help you reach your long-term goal. To pass the algebra course, you could write the action plan shown in Figure 4.5.

FIGURE 4.5

ACTION PLAN FOR PASSING ALGEBRA 101

1. **Long-term goal:** I want to pass Algebra I with a grade of A or B.

2. **How my goal meets the six characteristics of reachable goals:**
   a. It is *realistic* because I like math, and my basic math skills are good.
   b. It is *believable* and *possible* because I have made good grades in math classes before, and common sense tells me that I can succeed in this course.
   c. It is *measurable* because I have the entire term to reach my goal and have built in checkpoints at midterm and after each unit test.
   d. It is *flexible* because I realize that this course will be difficult, and I may have to settle for a B instead of the A that I would prefer.
   e. It is *controllable* because my motivation and effort will determine my performance and results.
   f. It is *ethical* because I am willing to do the work, and I do not expect the instructor to give me a grade that I don't deserve.

3. **Short-term goals:** I will do the following to achieve the outcome that I want.
   a. Attend class regularly and arrive on time.
   b. Do all required work and extra problems for practice.
   c. Make and follow a study schedule that allows me to review daily, weekly, and just before a test.
   d. I will chart my grades on homework and tests. If I lose points or miss problems, I will correct my mistakes before moving on.
   e. Keep up with the work and seek help if I have problems.

4. **Evaluate action plan:** I will review my plan every Friday to evaluate my progress. If I am falling behind in Algebra, or if I am having trouble following my plan, I will determine what is wrong, get help if I need it, and revise my plan or write a new one.

EXERCISE 4.5

WRITE AN ACTION PLAN FOR achieving a long-term goal. Use your major from Exercise 4.3 and the goal you selected for Exercise 4.4 or choose another goal. Using Figure 4.5 as a model, write your responses to the following items:

1. State your long-term goal, and be specific.

2. Explain how your goal meets the six characteristics of reachable goals.

3. Write three or more short-term goal statements that explain specifically what you will do and how these goals will help you reach the long-term goal.

4. Explain how and when you will evaluate your action plan.

Exercise Overview

Goal setting and problem solving are linked. Once you have identified a problem, you can choose a strategy for solving it. Your plan can include long-term and short-term goals that will help you reach your desired outcome.

Exercise Background

As a college student, your face pressures from many sources. Living with room-mates, keeping up with assignments, and managing your finances can be stressful. As an adult learner, you may be juggling family, college, and work obligations. The expectations that you place on yourself are often the hardest challenges to meet. Acknowledging these pressures and facing problems head-on will help you set realistic goals.

Exercise Task

The following scenarios illustrate common problems that students face. Read the scenarios and then choose one to discuss with a partner. Using the COPE strategy explained in Chapter 3, the goal-setting strategies explained in this chapter, or a combination of each, write out your solution to the student's problem.

1. My roommate sleeps in the afternoon and stays up all night studying, which interferes with my sleep. My roommate also has friends over when I am trying to study. Their loud talking and music or TV programs distract me. I'm tired all the time, and can't get much work done.

2. I am always low on cash, and I sometimes skip meals because I don't have enough money to pay for food. Tuition and books plus an unexpected medical expense have really depleted my savings. I am worried that I will have to drop out of college and go to work to save the money that I need to complete my education. I would hate to do this because my grades are good despite my financial woes, and I don't want to interrupt my momentum.

3. I am in my second semester of college, and I still don't have a major. I enjoy the outdoors, I like working with plants and animals, and I wish I could find a major that would allow me to explore these interests. Money is less important to me than doing something that I really enjoy. I hope to have a job someday that will allow me to spend time outdoors or to travel to distant places. Of course, I can't make progress until I select a major and make some plans.

4. I am a divorced father of two. My salary as a claims adjuster supports me and pays child support. I share custody of the kids with my ex-wife, and they spend most weekends with me. Although I like having the kids around, weekends are my only time to study. I attend community college part-time. My goal is to transfer to a four-year college and pursue a law degree, something I've always wanted to do. With my hectic schedule, I wonder if I'll ever make it.

Thinking ahead about Career

Purpose and Instructions

A workplace focus in Chapter 4 is on self-management, which is a personal quality you can develop by clarifying your values and setting goals. Use the knowledge you have gained from this chapter to solve career-related problems such as the one explained in the following case study. Read the case study on your own or with a partner, and then answer the case questions.

Case Study

Tyrone's father is a surgeon. He enjoys his work and its financial rewards. He has provided well for his family and has sent three children to college. His older son and daughter are both physicians. Tyrone, the youngest, is a sophomore in college. His family expects him to enter the medical field also. Tyrone has no interest in medicine, but he doesn't want to disappoint his family. After all, they are paying for his tuition. Tyrone's father has mapped out a course of study for Tyrone so that he can complete his required courses during the first two years, leaving the last two years to concentrate on his major. Tyrone's grades are good, but he dreads taking the science courses that will prepare him for medical school. Tyrone is good in math, enjoys working with computers, and knows he would be much happier as a business analyst or a purchasing manager for a large company. He would much rather seek a degree in business administration than in medicine. However, his earning capacity would be greater as a doctor—and his father would be proud, Tyrone doesn't know what to do.

Case Questions

1. As reflected in this case study, what are Tyrone's values? What are his father's values? How are their values in conflict?

   _____

   _____

2. What are Tyrone's academic/career options as stated in the case study?

   _____

   _____

3. Of these options, which one seems best for Tyrone? Does it meet the six characteristics of reachable goals? Explain your answer.

   _____

   _____

4. Access the Career Resource Center and read the article entitled "Your Major: Is It 'Til Death Do You Part?" in the *From College to Career Success* section of *The Bridge*. Based on this article, what would you suggest Tyrone do if he decides to change his major that would show his family he is taking personal responsibility for his actions?

   _____

   _____

Your *Reflections*

R **eflect on what you have learned from this chapter about values and goals.** Use the following questions to stimulate your thinking; then write your reflections. Include in your writing specific information from the chapter.

- Describe one of your best accomplishments. How did you achieve it, and was goal setting part of the process?

- Read the values listed in Figure 4.1. Which one of the values is most important to you and why?

- Why are you attending college, and what specific value do you place on your education?

- What is one skill or attitude explained in this chapter that you would like to develop, and what can you begin doing today to make that happen?

_____

_____

_____

_____

_____

_____

_____

_____

_____

_____

_____

_____

_____

_____

_____

_____

Chapter review

To review the chapter, reflect on the following confidence-building attitudes and skills. Complete **Concepts to Understand** by filling in the blanks with words or terms from the list provided. Then practice your new skills at every opportunity.

ATTITUDES TO DEVELOP
- positive thinking
- self-motivation
- personal responsibility

SKILLS TO PRACTICE
- setting goals
- writing action plans
- defining and building values

CONCEPTS TO UNDERSTAND

believable	long-term	goal	academic
personal	measurable	ethical	realistic
flexible	short-term		

Knowing why you are attending college, learning to set goals, and defining your values will help you to become a more confident student. Students have many reasons for attending college. It is important that the reasons you identify be your own and that you use them to motivate yourself.

A (1) _____ is an outcome, the result of a plan, something you want and are willing to work for. (2) _____ goals take some time to accomplish and may include such things as graduating from college, changing careers, or planning for a child's education. (3) _____ goals are intermediate steps between the initiation of a plan and its outcome. Goals fall into three general categories: (4) _____ goals, (5) _____ goals, and career/work-related goals.

Success is more likely if you set reachable goals. A reachable goal has six characteristics. A goal is (6) _____ if you can reasonably expect to achieve it given your abilities. A goal is (7) _____ and possible if you know what it takes to achieve it and where to begin and end. For example, it is possible to complete a bachelor of arts program in four years, perhaps even in three years. But a goal of completing the program in one year would be both unbelievable and impossible. To set (8) _____ goals, give yourself a time limit. Keep your goals (9) _____ and controllable by deciding what you want to do and by being willing to change your plans if necessary. (10) _____ goals are fair to all concerned.

To access additional review exercises, go to **college.hmco.com/pic/KanarTCS6e.**

Online Study Center
Review Exercise
ACE Self-Test

Online Study Center

Prepare for Class, Improve Your Grade, and ACE the Test. This chapter's *Student Achievement* resources include

Chapter exercises/forms	Review exercise	Confidence Builder Web search
ACE Self-Test		

To access these learning and study tools, go to **college.hmco.com/pic/KanarTCS6e.**

5 Sharpening your classroom skills

Your active involvement in learning brings you closer to your goals.

Improve your understanding of lectures, get more out of discussions, and earn better grades by coming to class prepared.

Define active listening; become an active listener by controlling your attention and concentration.

Know how to take notes and use a note-taking system that is compatible with your learning style.

▶ PREPARE FOR CLASS

▶ BECOME AN ACTIVE LISTENER

▶ DEVELOP A PERSONAL NOTE-TAKING SYSTEM
Guidelines for Note Taking
The Informal Outline/Key Words System
The Cornell Method
Matching Note-Taking Style and Learning Style

▶ MAKE EFFECTIVE ORAL PRESENTATIONS

▶ PARTICIPATE IN CLASS AND GROUP ACTIVITIES

▶ *Understand how participation affects learning and become more active in class and group activities.*

▶ *Learn strategies that will help you reduce stage fright and speak confidently in front of a group.*

Interpersonal skills valued in the workplace include teamwork, teaching and leadership abilities, and working cooperatively with others from diverse backgrounds.

Communication skills employers expect include reading, writing, listening, and speaking.

Because most exams and class activities are based on information presented in lectures, your ability to listen and take notes is closely linked to your performance in a course. If the lecture method is not your preferred mode of instruction, then you may need to improve or develop listening and note-taking skills that will enable you to gain as much from lectures as you do from other instructional modes.

In many classrooms learning is a collaborative activity. Sharing your ideas with others builds confidence. Moreover, group work, oral presentations, and class discussion are significant parts of the assessment and learning processes. The give-and-take of these activities helps you build the **interpersonal skills** and **communication skills** needed for effective interaction in class as well as in the workplace.

KEY TERMS

punctuality, *p. 105*
etiquette, *p. 106*
syllabus, *p. 106*
active listening, *p. 107*
passive listeners, *p. 107*
active listeners, *p. 107*
clustering, *p. 118*

SCANS TERMS

interpersonal skills, *p. 103*
communication skills, *p. 103*

To sharpen your classroom skills, make a commitment to learn, take responsibility for the outcome of every course, and be an active participant in all classroom activities.

Take the first step toward becoming more actively involved in your own learning process by evaluating your current performance in the classroom with Awareness Check 8.

AWARENESS CHECK 8

Are You Prepared for Classes and Lectures?

Points

To explain how closely each statement applies to you, choose one of the following as your response: *always* **(4 points)**, *usually* **(3 points)**, *occasionally* **(2 points)**, *rarely* **(1 point)**. Write your number of points in the box beside each statement. When you are finished, add your score.

1. I attend class regularly, and I am absent only in case of emergency.

2. I make a point of arriving to a class or a lecture on time and staying until the end.

3. I use my syllabus to review requirements and keep up with assignments.

4. I begin studying for a test as soon as it is announced.

5. I do not forget to bring my book and other materials to class.

6. I always complete assigned work and hand it in on time.

7. I usually know what the instructor expects me to do.

8. I can pick out the important ideas in a lecture.

9. I can easily ignore distractions when I am listening to a lecture.

10. Even if I don't agree with an opinion that is expressed or don't understand everything that is said, this situation doesn't interfere with my ability to listen and learn.

Total

Add your score. If your total is 35–40, you have a solid foundation of classroom preparation and listening skills. If your total is 30–34, you have some strengths but also some weaknesses. If your total is 25–29, practicing this chapter's strategies will improve your classroom performance. If your score is 10–24, you may have had difficulty in the past with meeting course requirements. It is never too late to make a new start. Whatever your level of skill, if you apply this chapter's strategies, you should see improvement not only in your grades but also in your level of confidence.

PREPARE FOR CLASS

▶ *Improve your understanding of lectures, get more out of discussions,
and earn better grades by coming to class prepared.*

Your first strategy for success in any course is to come to class prepared. Although the following tips may seem obvious, many students sabotage their learning by ignoring them.

Attend Regularly and Be Punctual. Absenteeism has always been a problem in college. Students who cut classes cite many reasons: boredom, dislike of the course or instructor, time constraints, tiredness, and off-campus jobs. Students whose classes meet in a large lecture hall may think that their absence won't be noticed or that they can get the notes from friends. Because many instructors post lectures online, class attendance may seem unnecessary. The reality is that absence hurts you in several ways.

First of all, cutting classes can be habit-forming. The first couple of times you do it, you may not notice any ill effects. However, with repeated cuts, you begin understanding less and less. When you finally do decide to show up, the class will have passed you by, and it may be too late to pull up your grade. Second, in many courses the material is presented sequentially: Each day's lesson builds upon previous lessons. Basic concepts and foundational skills are taught early in the course, and the level is raised gradually over the entire term. Cutting class cuts you out of the information loop. Third, an essential part of any course is the interaction you have with other students as you work cooperatively to solve problems and apply concepts. Students who have been absent often ask, "Did I miss anything?" Students who plan on being absent often ask, "Will we be doing anything important?" The answer to both questions is "Yes."

Punctuality is as important as attendance. Emergencies will happen, and once in a while you may have to be late, but if you make lateness a habit, here's what can happen. Instructors usually state objectives during the first few moments of class. During the last few minutes, the instructor concludes the lesson and may announce a test or make a change in an assignment. Whether you arrive late or leave early, you miss something. Chronic lateness sends the message that you are irresponsible, not in control of your time and your life. Also, arriving late and leaving early are distracting, disruptive, and discourteous.

Punctuality is the quality of being on time.

Some students argue that since they are paying for the course, they have a right to attend or not. Don't make this faulty assumption. Your tuition buys you a place at the table. It does not buy you the right to behave any way that you choose. You are bound by the instructor's requirements and rules of etiquette, but since you do pay for every moment that you spend in class, why not get your money's worth? Come every day, arrive on time, and stay until the end.

Watch Your Etiquette. Enter class quietly, find your seat quickly, and arrange your materials with a minimum of fuss. Turn your cell phone off and your mind on. The classroom, like the workplace, is not a casual setting. Here you do not prop up your feet, kick back, and relax. Let your posture show that you are engaged, involved, attentive, and interested—even if you are not. It's the polite thing to do.

Be respectful of your classmates and instructor. Raise your hand and wait for acknowledgment instead of blurting out a comment or question. Take part in the class. Dozing at your desk, studying for another class, working on an assignment that should have been completed yesterday, or socializing with friends are activities that show disrespect for the serious work in which the class is engaged.

Etiquette means good manners, polite behavior, and rules of conduct that make people feel comfortable being together.

Syllabus refers to the document that lists general course requirements and specific assignments.

Observing classroom **etiquette** means thinking about what you do and how it affects others.

Use Your Syllabus. The course **syllabus** helps you keep up with assignments and tests, tells you what topics were covered if you were absent, and summarizes the instructor's requirements. Review it often to keep this information fresh in your mind. Bring it to class every day. Then, if the instructor makes a change or postpones a test, you can note the change directly on the syllabus. Your syllabus is a confidence builder because it gives you a plan to follow.

Bring Textbooks and Other Supplies to Class Every Day. Instructors often call attention to information in the textbook, or they may ask you to do an exercise from the textbook in class. Some instructors lecture on material contained in the book, especially if it's complicated or needs supplementing. If you bring your textbook to class, you will be able to follow along and mark important passages.

Do the Assignments. Assignments provide the practice you need to acquire new skills. They help reinforce ideas and concepts discussed in class. Most important, doing the assignments provides you with background information that will help you make sense of future assignments. Also, you may lose points on tests if you are not able to answer questions that come directly from your assignments.

Anticipate the Next Lesson. Follow two simple steps to anticipate what will be covered in class each day.

> ## CONCEPT CHECK 5.1
>
> Predicting outcomes is a critical thinking strategy explained in Chapter 3. You apply this strategy when you try to anticipate the next day's assignment.

1. **Review the previous day's work.** Read your notes from the last class. Review the previous chapter and the assignment, if any. The next class is likely to expand on this information. Reviewing the work from the previous class helps you retain the information and prepare for the next class.

2. **Preview the next day's assignments.** Review your syllabus to determine what will be covered and how it relates to what was covered in the previous class. Formulate some questions in your mind about the topic. Ask yourself, "What do I already know?" Also, skim assigned chapters before reading them to preview content and to determine whether new words or terms are introduced; then look up the terms and definitions to familiarize yourself with them before doing the reading. Considering past assignments, try to predict what the instructor's approach to the material will be—whether lecture, discussion, or group work—and prepare for class accordingly. Previewing helps you relate new information to your prior knowledge, placing it in a meaningful context.

If you attend class regularly, are punctual, use your syllabus, bring your textbook and other supplies to class, do the assignments, and anticipate the next lesson, you will always know what to expect from your classes, you won't feel lost, and you will be in the proper frame of mind to listen attentively.

BECOME AN ACTIVE LISTENER

▶ *Define* active listening; *become an active listener by controlling your attention and concentration.*

Your second strategy for classroom success is **active listening**. Since lecture–discussion is the preferred style of many college instructors, you will probably spend most of your class time listening. Listeners fall into two categories: passive and active. **Passive listeners** do more hearing than listening. They are aware that the instructor is speaking, but they aren't making sense of what he or she is saying. Passive listening is characteristic of the external locus of control. For example, passive listeners may expect instructors to motivate them and to interest them in the topic. On the other hand, **active listeners** pay attention to what they hear and try to make sense of it. Active listening is characteristic of the internal locus of control. For example, active listeners are self-motivated, and they expect to find their own reasons for being interested in a lecture topic. Figure 5.1 compares the traits of active and passive listeners. Which kind of listener are you?

To get more out of lectures, become an active listener. Follow these five steps:

1. **Decide to listen.** By deciding to listen, you are strengthening your commitment to learn. Also, by deciding to listen, you are taking an active role instead of waiting passively to receive information.

2. **Listen with a positive frame of mind.** Expect to find something in the lecture that will interest you. Assume that you will learn something useful, that you will expand your knowledge, and that you will increase your understanding of the subject.

Active listening is involved listening in which your vision, hearing, posture, and mind each play a role.

Passive listeners are uninvolved, inattentive, and detached from the process.

Active listeners practice active listening strategies.

FIGURE 5.1

TRAITS OF PASSIVE AND ACTIVE LISTENERS

PASSIVE LISTENERS	ACTIVE LISTENERS
Expect a lecture to be dull	Expect to find something in the lecture that interests them
Assume that information in a lecture will not be useful or pertain to their lives	Assume that information in a lecture will be useful—if not now, then later
Look for weaknesses in the speaker's style instead of listening to what the speaker says	May notice weaknesses in the speaker's style but pay attention to what the speaker says
Listen only for ideas that interest them	Listen for main ideas and the details that support them
Give in to daydreaming and become distracted	Resist daydreaming and ignore distractions
Tune out when they disagree with the speaker	Keep listening even when they disagree with the speaker
Tune out difficult or technical information; do not ask questions	Try to understand difficult or technical information; ask questions as needed
May doze in lectures if tired	Fight to stay awake if tired
Do not take good notes	Take well-organized notes

Online Study Center   www.college.hmco.com/pic/KanarTCS6e

When active listening is involved, you are engaging in whole-body and whole-mind listening.

3. **Assume the posture of involvement.** Sit straight but comfortably and make eye contact with the speaker. Concentrate on what is being said. Your effort to understand and follow the lecture will show in your expression, making you look interested even if you are not. Body orientation, expression, and gestures such as nodding when you agree or displaying a questioning look when you don't understand are cues that help the speaker determine whether the message is getting across. Your involvement will pay off. By trying to appear interested even when you are not, you may actually become interested. At that point, learning begins.

4. **Take notes.** Taking notes also helps you concentrate on the lecture. Taking notes activates your tactile sense, as explained in Chapter 2, so that you are more likely to retain the information, especially if you review your notes soon after the lecture. Take notes consistently when listening to lectures and adopt or develop a note-taking system that works for you. (More is said about note taking later in the chapter.)

5. **Decide what is important.** Listen for repeated terms or ideas. Speakers use repetition to emphasize important points. Watch for gestures and facial expressions that may also be used for emphasis. Listen for signal words or phrases. See Figure 5.2 for a list of signal words and phrases and explanations of what they mean.

Listening for signal words helps you listen for ideas. For example, if an English instructor says, "You can use seven different patterns to organize details in a paragraph," then you should number from one to seven on your paper, skipping lines between, and listen for the seven patterns and the instructor's explanations. If you get to the fifth pattern and realize that you don't have anything written down for the fourth one, then you know you have missed something in the lecture. At this point, you should ask a question.

FIGURE 5.2

SIGNAL WORDS AND PHRASES

1. **To indicate that another main idea or example follows:**

also	furthermore	another
in addition	moreover	

2. **To add emphasis:**

most important	above all	of primary concern
remember that	a key idea	most significant
pay attention to	the main idea	

3. **To indicate that an example follows:**

for example	to illustrate	such as
for instance	specifically	

4. **To indicate that a conclusion follows:**

therefore	in conclusion	finally
consequently	to conclude	so

5. **To indicate an exception to a stated fact:**

however	although	but
nevertheless	though	except

6. **To indicate cause or effects:**

because	due to	consequently
since	reason	result
for	cause	effect

7. **To indicate that categories or divisions will be named or explained:**

types	parts	groups
kinds	characteristics	categories

8. **To indicate a sequence:**

steps	numbers (1, 2, 3, . . .)
stages	first, second, etc.

9. **To indicate that items are being compared:**

similar	different	equally
like	in contrast	on the other hand
advantages	disadvantages	contrary to

EXERCISE 5.1   COLLABORATIVE ACTIVITY

APPLY WHAT YOU HAVE LEARNED about signal words by doing this exercise with group members. Follow the guidelines for group discussion that appear on the inside back cover. Read the following paragraph. First identify as many signal words as you can and discuss their meaning in the sentences in which they appear, using Figure 5.2 as a reference. Next, discuss and answer the questions. When you arrive at consensus, record your answers. Then write your evaluation on your own paper or download the group exercise form from the Online Study Center at college.hmco.com/pic/KanarTCS6e.

Most of us assume that listening is an innate skill. Aren't most people born with the ability to sleep, breathe, see, and hear? But is hearing the same act as listening? Although most of us can hear perfectly well, we are not all good listeners. What, you might ask, are the characteristics of a good listener? First, a good listener makes a commitment to listen. Second, a good listener focuses attention on the speaker. For example, a good listener is not reading the newspaper or watching television while listening to a friend explain a problem. Most important, a good listener is genuinely interested in the speaker and in what he or she says. In conclusion, listening is not something you should assume that you do well. It is a lifelong skill that can be improved with earnest practice and hard work.

1. **What signal words indicate that an example is to follow? What example does the writer give?**

   _____

2. **Write the signal word that indicates that categories or divisions will be explained.**

   _____

3. **Write the signal words that indicate sequence.**

   _____

4. **What does the writer believe is the most important characteristic of a good listener?**

   _____

5. **What is the writer's concluding idea about listening?**

   _____

Group Evaluation:
Evaluate your discussion. Did everyone contribute? Did you accomplish your task successfully? What additional questions do you have about signal words? How will you find answers to your questions?

Online Study Center
   Chapter Exercises/
   Forms

EXERCISE 5.2   COLLABORATIVE ACTIVITY

FORM A GROUP WITH FOUR or five students. Using the traits listed in Figure 5.1 as a guide, prepare a short demonstration on listening behavior. Let one person in the group be the lecturer. Let other group members demonstrate passive or active listening habits. The group member acting as the lecturer should be able to explain to the class which group members were good listeners and which were not. Practice your demonstration. Your instructor may call on one or more of the groups to present in class.

DEVELOP A PERSONAL NOTE-TAKING SYSTEM

▶ *Know how to take notes and use a note-taking system that is compatible with your learning style.*

The third strategy for classroom success is good note taking. There is no *best* way to take notes. The suggestions offered in this chapter have worked for many students. Experiment with them, and then adapt them to find the style of note taking that consistently gives you good results. Complete Awareness Check 9 before you begin reading this section.

AWARENESS CHECK 9

How Effective Are Your Note-Taking Skills?

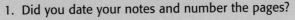

Yes	No	To see where you need improvement, evaluate your lecture notes from a recent class. Read them over and answer *yes* or *no* to the following questions.
☐	☐	1. Did you date your notes and number the pages?
☐	☐	2. Did you write the course name or number on your notes?
☐	☐	3. Did you write down the topic of the lecture?
☐	☐	4. Did you use 8½" by 11" paper to keep in a loose-leaf binder?
☐	☐	5. Did you take notes with a ballpoint pen?
☐	☐	6. Are your notes easy to read?
☐	☐	7. Is this set of notes in the same notebook as all your other notes for this class?
☐	☐	8. Are your notes organized into an informal outline or other logical format?
☐	☐	9. Are you able to distinguish the speaker's main ideas from the examples that illustrate them?
☐	☐	10. As you read your notes, are you able to reconstruct in your mind what the lecture was about?

If you answered no *to any of these questions—particularly the last two—then your note-taking skills may need improvement. Try the guidelines that follow for improving your note taking.*

Guidelines for Note Taking

▼ Keep track of your notes by heading your paper with the *date, name of course,* and *lecture topic.* Number consecutive pages. Later, when you study, you'll be able to match up class notes and textbook notes or assignments on the same topic.

▼ Use standard-sized paper—8½" by 11"—that will fit into most notebooks or folders. Small sheets of paper won't hold enough writing and may get lost or out of order.

▼ Keep the notes for one class separated from the notes for other classes. Use separate notebooks for each class or use dividers to distinguish different sections in one notebook. Some students like to use spiral notebooks. Others prefer to use a loose-leaf binder so that lecture notes, textbook notes, and the instructor's handouts may be taken out of it and reorganized for study purposes.

▼ Use a ballpoint pen for taking notes. Ink from felt-tip pens blurs and soaks through the paper, spotting the sheets underneath. Pencil smears and fades over time. Many students prefer to use blue or black ink because other colors, such as red or green, are hard on the eyes.

▼ If you know your handwriting is poor, print for clarity. Illegible or decorative handwriting makes notes hard to read.

▼ To speed up your note taking, use standard abbreviations and make up some of your own for words or phrases that you use often. Make a key for your abbreviations so you won't forget what they mean. See Figure 5.3 for a list of some common abbreviations. For even greater speed while taking notes, omit the periods from abbreviations.

▼ Copy into your notes anything that is written on the board or projected on a screen. Test questions often come from material that is presented in these ways.

FIGURE 5.3

COMMONLY USED ABBREVIATIONS AND SYMBOLS

1. equal: =	11. introduction: intro.
2. with: w/	12. information: info.
3. without: w/o	13. department: dept.
4. number: #	14. advantage: adv.
5. therefore: \	15. organization: org.
6. and: +	16. maximum: max.
7. and so forth: etc.	17. individual: ind.
8. for example: e.g.	18. compare: cf.
9. against: vs.	19. association: assoc.
10. government: gov't.	20. politics: pol.

Taking notes during a lecture involves your visual, aural, and tactile/kinesthetic senses that open multiple pathways to the brain.

▶ Take organized notes. Use a system such as one of those suggested later in this chapter or devise your own. Make main ideas stand out from the examples that support them. Do not write lecturers' words verbatim. Summarize ideas in your own words so that they will be easier for you to remember.

▶ As soon as possible after class, review your notes to fill in gaps while the information is still fresh in your mind. The purpose of taking notes is to help you remember information. If you take notes but don't look at them until you are ready to study for a test, you will have to relearn the information. To retain information in your long-term memory, review it frequently.

▶ To fill in gaps, compare notes with a classmate or see the instructor.

The Informal Outline/Key Words System

Ideas that are organized in a logical pattern are easier to remember than isolated facts and examples that don't seem to relate to one another. Try this simple, two-part system to improve your note taking.

Draw a line down your paper so that you have a 2½" column on the right and a 6" column on the left. Take notes in the 6" column, using an informal outline. Make main ideas stand out by indenting and numbering the details and examples listed under them. Skip lines between main ideas so that you can fill in examples later or add an example if the lecturer returns to one of these ideas later on. After the lecture, write key words in the right margin that will help you recall information from your notes.

Figure 5.4 on page 114 shows a student's lecture notes on the topic "Studying on the Right Side of the Brain." The student has used the informal outline/key words system. On the left side of the page, the student has outlined the lecture

Online Study Center   *www.college.hmco.com/pic/KanarTCS6e*

THE INFORMAL OUTLINE/KEY WORDS SYSTEM

FIGURE 5.4

Study Skills 1620 | Sept. 18

Studying on the Right Side of the Brain	
Visual thinking	
1. Use graphic techniques like diagrams, maps, etc. to organize information into a meaningful pattern.	def.
2. Visual learners need to make verbal information "visual" or they will have a hard time remembering it.	reason for using "visuals"
Fantasy	
1. The ability to create and use mental images is another kind of visual thinking.	def.
2. To understand the stages in an organism's life cycle, imagine you are the organism going through the stages.	ex. of fantasy
Hands-on experience	
1. Get involved in a direct experience of what you are learning.	def.
2. Do lab experiments, take field trips, role play, look at or touch objects as they are described. Go through the steps of a process.	hands-on activities
Music	
1. Common belief: music distracts while studying.	
2. Music can accelerate learning.	effect of music on learning
3. Studies show retention improved when students read to music.	
4. Instrumentals that match the feeling or mood of the information to be remembered are the best type of music.	

given in class. Later, on the right side of the page, in the margin, the student has written key words or abbreviations that show at a glance what the lecture covered.

When you use this system, wait to write in the key words until you are reviewing your notes.

The Cornell Method*

Developed by Dr. Walter Pauk of Cornell University, the Cornell method is a classic note-taking system that has worked for many students. One version of the system involves six steps: *recording, questioning, reciting, reflecting, reviewing,* and *recapitulating.*

Begin by dividing an 8½" by 11" sheet of notebook paper into three sections, as shown in Figure 5.5 on page 116. Then follow these steps for taking notes from a lecture:

1. **Record** facts and ideas in the wide column. After the lecture, fill in any gaps and neaten up your handwriting, if necessary, so that you will be able to read your notes when you review them later.

2. **Question** facts and ideas presented in lectures. Write questions about what you don't understand or what you think an instructor might ask on a test. Write your questions in the left margin beside the fact or idea in the wide column. Writing questions helps you strengthen your memory, improve your understanding, and anticipate test questions.

3. **Recite** the facts or ideas aloud from memory and in your own words. If you summarized them in your notes in your own words, then this will be easy to do. If you are an auditory learner, reciting will improve your retention because you will be using listening, your preferred mode. To see how much you remember, cover up the wide column of your notes and recite from the key words or questions in the left margin. Recite the key word or question first; then try to recall and recite the whole fact or idea. To check yourself, uncover the wide column and read your notes.

4. **Reflect** on what you have learned from the lecture by applying the facts and ideas to real-life situations. Determine why the facts are significant, how you can use them, and how they expand or modify your prior knowledge.

5. **Review** and recite your notes every day. A good way to begin a study session, especially if you have trouble getting started, is to review your notes. Reviewing reminds you of what you have learned and sets the scene for new information to be gained from the next assignment.

6. **Recapitulate** by writing a summary of your notes in the space at the bottom of your paper. You can summarize what you have written on each page of notes, or you can summarize the whole lecture at the end of the last page. Doing both a page summary and a whole-lecture summary is even better.

Now, clarify these steps in your mind by examining the student's lecture notes shown in Figure 5.6 on page 117.

---

*Walter Pauk, *How to Study in College,* Eighth Edition. Copyright ©2005 by Houghton Mifflin Company. Used with permission.

> **CONCEPT CHECK 5.2**
>
> A personal note-taking system that is compatible with your learning style may include drawings, diagrams, symbols, and abbreviations that are meaningful to you.

2 1/2" margin
for questions

6" column for taking notes

2" space for a summary

THE CORNELL METHOD: ONE STUDENT'S NOTES

FIGURE 5.6

Intro. to Literature 2010   Sept. 18

	The Five Elements of Fiction
	1. Plot
How does the	a. Events and setting
plot of the	b. Plot development
story develop?	* conflict
	* complications
	* climax
	* resolution
	2. Character
What is the	a. Dynamic
difference between	* well-rounded
a dynamic and a	* motives
static character?	b. Static
	* flat
	* stereotype
	3. Point of view
What are the	a. First person
four points	b. Omniscient
of view?	c. Limited omniscient
	d. Dramatic
How is the	4. Theme
theme of the	a. Meaning or significance
story revealed?	b. Revealed through interaction of five elements
What makes one	5. Style/Tone
writer's style	a. Mood or feeling
distinctive?	b. Choice of words, use of language

The writer uses five elements of fiction—plot, character, point of view, theme, and style/tone—to develop the story. Through the interaction of these elements, the meaning of the story is revealed and the reader can understand its significance.

Matching Note-Taking Style and Learning Style

Clustering is a visual form of outlining that is nonsequential.

What if you are not a linear thinker? What if a 1, 2, 3 order of information does not appeal to you because you don't think that way, and instructors don't always stick to their lecture outlines? You may prefer a more visual style of note taking. Try **clustering**. Start a few inches from the top of the page and write the speaker's first main idea in a circle near the middle of the page. If the speaker gives an example, draw an arrow to another circle in which you write the example. If the speaker presents another main idea, start a new cluster. Figure 5.7 shows an example of the cluster note-taking technique. The cluster technique will help you visualize the information you want to remember. An advantage of clustering is that if the speaker leaves one idea and returns to it later, it is easy to draw another arrow from the circle and add the example. Clustering is a nontraditional note-taking procedure, but if it works for you and if it makes note taking easy and pleasant, then don't hesitate to use it.

CLUSTERING: A VISUAL FORM OF NOTE TAKING — FIGURE 5.7

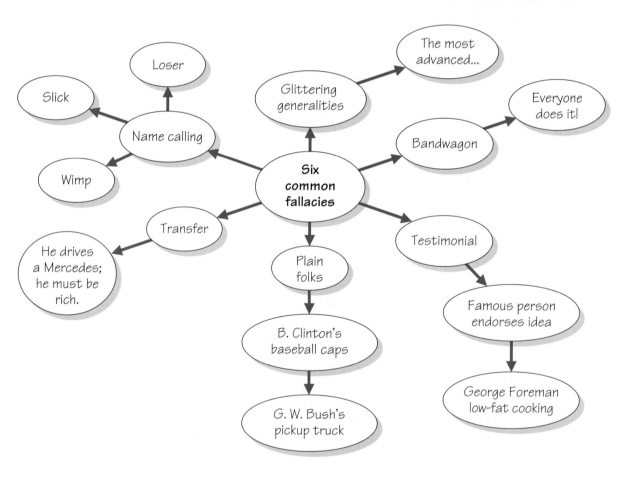

> ## EXERCISE 5.3   LEARNING STYLE
>
> **PRACTICE NOTE TAKING WITH A** classmate. During the next class meeting, both of you should take notes, using your preferred method. After class, compare your notes. Do your notes cover the same information? Are your note-taking styles similar or different? Whose notes are neater, better organized, and more thorough? What have you learned from this exercise that will help you improve your note-taking skills?

MAKE EFFECTIVE ORAL PRESENTATIONS

▶ *Learn strategies that will help you reduce stage fright and speak confidently in front of a group.*

Being able to make an effective oral presentation is the fourth strategy for success in the classroom. A speech course is a general education or liberal arts requirement at many colleges and universities because oral communication is an important academic and career skill. In a speech class you learn how to plan, organize, and make speeches. You also learn how to cope with *stage fright*, the fear of speaking or performing in front of an audience, and the stress that results from that fear. If it has been a while since you took a speech course, or if you have not yet had an opportunity to take one, then the following suggestions may help you prepare yourself for making an oral presentation.

Suppose your literature instructor asks you to give an oral interpretation of a poem you were assigned to read. Or maybe your biology instructor asks you to report to the class about the results of an experiment you performed in the lab. Perhaps a finance professor requests that you analyze and give an oral report on several properties that a company might purchase. You are to explain which purchase would net the company a greater return on its investment. In each case, you would first decide what your *purpose* is. For example, the purpose of your interpretation of a poem might be to explain what you think the writer's theme is. In your report about your lab results, your purpose would be to tell what conclusion you reached as a result of your experiment. In your report to your finance class, your purpose might be to convince class members that the purchase of one of the properties is best for the company.

Once your purpose is clear, you can *plan* and *organize* your speech. Outline your main idea and the details that support it. Recite from your outline several times until you know what you want to say. Try your speech out on a friend or family member and ask for suggestions about how to improve your delivery or how to explain your ideas more clearly. If you think you might forget something, summarize your main idea and details on 3" × 5" cards. The notes will jog your memory, and holding the cards will give you something to do with your hands.

In general, a good plan to follow in preparing an oral presentation is to use a three-part development:

1. **Tell your listeners what you're going to say.** Introduce your topic. State your purpose and main idea.

2. **Say it.** Support your main idea with details. State the facts, reasons, or examples that explain your opinions. Draw a conclusion from your evidence: Tell listeners why the information you have just given them is important and how they can use it.

3. **Tell them what you have just said.** Briefly summarize your main idea, details, and conclusion.

It is normal to feel some nervousness before giving a speech. Preparation is the best antidote to stage fright. Practice your speech in front of a roommate or friends until you feel comfortable with it. Before the speech, take a few deep breaths to relax yourself and clear your mind. To prevent dry mouth, put some lip balm on your lips. To control shakiness, hold your note cards. Most important, focus on your message and your audience instead of your feelings.

Remember that your audience is on your side. They are interested in what you have to say. You can make it easy for them to pay attention by making eye contact, speaking loudly enough to be heard in the back of the room, and speaking distinctly. Also, watch your pace because speaking too fast or too slowly is distracting and interferes with the flow of ideas. Making oral presentations is like any other skill. The more practice you have, the more you will improve.

C R I T I C A L   T H I N K I N G

Exercise Overview

This exercise will give you practice in preparing and making a short oral presentation. The exercise will also help you review one of the topics covered in your textbook.

Exercise Background

Speaking is an often-neglected skill. Students who have stage fright may avoid taking a speech course unless it is required, depriving themselves of the opportunity to develop and practice this skill. Being able to speak with confidence or to make a well-organized presentation is an asset in the workplace. Planning and making an effective speech or presentation involve critical and creative thinking.

Exercise Task

Make a brief presentation to the class on a topic of your choice from Chapters 1 through 4 of *The Confident Student*. Your purpose is to teach your classmates a skill or to help them gain greater understanding of a concept. To organize your presentation, follow the three-part development plan suggested in this chapter: *Tell your listeners what you're going to say, say it, and then tell them what you have just said.* Supplement your presentation with visual or other aids. Be creative.

EXERCISE 5.4   COMPUTER APPLICATION

FIND ONLINE RESOURCES TO HELP you prepare speeches and presentations. Some search words to try are *public speaking, stage fright*, and *oral presentations*. For a summary of the basics of public speaking from Toastmasters international, see http://www.toastmasters.org/tips.htm.

After reviewing these resources and any others that you may find, briefly explain in writing which ones were most useful. Also be prepared to present your findings orally to the rest of the class.

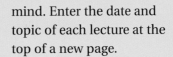

COMPUTER CONFIDENCE

Use a Computer to Organize Your Notes

Taking notes in class and while you're reading is an important first step toward understanding new material. But the next step is even more important—organizing your notes into a format from which you can study effectively. That's where a computer can make a big difference. Whichever note-taking style you prefer—the informal outline/key words system, the Cornell method, clustering, or a system of your own—using the computer to reorganize your notes offers several advantages:

1. It's easy to move whole blocks of words around to rearrange information into a format that makes sense to you.

2. It's easy to add new ideas to your notes as you go along or to combine class and textbook notes to give yourself the most complete coverage of the information.

3. The actual process of typing your notes on the computer improves your memory by engaging your tactile and visual senses.

Many word-processing programs offer easy-to-use outlining features that automatically provide an outline format into which you can type your notes. Or you can create your own outlines by following these simple steps:

1. Open a separate file for each of your courses. Create a name for the file.

2. Try to get to the computer soon after each class, while the lecture is still fresh in your mind. Enter the date and topic of each lecture at the top of a new page.

3. Review your class notes. No matter what note-taking system you're using, this is a good time to focus on the main ideas or key questions. Then type your notes into the computer, using a system. For example, use the boldface function to make main ideas stand out, use tabs to indent details, and set special margins for key words or questions.

4. At this point, you may wish to add comments, insert notes from your reading, or move sections of your outline around. To create a formal outline, insert Roman numerals and uppercase letters to mark major divisions, and move each line so that it aligns correctly. Then insert Arabic numerals and lowercase letters in front of the details and also align them.

5. Print out the final version. Double-space the printed copy so that you will have room to insert additional notes.

Other options for note taking with a computer include using voice-recognition software that allows you to dictate your notes. A hand-held computer is convenient to use between classes to enter a few ideas while on the run until you have time to sit down and review the lecture and organize your notes.

PARTICIPATE IN CLASS AND GROUP ACTIVITIES

> *Understand how participation affects learning and become more active in class and group activities.*

Chapter 1 introduces the idea of active learning. Chapter 4 encourages you to write action plans to achieve your goals. This chapter promotes active listening and involvement in class. Throughout *The Confident Student* you will see an emphasis on active processes to enhance learning. If you sit back passively in your class or group, letting others take the risks and do the work, you are not really involved. You may be taking in some information, but you aren't *doing* anything to promote learning and retention. The key to active learning is participation.

To become more active during class discussion, listen attentively, take notes, and make eye contact with whoever is speaking, whether it is the instructor or a student. Ask questions if appropriate and express your opinion when you have something to contribute. Avoid distracting behaviors such as socializing. Good classroom etiquette requires that you treat your classes with the same seriousness as you would a job. Be professional at work; be academic in class.

Small group work also calls for a serious attitude and polite behavior. The group is not a social gathering; it has a task to perform. Clearly define the task and your role within the group—leader, recorder, timekeeper, and so on. Understand what part of the work is your responsibility and stay on task. In addition, follow these guidelines for successful work within groups:

1. Allow each person to contribute to the discussion; take turns and don't interrupt.

2. Question facts, argue the details, but do not engage in personal attacks.

3. When it is your time to share, be precise and to the point, and do not monopolize the discussion.

4. If you are the group leader, keep the discussion focused, encourage everyone to contribute, and summarize the group's conclusions at the end of the discussion.

5. Do your part to keep the group on task. Do not let the discussion degenerate into a social exchange.

Participation in class and group work helps you build interpersonal skills and also keeps you actively involved in the learning process. Through participation you become a part of something larger—people working together to reach common goals.

CONFIDENCE BUILDER

Interpersonal Skills for College and Career

When you interact with others in class, especially in small group activities and on collaborative projects, you are building interpersonal skills that will give you an edge in the workplace. The days of isolated workers sitting in their cubicles are giving way to work teams in which work is shared by a group of colleagues, each contributing his or her expertise. At companies such as Lockheed Martin much of the work is done in teams, and employees are expected to have the necessary interpersonal qualities and leadership skills. In 1991, the U.S. Department of Labor, through the Secretary's Commission on Achieving Necessary Skills (SCANS), issued a report on the skills students will need to succeed in the high-performance workplace of the twenty-first century. The Department of Labor calls these skills, collectively, "workplace know-how." One of the skill areas cited as being necessary for solid job performance is *interpersonal skills*.

Participating in class and working collaboratively on projects in and out of the classroom can potentially help you develop two of the SCANS' interpersonal skills: *working as a member of a team* and *exercising leadership*.

What behaviors promote effective teamwork? The SCANS report lists the following:

- Share the work.

- Encourage others by listening and responding appropriately to their contributions.

- Recognize each other's strengths and build on them.

- Settle differences for the benefit of the group.

- Take responsibility for achieving goals.

- Challenge existing procedures, policies, or authorities—but do so in a responsible way.

How do you exercise leadership within a group? The SCANS report says that competent leaders do the following:

- They make positive use of the rules and values followed by others.

- They justify their positions logically and appropriately.

- They establish their credibility through competence and integrity.

- They take minority opinion contributions into consideration.

In plain language, what do these competencies for participating and leading mean? Simply put, if you are the leader of a group discussion in class, you can make "positive use of rules and values" by making sure that your group follows the guidelines your instructor has given for completing the assignment. As a leader, you "justify" your position "logically and appropriately" by not monopolizing the discussion and by keeping order when things get out of hand. You "establish credibility" by doing your share of the work, and you show "integrity" by seeing that the work gets done. If someone in the group expresses an opinion different from that of the majority of group members, you treat that "minority contribution" fairly and do not dismiss it out of hand.

Suppose that you don't understand the instructions or that you see an easier, better way to accomplish the task than to follow the guidelines you've been given. How do you "challenge existing procedures" responsibly? Discuss your concerns with your instructor, asking in a polite way whether the guidelines can be modified and being willing to proceed as instructed if necessary.

Respect for others and their opinions is the key to effective participation in groups, whether in class or at work. To learn more about SCANS online, go to AltaVista or another search engine and type *SCANS report* as your keyword. Also, see Chapter 14 for additional information on SCANS.

Online Study Center
Confidence Builder
Web Search

Online Study Center   *www.college.hmco.com/pic/KanarTCS6e*

EXERCISE 5.5   LEARNING STYLE

HOW WELL DO YOU PARTICIPATE in your classes? Read about three members of a sociology class and see if you find yourself mirrored in their profiles. Then answer the questions that follow.

> *Bob always sits at the back of the classroom so that he can nap quietly if he has stayed out late the night before. He rarely makes a comment or asks a question. If he doesn't understand something the instructor says, he forgets about it. He's sure that he'll figure the problem out when he does the reading just before the final exam. He would probably forget about it anyway before the exam rolled around.*
>
> *Sam can't wait to get to class. He has done all the reading, and he has millions of questions to ask. Sam's voice is always the first one heard. His hand is raised many times each class hour, whether there's a lecture or a discussion. Often frustrated, Sam does not listen to either his peers or his instructor. If he did listen, he'd realize that many of his questions had already been addressed. Sometimes Sam is so interested in getting his point across that he interrupts his classmates' remarks, or he attacks them for challenging his views.*
>
> *Carmen loves sociology class. She enjoys listening to the lecture, but she also enjoys the give-and-take of class discussions. At first, she was hesitant to speak out, but once she became convinced that she could learn a great deal from the questions and comments of her peers, she tried participating. When she leads a discussion, Carmen makes sure that everyone has a chance to contribute, keeps the discussion focused, and summarizes the discussion at its close.*

1.   **List three negative behaviors that Bob exhibits in class.** _____

_____

_____

2.   **How could Bob change his behavior so that he could participate more fully in class?** _____

_____

_____

3.   **Why is Sam's behavior negative? How could he change his behavior to participate in a more positive way?** _____

_____

_____

4.   **How does Carmen play an active role in class?** _____

_____

_____

5.   **Why is Carmen a good discussion leader?** _____

_____

_____

6.   **Where do you place each students' locus of control (internal or external), and why?** _____

_____

_____

Thinking ahead about Career

Purpose and Instructions

A workplace focus in Chapter 5 is on listening, which is a communication skill. Active listening is the key to getting information that is presented orally. Use the knowledge you have gained from this chapter to solve work-related problems such as the one explained in the following case study. Read the case study on your own or with a partner and then answer the case questions.

Case Study

Paula has been working at a toy company's manufacturing plant as a troubleshooter who corrects defects observed during a toy's assembly. Her creativity, people skills, and fine arts background have earned her a promotion to the company's research team whose job is to brainstorm and recommend new product ideas. Now she spends hours in meetings where she must present her own findings, listen to others' ideas, and report back to her team leader. Paula has no trouble presenting her own ideas, but her listening skills are rusty. As a result, she has trouble maintaining concentration, following everyone's ideas, and determining what is most important. She wishes she could remember some of the listening strategies she learned in college.

Case Questions

1. **What is Paula's problem?**

   _____

   _____

2. **What difficulties does Paula's problem cause for her?**

   _____

   _____

3. **How can Paula use one or more of her strengths to overcome her problem?**

   _____

   _____

4. **Access the Career Resource Center and read the article entitled "Become a Better Listener" in the** *Building Learning Strategies* **section of** *The Bridge.* **Based on this article, suggest two ways that Paula could improve her listening skills.**

   _____

   _____

Your *Reflections*

Reflect on what you have learned from this chapter about classroom skills that can improve your performance. Use the following questions to stimulate your thinking; then write your reflections. Include in your writing specific information from the chapter.

- Of the skills presented in this chapter—class preparation, active listening, note taking, making oral presentations, and participating in groups—which is your strongest? Explain your answer.

- What relationship do you see between punctuality in the classroom and in the workplace?

- How has your preparation for classes either led to or prevented your success?

- What is one skill or attitude explained in this chapter that you would like to develop, and what can you begin doing today to make that happen?

_____

_____

_____

_____

_____

_____

_____

_____

_____

_____

_____

_____

_____

_____

_____

_____

_____

_____

Chapter review

ATTITUDES TO DEVELOP

- positive thinking
- consideration for instructors and classmates
- willingness to get involved

SKILLS TO PRACTICE

- active listening
- effective note taking
- making oral presentations

CONCEPTS TO UNDERSTAND

Cornell	signal	clustering	regularly	positive
prepare	purpose	personal	say it	oral

The five strategies for successful classroom performance are (1) _____ for class, become an active listener, develop a (2) _____ note-taking system, make effective (3) _____ presentations, and participate in class and group activities.

To prepare for class, do the following things. Attend (4) _____ and arrive on time. Use your syllabus to keep up with assignments and bring your textbooks and other supplies to class every day.

Do all assignments and anticipate the next lecture or assignment. Improve your listening skills by listening with a (5) _____ frame of mind, focusing your attention on the speaker, encouraging the speaker, taking notes, and deciding what is important in a lecture by listening for (6) _____ words and phrases.

To take notes effectively, you need a note-taking system. Students have used many such systems successfully. For example, you can use the informal outline system, the (7) _____ method, or the (8) _____ technique discussed in this chapter. Any of these systems—or one that you adapt from them—will work.

To make an effective oral presentation, have a (9) _____ for speaking on the topic you have chosen. Then plan and organize your presentation by using this three-part development: Tell listeners what you are going to say, (10) _____ , and then tell them what you have just said.

Take part in group activities and discussions, and ask questions as needed. Do your share of the work and don't monopolize the discussion. Your involvement in class will help you add to your background of knowledge, which is the framework on which you can build effective listening and note-taking skills.

To access additional review exercises, go to **college.hmco.com/pic/KanarTCS6e.**

Online Study Center
Review Exercise
ACE Self-Test

Online Study Center

Prepare for Class, Improve Your Grade, and ACE the Test. This chapter's *Student Achievement* resources include

Chapter exercises/forms   Review exercise   Confidence Builder Web search
ACE Self-Test

To access these learning and study tools, go to **college.hmco.com/pic/KanarTCS6e.**

6 Making the most of your time

You can manage your time, or time will manage you.

Take control of your time by setting goals that help you meet responsibilities and keep your life in balance.

Learn about different types of schedules and how you can use them to manage your time.

▶ *Define procrastination, identify the reasons for it, and develop ways to avoid it.*

▶ *Recognize that community college students and all those who commute to campus have special time-management challenges.*

Resource means *asset.* In the workplace, as in college, resources include time, money, and materials to be managed.

Much of Lewis Carroll's *Through the Looking Glass* takes place on a giant chessboard. Alice is a pawn who wants to win the game and become a queen. Choosing a square and trying to hold her position, she finds herself on the other side of the board. Frustrated, she turns to the Red Queen for advice. Explaining the rules of the game, the Red Queen says, "Here it takes all the running you can do to keep in the same place." Do you sometimes feel, like Alice, that you are just running in place, never getting ahead?

What are the factors that make time management difficult? Course requirements, work demands, family responsibilities, and personal needs all compete for your time. Nevertheless, time is a **resource** you can learn to manage. By

---

KEY TERMS

fixed times, *p. 131*
flexible times, *p. 131*
schedule, *p. 131*
semester or quarter calendars, *p. 133*
weekly schedules, *p. 133*
daily lists, *p. 133*
procrastination, *p. 145*
avoidance tactics, *p. 147*

SCANS TERM

resource, *p. 129*

taking control of your time now, you can establish efficient work habits that will lead to success in college and in your career. You already possess several keys to effective time management. Use your assessment skills to identify your time management strengths and weaknesses. Your understanding of learning styles can open the door to your and others' time management styles. Finally, by thinking critically and using the strategies explained in this chapter, you will be able to manage your time instead of letting time manage you.

HOW TO GRAB SOME TIME

> *Take control of your time by setting goals that help you meet responsibilities and keep your life in balance.*

CONCEPT CHECK 6.1

Define *time* as you see it: What is time? Why do people seem to have so little of it? What would you do if you had more time?

To take control of your time, you must be aggressive, especially if you are a chronic procrastinator—someone who consistently puts off doing difficult, boring, or time-consuming tasks. Unless you live alone, you may have to fight for study time. Talk honestly with family members about your goals. Ask for their suggestions. Make it clear that their support, cooperation, and encouragement will increase your chances for success. Talk plainly to roommates about your and their study needs and arrange your schedule accordingly. Above all, be candid with yourself about your own time management issues. Time will slip away from you unless you GRAB it and hold tight (see Figure 6.1).

Goal

To GRAB study time, set a goal. What do you want to do? Would you like to set aside a block of time each day for completing your assignments? Would you like to have Tuesday and Thursday evenings free for study? Do you want to set aside one afternoon a week, in the library, to write drafts of essays for your composition class? The goal is up to you; it should be a reachable goal, one you can reasonably expect to achieve. The time limit you set should be one you can live with. For more information on how to set reachable goals, see Chapter 4.

FIGURE 6.1

HOW TO GRAB SOME TIME	
G GOAL	Set a goal.
R RESPONSIBILITIES	Determine your responsibilities.
A ANALYSIS	Analyze where your time goes.
B BALANCE	Balance work, class, study, and leisure time.

Responsibilities

Determine your responsibilities. To manage time, you must first determine what your responsibilities are. Do you live alone? If not, then you have responsibilities to those with whom you live. Do you work? If so, then you have obligations to your boss and coworkers. As a student, you have course requirements to meet. All of these responsibilities—which may include child rearing, cooking, cleaning, working, and studying—somehow have to be met. Sharing household tasks with family members will leave you more time for study. By considering your roommate's needs, you can work out a study schedule that is mutually agreeable. Your employer may be willing to adjust your hours to accommodate your course schedule. Enlist the aid of family members, roommates, your boss—whoever is in a position to help you reach your goals. With a little effort, you can manage your time so that you can meet all your responsibilities.

Analysis

Analyze where your time goes; then you may be able to find a more efficient way to use your time. What are the fixed times in a typical day for you? **Fixed times** include the hours you spend working, attending classes, and traveling to and from each activity. These are the time slots that may be difficult or impossible to change. For example, if you are an athlete, then your fixed times will include practice and participation in games or events. If you are a parent, then your fixed times may include driving children to and from school and to other regularly scheduled activities. If you are working full-time and attending college part-time, then your fixed times include the hours you spend in classes and at work. For many students, regular exercise warrants a fixed time in their schedules. **Flexible times** include the hours you spend doing things such as sleeping, eating, watching television, and studying. You can choose when you do these activities and how much time you spend on each.

Fixed times are times you cannot change, such as work hours or class times.

Flexible times are the hours of a day that you can control, such as when to sleep or eat.

Balance

Balance your time through scheduling. A **schedule** is a structure that you impose on the events of one day, week, semester or quarter, or any other block of time you choose. A schedule is a plan for getting things done. Think of a schedule as your commitment to complete certain tasks at certain times so that you make steady progress toward your goals.

Schedule means timetable, plan, or program of events or activities.

Managing your time will allow you to balance work and leisure so that you meet your responsibilities and still have time for yourself. To bring work, classes, study time, and leisure into balance, first determine how much time you usually spend on these activities. When you have a clear picture of the fixed and flexible times in your day, then you will be able to set more realistic goals and create the schedules you can live with. Now complete Awareness Check 10 to assess your use of time.

AWARENESS CHECK 10

Where Does Your Time Go?

Estimate the number of hours you spend each week on the following activities. When you are finished, subtract your total hours from 168, the number of hours in a week. How much time is left? How can you use this time to reach your goals?

Activity	Hours per Week
1. Attending classes	_____
2. Working	_____

 3. Sleeping   _____

 4. Dressing, showering, etc.   _____

 5. Traveling to and from work, college, etc.   _____

 6. Studying   _____

 7. Eating   _____

 8. Watching television   _____

 9. Engaging in leisure activities   _____

10. Caring for family   _____

11. Cleaning and doing laundry   _____

12. Socializing   _____

13. Attending athletic practice   _____

14. Surfing the Internet   _____

15. Other   _____

                              Total =   _____

                168 Hours minus Total =   _____

Now answer the following questions:

 1. On which activity do you spend the least amount of time?

 _____

 2. On which activity do you spend the most time?

 _____

 3. Is the amount of time that you spend studying producing the grades you want?

 _____

 4. Overall, are you satisfied with the way you spend your time? Why or why not?

 _____

 5. If you could make some changes, what would they be?

 _____

After completing the Awareness Check, you may find that you have some surplus time during the week. You might use this time for scheduling additional study hours as needed; for setting aside a block of regular, consistent study time; or for completing a task or activity you did not think you had time to do. Schedules can make your life easier, not harder, because they help you organize your time.

SCHEDULING YOUR TIME

▶ *Learn about different types of schedules and how you can use them to manage your time.*

Schedules put you in control of your time and your life. Your schedule is the result of the inward decision you make to control events instead of letting external circumstances control you. **Semester** or **quarter calendars, weekly schedules,** and **daily lists** are three time-honored plans that have helped thousands of students become better time managers. Build confidence in your ability to manage your time by trying out each of these plans.

The Semester or Quarter Calendar

A calendar for the current term allows you to see at a glance what you need to accomplish each month in order to complete your course requirements. A semester is about sixteen weeks long, a quarter about ten weeks long. If your college is on a semester system, you probably attend different classes on alternate days: Monday, Wednesday, and Friday or Tuesday and Thursday. On the quarter system, however, you may attend some classes every day. The system your college uses will determine what your calendar will look like and how you will be able to schedule the rest of your time around your classes. To make a complete semester or quarter calendar, you need the following three items:

1. *Your college calendar*, which is printed in the college catalog or posted on your college's web site.

2. A *syllabus*, or instructor's outline, for each course.

3. A *personal calendar*, one you either buy or make yourself, that contains squares big enough for you to record information.

Use your semester or quarter calendar as a quick reference to remind you of upcoming tests and the due dates of assignments. Keep the calendar on your desk, on a wall above your desk, or on a bulletin board where you will see it every day when you sit down to study. Always have two months visible so that by the last week of the current month, you will also be aware of what's ahead in the next month. Follow these steps to make your calendar:

1. Enter the following information in the appropriate squares: when classes begin and end, holidays, registration, exam times, and any other important dates or deadlines. Your college's catalog or web site may contain most of this information.

2. Review the instructor's syllabus that you received for each course. The syllabus, or course information sheet, may list test dates and major assignments such as essays, research papers, or projects that are due throughout the term. Some instructors do not plan very far ahead. They may wait to announce test dates several days beforehand. If that is the case, you will want to update your calendar as you receive this information.

3. Enter any other information, event, or activity you want to include. For example, if you plan to attend sports events or concerts, fill in those dates on the calendar. If you take part in any regularly scheduled activities such as sports practice and club or organization meetings, add them to your calendar.

4. Be sure to leave enough space in each square. You may have to list more than one item under each date.

Semester or quarter calendars provide an overview of an entire term at a glance.

Weekly schedules help you manage your assignments and other obligations one week at a time.

Daily lists help you prioritize tasks on a daily basis.

ONE MONTH IN A STUDENT'S SEMESTER

FIGURE 6.2

October						
Sunday	**Monday**	**Tuesday**	**Wednesday**	**Thursday**	**Friday**	**Saturday**
	1	2	3	4	5 Comp. essay due	6
7 2 p.m.–4 p.m. Charity walk/run	8 Dentist appt. 4:00 p.m.	9 Hum. paper due	10 Concert 8:00 p.m.	11	12 Comp. 1 midterm 10:00 a.m.	13
14	15 Alg 1 midterm 8:00 a.m.	16	17 Psych. midterm 7:00 p.m.	18	19 Hum. midterm 10:00 a.m.	20
21	22	23	24	25	26	27 Homecoming
28	29	30	31			

Be creative with your calendar. Make planning your semester or quarter an enjoyable activity. Either purchase a calendar that you find attractive or make your own. Use different colored inks or marking pens for each kind of information you enter. If you type your calendar on the computer, add some graphics. Figure 6.2 shows one month from a student's calendar for a typical semester.

Your Weekly Schedule

The main purpose of the weekly schedule is to help you plan your study time. By scheduling your study time and making a commitment to stick to your schedule, you will be giving studying the same importance that you give to working or attending classes. Without a schedule, you may begin to study only when you have nothing else to do, at the last minute before a test, or late at night when you are tired. If you are a procrastinator, a weekly schedule may provide the extra motivation you need to get your work done. Your schedule is your commitment to learn. Figure 6.3, page 135, is an example of a student's weekly schedule.

Omar's Weekly Schedule

Figure 6.3

	Sunday	Monday	Tuesday	Wednesday	Thursday	Friday	Saturday
6:00 – 7:00	Sleep	Run, Dress, Eat	→				→	Sleep
7:00 – 8:00	Sleep	← Transportation to class →					Sleep
8:00 – 9:00	Sleep	Algebra class	Study in library	Algebra class	Study in library	Algebra class	Eat, Run
9:00 – 10:00	Run, Dress	Comp. 1	French 1	Comp. 1	French 1	Comp. 1	Study
10:00 – 11:00	Eat, Trans. to church	Biology class	Biology lab	Biology class	French lab	Biology class	Study
11:00 – 12:00	Church	Lunch/ Trans.	↓	Lunch/ Trans.	↓	Lunch/ Trans.	Lunch
12:00 – 1:00	Trans. church to home	Home		Home		Home	
1:00 – 2:00	Lunch						
2:00 – 3:00	Clean apartment	Study	Study	Study	Study	Study	
3:00 – 4:00	Free	→ Laundry, other chores →				→	Leisure
4:00 – 5:00	Free					→	or study
5:00 – 6:00	Free					→	May go
6:00 – 7:00	Dinner					→	out later
7:00 – 8:00	↑					→	
8:00 – 9:00	Study or					→	
9:00 – 10:00	Watch TV					→	
10:00 – 11:00						→	
11:00 – 12:00	↓					→	
12:00 – 1:00	Sleep						→

This student, Omar, has fixed times for classes and church attendance. He has flexible times for his other regular activities. In the time remaining, he has allotted the same block of time each day for studying. He has made a commitment to treat studying like a job. If Omar sticks to his schedule, then, over time, studying will become a habit for him. When he sits down to study at his regular time, he will be able to get to work quickly and to give his assignments maximum concentration. During some weeks, Omar may need additional time to study for a test or to complete an especially lengthy assignment. On these occasions he can use some of his "free" hours for more studying. What if Omar decides to take a part-time job? Then he will have to modify his fixed, flexible, and free times. Omar's schedule puts Omar in control of his time and his life.

As you experiment with making schedules, keep in mind that for maximum performance, most instructors recommend at least two hours of study time for every hour spent in class. For a class that meets three times a week, this would mean six hours of studying per week. So if you are taking five three-hour courses, and you want to do your best, you would need to schedule thirty hours a week of study time. If you are a working student, you may have difficulty finding that much time to study. To reach your goals, you may be forced either to take fewer courses or to reduce your working hours.

If the ratio of study time to class time seems high, remember that it takes a lot of time and effort to acquire knowledge and to learn skills. However, you may spend less time studying subjects that are easy for you than you spend studying difficult ones.

A Daily List

Keep a daily list of things to do and appointments to keep. Nearly everyone makes lists: grocery lists, appointment lists, errand lists. As a student, you need to make lists, too—when to return library books, specific study tasks you must complete, counseling appointments, and so on. Consult your lists frequently and check off items as you complete them. A list is a motivational aid that reminds you to stay on track. Each item you complete and check off brings you closer to achieving your day's goals, boosting your confidence.

EXERCISE 6.1   COMPUTER APPLICATION

CREATE A SEMESTER OR QUARTER calendar. Either buy a calendar or make copies of the template in Figure 6.4, page 137, for each month in your semester or quarter. Also see college.hmco.com/pic/KanarTCS6e to download copies of the calendar. Write in the month and each day's date on each calendar page; then staple the pages together. Look again at Figure 6.2, and then enter the following information on your calendar:

1. **When classes begin and end, holidays, final exam dates**

2. **The registration date for the next semester or quarter**

3. **Test dates and dates when major assignments are due**

4. **Dates of activities or events that you want to participate in or attend**

5. **Any other dates or deadlines you want to remember**

Online Study Center
**Chapter Exercises/
Forms**

	Sunday	Monday	Tuesday	Wednesday	Thursday	Friday	Saturday

EXERCISE 6.2   **COMPUTER APPLICATION**

MAKE A WEEKLY SCHEDULE. See Figure 6.5 on page 138 for the template that accompanies this exercise or download copies of the template from college.hmco.com/pic/KanarTCS6e If you prefer, use a word-processing program to make your own schedule template, either by setting up a table or by using your program's graphics. Programs differ; therefore, if you need more specific instructions, either see your instructor or consult with someone in your college's computer or media center. To fill in your schedule, follow these directions:

1. **Fill in your fixed-time activities. These are the things you must do at scheduled times—for example, working and attending classes.**

2. **Fill in your flexible-time activities. These are the things you need or want to do that you can schedule at your own discretion.**

3. **The squares remaining are your free times. Schedule a regular time each day for studying.**

4. **Be sure to schedule some time for leisure activities.**

5. **Fill in every square.**

Weekly Schedule Template

FIGURE 6.5

	Sunday	Monday	Tuesday	Wednesday	Thursday	Friday	Saturday
6:00 – 7:00							
7:00 – 8:00							
8:00 – 9:00							
9:00 – 10:00							
10:00 – 11:00							
11:00 – 12:00							
12:00 – 1:00							
1:00 – 2:00							
2:00 – 3:00							
3:00 – 4:00							
4:00 – 5:00							
5:00 – 6:00							
6:00 – 7:00							
7:00 – 8:00							
8:00 – 9:00							
9:00 – 10:00							
10:00 – 11:00							
11:00 – 12:00							
12:00 – 1:00							

Some people make lists on little scraps of paper. Others use fancy note pads, small spiral-bound notebooks, daily planners, or appointment books which they buy in bookstores or office supply stores. (If you buy a daily planner or appointment book, be sure to get one with squares that are big enough to hold several items or one that includes a separate note pad.) Whatever you use for making your daily lists, make sure it is a convenient size and keep it handy.

If you have a personal computer, you might want to invest in an electronic calendar. Several programs allow you to keep records of important dates and appointments online and to set up your calendar in a variety of formats. When you turn on your computer, for example, the calendar could tell you the day's date and list your schedule for the day. In some programs, you can instruct the computer to beep to remind you of an appointment.

Keeping a daily list can be a quick and easy way to start planning your time effectively. Your daily lists should include whatever you want to do or whatever you need to remember that you might otherwise forget. Figure 6.6 on page 140 shows a student's list for one day.

Online Study Center
Chapter Exercises/ Reviews

EXERCISE 6.3

REVIEW YOUR RESPONSES TO AWARENESS Check 10 on pages 131–132. Notice how many hours per week you estimated that you spend on each of the activities listed. For one week, keep track of the *actual* hours you spend on those activities. Write down the actual amounts of time as you spend them (*not* later that day, or you could easily end up estimating your time again). At the end of the week, write your original time estimates and the exact hours you spent on the following lines; then complete the lists and answer the question.

Activity	Estimated Time	Actual Time
1. Attending classes	_____	_____
2. Working	_____	_____
3. Sleeping	_____	_____
4. Dressing, showering, etc.	_____	_____
5. Traveling to and from work, college, etc.	_____	_____
6. Studying	_____	_____
7. Eating	_____	_____
8. Watching television	_____	_____
9. Engaging in leisure activities	_____	_____
10. Caring for family	_____	_____
11. Cleaning and doing laundry	_____	_____
12. Socializing	_____	_____
13. Attending athletic practice	_____	_____
14. Surfing the Internet	_____	_____
15. Other	_____	_____

1. List the activities in which you spent more time than you had estimated.

   _____

   _____

2. List the activities in which you spent less time than you had estimated.

   _____

   _____

3. How can you use this new information to revise your weekly schedule?

   _____

   _____

A LIST FOR ONE DAY

FIGURE 6.6

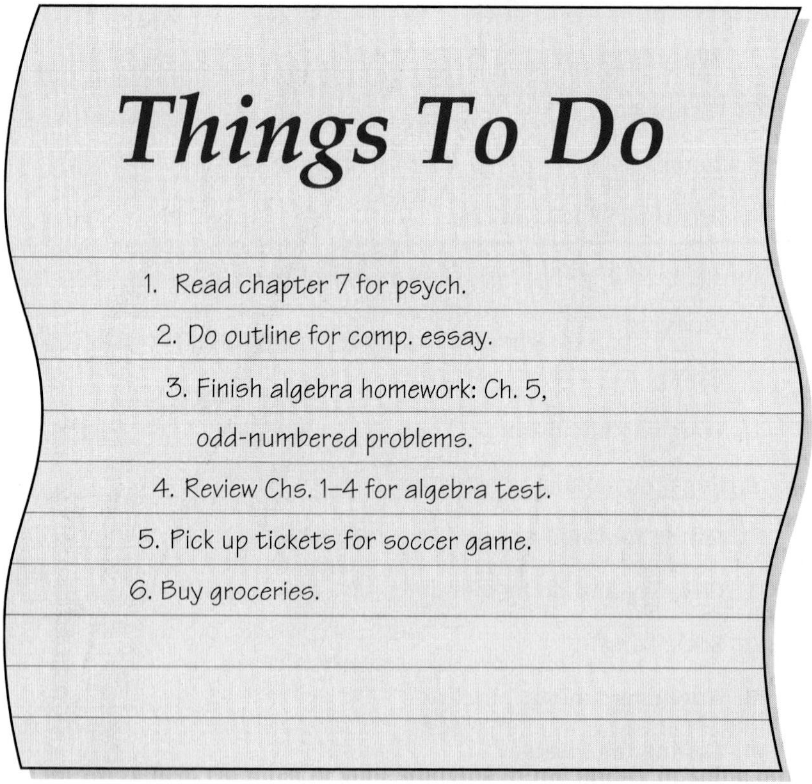

Things To Do

1. Read chapter 7 for psych.
2. Do outline for comp. essay.
3. Finish algebra homework: Ch. 5, odd-numbered problems.
4. Review Chs. 1–4 for algebra test.
5. Pick up tickets for soccer game.
6. Buy groceries.

| EXERCISE 6.4 | COLLABORATIVE ACTIVITY |

APPLY WHAT YOU HAVE LEARNED about schedules by doing this exercise with group members. Follow the guidelines for group discussion that appear on the inside back cover. Discuss the following questions, and write your answers on the lines provided. Then write your evaluation on your own paper or download the group exercise form from the Online Study Center at college.hmco.com/pic/KanarTCS6e.

1. **What are your experiences with making and following schedules? Which group members have used schedules, and which have not?**

   _____

   _____

2. **What are the advantages and disadvantages of making daily, weekly, and semester or quarter schedules?**

   _____

   _____

3. **Which type of schedule do you find most useful, and why?**

   _____

   _____

4. **Discuss a specific problem you have had with time management. How could you use schedules to overcome this problem?**

   _____

   _____

Group Evaluation:
Evaluate your discussion. Did everyone contribute? Did you accomplish your task successfully? What additional questions do you have about making and following schedules? How will you find answers to your questions?

Time Management and Learning Style

Chapter 2 explains that your body's reactions affect your learning style. For example, you probably have an optimum time of day when your concentration seems to be at its peak, and you are most productive. But being a morning person or a night person isn't just a preference, nor do you have a choice about it.

You have a biological clock that regulates your internal rhythms, telling you when to eat, when to sleep, and when to get up and get moving. The time of day when your temperature is highest is what determines whether you are an "early bird" or a "night owl." Since you can't control fluctuations in your body's temperature, you may as well take advantage of them. Do important activities that require critical thinking and concentration during your optimum time of day. Try to schedule your classes, especially ones that you expect to be difficult, at the time of

Online Study Center
Chapter Exercises/ Forms

EXERCISE 6.5　　LEARNING STYLE

WRITE A SHORT ESSAY IN which you explain how your present schedule of classes and study times either do or do not conflict with your learning style and personal habits. Consider which classes require the most work, which assignments need greater concentration, your optimum time of day, and whether your schedule permits you to eat regularly and to get enough rest. What are your schedule's strengths and weaknesses? How can you improve your schedule next semester or quarter? Give your essay a title.

day when you are most alert. If you have to take a class at a time when you know you will be working at a disadvantage, try these suggestions:

▼ When you feel yourself getting drowsy, take a few deep breaths.

▼ Change your position every few minutes: cross and uncross your legs, sit up straight, and make other adjustments in the way you are sitting.

▼ Eat a snack such as a handful of raisins or a piece of fruit before you go to class. This will raise your blood-sugar level and your body temperature, making you feel more alert.

▼ Take deep, rhythmic breaths to get more oxygen into your bloodstream.

Try these suggestions whenever you must study at a time when you are tired. In addition, when you are at home, prop up your feet to increase the blood flow to your brain.

Making Time for Reading

One of the big differences between high school and college is the amount of reading assigned. You may be frustrated by the number of pages per week that each instructor assigns. A common complaint you will hear from college students of all ages is "Each of my instructors must think his or her class is the only one I have."

Nevertheless, the reading has to be done. Are there any short cuts? No. Reading takes time. The more difficult the reading, the more time it takes. However, you can learn to read more efficiently. Try these strategies:

▼ Determine the time you will need for reading.

▼ Schedule your reading time.

▼ Develop active reading habits and study skills so that you do not waste time.

To calculate your reading time, follow the steps given in Figure 6.7 on page 143. For example, suppose you have been assigned a fifty-page chapter from your biology text. The assignment is due at the next class meeting. You have determined that it takes you two hours to read twenty-five pages from this book. Sometime between now and the next class meeting, you should schedule four hours of reading time for biology.

Active reading habits include underlining, making notes in the margins of your textbooks, outlining, and other activities such as using a reading system and organizing information for study—strategies explained in Chapters 8 and 9. These strategies lead to concentrated review and may eliminate the need for re-reading entire chapters. In fact, re-reading is an inefficient way to study and one you should avoid. If you take the time to read, mark your text, and make notes, you may be able to shorten your review time. If you think that you have missed something, you can always re-read just those sections of a chapter that contain the information you need.

FIGURE 6.7

CALCULATE YOUR READING TIME

1. Choose three consecutive textbook pages that contain mostly print.

2. Time yourself on the reading of these three pages.

3. Jot down your starting time in minutes and seconds. When you have read three pages, jot down the time and subtract your starting time to get the total reading time. Divide the total time by 3 to get the time that it takes you to read one page.

4. To get the time needed to complete a reading assignment, multiply the number of pages by your time per page. Divide by 60 to get the number of hours and minutes it will take you to finish your reading.

Example: You have twenty pages to read. How long will it take you?

Here are the results of your initial calculation:

Starting time: 3:00
Finishing time: 3:18

Subtract starting time from finishing time:

$$\begin{array}{r} 3:18 \\ -3:00 \\ \hline \end{array}$$

0:18 ÷ 3 = 6 minutes per page

Multiply the number of minutes per page times the number of pages in the assignment and divide by 60:

6 × 20 = 120 ÷ 60 = 2 hours (time needed to read twenty pages)

TIME MANAGEMENT FOR COMMUNITY COLLEGE STUDENTS

▶ *Recognize that community college students and all those who commute to campus have special time-management challenges.*

If you are a community college student—or anyone who commutes to campus—building travel time into your schedule may be a challenge. The time you spend traveling to and from campus or from campus to work to home leaves less time for studying and other activities. You may also need to transport your children to and from school. Because it is easy to underestimate the time it takes you to get from place to place, give special consideration to travel time as you plan your schedule and select courses.

Adding college courses and study time to an already busy schedule is another challenge. You may be tempted to meet it by scheduling all your classes on one or two days. Although this may seem like a good idea at the time, you may encounter one or more common problems. Suppose you schedule all your classes on the same day. If you are absent one day, then you will miss *all* your classes for the whole week. Also, papers, tests, and other assignments for those classes will always be due on the same day. Instead of having a paper due on Monday, several math problems due on Wednesday, and a test on Thursday or Friday, you will have to turn in the paper and the problems and take the test all in one day. Spreading your classes over two days is not much better; you still may have several assignment deadlines or tests on the same day.

Time Management Tips for Student Athletes

College takes a physical and mental toll on student athletes. Self-discipline and the use of effective time management techniques can help to alleviate this.

College challenges student athletes physically. The hours spent practicing, weight training, competing, and traveling to and from sports events leave these students physically exhausted. As a result, they are often too tired to participate fully in classes, remain attentive during lectures, or study with maximum concentration. Exhaustion may also lead to poor eating and sleeping habits which sap students' energy, making study even more difficult.

In addition to the physical toll, student athletes may also pay a mental toll. For one thing, these students are under pressure to earn good grades on which their scholarships and their eligibility to play depend. Also, negative stereotyping in the form of taunts ("dumb jock") and lowered expectations on the part of some instructors and classmates may lead to depression and a loss of self-esteem in all but the most confident students.

What we all need to remember is that every student has strengths and weaknesses, and on any college sports team, as wide a range of abilities will be represented as in any other area of campus life. Nevertheless, the student athlete who *is* underprepared for college work carries a double burden; the need to develop academic skills and the need to resist being dragged down by others' negative attitudes toward him or her.

If you are a student athlete, follow these time management tips to meet your physical and mental challenges so that you can be successful in your sport and in your academic program. If you are not an athlete, pass these tips on to a friend who is and be supportive of his or her efforts to succeed.

- Use daily lists, weekly schedules, and semester or quarter calendars to manage your time. Remember that if you don't manage time, time will manage you.

- Although it may be too late to do anything about this term's classes, you can plan ahead for next term. Keep track of where your time goes and when you are most alert, and use this information to build your ideal schedule next term.

- Put studying first. You can't maintain eligibility without grades, so schedule regular study time. If your coach requires you to attend group study sessions, great! If not, form your own study group. Be sure to include one or more nonathletes in your group so that different perspectives are represented. Schedule a meeting time for your study group and follow through on your schedule.

- Arrange your schedule so that you have regular meal times and get adequate rest. If you don't, exhaustion will overtake you.

- If you have weaknesses in any basic skills (reading, writing, mathematics), take any required courses in these subjects as soon as possible. Schedule regular meetings with a tutor if necessary. It's more efficient to take care of basic skills *now* than to risk getting more and more behind. As you build skill, your grades will improve, and with improved performance comes confidence.

- Use *all* your time, Write information for studying on 3" × 5" note cards that you can carry with you everywhere. While waiting in lines, between classes—anywhere you have extra time that you might otherwise waste—

review your notes. In other words, be efficient in your use of time.

- Other people's negative attitudes and stereotypical thinking may be difficult to overcome, but you can control how you respond to them. Let nothing stand in the way of your own success. Arrange your schedule so that you are able to do the studying and skill building needed to ensure successful classroom performance. Scheduling time for adequate rest and proper nutrition will keep you alert and ready to participate in class. Be punctual and prepared, and you may change a few minds about the seriousness of student athletes.

To learn more ways to manage time, do an online search using these keywords as a starting point: *college sports, student athletes and study skills, time management and sports.*

What happens at the end of the one or two days when you attend class? For one thing, you are probably exhausted and have so many other things to do that you don't or can't take time to review your notes from each class or begin doing the assignments. Also, you may postpone the work until the night before your classes meet, leaving you only enough time to do a portion of the work. You may even skip one or two assignments, thinking you'll catch up later. This almost never happens. One- or two-day schedules often lead to scheduling classes back to back, which may seem like another good way to save time. Unfortunately, when you attend one class right after another, you don't have time to absorb and process the information covered in the previous class. You set yourself up for *information overload*, a condition in which the material explained in one class gets confused with that covered in another.

Ideal schedules are those that spread classes and study times over the whole week and that alternate class periods with free periods. During your free periods, you can either review notes from your previous class or do some last-minute review for a test you must take in the next class. Because you have free time between classes, you must remain on campus. This puts you in a good position to form a study group that you'll meet with at a regular time or to set up a standing appointment with a tutor if you are having difficulty in one of your classes. You may find that by scheduling classes over the whole week, you are actually *saving* time. This can happen because it's easier to schedule study time around one or two classes a day and still meet your other obligations than it is to try to pack in some study time after having attended four or five classes. However, if you absolutely have to attend classes on a two-day schedule because of work or other obligations, at least try to schedule a free hour between classes.

Online Study Center
Confidence Builder
Web Search

AVOIDING PROCRASTINATION

▶ *Define* procrastination, *identify the reasons for it, and develop ways to avoid it.*

Procrastination means needlessly postponing tasks until some future time. Although procrastinating once in a while may not hurt you, if you delay studying and put off doing important assignments too often, you will sabotage your efforts to succeed. Complete Awareness Check 11 on pages 146–147 to gauge your tendency to put off tasks.

Procrastination is a behavior characterized by the needless avoidance of obligations and by putting off tasks.

If you budget your studying time wisely, you will have more time for leisure activities.

AWARENESS CHECK 11

Are You a Procrastinator?

Choose one of the following as your response to each statement: *always* (4 points), *usually* (3 points), *sometimes* (2 points), *rarely* (1 point). Write your number of points in the box beside each statement. When you are finished, add your score.

Points

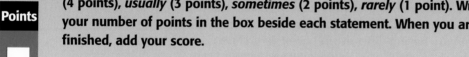

1. If I know that an assignment will be difficult, I will put off doing it.

2. If an assignment is going to take a lot of time, I will procrastinate.

3. I will put off studying if I don't like the subject or the course.

4. I can't start studying until I am in the mood to do it.

5. Writing papers is hard for me, so it takes me a lot of time to get started.

6. I often wait until the last minute to study for a test.

7. Being too hungry or too tired is reason enough for me to delay studying.

8. If I have a slight cold or am not feeling my best, I won't study.

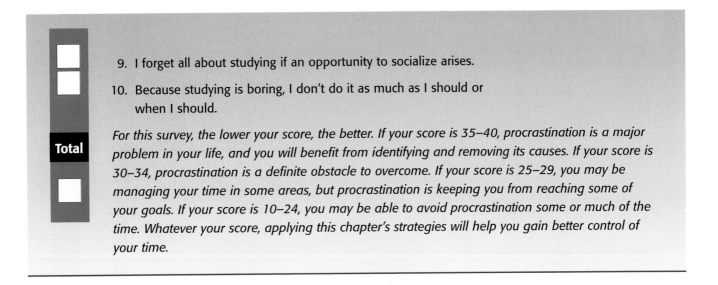

9. I forget all about studying if an opportunity to socialize arises.

10. Because studying is boring, I don't do it as much as I should or when I should.

Total

For this survey, the lower your score, the better. If your score is 35–40, procrastination is a major problem in your life, and you will benefit from identifying and removing its causes. If your score is 30–34, procrastination is a definite obstacle to overcome. If your score is 25–29, you may be managing your time in some areas, but procrastination is keeping you from reaching some of your goals. If your score is 10–24, you may be able to avoid procrastination some or much of the time. Whatever your score, applying this chapter's strategies will help you gain better control of your time.

Why Do People Procrastinate?

Ann has to write a research paper for her composition course. The paper is due in six weeks. She thinks she has plenty of time, so for the first two weeks, she doesn't even think about the project. That leaves her only a month in which to choose a topic, do her research in the library, make an outline, and write the paper. It takes her another week to select a topic, but when she gets to the library, she finds that several of the books she wants have been checked out. By the time Ann chooses another topic and compiles her research materials, she has only one week left to complete the paper. She *does* hand it in on time, but she knows it's not her best effort. She doesn't like to write anyway and is not expecting to receive a very good grade. "Next time," she swears, "I'll get started sooner." But next time Ann will probably procrastinate again because that is her pattern of behavior. She doesn't like to do difficult or lengthy assignments and will put them off until the last minute. Like many students, Ann procrastinates for one of four common reasons. Perhaps you also procrastinate for one of these reasons:

▼ Your tasks seem difficult or time-consuming.

▼ You have trouble getting started.

▼ You lack motivation to do the work.

▼ You are afraid of failing.

Putting off difficult or time-consuming assignments makes them even harder to do when you actually get started and further ensures that you won't be able to do your best because you will not have enough time. However, a task may be less difficult than you think if you break it down into segments that you can handle during short periods of time. If you have trouble getting started on an assignment, or if you waste a lot of time before sitting down to study, then you may be using **avoidance tactics.** Why are you avoiding what you have to do? Perhaps you aren't interested in the subject, or perhaps you'd simply prefer to be doing something else. You may be insufficiently motivated to perform the work.

Avoidance tactics are habitual behaviors we've developed over time to keep from doing difficult or unpleasant things.

You may not see a direct connection between the assignment and your goals or your overall grade in the course. Or you may be afraid of failure. If you believe that you will not get a good grade—no matter what you do—you may delay getting started on an assignment. Complete Awareness Check 12 for more insight into why you procrastinate.

COMPUTER CONFIDENCE

Use the Computer to Save Time

Effective time management is crucial to success in college, especially when it comes to writing papers. For many students, paper writing is the most time-consuming part of any course. How about you? Does the process of planning, researching, drafting, revising, editing, and rewriting seem endless? Do you find yourself waiting until the last minute to get started? If so, try using a computer. You'll be surprised at how efficient your planning and writing will become and how much better your results will be.

Using a computer for writing assignments is a good idea for several reasons. A computer lets you make changes almost instantly. You can move words, sentences, and even whole paragraphs in seconds. A computer gives you a neatly printed draft whenever you want one, quickly and painlessly. Spell-checking, grammar, and writing style programs can help you spot errors, but beware. A misused homophone (*their*, *there*, or *they're*, for example) may not be recognized as an error. Grammar and style programs are not perfect and either may cite as wrong a sentence that is actually correct or may fail to recognize a sentence error.

Before you start writing, use a computer to organize your notes. Suppose you have taken notes from several books and magazines. If you enter those notes on disk, integrating them into a coherent outline will be easy, and using your outline may help you write a logically organized paper. (See Computer Confidence, Chapter 5, for more information about outlining.)

Whenever you use a computer to write a paper, follow these steps to make sure that you don't accidentally "lose" your work:

1. Use the "Save" command frequently. Save every five or ten minutes. Save every time you complete a page. And save whenever you leave the computer, even if you will be away for only a few minutes. Remember: Save it; don't lose it!

2. Give your files easily recognizable names that clearly indicate the project and its stages of development—for example, the file name *ENG2DR1* might stand for "English class, paper number two, first draft." Date each file so that you can quickly and easily find the most recent one.

3. Before you revise a draft, copy it in case you want to refer to your original version. Renaming each draft automatically saves all your drafts in separate files. At the end of every writing session, print out a paper copy of your new work. This "hard copy" is always useful for revisions. If you have a hard copy, and something goes wrong with your disk, you will still have your work.

4. Keep backup files of all of your work. At the end of every writing session, always back up your completed work.

What Is Your Attitude Toward Studying?

Read all of the following study situations and imagine that they apply to you. Put a check in the column that best describes how you feel about each one; then add up your checks. An explanation of your results follows.

Positive	Negative	Study Situation
■	■	1. A term paper is due at the end of the term.
■	■	2. Midterm exams are next week.
■	■	3. You have major tests in two classes this week.
■	■	4. In one of your classes, the final exam will determine whether you pass or fail.
■	■	5. You are in a self-paced math course. You have a list of assignments and several tests to complete by semester's end.
■	■	6. You have a sixty-page chapter to read in your psychology text for tomorrow's class.
■	■	7. You have a speech to prepare for your speech class.
■	■	8. You have a five-hundred-word essay to write for your composition class.
■	■	9. You have final exams to study for in all of your classes.
■	■	10. You are taking an anatomy course. You must learn the names of all the bones in the body.

Totals: Positive _____   Negative _____

All of these study situations represent tasks that are difficult or time-consuming. Look at your totals in each column. In general, based on this exercise, what do you think about difficult or lengthy assignments? Specifically, if you checked negative for items 1 and 8, perhaps writing is difficult for you, and you avoid getting started for that reason. If you checked negative for items 2, 3, 4, and 9, perhaps you avoid studying for tests because you have test anxiety or are afraid that you will fail. See Chapter 12 for some suggestions to ease test anxiety. If you checked negative for item 5, maybe the self-paced learning situation seems overwhelming, and you need the structure of a classroom setting, in which the instructor sets the pace for you. If you checked negative for item 6, it could be that the length of a reading assignment affects the way that you approach it. Perhaps you'd be more motivated to start sooner if you divided the reading assignment into smaller segments with breaks in between. If you checked negative for item 7, perhaps you don't like giving speeches, can't think of what to say, or are afraid you will get nervous and do a poor job. The sooner you start writing your speech, and the more time you give yourself to practice it, the more confident you will feel about your ability to do a good job. If you checked negative for item 10, perhaps you avoid starting assignments like this one because the number of items you have to learn and remember seems like more than you can handle. One of the memory techniques suggested in Chapter 10 may make it easier for you to get started.

Tips to Beat Procrastination

To avoid procrastination, change your behavior. If you procrastinate when assignments are too difficult or too long, or if you have trouble getting started or lack the motivation to do the work, then instead of focusing on your feelings about the assignment, focus on the advantages of completing it on time. If you get started right away, you will have the advantage of enough time to do your best. You may even complete the assignment with time left over to do something else. However, if you wait too long to begin, then you won't be able to do your best, or you may not finish at all. Fear of failure is sometimes the result of not knowing what to do. If you are not sure about what is expected of you, then you may not know how to begin the assignment. To help you overcome the fear of failure and get started, try using these tips that have worked for many students:

1. Break a large assignment or project into smaller units of work that you can complete in one sitting.

2. Plan rewards for yourself for completing each part of the assignment. Take a break, call a friend, or do something else you enjoy.

3. Schedule enough time for completing a long assignment. Set a goal to spend a certain amount of time working each day until the assignment is finished.

4. Get organized. Your attitude toward studying will improve if you have an orderly work area with everything you need at your fingertips—books, pens and pencils, paper—so that you will be ready to begin the moment you sit down.

5. If you put off assignments because you don't know where to start or aren't sure how to do the work, find out what you need to know. Make an appointment with your instructor. Explain the difficulty you are having and ask for advice. If you have started the assignment, show your instructor where you are having trouble. Or talk to someone in the class. If you missed a lecture or have gaps in your notes, your friend might be able to fill you in.

6. Assume an attitude of confidence, and you will be confident. Instead of thinking, "This is too difficult" or "I'll never finish this," think, "I can do this if I get started right now" or "There's a lot of work to do, but if I can do a little bit at a time, I'll be finished before I know it."

Learning to manage time and avoiding procrastination require some effort. Do not be discouraged if your first efforts are unsuccessful. Try to pinpoint your reasons for procrastinating. Identify your avoidance tactics and try to eliminate them. Experiment with schedules until you come up with a plan that works for you. With determination, you will take control of your time and your life—and you will reach your goals.

Managing Your Study Environment

Managing your time well also means choosing a quiet place to study. If you are a resident student, you probably do most of your studying in your room or in the library. If you are a commuter, chances are you do the majority of your studying at home. In either case, you probably have to fight distractions, and the best way to do that is to schedule your study time when and where you are least likely to be disturbed.

If you are a commuter, set up a study area in a quiet part of your home. Your study place doesn't have to be elaborate. A desk or small table in your bedroom or

Your study place should be comfort-able, quiet, well lighted, and supplied with everything you need to study.

in a guest room will do. Avoid studying in bed because you will probably fall asleep. Avoid places in high-traffic areas such as the kitchen or family room. Not only will you be distracted, but your family may also conclude that your studying is not serious business and that you won't mind being interrupted. Having a study area away from the family and the noise of the TV and children's play—a place where you do nothing but study—sends a subtle message that you are treating studying like a job and do not want to be distracted.

Let your family know that you need quiet time to do your work. Schedule a regular time for studying at home and make studying a routine. Soon your family will get used to the idea that when you are in your study place, you are unavailable except in an emergency. If you can plan your study time for when your children are asleep or when no one else is at home, so much the better.

To help fight procrastination, outfit your study place with everything you might need to get the job done: pens, pencils, paper, a dictionary, a good desk lamp, and whatever other supplies you will need. When you come in from class, go immediately to your study place and unload your books. Then they will already be there waiting for you when you are ready to study.

If you are a resident student, set up a study area in your part of the room. Put your desk against a wall, away from a window or door if possible, and keep the door closed while you are studying. Then you won't be tempted away from your books by whatever is going on outside the window or in the hallway. Like the commuter, you should avoid studying in bed. Like the commuter's family, your roommate and friends across the hall are your temporary "family" and therefore a source of distractions. Early in the term, work out mutually agreeable study times with your roommate. For example, one of you might study while the other is in class. On the other hand, you may want to schedule some of your studying so that you can work together or both study at the same time.

C R I T I C A L

T H I N K I N G

Exercise Overview

Procrastinating only now and then won't hurt you. But if it becomes chronic, you are in for trouble. Most people can find excuses for putting off doing their work, and students are no exception. This exercise will help you reflect on your own excuses so that you can recognize them as avoidance tactics to be overcome.

Exercise Background

Most instructors who have taught for a while think they have heard it all. It takes a very clever student to come up with a unique excuse for not being prepared for a test, not completing an assignment, or not handing in a paper when it is due. As you read the following two lists of excuses, see how many you have heard or used yourself.

Exercise Task

Listed next are two questions instructors often have to ask, followed by the excuses students make. Read all of the excuses with a partner. Be able to explain why each excuse is invalid and what students can do to beat procrastination.

"Why were you not prepared for today's exam?"

1. I didn't know what to study.
2. I didn't know we were having a test.
3. I forgot.
4. I was too tired.
5. I didn't understand the material.
6. I knew I wouldn't make a good grade.

"Why haven't you done today's assignment?"

1. I wasn't here when it was assigned.
2. It was too difficult.
3. I didn't know how to do it.
4. I had to go to work.
5. My computer crashed.
6. I lost it.

Thinking ahead about Career

Purpose and Instructions

A workplace focus in Chapter 6 is on time as a resource you can manage. Use the knowledge you have gained from this chapter to solve work-related problems such as the one explained in the following case study. Read the case study on your own or with a partner and then answer the case questions.

Case Study

Marsha wants a career in advertising. She'd like to work for a big company in a major city. Marsha has done well in her courses in art and advertising and believes that she has the skills necessary to mount a successful ad campaign. In fact, her sketches and designs have won several contests and awards. She made an appointment with a career counselor to find out what additional skills would prepare her for her chosen career. The career counselor told her the following:

Much of the work done in businesses today is accomplished as team projects. A project manager oversees the work, breaking it down into segments for which each member of the project group is responsible. A successful project begins with setting goals both for achievement of the project's purpose and for its completion on time. People who come into the workplace lacking goal-setting and time management skills are at a disadvantage. Through goal setting and time management, people can direct and change the courses of their lives—and most important to employers, they can get the job done.

Wow, thought Marsha. I figured I'd be working alone most of the time. Although Marsha sets goals, she often has trouble reaching them because she does not manage her time effectively and sometimes hands in assignments late. Also, she has had limited experience working with a team. "What can I do?" She asked.

Case Questions

1. **What are Marsha's strengths and weaknesses in terms of her preparedness for her career?**

   _____

   _____

2. **How will her strengths help her in her career?**

   _____

   _____

3. **If you were Marsha, would you continue to pursue your goals, or would you change your career plans? Explain your answer.**

   _____

   _____

4. **Access the Career Resource Center and read one or more of the articles in the *Managing Time* section of *The Bridge*. Based on the new information you have learned from these articles, what can Marsha do to overcome her weaknesses?**

   _____

Your *Reflections*

Reflect on what you have learned from this chapter about time management and how it can improve your performance. Use the following questions to stimulate your thinking; then write your reflections. Include in your writing specific information from the chapter.

- What is one type of schedule you have used for managing your time, and has it been helpful?

- What time management tip or method have you used that is not explained in this chapter?

- Do you believe that procrastination has more to do with attitude and emotions than with time availability? Explain your answer.

- What is one skill or attitude explained in this chapter that you would like to develop, and what can you begin doing today to make that happen?

Chapter review

To review the chapter, reflect on the following confidence-building attitudes and skills. Complete **Concepts to Understand** by filling in the blanks with words or terms from the list provided. Then practice your new skills at every opportunity.

ATTITUDES TO DEVELOP
- commitment
- self-confidence
- positive attitude toward studying

SKILLS TO PRACTICE
- managing your time
- avoiding procrastination
- making and following schedules

CONCEPTS TO UNDERSTAND

procrastination	responsibilities	semester	quarter	balance
analyze	weekly	goals	daily	motivation

Time management and procrastination present major problems for many students. Managing your time effectively and beating procrastination call for aggressive action. *You can GRAB time by following four steps:* First, set (1) _____ and give yourself a time limit to reach them. Second, determine your (2) _____ to the important people in your life and find ways to involve them in your plans to reach your goals. Third, (3) _____ where your time goes so that you can find more efficient ways to use it. Finally, (4) _____ your fixed, flexible, free, and study times by making and following schedules.

Semester or quarter calendars, weekly schedules, and daily lists can help you remember important dates, deadlines, assignments, events, and appointments. Make out a (5) _____ or (6) _____ calendar early in the term so that you can see at a glance what you have to accomplish each month. Use your (7) _____ schedule to help you keep up with weekly assignments and plan reviews for tests. Your (8) _____ list can be a reminder of all the things that you need to do during the day that you might forget—phone calls you need to make or appointments you must keep, for example. Schedules help keep you organized and on track.

People procrastinate for four common reasons that may also apply to you. Your tasks seem difficult and time-consuming; you have trouble getting started; you lack (9) _____ to do the work; you are afraid of failing. Avoid (10) _____ by understanding the reasons why you delay performing required tasks and by changing the behaviors that may contribute to the problem.

To access additional review exercises, go to **college.hmco.com/pic/KanarTCS6e.**

Online Study Center
Review Exercise
ACE Self-Test

Online Study Center

Prepare for Class, Improve Your Grade, and ACE the Test. This chapter's *Student Achievement* resources include

Chapter exercises/forms   Review exercise   Confidence Builder Web search   ACE Self-Test

To access these learning and study tools, go to **college.hmco.com/pic/KanarTCS6e.**

When your physical, emotional, and social needs are balanced, well-being and improved academic performance will follow.

Emotions can cause you to lose sight of your goals. Learn how you can manage your feelings and regain your perspective.

Understand the connection between success in college and your health and well-being so that you can make good choices.

*Confident students are **emotionally intelligent**. They control their impulses rather than allowing their impulses to control them.*

▶ HEALTH, WELL-BEING, AND SUCCESS IN COLLEGE

Eating Sensibly
Improving Fitness
Managing Stress
Avoiding Harmful Substances

▶ MANAGING YOUR EMOTIONS

Understanding Your Feelings
Leading a Purposeful Life
Accepting the Need for Change

▶ DEVELOPING YOUR INTERPERSONAL SKILLS

▶ BUILDING HEALTHY RELATIONSHIPS

Your Sexuality
Understanding Acquaintance Rape
Dealing with Sexual Harassment

▶ *Develop and follow guidelines that will help you maintain healthy relationships with your friends and intimate partners.*

▶ *Develop the interpersonal skills essential to success and well-being in college and at work.*

O ne of the values of a college education is that it exposes you to diverse students and ideas. It offers you a chance to develop socially, culturally, and intellectually—to become well-adjusted. *A well-adjusted person has achieved a balance among physical, emotional, and social needs.* Some students are not managing their lives as well as they could. Other students' emotional and physical well-being are out of balance. Some may place excessive emphasis on their friends' and family's needs and neglect their studies. Still others may be a little too conscientious, neglecting the importance of social relationships and leisure-time pursuits.

Your physical self is linked with health, diet, fitness, and stress management. Your emotional self involves your feelings, your degree of satisfaction in life and career, and your locus of control—your source of motivation—all keys to success in college. Your social self derives from your relationships and your behavior. This chapter explains how you can develop the **personal qualities** and interpersonal skills needed to keep your physical, emotional, and social selves in balance:

Personal qualities are traits or characteristics such as personal responsibility, self-esteem, and sociability. These qualities and others like them can be developed.

<table>
<tr><td>

KEY TERMS

well-being, *p. 158*
glucose, *p. 161*
aerobic exercise, *p. 163*
stress, *p. 164*
binge drinking, *p. 170*
aggressive behavior, *p. 179*
assertive behavior, *p. 179*
acquaintance rape, *p. 183*
sexual harassment, *p. 184*

</td><td>

SCANS TERM

personal qualities, *p. 157*

</td></tr>
</table>

HEALTH, WELL-BEING, AND SUCCESS IN COLLEGE

> *Understand the connection between success in college and your health and well-being so that you can make good choices.*

Getting an education means more than gaining academic skills. If you are a first-time college student, you are also learning how to live on your own, and you can take advantage of unique opportunities for establishing good health habits, building self-esteem, and forming close friendships. If you are an adult learner, college is one more responsibility you are adding to those you already have. Your health, relationships, and self-esteem may be put to the test as you struggle to cope with the challenges of being a student.

Whatever your age, health and well-being can affect your ability to do well in college. If you don't eat sensibly, stay physically fit, manage your stress, and avoid harmful substances, then your health and grades will suffer. Similarly, if you have troubled relationships, allow your emotions to rule, and resist change, then you will not have the sense of **well-being** that keeps you optimistic, hopeful, and motivated. To do well academically you need a good balance among the physical, emotional, and social factors that contribute to your sense of well-being. This section focuses on your physical self and keeping it healthy.

Health is a basic need. If your body doesn't work properly, your mind can't function at its best. Good or bad health is rarely something that just happens; it

Well-being refers to your emotional state. High self-esteem, confidence, optimism, and positive feelings about your health and abilities—all contribute to your sense of well-being.

AWARENESS CHECK 13

Are You Leading a Balanced Life?

Check the statements in each part that describe you.

Part I: Your Physical Self

☐ 1. I exercise regularly, three times a week or more.

☐ 2. I think that I am getting enough sleep most nights.

☐ 3. As far as I know, I eat a balanced diet.

☐ 4. I limit my intake of foods that are high in fat, salt, and sugar.

☐ 5. I feel well most of the time.

☐ 6. I believe that I am not under a great deal of stress.

☐ 7. When I do have stress, I am able to manage it.

☐ 8. I am neither overweight nor underweight.

☐ 9. I do not smoke.

☐ 10. I do not abuse alcohol, caffeine, or other drugs.

Part II: Your Emotional Self

☐ 1. Basically, I am a confident person.

☐ 2. Generally speaking, I am happy.

☐ 3. When I am angry or depressed, I can get over it quickly and go on with my life.

☐ 4. My outlook for the future is positive.

☐ 5. I am rarely, if ever, overcome by nervousness, stress, or anxiety.

☐ 6. Overall, my self-esteem is high.

☐ 7. For the most part, I believe that I am in control of what happens to me.

☐ 8. I am not a fearful person by nature.

☐ 9. I am able to take criticism.

☐ 10. I can cope with change.

Part III: Your Social Self

☐ 1. It is fairly easy for me to make friends.

☐ 2. I have several friendships that mean a lot to me.

☐ 3. I am not uncomfortable if I am at a party where I don't know many people.

☐ 4. People would probably not describe me as shy.

☐ 5. I am a good listener.

☐ 6. I can also contribute to a conversation.

☐ 7. Most of the time I get along well with the significant people in my life.

☐ 8. I understand and accept my responsibilities in a sexual relationship.

☐ 9. I believe I am assertive about what I want without being overbearing.

☐ 10. If a friend points out a fault that I have, I don't take offense; instead, I try to change my behavior if I agree with my friend.

All of these statements are positive ones, so if you have checked most of them, you may be managing your life successfully. The statements are grouped into three parts, reflecting the physical, emotional, and social aspects of your health and well-being. Therefore, fewer checks in one section could indicate a need for greater balance in that part of your life. Of course, the Awareness Check is an informal survey that does not begin to cover all of the possible aspects of adjustment, but your responses should give you a starting point for improving your health and well-being.

is partly the result of choices and actions. The four questions that follow embody four goals of healthful living that can lead to improved brain functioning. Think about your life and your habits; then, mentally answer the questions *yes* or *no*.

1. **Do you eat nutritionally sound, balanced meals?**

2. **Are you physically fit?**

3. **Are you able to manage stress?**

4. **Do you avoid the use of harmful substances?**

Eating Sensibly

A nutritionally sound, balanced diet is one that includes more fish and poultry than red meat, plenty of fruits and vegetables, whole grains, nuts, and low-fat dairy products. A balanced diet contains a variety of foods. It also contains more complex carbohydrates than protein and less fat than either carbohydrates or protein. A fast-food meal of a hamburger, french fries, and a soft drink, for example, is not a balanced meal because it contains too much fat. A more balanced meal would consist of broiled lean meat (chicken or fish), two cooked vegetables or a cooked vegetable and a salad, a whole grain roll, and a piece of fruit for dessert (see Figure 7.1).

Not only should you eat balanced meals, but you should also eat at regular intervals spaced throughout the day so that your brain is continually supplied with the nutrients it needs to function properly. Skipping breakfast, for example, or going into an exam hungry can interfere with your concentration and memory function and make you feel drowsy and less alert. Your brain responds to highs and lows in your blood sugar levels. When you haven't eaten, the level of glucose in your blood is low, and your mental alertness is diminished.

FIGURE 7.1

NUTRITION CHART: GUIDELINES FOR GOOD EATING

GUIDELINES	FOODS	REASONS
Eat some of these foods every day.	Fruits, vegetables, fish, poultry, nuts, beans	To achieve a varied, balanced diet that supplies enough energy and essential nutrients for optimum brain functioning
Increase complex carbohydrates.	Fruits, vegetables, nuts, whole grains	For maintaining energy throughout the day
Avoid simple carbohydrates.	White flour, refined sugar	To reduce risk of diabetes, heart disease
Choose good sources of protein; limit red meat.	Lean meat, fish, chicken, eggs, peas, and beans	For the growth and repair of tissue and to help fight infections
Choose *good* fats over *bad* fats, and limit fat intake.	Vegetable oils instead of butter; low-fat dairy products instead of whole-milk products	To reduce risk of high blood pressure, heart disease, and diabetes

Glucose is a sugar best synthesized from proteins and fats. Eating a candy bar before a test will temporarily raise the level of glucose in your blood, but the burst of energy you get from it will be short lived and will leave you feeling sluggish. Instead, eat balanced meals three times a day with snacks in between. A piece of fruit, which is high in fructose (another sugar), or a cup of yogurt is a good high-energy snack.

What can you do to maintain a healthful diet while you are in college? Try these suggestions:

Glucose is a sugar and is the body's main energy source.

1. Schedule your classes and other activities so that you have time for meals.

2. Eat balanced meals. You may be able to get a nutritious meal in your college's cafeteria. A variety of vegetables is usually available, and you can select your own combination of foods. If you live off campus, select foods according to the guidelines in Figure 7.1.

3. Avoid rich, high-calorie snacks. If you get hungry between meals, eat an apple or another fruit; carrot or celery sticks; or unbuttered, unsalted popcorn. For an energy boost, try low-fat yogurt or a few unsalted nuts instead of sugary or salty snacks.

4. If you live off campus, go home for lunch or bring your lunch. Be in control of what you eat.

5. If you go to parties, go easy on the snacks and alcoholic drinks. You may not know this, but alcohol converts to sugar in the blood-stream and is stored as fat. Apart from its other dangers, too much alcohol can make you gain weight, and it can interfere with your body's absorption of essential nutrients.

6. Don't make a habit of skipping meals. Fatigue, fuzzy thinking, and diminished concentration are among the problems this habit can cause.

7. If you are overweight and would like to reduce, ask your doctor to help you select an appropriate weight-loss program.

8. Exercise regularly; it will increase your level of fitness, make you feel positive and energetic, and help reduce stress. If you are trying to lose weight, combining a sensible diet with exercise will speed up the process and help keep the weight off.

9. Put food in perspective. Eat for good health. Don't eat because you feel depressed, because you want to celebrate, or as a social activity.

10. Drink eight to ten glasses of water a day to aid the digestive process, help eliminate wastes and toxins from your body, and supply needed moisture to the tissues.

Improving Fitness

Exercise has many benefits; fitness is just one of them. Regular exercise strengthens your heart, improves circulation, and helps reduce your risk of cardiovascular illness or death from a heart attack or stroke. Exercise can make you strong and able to withstand other diseases, and it can relieve stress. In addition, it helps you lose weight and improves your appearance.

Online Study Center   *www.college.hmco.com/pic/KanarTCS6e*

Exercise 7.1

FIND OUT WHAT YOU EAT and whether your diet is as balanced and healthful as it could be. Keep a record of what you eat for one week; then determine ways to eat more sensibly if necessary. For example, if you discover that most of your calories are coming from fats, decrease your intake of fatty foods such as butter, cheese, ice cream, margarine, salad dressings, luncheon meats, or other meats rich in fat, and increase your intake of whole grains, fruits, vegetables, lean meats, fish, and poultry. Keep recording your meals and attempting to adjust what you eat until you achieve a balanced diet.

Make copies of this charts so that you can record what you eat throughout the day. (If you wait until evening, you may forget what you've eaten.) To download copies of the chart, go to college.hmco.com/pic/KanarTCS6e.

	Sunday	Monday	Tuesday	Wednesday	Thursday	Friday	Saturday
Breakfast							
Lunch							
Dinner							
Snacks							

Online Study Center
Chapter Exercises/
Forms

Walking is one of the simplest forms of aerobic exercise. Thirty minutes of brisk walking daily can raise your fitness level.

The best exercise is aerobic. An **aerobic exercise** lasts for a minimum of twenty minutes during which your heart rate is elevated and your muscular activity is continuous. You should not do aerobic exercises without checking your pulse frequently and without first receiving instructions on how to perform the activities. Overstressing your heart can have serious, even fatal, effects. "No pain, no gain" is a dangerous myth. "FIT" is a much better guideline.

Aerobic exercise is continuous muscular activity that elevates the heart rate. Running and walking are examples.

F = Frequency	How often you exercise—three times a week is the generally recommended starting frequency
I = Intensity	Your target heart rate, based on your age and present level of fitness
T = Time	The amount of time you spend exercising—start with fifteen minutes or less, depending on your age and condition, and then gradually increase the time as you are able

Exercise is great for you if you do it correctly. An excellent place to get started is in your college's athletic department. Courses and individual counseling may be available at a lower cost than you are likely to find at one of the commercial health clubs or spas and may even be offered free of charge. If you don't have time for exercise that requires a change of clothes or a special place or type of equipment, try walking. You can walk anywhere; just thirty minutes a day of brisk, uninterrupted walking greatly reduces your risk of heart problems and improves your overall level of fitness. Here is a list of aerobic activities, some of which you may already be doing:

Aerobic dancing

Rowing

Swimming

Bicycling

Running

Walking

Jumping rope

CONCEPT CHECK 7.1

Would you like more information on improving diet and fitness? Go to http://www.Nutrition.gov for the latest U.S. Government nutrition guidelines.

Managing Stress

Some stress won't hurt you. In fact, you should expect to experience stress now and then. For example, it is normal to feel a little anxious before getting up in front of a group to speak. You want to do your best, and you may be wondering whether you will be able to remember everything you want to say. Once you get started, this anxiety should quickly pass as you begin to focus your attention on giving the speech. It is also normal to feel a little anxiety on the day of an exam. But once you have the exam in front of you and get down to the business of taking the test, the anxiety should pass. Real **stress** is unrelieved anxiety that persists over a long period of time. Stress is especially harmful if you are unable to manage it. Unrelieved stress can weaken you physically so that you become vulnerable to disease, and it can impair your ability to think clearly so that your performance in class and at work suffers.

Stress is persistent, unrelieved anxiety that interferes with normal functioning.

Many warning signs can tell you if your stress is getting out of control. Look at the brief list that follows and see whether you have any of these common symptoms of stress. The more of these symptoms that you have, the more likely it is that you need to learn some strategies for coping with stress.

Depression	Loss of pleasure in life
Difficulty falling asleep	Increase or decrease in appetite
Extreme tiredness, fatigue	Muscular aches for no apparent reason
Feelings of anger or resentment	Stomach or intestinal disturbances
Frequent absence from work or classes	Sweaty palms
Impatience	Tension headaches
Inability to concentrate	Test anxiety

Many students find adjusting to college and meeting course requirements extremely stressful, especially if they are also working, raising a family, or trying to cope in an environment in which they feel out of place. Some students are chronically anxious about tests, and their nervousness prevents them from doing their best. Test anxiety is a special kind of stress related to testing situations. Chapter 12 explains test anxiety and how to overcome it. It is important that you find ways to manage stress so that you can reach your goals and enjoy yourself in the process. Try the following tips for managing stress.

Ten Stress Beaters

1. **Be realistic.** You know what you can and cannot do. Don't waste energy worrying about matters that are out of your control. Instead, use your energy to alter those situations that you have the power to change. Unrealistic goals, perfectionism, and believing you have to do everything right the first time will set you up for failure. Be reasonable about what you expect of yourself, and don't be afraid to make mistakes.

2. **Exercise tensions away.** When you are under stress, your muscles tense involuntarily. Exercise has a natural calming effect that is accompanied by a positive feeling. For example, you may have heard about or experienced "runner's high," the feeling of euphoria and the sudden burst of energy runners get after they have been running for a long time.

   To help you relax, try the desktop relaxation technique and the chair-seat relaxation technique explained in Chapter 10. Also try this simple deep-breathing technique for calming yourself in any situation: Breathe slowly through your nose, filling your lungs. Then slowly exhale through your mouth. As you take ten deep breaths in this manner, think to yourself: "I am relaxed; I am calm."

3. **Learn to say *no*.** For whatever reason, many of us have difficulty saying *no*. When you are under stress because of work, family, course requirements, and other obligations, the last thing you need is to take on more responsibilities. When someone makes demands on your dwindling time, ask yourself, "Do I really want or need to do this?" If the answer is "No," don't be afraid to say so. If you have trouble saying *no*, you may need to become more assertive, as explained later in this chapter.

4. **Ask for help.** Some problems may be more than you can handle by yourself, so you may need to seek financial, medical, or some other type of help or advice. If you are the kind of person who hates to ask for help, try to get over this attitude. Many times we worry needlessly and cause ourselves even more stress by living with problems that we consider unsolvable when asking for and getting help might bring a solution.

5. **Learn to deal with negative people.** People who display negative attitudes, a pessimistic outlook on life, and a constant state of nervousness can make you experience negative feelings that add to your stress. If you can eliminate negative people from your life, do so. If they are friends or family members, try to counter their negative remarks with positive ones of your own. When they do behave in a more positive way, comment on what you like about their behavior, thereby positively reinforcing a behavior that you want them to continue.

6. **Lose yourself in activity.** When you are under stress, engage in some activity that causes you to lose all track of time. During those

> **CONCEPT CHECK 7.2**
>
> People experience stress from many sources. What makes you feel stressed? How do you cope with the stress in your life? What works best for you?

EXERCISE 7.2

FIND AN EXERCISE PROGRAM THAT works. Choose a form of exercise that you enjoy and can easily fit into your schedule. Try out some of the aerobic exercises listed on page 164; then use the following chart to summarize and comment on your experiences. You can also download the chart from college.hmco.com/pic/KanarTCS6e. The chart will help you determine which type of exercise works best for you and why.

Type of exercise	Aerobic dancing					
Time of day	7:00 p.m.					
Amount of time spent	1 hour					
Reaction	I went to an aerobics class with a friend, and I liked it so much I decided to join too.					

Online Study Center
Chapter Exercises/ Forms

moments, you can forget your worries and experience happy, calming feelings. Reading, playing a sport, and spending time pursuing a hobby or special interest are all activities in which you can lose yourself.

7. **Reward yourself.** Ideally, you should always be prepared for tests, complete assignments on time, and follow your study schedule. Realistically, you may fall short of meeting these goals. When that happens, get back on track as soon as you can; then reward yourself with a break or another treat. A completed task followed by a reward is a great stress reducer.

8. **Get your life in order.** You've probably been meaning to do this anyway. If you are off schedule or behind in your courses, resolve

to get organized. Make out a new study schedule that includes time to catch up on work you've missed. Make a list of all the other tasks that need doing; then tackle them one at a time. Don't worry if it takes you a while to get organized. After all, it took a while to get off schedule.

9. **Make a wish list.** We all have a tendency to say to ourselves, "If only I had the time, I'd do _____." How would you complete this sentence? Make a list of all the things you'd do if you had the time. When stress has become more than you can handle, and you have to get away for a while, do one of your wish-list activities.

10. **Help someone else.** It's no secret that doing something for someone else can make you feel good and can take your mind off what is worrying you. Take the opportunity to help a friend who has a problem. Volunteer or participate in service learning projects. The things you do for others not only help them but also help you build self-esteem, an important personal quality.

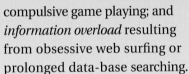

COMPUTER CONFIDENCE

Are You Spending Too Much Time on the Net?

Internet addiction is a student health issue that causes concern on college campuses. Cruise by your college's computer lab at any time of day, and you are likely to see all stations occupied. What are these students doing? Some undoubtedly are researching and writing. Many, however, are playing games and visiting chat rooms. Though harmless in themselves, when taken to extremes, these activities can put students at risk for failing grades and failed relationships. College counselors are troubled by the attrition rate of students whose misuse of the Internet has disrupted their lives and curtailed their education.

A person who uses the Internet obsessively to the point of losing self-control suffers from *Internet addiction*. Four types of addictive online behavior are *cybersexual addiction*, which involves visits to adult chat rooms and pornography web sites; *cyber-relationship addiction*, whereby online friendships become more important than real-life relationships with friends and family members; net *compulsions* such as online auctions, trading, and compulsive game playing; and *information overload* resulting from obsessive web surfing or prolonged data-base searching.

Why do people become addicted to the Net? Cyberspace is a virtual community in which one can escape from reality and the complexities of real-world human relations. In cyberspace, people can create new identities, concealing their real names, ages, personalities, and socioeconomic status. The intimacy that develops between friends who meet in chat rooms is, therefore, an illusion. Real intimacy comes from closeness with another. But cyber-relationships are, by their nature, at arm's length.

Who is at risk? The same risk factors that apply to drug and alcohol use apply to Internet addiction. Depression, anxiety, or lack of self-confidence and self-esteem may cause people to seek relief in the stimulating world of cyberspace. People who have abused drugs, alcohol, or tobacco may have an increased susceptibility to Internet addiction.

What can you do? As with any other activity that has a potential for abuse, use caution. Have a purpose for using the Internet and schedule your online time so that it doesn't interfere with your other activities. Use the Internet as a research tool or for an occasional game, but don't let it become a substitute for social interaction. Email, too, can get out of hand if reading and sending messages consumes too much of your time or if you use email not as a convenience but rather as a way to keep the people closest to you at a distance. If you are concerned that your Internet use may be excessive, seek help.

The Internet is a helpful tool for researching and fact finding; it can also be a pleasant distraction similar to watching a movie or a favorite TV program. But when your Internet use becomes obsessive, it may also become addicting. Watch for these warning signs:

- Internet activities are on your mind more often than not.

- The amount of time you spend on the Net has gradually increased.

- After deciding that you were spending too much time on the Net, you tried to stop or cut back but were unsuccessful.

- Just the thought of limiting your Internet time makes you feel anxious or depressed.

- Friends, family members, or others close to you have expressed concern about the amount of time you spend on the Net.

- You often turn to the Net for relief from stress, life's problems, or feelings of depression.

Do four or more of these warning signs apply to you? If so, you may be spending too much time on the Net.

To learn more about Internet addiction, see the following web sites for a list of resources, including an online test for Internet addiction that you can take: www.netaddiction.com and www.virtual-addiction.com.

EXERCISE 7.3   COMPUTER APPLICATION

ADDICTIVE BEHAVIOR—WHETHER IT INVOLVES binge drinking, smoking, overeating, using drugs, or surfing the Net to excess—interferes with your health and undermines your performance. If you are struggling with an addiction, or if someone you know is, research the addiction online. Find out what support groups may be available and what other useful information exists. As a starting point, use *addiction* as one of your search words and the name of the behavior or substance in which you are interested. If your topic is "Internet addiction," try the suggestions in this chapter's Computer Confidence. Then share what you find with the rest of the class.

Avoiding Harmful Substances

When it comes to drugs, both legal and illegal, it's best to take a realistic approach. What are the facts and misconceptions surrounding alcohol, tobacco, caffeine, and illegal drugs such as marijuana and cocaine? What are the risks and perceived benefits of using one or more of these substances? Arming yourself with knowledge enables you to deal with issues of substance use and abuse on your own terms.

Tobacco. Smoking places you at risk of getting lung cancer, heart disease, and a host of other illnesses, according to the American Cancer Society, the American

Lung Association, the American Heart Association, and many other health organizations and professionals. Because second-hand smoke poses similar risks for nonsmokers, smoking is prohibited or limited in all public buildings, many restaurants, and other establishments. Public awareness about the dangers of smoking has increased, and a growing social stigma against smoking prevails. All states have laws prohibiting the sale of tobacco products to minors. Those are the facts.

A misconception some people have is that they can quit smoking whenever they want to. According to a report issued by the Surgeon General of the United States some years ago, nicotine is as addicting as the illegal drug heroin. If you smoke, ask yourself this question: What is this habit doing for me? If, after considering the risks and benefits, you decide to quit, ask your doctor to suggest a smoking cessation program.

Caffeine. How many students do you know who can't face the morning without a cup of coffee? How many students need caffeine to keep them going throughout the day or to keep them awake during late-night study sessions? Here are the facts about caffeine: It is present in coffee, tea, chocolate, some soft drinks, and certain over-the-counter drugs. When used in moderation, caffeine reduces drowsiness and increases energy. When abused, caffeine can produce anxiety and tremors, and may aggravate certain conditions such as heart disease and high blood pressure. Caffeine can be addicting: an abrupt decrease or cessation of use produces withdrawal symptoms such as headaches and jitters, but one or two cups a day may produce few if any negative side effects. As you weigh the benefits and risks of using caffeine, consider two alternatives to morning coffee: switch to decaffeinated or manage your time so that you get enough rest, eliminating the need for a caffeine boost.

Illegal Drugs. What is the allure of drugs such as marijuana, cocaine, heroin, amphetamines, and crystal meth? They stimulate the brain's pleasure centers, generating feelings such as alertness, euphoria, or relaxation. But the "high" users get is short lived and may be followed by feelings of depression or anxiety. Because these drugs are both psychologically and physically addicting, abuse can lead to a habit that is extremely hard to break. Because the drugs are illegal, the Food and Drug Administration has no control over their manufacture. As a result, they may be produced in unsanitary conditions and may contain toxic additives that increase users' health risks.

Some students who have experimented with illegal drugs have experienced few, if any, ill effects. But some have become addicted, some have died of overdoses, some have been sexually assaulted while under the influence, and others have served jail terms and have had their academic careers and future prospects forever curtailed as a result. Keeping these facts in mind, ask yourself whether the short-term benefits students may think they are getting from drug use are really worth the considerable risks involved and their long-term consequences.

Alcohol. We have saved this drug for last because its use and abuse are of greatest concern to college students. Because binge drinking on college campuses, alcohol abuse at campus social events, and alcohol-related deaths and other incidents during Spring Break get a lot of media attention, it's easy to get the impression that "everybody does it." The reality is that many college students do not drink, and many who do drink do so responsibly. But for others, alcohol abuse has resulted in dangerous behavior—and even death. Because students are often pressured to drink in social situations and because the opportunities to abuse alcohol are readily available, your best defense is knowledge.

Why do students drink? Psychologists and other professionals cite several reasons. For one thing, children of alcoholics and children who grew up in homes where alcohol was used at family occasions may be more prone to use alcohol. Also, some experimentation with "the forbidden" is a normal part of growing up. Drinking, for some students, is a rebellious act through which they establish their independence. Third, despite the risks of drinking, some students turn to alcohol to relieve stress or to escape unpleasantness. Peer pressure is another reason. Students may feel that they must drink in order to be accepted. Finally, the media and the campus atmosphere exert powerful influences. The media are filled with images that make drinking seem glamorous. Beverage companies sponsor social events that make alcohol consumption by young people seem normal, average. Social organizations on campus, Greek organizations in particular, may sponsor events that revolve around drinking. Too often, college administrators look the other way, ignoring the underage drinking that may be occurring on campus.

Although light drinking may pose few health risks, binge drinking is dangerous. What is binge drinking? Ingesting five or more drinks in a short time period constitutes **binge drinking.** This behavior can result in injury, illness, and even death from alcohol poisoning. Binge drinking has negative academic effects as well, impairing performance and judgment.

What are your choices? As a student, you must make your own decisions about alcohol use. You don't have to drink, but if you choose to, know the risks. Know the difference between light-to-moderate drinking and abusive or binge drinking. Consider also your religious beliefs and personal values. Be aware of legal limits and campus policies regarding alcohol use and make ethical choices. If you do drink, the following guidelines may help you drink safely and responsibly.

> **Binge drinking** is the consumption of five or more drinks within a short time period.

▼ **Know what you're drinking.** It's easy for someone to slip a drug into a drink and easy for someone to spike a drink with more alcohol than you had intended to consume. Therefore, do not accept a drink from anyone. Get your own drink.

▼ **Time your drinking.** Don't drink too much too fast. Drink slowly, making one or two drinks last at least an hour.

▼ **Do not drink on an empty stomach.** Eat or nibble while drinking. Eating slows the absorption of alcohol into the bloodstream.

▼ **Opt out of drinking games.** Games such as chug-a-lug contests are risky because they introduce too much alcohol into your system too rapidly.

▼ **Say "No" when you've had enough.** A simple *no* is all you need to say to refuse a drink. You don't owe anyone an explanation.

▼ **Do not drink and drive.** If you and your friends are out drinking, let someone who has not been drinking be your designated driver. Do not drive drunk, and don't ride with a driver who is.

Choosing not to drink is a valid option. If you make this choice, you can still attend parties and other social events where alcohol is consumed without participating in drinking. Take someone with you who is also a nondrinker. In addition, choose other, positive ways to find escape, relaxation, excitement, and pleasure. For example, plan activities with your friends that involve physical and mental stimulation. Attend sports events, take bicycle or hiking trips, go to the beach for a day of surfing and sunning, or go to a movie. Solitary pursuits that provide escape, adventure, and excitement include reading; writing poems, essays, and stories; and learning a new hobby, craft, or sport. For example, you might enjoy taking a course in creative writing or drawing.

Like everything else, deciding whether or not to drink is *your* choice. In this behavior, as in all others, by being informed and by making responsible choices, you are taking control of your life.

EXERCISE 7.4

HOW PREVALENT IS DRINKING ON your campus? Take this informal survey to gather information about your own habits and assumptions. Do not identify yourself on the survey. Your instructor will compile all students' answers and report back to the class.

To take the survey, read each question and circle your answer.

1. **Do you drink?**

   a. never   b. occasionally   c. regularly

2. **How many drinks do you have in a week?**

   a. none   b. 1 or 2   c. more than 1 or 2

3. **When are you most likely to drink?**

   a. at social events   b. on special occasions

   c. with meals   d. whenever I'm with friends

4. **How many drinks do you usually have at a social event or during an evening spent with friends?**

   a. 1 or 2   b. 2 to 5   c. more than 5

5. **Have you ever engaged in binge drinking?**

   a. never   b. occasionally   c. regularly

6. **Have you ever engaged in drinking games?**

   a. never   b. occasionally   c. regularly

7. **To the best of your knowledge, how prevalent is binge drinking among the students on your campus?**

   a. not prevalent at all   b. somewhat prevalent   c. quite prevalent

8. **In general, what would you estimate to be the percentage of students on your campus who drink regularly?**

   a. fewer than 50 percent   b. about 50 percent   c. more than 50 percent

9. **Do you believe that a student on your campus has to drink in order to be accepted or to have a social life?**

   a. not at all   b. in some cases   c. definitely

10. **Based on your own experience, how would you describe college students' drinking behavior?**

    a. Most students do not drink.

    b. Most students engage in light-to-moderate drinking.

    c. Most students drink to excess.

11. **How does drinking behavior on your campus compare with that on other campuses?**

   a. **There is less drinking among students on my campus.**

   b. **About the same amount of drinking occurs among students on my campus as on others.**

   c. **Students on my campus drink more than students on other campuses.**

12. **If you are out with friends, how likely is one of you to abstain from drinking so that he or she can be the designated driver?**

   a. **not likely**   b. **somewhat likely**   c. **very likely**

13. **How much underage drinking do you see at campus events or other social events at which college students are present?**

   a. **hardly any**   b. **some**   c. **a great deal**

14. **Among the students on your campus, how much pressure is there to engage in drinking?**

   a. **none**   b. **some**   c. **a great deal**

15. **Do you know anyone on your campus who has been involved in one or more of the following while drinking? Circle all that apply.**

   a. **acquaintance rape**   b. **an automobile accident**

   c. **a serious injury**   d. **unsafe sexual activity**

16. **Do you know anyone on campus whose drinking has led to one or more of these outcomes? Circle all that apply.**

   a. **missed class or was late**   b. **scored poorly on a test**

   c. **failed to hand in course work**   d. **had a loss of memory**

MANAGING YOUR EMOTIONS

> *Emotions can cause you to lose sight of your goals. Learn how you can manage your feelings and regain your perspective.*

Although you may be faced with a situation you cannot change, you *can* change how you react to it. For example, if you are having trouble getting along with a roommate, you may be losing study time because of arguing or worrying about the problem. Soon your grades will suffer if you can't resolve your differences and get back on schedule. Obviously, you can't change your roommate's behavior, but you can change your feelings about that behavior. You can decide not to let it get to you. Focus your attention on doing well in your courses. Concentrate on meeting every requirement, completing every assignment, and preparing for every test. Do most of your studying in the library or some other place away from your roommate. Try to resolve your differences, but if you cannot, make the best of the situation until you can make other living arrangements. Avoid getting into arguments and say to yourself, "I am in charge of my feelings, and I will not let my conflict with my roommate interfere with my success in my courses."

Similarly, if you are an older student who lives off campus, you may have a family member or friend who tries to undermine your efforts to be successful by making comments such as "You'll never make it" or "You shouldn't put yourself through this." Negative comments like these don't have to upset you. Your emotions belong to *you*. People cannot control how you feel unless you give them that power.

Understanding Your Feelings

To begin taking control of your emotions, determine what causes you to feel one way or another. Begin by listening to yourself think and talk. Are your thoughts and words dominated by statements that begin with *they, he, she,* or *you*? Do you often make statements such as these?

You make me angry because you don't listen to what I say.

She doesn't care how I feel.

He really hurt my feelings.

They make it hard for me to get the schedule that I want.

She gave me a D on that paper, but I deserved better.

When you make statements like these, you place all the blame for your feelings on someone else. You place yourself at the mercy of others' whims. If they choose to, they can make you feel great. If they choose to, they can make you feel awful. You never know where you stand with people, and consequently, your self-esteem is undermined.

Chapter 2 explains locus of control as a factor that influences your motivation. *Locus of control* is a psychological term that describes where you place responsibility for the control of your life's events. For example, if your locus of control is *external*, you expect someone or something to motivate you. If your locus of control is *internal*, you are self-motivated. Locus of control may also explain, in part, *what* controls your feelings. Externally motivated students tend to blame others for the way they feel. Internally motivated students are more likely to examine their own behavior to find the source of their feelings.

One way to take control of your emotions is to replace any statements of feeling that begin with *they, he, she,* or *you* with statements that begin with *I*. You will then be able to determine what actually caused the feeling. For example, here are the same statements you read before, but the word *I* has replaced the first word, and the statement has been altered to shift the cause of the feeling to the person making the statement:

I get angry when I think you're not listening to what I say.

I believe she doesn't care how I feel.

I feel hurt by some of the things he does.

I find it hard to get the schedule that I want.

I made a D on that paper, but I could have done better.

Pretend for a moment that you made these statements. Notice how you have accepted responsibility for the feelings. For example, by accepting that the D is the grade that you earned, you are likely to do better next time. But if you blame someone else for the D, then you are off the hook and have no control over your future in the course. Similarly, if "they" are not responsible for your schedule, then you must determine what actions you should take to get the schedule you want. This kind of thinking puts *you* in control of the outcome.

For example, in the first three statements, you accept responsibility for your feelings that seem to result from others' actions. The value of doing this is that it opens a discussion about behavior you don't like without blaming the other person. For example, if it turns out that your friend really doesn't listen, doesn't care how you feel, or does things that hurt you, then you can decide what you are going to do about the situation, whether it is worthwhile to try to improve the relationship or to end it. In either case, you open the way for communication rather than for more arguments and bad feelings.

Leading a Purposeful Life

When you control your emotions and accept responsibility for your feelings, you increase your chances for happiness and decrease your chances for disappointment. A sense of well-being results from having goals to reach and making plans to achieve them. As explained in Chapter 4, setting reachable long-term and short-term goals will give you a purpose for attending college, completing your tasks at work, and realizing your dreams and plans. When your purpose is clear, you are more likely to schedule your time, follow through on your action plans, and avoid procrastination.

If your life seems to lack purpose, examine what you are doing in your courses, at work, or at home. Ask yourself, "Why am I doing this?" Answers may not come right away, but when they do, they may remind you of your goals or indicate a need to make some changes in your life. This knowledge will give you a renewed sense of purpose.

Accepting the Need for Change

Negative feelings, a sense of helplessness, and lowered self-esteem result when something you are doing isn't working out, but you are afraid to make a change. An unhappy wife or husband may continue without help in a relationship that makes both partners miserable because one or the other is afraid of the changes that counseling might require. A person who has been offered a new and better job or a transfer to a higher-paying job out of state may turn down the offer because he or she fears change. You may keep working on a research paper—even though you may realize that you have chosen an unworkable topic—because you don't want to start over. If you are "test anxious," you may avoid seeking help because you believe that the problem will go away or that there is nothing you can do about it. Trying to avoid change by ignoring a problem can be self-destructive. Negative feelings breed more negative feelings, encouraging the mistaken belief that a bad situation can only get worse.

Accept the need for change when it becomes clear that you have done all you can do in a situation that is not working. Acceptance is the hard part. Once you're committed to making a change in your life, exploring your options and deciding what to do next can be fun and challenging.

C R I T I C A L

T H I N K I N G

Exercise Overview

What are the most common sources of stress? What can people do to cope with stress? This exercise will help you think through these questions to find answers.

Exercise Background

Stress affects people in different ways. A situation that is a major stressor for one person may not be a source of worry for another. However, some events are universally stressful because they disrupt the orderly pattern of our lives and relationships. How we handle the stress following one of these events determines how well we are able to move on with our lives and reach our goals.

Exercise Task

Listed next are some life-changing events that can upset the balance of a person's health and well-being and cause stress. Have you experienced one of these events within the last six months or year? Write a short essay about the changes in your life resulting from the event and explain what you are doing to adapt to your new circumstances. If you prefer, you can write about a stress-causing event that is not listed.

Death of a spouse or partner

Death of a parent

Death of other close family member

Divorce

Unwanted pregnancy

Major injury or illness (self)

Major injury or illness (family member or partner)

Loss of a job or financial support

Breakup of a relationship other than marriage

Serious argument with someone

Legal problem

Academic difficulties, probation

Relocation of residence

EXERCISE 7.5   LEARNING STYLE

IN THE FOLLOWING STATEMENTS, the pronouns *they, he, she,* and *you* suggest that the people making the statements are not taking responsibility for their feelings and behavior. Rewrite each statement so that the focus is on the person making the statement. Replace any pronouns with the first-person pronoun *I* and change any other wording as needed.

1. **You didn't tell us that we had to do the exercises.**

   _____

   _____

2. They told me that the department chair would let me in the course even though it's full.

_____

_____

3. You are not paying attention to me.

_____

_____

4. Brown is a boring lecturer.

_____

_____

5. Greene never is in the office when I go there.

_____

_____

EXERCISE 7.6

LIKE MOST PEOPLE, YOU PROBABLY have times in your life when you feel disappointed, depressed, angry, frustrated, lonely, incompetent, or unloved. Like many people, you may tend to blame others for making you feel this way. In fact, no one needs to have that much power over you if you assume responsibility for your own well-being. Complete the statements that follow to remind yourself of what you have and the things that make you feel good. Think about these positive qualities and accomplishments whenever you lack confidence.

1. My finest character trait is _____.

2. My favorite possession is _____.

3. My closest friend is _____.

4. I am proud of myself for _____.

5. I feel happiest at home when I _____.

6. I feel most comfortable at work when I _____.

7. The course in which I am doing my best is _____.

8. Something I enjoy doing by myself is _____.

9. A skill I have mastered very quickly is _____.

10. One thing I can really do well is _____.

11. On my next vacation I will _____.

12. One of my plans for the future is _____.

Emotional Intelligence—Another Way of Being Smart

Why do some highly intelligent people fail? Why do some whose IQs are not so high still manage to do well? What makes one person moody and another person more even-tempered?

Emotional intelligence, or EQ, may be the answer. Daniel Goleman, author of *Emotional Intelligence*, draws on Howard Gardner's theory of "personal intelligences," Peter Salovey's definition of *emotional intelligence*, and the research of many others to explain why your EQ may be more important than your IQ.

According to Goleman, "IQ contributes about 20 percent to the factors that determine life success, which leaves 80 percent to other factors." One of those factors is emotional intelligence: the qualities that enable you to control your emotions instead of letting them control you. For example, you could have the IQ of an Einstein and still find yourself on academic probation if you could not control the emotions that make you want to party instead of study. What exactly is emotional intelligence, and can it be developed? Goleman says it can. Emotional intelligence adds up to *character*, and it includes these qualities:

- **Self-motivation.** You alone are responsible for paying attention, maintaining concentration, and relieving yourself of boredom.

- **Persistence.** Following through on schedules and commitments, living up to obligations, and continuing to make progress despite temporary setbacks will help you to achieve your goals.

- **The ability to control impulses and delay gratification.** Now and then we all do things on a whim or "in the heat of the moment." But some people let passion rule, with disastrous results: the student who drinks too much, has unprotected sex, or acts first and thinks later. To control your impulses, you have to think ahead to the consequences and ask yourself, "Is it worth it?"

- **The ability to regulate moods.** How fast can you bounce back from disappointment and frustration? Do you allow yourself to be overcome by sadness, anxiety, or anger? Constantly giving in to your emotions produces stress that has harmful physical and mental effects. If your inclination is to say, "But I can't help how I feel," think again. The answer is to know yourself. Learn to recognize what your feelings are and what causes them. When you know *why* you are depressed, for example, you can figure out what it will take to eliminate the cause.

- **Empathy.** *Empathy* is another word for *caring*, and it is a valuable interpersonal skill. People who are empathetic have a high degree of self-awareness that enables them to sense the feelings of others. They are able to put themselves in another's place so that they can tell what he or she wants or needs.

- **Hope.** You have to believe that things will get better, that life is basically good, and that with hard work and persistence, you will achieve your goals. Without hope, it is unlikely that you will have either the will or the self-discipline to make a plan and follow it through.

Do you see a connection between Goleman's emotional intelligence and the internal locus of control? Remember that internally motivated people take responsibility for their own successes and failures. They manage their lives, as opposed to allowing life's circumstances to manage them. Goleman's qualities of self-motivation and persistence are also characteristic of the internal locus of control.

To learn more about this topic, see Goleman's book *Emotional Intelligence* or do an online search using these keywords as a starting point: *emotional intelligence* and *Daniel Goleman*.

DEVELOPING YOUR INTERPERSONAL SKILLS

Develop the interpersonal skills essential to success and well-being in college and at work.

The most influential people in your life may include your parents, your spouse or other intimate partner, your children, your roommate, and your friends. You depend on these people for many things, and they depend on you. Your relationships with these people can span the entire range of emotions, from great happiness to extreme disappointment. What makes a relationship succeed or fail? Educators, philosophers, psychologists, writers, and many others have explored this question. Perhaps you have also explored it. Though each relationship is based on a complex system of need satisfaction, and though each type of relationship has characteristics that distinguish it from other types, five interpersonal skills that you can develop will lead to more satisfying relationships.

Listen. Give all of your attention to the people you are with. Spend an equal amount of time listening and talking. In this way you will be sharing your ideas, but you will also be giving others an opportunity to share theirs. Listen actively and make eye contact. Show interest by asking questions and commenting on the ideas expressed. Encourage people to explain their opinions; then listen without judging. Respond by giving your opinions. When you are not sure what the other person means, paraphrase (restate) and preface your remarks with "Did I hear you say . . . ?" or "Did you mean that . . . ?"

Converse. Don't "hold forth"; don't deliver long, rambling monologues; and don't interrupt. A conversation is an interchange of ideas and opinions. Remember to listen 50 percent of the time and to talk 50 percent of the time. Avoid making critical or judgmental remarks. If talking with you is unpleasant, people will avoid conversation, believing that they won't be understood or appreciated. A breakdown in communication is the first sign that a relationship is in trouble. When people are asked what they like most in a relationship, a frequent answer is "Someone I can really talk to."

Have Fun. Create opportunities to have fun together. Make a mental list of interests you have in common with each of your relatives and friends, and plan trips or outings that focus on those interests. Or plan an adventure with someone. Go someplace new or try out a sport or activity together that neither of you has ever done before. When you discover a new activity that you both enjoy, set aside time to pursue it together. And make sure that you don't change or cancel plans at the last minute.

Be Supportive. You know how you feel when you have a problem, and the person you turn to for help lets you down. You know how you feel when you come home from work excited about some small but important accomplishment, and the person you were hoping would share this excitement acts uninterested. Don't be that kind of person. Encourage others' dreams. Share each triumph and disappointment as if it were your own. Don't assume someone you love knows you care; let your feelings show.

Being supportive is especially important in a diverse learning community or workplace in which people of different cultures and backgrounds share assignments and tasks. Being supportive means respecting others' opinions, being receptive to new ideas, and seeking points of agreement.

Be Assertive. Being assertive means being able to ask for what you want. It also means not giving in to people who try to make you do something you don't want to do. But don't confuse assertiveness with aggressiveness. **Aggressive behavior** is rude, domineering, and intimidating. **Assertive behavior** is polite but strong and independent. Being assertive means standing up for your rights without denying the rights of others. As an assertive person, you have the right to express your feelings and opinions, to ask for what you want, and to say *no*. At the same time, you must respect the fact that others have the same rights.

Few college students are truly aggressive, and far more students are passive than assertive. Being passive is taking the easy way out by letting other people make decisions for you. If you're at a party, and someone pushes another beer on you when you don't want it, do you take the beer so that you won't seem unsociable? If you don't want another beer, say so assertively and mean it: "No thanks, I've had enough." If you're a mother who comes in from classes to find dishes stacked in the sink and laundry piled up by the washer, do you start rinsing the dishes and sorting the clothes? Only if that's what you *want* to do. You should make it clear to your family that you need some help. Getting them to share the problem and its solution rather than demanding their help increases your chances of success.

Assertive behavior is responsible behavior. When you are assertive, you accept responsibility for what you will or will not do and for the consequences of your actions. Aggressive people, on the other hand, are irresponsible because they attempt to get what they want by intimidation. This approach may lead to outright refusal or a fight, a consequence the aggressor may not have intended. Aggressive people are less likely to predict or control the outcome of events than assertive people are because they don't take into account others' feelings or reactions. Passive people are also irresponsible because they give up control over their lives.

In college and at work, the more assertive you become, the more likely you are to be successful. As an assertive person, you will ask questions, seek out information, and be able to express clearly to others what you do not understand and what help you need from them.

> **Aggressive behavior** is rude, domineering, intimidating, and inconsiderate behavior.
>
> **Assertive behavior** is polite but forceful, independent, responsible, and considerate behavior.

EXERCISE 7.7   COLLABORATIVE ACTIVITY

APPLY WHAT YOU HAVE LEARNED about interpersonal skills by completing this exercise with group members. Remember to follow the guidelines for successful collaboration that appear on the inside back cover. Read the following scenario, discuss the questions, and answer them on the lines provided. Then write your evaluation on your own paper, or download the group exercise form from the Online Study Center at college.hmco.com/pic/KanarTCS6e.

> *Jack was exhausted. He had three college courses on Mondays and worked the lunch shift at the cafeteria. Then he had to rush to pick up his girlfriend Bonita at her part-time nursing job. Today Bonita seemed particularly disgruntled. "I hate the hospital. I hate my supervisors," she said. "I just want to be home practicing my guitar."*
>
> *"Your supervisors work hard all day, too," Jack snapped.*
>
> *"Why don't we stop for coffee on the way home?" asked Bonita.*
>
> *Jack sighed and answered, "Not today. I have a paper to finish. And maybe you should spend some time on those job applications."*
>
> *Bonita turned her back and looked out the window.*

1. **At what point could Jack have listened more actively to what Bonita was saying?**

_____

_____

2. What could Jack have said to start a positive conversation with Bonita?

_____

_____

3. How could Bonita have been supportive of her boyfriend?

_____

_____

4. How could Jack and Bonita have spent time together before going home to do their work?

_____

_____

Group Evaluation:

Evaluate your discussion. Did everyone contribute? Did you accomplish your task successfully? What additional questions do you have about interpersonal relationships? How will you find answers to your questions?

Online Study Center
**Chapter Exercises/
Forms**

EXERCISE 7.8

THE FOLLOWING IS A LIST of behaviors typical of assertive people. Put a check beside those that are typical of you. For any behaviors that you did not check, summarize on the lines that follow why you would or would not feel comfortable engaging in those behaviors.

Assertive people:

☐   1. Turn down invitations without feeling guilty

☐   2. Politely refuse an offer of food or drink if they don't want it

☐   3. Do not let themselves be talked into doing something that goes against their values

☐   4. Make choices and decisions based on what they think is the right thing to do

☐   5. Have little difficulty saying *no*

☐   6. Reserve the right to express their opinions while respecting others' rights to do the same

☐   7. Reserve the right to change their opinions

☐   8. Are not afraid to speak up, ask questions, or seek information

☐   9. Are not afraid to make mistakes or to take action to correct them

☐ 10. Do not feel compelled to share others' feelings, beliefs, or values that go against their own

_____

_____

_____

BUILDING HEALTHY RELATIONSHIPS

Develop and follow guidelines that will help you maintain healthy relationships with your friends and intimate partners.

College offers the opportunity to build new relationships and to test old ones. Your well-being depends, in part, on the relationships you are able to establish and maintain. When you are new in college, you may have trouble meeting people at first, but don't be discouraged. Many students are in the same situation as you are, and they are just as eager to make friends. In the student center or cafeteria, resist the temptation to sit by yourself. Join a group at a table and introduce yourself. Offer to exchange phone numbers with one or two people in each of your classes so that you can compare notes if one of you should be absent. Participate in as many campus activities as you can. You will meet people who share your interests, which is the basis of any long-lasting relationship. If you live in a residence hall, introduce yourself to the students living on either side of you and across the hall. Invite someone to go home with you one weekend. As you extend these offers of friendship to others, you will find them responding to you with similar offers of their own.

Friends offer support and companionship and are an important part of your college experience.

EXERCISE 7.9

COLLEGE OFFERS A VARIETY OF situations and settings for meeting new people. But college students often spend hours in solitary studying and miss out on or ignore many opportunities for socializing. Imagine that you are a new transfer student at your college and don't know a soul. How would you go about meeting new people? Using your student handbook, college newspaper or web site, student bulletin, and posted flyers as resources, list places and situations for meeting new people. Find examples in the following three categories.

1. **Academic activities**

   _____

   _____

2. **Social events**

   _____

   _____

3. **Recreational activities**

   _____

   _____

Are you the kind of person who meets new people easily, or do you take a long time to "warm up" to someone? Think about the three newest friends in your life. Describe where and how you met these people. Can you draw a conclusion about what kinds of situations you find most conducive to meeting new friends? Write your conclusion in one or two sentences.

Friend 1: _____

_____

Friend 2: _____

_____

Friend 3: _____

_____

Conclusion: _____

_____

_____

Your Sexuality

Sex takes a relationship to a new level of physical and emotional intimacy. Whatever your sexual orientation, you probably want the same thing that most people want from an intimate relationship: mutual acceptance, trust, respect, and—given the prevalence of sexually transmitted disease (STD)—honesty about past relationships. Although some people may profess a desire for recreational sex or sex without emotional intimacy or commitment, the truth is that sex is rarely, if ever, "just physical" for both people involved. Sexual behavior carries with it emotional issues of self-esteem, self-respect, and self-confidence. Moral values and ethics, too, play an important role. In fact, the kind of person you are and your character—or lack of it—are revealed in the way you handle *all* your relationships. Here are some guidelines to follow:

▸ **Don't rush sex.** If you become physically involved with someone for whom you don't feel real affection, you will probably suffer a loss of self-esteem.

FIGURE 7.2

CONTRACEPTIVE METHODS AND THEIR EFFECTIVENESS RATES

METHOD	EFFECTIVENESS RATE
Oral contraceptive	97–99%
Intrauterine device (IUD)	94–98
Condom	90
Diaphragm	80–95
Cervical cap	80–90
Spermicidal creams, foams, jellies	75–80
Natural family planning (refraining from sexual intercourse during a woman's period of ovulation)	80
Coitus interruptus (withdrawal before ejaculation)	80

▼ **Listen to your feelings.** Anxiety before sex, guilt afterward, and a lack of desire or pleasurable feeling at any point along the way signal that something is wrong.

▼ **Stand by your values.** Don't let someone pressure you into any type of sexual activity if you don't want it or if it goes against your morals, and don't pressure others. Sexual activity should be mutually desired by both partners. Anything less is sexual harassment or acquaintance rape.

▼ **Practice safe sex.** Take precautions to avoid pregnancy and disease. Either of these can limit your possibilities for the future. Figure 7.2 lists contraceptives and their effectiveness rates, which are based on consistent use according to directions. Remember that no birth control method, short of abstinence, is 100 percent effective. To guard against STDs, condoms offer some protection, but, again, they are not 100 percent reliable. Your risk of contracting an STD increases with the number of sexual partners you have had. If you and your partner are honest about past relationships, you will both be in a better position to make a wise decision about whether to become sexually involved.

Understanding Acquaintance Rape

Acquaintance rape is forced sexual intercourse involving people who know each other. Studies done on campuses place the percentage of women who may become the victims of rape or attempted rape before they graduate at anywhere from 15 to 35 percent.

In any discussion of acquaintance rape, you need to keep in mind three things. Rape is a crime, no matter who is involved. A person who forces sexual intercourse on an acquaintance is just as guilty of a crime as someone who sexually assaults a stranger. Second, a person has a right to say *no* to sex at any point during a date or in a relationship, regardless of any previous sexual activity that may have occurred. Finally, because alcohol lowers inhibitions, acquaintance rape may be more likely to occur in situations where one or both parties involved may have had too much to drink. The following guidelines should serve as a first step toward acquaintance rape prevention:

Acquaintance rape is forced sexual intercourse involving people who know each other.

▸ **Set standards for sexual conduct.** Decide how far you will go both physically and emotionally before getting involved with someone.

▸ **Communicate with each other.** Talk with each other about your expectations. Don't expect your partner to read your mind. Sex is too important to leave to chance.

▸ **Stand your ground.** If you don't want to respond to someone's sexual advances, your responsibility is to be assertive. Say *no* and mean it. Don't be hesitant, and don't back down. Even if you *do* want to have sex, your responsibility is to listen when your date says *no* and to believe that *no* means *no*, even if your date's nonverbal signals seem to say *yes*.

▸ **Treat each other with respect.** You have a right to your opinions and should trust your feelings. When something feels wrong, it probably is. Demand respect from your partner. At the same time, respect his or her choices as well. Don't let sexist notions or social pressures determine your behavior. Stick to your standards.

If you are a victim of rape, realize that you are not at fault and that you have options. Seek help immediately. Get medical attention. Do not shower, douche, or change clothes. Then call the police. To help yourself cope with the aftereffects of sexual assault—which may include nightmares, depression, mood swings, feelings of guilt or shame, and various physical symptoms—call a rape crisis center.

Dealing with Sexual Harassment

Sexual harassment is unwanted teasing, touching, or inappropriate remarks.

Sexual harassment is any kind of unwanted teasing, touching, or inappropriate remarks. Sexist jokes, sexist remarks, unwanted touching, or unwelcome requests for sexual favors are forms of sexual harassment and are inappropriate behaviors in any relationship. Your college probably has a policy on sexual harassment, which may be stated in a pamphlet, student handbook, or college catalog or on a web site. Your college may have a designated advisor or other official on campus who deals with sexual harassment issues and complaints.

Once sexual harassment starts, it will probably continue until you demand that it stop. Dropping a course to get away from an offending professor or changing your major because you are the recipient of sexist remarks and behaviors are ineffective ways of coping with sexual harassment. Instead, you should speak up at the first sign of sexism and confront the harasser by making it clear that you want the behavior to end. Don't keep sexual harassment to yourself. Talk to an advisor or report the behavior to the person at your college who handles complaints of sexual harassment. Make sure you have kept a record of the date, time, and place where the harassment occurred and of those people present who can act as witnesses.

Sexual harassment is everyone's problem, and creating a friendly, nonsexist environment is everyone's responsibility. Speaking out against sexism is one way students can let professors and each other know that sexism has no place in the classroom or on the campus and that harassers will be held accountable.

Thinking ahead about Career

Purpose and Instructions

A workplace focus in Chapter 7 is on sociability, a personal quality that can help you balance your physical, emotional, and social selves. Use the knowledge that you have gained from this chapter to solve work-related problems such as the one explained in the following case study. Read the case study on your own or with a partner and then answer the case questions.

Case Study

After high school, Wes attended a technical college, where he prepared for a career in the building industry. He now works for a company that makes cabinets. Lately, he has begun stopping off at a bar after work with two of his buddies. At first he had one or two beers, then went home to his family. Evenings were a special time when Wes and his wife would play with their children, feed them dinner, and put them to bed. Then Wes and his wife could spend time together.

But recently his after-work drink with the guys has been getting out of hand. Now Wes has several beers, stays later and later, and is missing dinner and playtime with his family. His wife is angry and says so, which makes Wes angry. He snaps at her and the kids. To compound these problems, he often wakes up with a hangover.

Wes knows he must do something. Not only is he afraid of losing his family, but he also worries about driving under the influence. He'd like to stop going out after work, but he wonders how the guys would feel. Would they think he's a wimp? Would his abstinence affect his relations at work? He needs the job and likes the company and his coworkers. What can Wes do?

Case Questions

1. State Wes's problem as you see it.

   _____

   _____

2. What are Wes's options?

   _____

   _____

3. What are the advantages and disadvantages of these options?

   _____

   _____

4. Access the Career Resource Center and read the article entitled "Stress Management Strategies" in the *Self-Responsibility and Self-Management* section of *Skills for Your Future*. Based on the suggestions in the article, what advice would you give to Wes?

   _____

Your *Reflections*

Reflect on what you have learned from this chapter about health and well-being and how you can find balance in your life. Use the following questions to stimulate your thinking; then write your reflections. Include in your writing specific information from the chapter.

- Are your physical, emotional, and social selves in balance? Explain your answer.

- Do you have a habit that needs changing? What self-improvement goal will you set?

- Review the interpersonal skills listed on pages 178–179. Which skill is your strongest? Give a specific example of how you use this skill.

- What is one skill or attitude explained in this chapter that you would like to develop, and what can you begin doing today to make that happen?

Chapter review

To review the chapter, reflect on the following confidence-building attitudes and skills. Complete **Concepts to Understand** by filling in the blanks with words or terms from the list provided. Then practice your new skills at every opportunity.

ATTITUDES TO DEVELOP
- personal responsibility
- self-motivation
- positive attitude

SKILLS TO PRACTICE
- making wise health and fitness choices
- controlling your emotions
- being assertive

CONCEPTS TO UNDERSTAND

assertive	balanced	aerobic	purposeful	emotional
physical	listen	social	fat	stress

Your health and well-being are within your power to control, and they affect your ability to do well in college. Successful adjustment depends on achieving a balance among your (1) _____, (2) _____ , and (3) _____ needs. This chapter suggests ways to maintain good health and increase your well-being.

To become healthy and stay healthy, choose a (4) _____ diet that includes a variety of foods and is low in (5) _____. Become physically fit by following a fitness program you can live with that includes (6) _____ exercises such as running or swimming. Learn to manage (7) _____ by first determining what circumstances and conditions make you feel stressed, then by trying the stress beaters suggested in this chapter. Avoid using harmful substances such as illegal drugs, alcohol, nicotine, and caffeine.

To increase your well-being, learn to take control of your emotions by understanding your feelings, leading a (8) _____ life, and accepting the need for change. To improve your relationships, try these five strategies:

1. (9) _____ to your friends and important others.
2. Converse and have fun with them.
3. Be supportive of them.
4. Take advantage of the opportunity college offers for making new friends.
5. Be (10) _____ about what you want.

Online Study Center
Review Exercise
ACE Self-Test

Protect yourself by making good decisions about sexual behavior. Practice safe sex, reduce your risk of date rape, deal assertively with sexual harassment, and avoid unwanted pregnancy.

To access additional review exercises, go to **college.hmco.com/pic/KanarTCS6e.**

Online Study Center

Prepare for Class, Improve Your Grade, and ACE the Test. This chapter's *Student Achievement* resources include

Chapter exercises/forms	Review exercise	Confidence Builder Web search	ACE Self-Test

To access these learning and study tools, go to **college.hmco.com/pic/KanarTCS6e.**

8 Creating your study system

Having a study system and using it consistently will keep you on target.

Learn the role that textbook graphics play, and follow guidelines for reading graphics with understanding.

Identify and use the common parts of textbooks and chapters as convenient learning and study aids.

*Confident students are **studious**. They know when, where, how, and what to study; and they use a study system.*

▶ *Start with a basic system like SQ3R and adapt it to your learning style. Vary the system's steps to meet the reading and study needs of different courses.*

How often do you finish reading a textbook chapter wondering what you were supposed to learn? How often do you skip a table, chart, or diagram either because you don't think it's important or because you're in a hurry to get done? If your answer to these questions is "frequently" or "all the time," then you probably also have trouble deciding what to study and are often unprepared for tests. You can turn all this around by studying with a system. Adopt a proven system such as SQ3R, which is explained in this chapter, or create a system that fits your learning style and meets your course requirements.

As explained in Chapter 2, not everyone learns in exactly the same way. Students' preferred learning styles, most productive times of day, and favorite study environments differ. Whatever your preferences, you will learn more and retain information longer if you are actively involved in the

Study system refers to the learning strategies or a process used to access information from reading. One example of a study system is SQ3R.

Acquire information means to gather facts or other data from a source for the purpose of interpreting and communicating what you have learned.

process. A **study system** focuses your attention on certain parts of a textbook or chapter where the most important information is contained. A good study system employs active learning strategies such as questioning and note taking.

Reading and study systems are also helpful in the workplace, where the need to **acquire information** from print or online sources is essential to success in most fields. Whether you need to gather data for a report or a presentation, you can adapt your study system to meet these needs.

AWARENESS CHECK 14

Are You Using Your Textbooks Efficiently?

Part 1

Can you identify and use the parts of a textbook? Match the textbook parts in Column A to their functions in Column B.

Column A

_____ 1. title page

_____ 2. copyright page

_____ 3. contents

_____ 4. introduction

_____ 5. glossary

_____ 6. index

_____ 7. appendix

_____ 8. bibliography

Column B

A. contains supplementary material

B. lists topics, terms, names of people, and their page numbers

C. tells when a book was published

D. lists chapter titles, main headings, and page numbers

E. lists author's sources or references

F. tells author's purpose for writing the book

G. identifies title, author, and publisher

H. contains terms and definitions

Part 2

Can you identify and use the common parts of most textbook chapters? Match the chapter parts in Column A to their functions in Column B.

Column A	Column B
_____ 1. title	A. restates and condenses author's ideas
_____ 2. introduction	B. helps explain or illustrate
_____ 3. heading	C. identifies overall topic covered
_____ 4. graphic aid	D. used for review or skill practice
_____ 5. summary	E. identifies section topic or main idea
_____ 6. questions and exercises	F. states author's purpose and gives overview

Part 3

Yes	No	
☐	☐	**Do you have a study system? Respond *yes* or *no* to the following statements.**
		1. When I sit down to read or study, I often have trouble getting started.
☐	☐	2. My studying is hit or miss. I don't have any set way to study; I do it when and if I have time.
☐	☐	3. I underline or highlight when I read.
☐	☐	4. I know how to tell what is important in a chapter.

Check your answers to Part I: 1.G, 2.C, 3.D, 4.F, 5.H, 6.B, 7.A, 8.E. The answers to Part II are 1.C, 2.F, 3.E, 4.B, 5.A, 6.D. In Part III, if you checked yes for either statement 1 or 2 and no for either statement 3 or 4, you will benefit from learning how to use a study system.

SQ3R: THE BASIC SYSTEM

▶ *Identify and use the common parts of textbooks and chapters as convenient learning and study aids.*

It's easy to see why students who don't read textbook assignments make poor grades. It may be a little harder to see why students who do read all assigned material may still not make the grades they want. There is a big difference between reading and studying. You can't merely read a chapter from first word to last and expect to retain the information. You must read *actively* by underlining, making notes, asking questions mentally, and then looking for the answers. Studying with a system guides your reading so that you can find the information you need to complete assignments and prepare for tests.

Perhaps you've heard of SQ3R. Developed by Francis P. Robinson in 1941, SQ3R is a classic system that millions of students have used successfully to improve their reading and studying. SQ3R is not just a study system; it is an active learning process that includes these five steps: *Survey, Question, Read, Recite,* and *Review.*

Survey

Survey means *preview* or *overview*. The first step of SQ3R is to take a quick survey of a book or chapter to see what it covers.

A **survey** is a quick review or brief overview of an entire textbook or a single chapter. You can survey a textbook in about ten minutes, and you need do it only once to determine what it covers and what helpful aids it contains. This knowledge will help you begin your courses with confidence. Surveying also has a practical advantage beyond the classroom. You can survey *any* book that you are thinking of buying. To survey a work of fiction, read the title and the plot summary to get an idea of what it is about. The plot summary appears on the back of a paperback or inside the jacket of a hardcover book. Read any comments from reviewers to find out what they think of the book. Read the first paragraph to see if the author's style and subject matter arouse your interest. Your survey will help you determine whether you want to read the book. You can also survey books online at sites like http://www.amazon.com or http://www.barnesandnoble.com.

Surveying also has a practical application in the workplace, where a significant amount of information processing occurs. Surveying printed or online materials is a quick way to assess their importance or usefulness.

How to Survey a Textbook. Survey a textbook one time only—as soon as you buy it—before the first chapter is assigned. Then you can start the class with an advantage: You will already know what topics the course is likely to cover. You will also have determined which of the eight common parts your textbook has and how they may be useful to you. For example, if you are taking a biology course, and you find out by surveying your textbook that the book has a glossary, then you know that you will be able to save time while studying. It is much quicker and easier to look up specialized terms in a glossary than in a dictionary. Also, glossary definitions fit the author's use of terms within the context of a book's subject matter.

To survey a textbook, examine its parts in the order in which they appear as you leaf through the book from beginning to end. Figure 8.1, page 193, lists features common to most textbooks, their purposes, and how to survey them.

How to Survey a Textbook Chapter. Survey a chapter before you read it for the first time. Then resurvey chapters that you are reviewing for a major exam. Resurveying material that you have not read for a while will refresh your memory.

Your chapter survey will not take long, it will focus your attention, and it will help you determine a purpose for reading. To survey a chapter, examine its parts in the order in which they appear. Figure 8.2 on page 194 lists the parts of most chapters and a purpose for surveying them.

Surveying helps you make assumptions about what a chapter covers. It is a prereading activity that focuses your attention on a topic. By relating the topic to what you already know, you prepare yourself for the next step in the SQ3R system: asking questions to guide your reading.

Question

During your chapter survey, as you read each heading, turn it into a question. The heading of a section identifies the topic covered in that section and may serve as a clue to the author's main idea. For example, three questions you could ask about the heading "Concentration" are "What is concentration?" "How can I improve my concentration?" and "Why is concentration important?" The "what" question asks you to read for a definition. The "how" and "why" questions stimulate you to think critically about the value of concentration and how to improve it.

FIGURE 8.1

HOW TO SURVEY A TEXTBOOK—FEATURES AND PURPOSES

TEXTBOOK FEATURE	PURPOSE	HOW TO SURVEY
Title Page	Lists title, author, publisher	Look at the title. Ask yourself what the book is about. Find out what you can about the author's qualifications, such as his or her college affiliation or degrees.
Copyright Page	Tells when book was published	Look at the copyright date to see how recent the book is and how many editions there have been. (If the book is in its second edition, it has been updated once.)
Introduction (Preface, To the Student)	Tells author's purpose and audience	Read the introduction to find out why the author wrote the book, for whom, and what the author expects readers to learn. The author may also explain how to use the book.
Table of Contents	Lists parts and chapters	Look over the contents to see what topics are covered. Be thinking about how these topics relate to your course.
Glossary	Lists special words, terms, and definitions	Look for a glossary. If there is one, you should use it for looking up words and terms to learn any special meanings the writer wants you to know.
Appendix	Contains material that supplements topics covered	Look for an appendix to see what additional materials the author has included.
Bibliography	Lists sources the author consulted to write the book	Look for a bibliography. You may need to refer to it later if you need more information.
Index	Lists author's topics alphabetically and their page numbers	Look at the end of the book for the index and use it when you need to find a topic quickly.

Carol C. Kanar, *The Confident Reader*, Second Edition. Copyright © 2000 by Houghton Mifflin Company. Reprinted by permission.

Turning headings into questions guides your reading so that you can find important details and examples. Later, as you read each section carefully, try to find the answers to your guide questions. You may discover that some of your questions are off the topic; but even if they are, you will win. Right or wrong, your questions can help you follow the author's ideas and correct errors in your comprehension.

FIGURE 8.2

HOW TO SURVEY A CHAPTER—FEATURES AND PURPOSES

CHAPTER FEATURE	PURPOSE	HOW TO SURVEY
Title	Tells you what topic the chapter covers	Read title to activate your background knowledge on the topic and create a context for reading.
Objectives or Goals	Tell what the author expects you to learn	Read goals or objectives, if any, to focus your attention on what you need to find out.
Introductory Material	Tells you the author's purpose and central idea	Read first paragraph or introductory section to determine the author's central idea—what the whole chapter explains.
Major Headings and Subheadings	Tell how the central idea is broken down	Read headings and subheadings to reveal the author's organization and major support for the central idea.
Graphic Aids	Illustrate topics or ideas that need clarification	Look over charts, graphs, diagrams, photos, and other visuals.
Key Words and Terms	Call attention to key ideas and concepts	Look for boldface or italicized words or terms. Some may be printed in color or in a different typeface.
Summary	Gives an overview of the author's central idea and supporting information	Read the summary, if there is one, so that you know what to look for when you read the chapter.
Questions or Problems	Ask you to apply concepts or to practice skills covered in the chapter	Read over the questions or problems at the end of the chapter to see what the author expects you to be able to do with the information you have learned.

Carol C. Kanar, *The Confident Reader*, Second Edition. Copyright © 2000 by Houghton Mifflin Company. Reprinted by permission.

EXERCISE 8.1

BORROW A TEXTBOOK FROM A friend who is taking a course that you plan to take. Survey the textbook from beginning to end and then respond to the following items.

Book Title: _____

Name of Course: _____

1. Can you tell from the title whether the book is an introductory text or an advanced text? Explain your answer.

_____

_____

2. How current is the information in the text? In what part of the book did you find your answer?

_____

_____

3. **What is the author's purpose? In what part of the book did you find your answer?**

_____

_____

4. **Where are chapters listed? Write the title of a chapter whose topic interests you.**

_____

_____

5. **Does the book contain a glossary? If so, on what page does it begin?**

_____

_____

6. **Does the book contain a bibliography? If so, on what page does it begin?**

_____

_____

COMPUTER CONFIDENCE

Survey to Save Time on the Net

Surveying is an important prereading step not only for textbooks but also for *any* reading you might do. Surveying before reading on the Internet is yet another practical application of this essential prereading strategy. Whether you are reading your email or researching a topic on the Web, surveying is a time-saving first step that will help you sift through irrelevant data to find desired information quickly.

Survey Email

Log on to the Internet and start your mail program. Any new messages are usually listed by date and time, along with the subject lines of their message headers. Survey the subject lines to determine which messages may be urgent and which ones can wait. Then you can decide which messages to read first, saving the rest for a more convenient time.

Survey Web Sites

As an information-gathering and communication tool, the World Wide Web provides access to resources located throughout the world's libraries, universities, and research institutions. You can browse these resources in search of books, periodicals, and other materials. Because resources are so extensive and because not all Internet connections provide access to the Web, tools such as *search engines* and *web indexes* can help you find information quickly.

A search engine collects, categorizes, and indexes information from web pages, allowing you to generate a list of sites relevant to a subject. You are probably already familiar with Google (http://www.google.com) and Yahoo! (http://www.yahoo.com).

Google evaluates web sites and Internet documents based on the number of links to them from other sites, and it is the largest search engine on the Web. The sites on any list generated are ranked according to their popularity, so the first few listed may be more useful or reliable.

Yahoo! is a popular subject directory that classifies thousands of sites. For most purposes, these two search engines may be all you need. To narrow your search, try AltaVista, Excite, InfoSeek/Go or other search engines that list or organize information in different ways.

Whatever search engine you use, remember two things: When you use a search engine, you are searching only through that engine's collection of documents, not the entire Web. Therefore, it is a good idea to use at least two search engines. Second, a search engine selects documents based on the exact words they contain, so the search words you choose are instrumental in generating a list that is truly useful. Here are some tips for enhancing your use of search engines:

- **Be specific.** A focused search will yield the best results. The more specific your search words are, the more likely it is that your results will accurately reflect what you want. For example the phrase *abnormal psychology* is too general, but *bipolar disorder* focuses the search on one abnormality. Short phrases are usually better than single words, and a phrase that resembles the title of a book or magazine article may produce the best results. Two good examples are *symptoms of bipolar disorder* and *treatments for bipolar disorder.*

- **Use mathematical symbols.** For most search engines, using the plus sign will allow you to find pages that contain all the words in your search phrase: *bipolar disorder + symptoms + treatments.* Use the minus sign to indicate that you don't want to see listings containing a certain word: *bipolar disorder + symptoms – treatments.*

- **Use quotation marks.** If you want listings in which your search words appear in exactly the order that you specify, put them in quotation marks: "*Walt Disney World resort hotels,*" "*World War Two generals,*" and "*Honda motorcycles*" are some examples.

- **Get to know your search engine.** If you have a favorite search engine, learn everything you can about its features and how they work. The more you know about a search engine, the more proficient you will become in using it. Most search engines have a "Help" function that explains their use.

Not all searches are fruitful. If you don't find exactly what you need at first, keep modifying your search words until you get the results you want. Survey your list, looking for words and phrases in the listings that suggest that a site may contain the information you need.

For strategies and tips to help you be more effective using search engines, go to http://searchenginewatch.com, or do your own search for best practices!

EXERCISE 8.2   COMPUTER APPLICATION

TO PRACTICE SURVEYING WEB SITES, try the following two browsing activities. Then discuss your results with the rest of the class.

1. **Many people have web sites and home pages. Find someone on the Net.** Choose a person who interests you: an athlete, an entertainer, a senator or representative, an artist, or an author. Survey the information that is available on the person of your choice, read what interests you, and write a brief summary of it. If you need help getting started, see your instructor or visit your college's computer or media center.

2. **Most colleges and universities have web sites.** A university's home page is a directory to the information available on the site. Find the home page of a university of your choice; then survey the home page to find out what information or courses are offered to help students improve their learning and study skills. If the institution you chose has no such information or courses, try another one. Report your findings to the rest of the class.

EXERCISE 8.3   COLLABORATIVE ACTIVITY

THE PURPOSE OF THIS EXERCISE is for you to practice surveying a textbook chapter with group members. Follow the guidelines for group discussion that appear on the inside back cover. Your tasks are as follows: Select from *The Confident Student* a chapter that you have not yet read. Each person must survey the chapter and write answers to items 1–7 within a time limit of ten minutes. Let one group member serve as timekeeper. Discuss your answers, and compile the best ones on a separate sheet of paper to be handed in along with the group evaluation, or you can download the form at the Online Study Center at college.hmco.com/pic/KanarTCS6e.

Chapter Title: _____

1. **What are the chapter goals or objectives?** _____

   _____

2. **According to the introductory section or paragraph, how will the information contained in this chapter help you?** _____

   _____

   _____

3. **List three major headings and turn each one into a question to guide your reading.**

   Heading   **Questions**

   _____   _____

   _____   _____

   _____   _____

4. **How many visual aids are there? What kind?**

   _____

   _____

5. **List two key words or terms that you should remember.**

   _____

   _____

6. **List a major point that is emphasized in the summary.**

   _____

   _____

7. **What skill or topic is covered in the first exercise?**

   _____

   _____

Group Evaluation:
What have you learned about surveying? Is surveying a strategy that you will use? Why or why not? Did your group complete its tasks successfully? What improvements can you suggest? What additional questions do you have about surveying? How will you find answers to your questions?

Online Study Center
Chapter Exercises/
Forms

Read

Read slowly and carefully, concentrating on one section at a time. Don't worry about how long you take. Although you may wish you could read faster, it takes time to absorb new ideas. Do not skip unfamiliar words or technical terms. If you can't infer their meanings from context, look them up in the book's glossary or in a dictionary. Then, be sure to reread the sentence in which each new word appears to make sure that you understand it. Carefully examine each diagram, chart, illustration, table, or other visual aid. Often, ideas that are hard to understand when you first read about them are easier to comprehend in a diagram or other graphic.

After reading, try to determine the main idea of the section. Summarize this idea in a marginal note that will aid your recall when you review. Read through the section again and underline the main idea and key details or examples. If you have difficulty deciding what is important, see Chapter 13 for a complete explanation of how and what to underline or highlight.

If a section seems particularly technical or complex, you may have to read it more than once. You may also have to restate the author's ideas in your own words to get the information into your long-term memory. Chapter 9 explains how to make study guides to aid your recall.

Making notes, underlining or highlighting, and constructing study guides are essential steps of active reading. They help you think critically about what you read, make studying a productive activity, and enhance memory.

Recite

Recitation is an essential aid to memory. After reading a section, try to state—aloud or silently—the important ideas covered in that section. If you find this hard to do, you probably have not understood the section and need to reread it.

Before you sign up for a course, visit the campus bookstore to survey the text the instructor has chosen. This will enable you to see what the course will cover and whether the level of the material is suited to your background and skills.

However, if the important ideas stand out, then you are probably comprehending what you read. Reciting not only increases your memory's power; it also helps you monitor your comprehension.

Review

Review a chapter immediately after reading it. One quick way to review it is by resurveying the chapter. Go over any notes you made in the margins and see if they still make sense to you. Reread any underlined or highlighted passages. Also, review a chapter before you take a test. It is a good idea to review a chapter at least once between your first reading and your last pretest review. With practice, you will discover how often you must review a chapter in order to keep the information in your long-term memory.

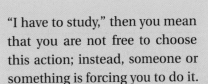

CONFIDENCE BUILDER

Be Proactive about Studying

Stephen R. Covey, author of *The Seven Habits of Highly Effective People*, says that people are either proactive or reactive in their responses to life's circumstances. *Proactive* people take initiative and accept responsibility for what happens to them. *Reactive* people lack initiative; instead of taking responsibility for what happens, they blame other people or outside events. The first and most important of Covey's seven habits is to *be proactive*. Being proactive means being in control of how you feel, what you think, and what you do. Being proactive means accepting responsibility for your own success or failure. Being proactive also means choosing your actions, accepting the consequences, and modifying your behavior as needed to achieve success.

When it comes to studying, are you *reactive* or *proactive?* Language is a key. The language of reactive people, according to Covey, relieves them of responsibility. For example, if you say, "I can't make a good grade in that class," then you are saying that you are not responsible. Rather, someone or something is preventing you from making good grades in the class. If you say, "I don't have time to study," instead of managing your time, you are allowing the factor of limited time to control you. If you say,

"I have to study," then you mean that you are not free to choose this action; instead, someone or something is forcing you to do it.

To be proactive about studying, you must first take control of your language. The following is an example of how language can either limit or expand your horizons. When you say, "I can't make a good grade in that class," you convince yourself that there is no reason to try. As a result, you give up. You stop studying. The belief that you can't make a good grade becomes a self-fulfilling prophecy. But if you become proactive and instead say, "I choose to make good grades in that class," then you realize that grades are the result of your own decisions and your own effort. You can then accurately assess what your strengths and weaknesses are and choose appropriate study systems or learning strategies that will get you the results that you want.

The following chart lists reactive statements about studying and their proactive counterparts. Use the chart to assess your own language. Ask yourself, "Am I reactive or proactive?" Then take steps to modify your language and behavior as needed.

Reactive Statements	Proactive statements
I don't have time to study	I can make time for studying.
I have to study.	I can choose whether, when, and how to study.
I must pass this test.	I will study and do my best to pass this test.
I'm just no good at math.	I can improve my math skills.
I can't understand this chapter.	I will use a study system to understand this chapter.
My instructor gave me a B on the test.	I earned a B on the test.

How does Covey's advice, *be proactive*, relate to locus of control? Those who have an external locus of control are *reactive* because they expect others to motivate them. Those who have an internal locus of control are *proactive* because they are self-motivated. How does proactivity relate to goal setting, time management, and problem solving? In every case, the proactive response of selecting a desired outcome and taking the steps necessary to achieve it puts *you* in control of your life and learning. With control comes confidence and increased self-esteem.

To learn more about this topic, do an online search using the keywords *Stephen R. Covey, Seven Habits of Highly Effective People, motivation,* and *values.* Also see Covey's latest book *The 8th Habit.*

Online Study Center
Confidence Builder
Web Search

UNDERSTANDING GRAPHICS

> *Learn the role that textbook graphics play, and follow guidelines for reading graphics with understanding.*

Textbooks and other printed sources of information are filled with graphics that are essential to your understanding of what you read. Graphics condense and summarize a great deal of information. Graphics illustrate relationships among ideas, and they provide a visual supplement to the text they accompany. Make reading graphics an important part of your study system. Figure 8.3, on pages 202–203, shows five common types of graphics you can learn to recognize.

Circle or "Pie" Charts. Pie charts illustrate part-to-whole relationships. Slices of the pie represent amounts and percentages. The size of each slice in relation to the other slices and to the whole pie indicates its significance. For example, where a student's monthly income goes could be illustrated on a pie chart, with each slice representing a different expenditure.

Bar Graphs. Bar graphs illustrate relationships between *variables,* or quantities, such as time and amount. They also show trends such as an increase or decrease in amount over a period of time. One variable is measured on a vertical axis; the other variable is measured on a horizontal axis.

Line Graphs. Like bar graphs, line graphs illustrate relationships among variables. Trends are represented by lines instead of bars or columns. Voter turnout among different age groups over several presidential elections could be illustrated by either a line graph or a bar graph.

Diagrams. Diagrams are drawings that illustrate functions or processes. A *process diagram* may illustrate the steps and stages of a process or trace a sequence of events. The stages of pregnancy and the events that occur during cell division are two examples. *Function diagrams* illustrate parts of a whole, such as the separate bones of a skeleton.

Tables. Tables are organized lists or rows of numbers or text. They classify and compare large amounts of information or statistical data. A table that lists contraceptive methods and their rates of effectiveness is one example.

To read a graphic with understanding, determine its *purpose*, discover what *relationship* of ideas it illustrates, and read the *text* that accompanies it. To help you recall these steps, remember the acronym **PRT:**

1. To determine the **purpose,** read the title of the graphic and its caption for any clues they may provide.

2. To help you discover the **relationship,** determine the graphic's type. For example, if you have identified a graphic as a process diagram, then determine what process is illustrated, trace the steps, and understand what happens at each stage.

3. For an explanation of the graphic, read the **text** that accompanies it. For each part of the explanation in the text, find its counterpart in the graphic. To test yourself, recite the explanation in your own words while looking at the graphic. Then close your eyes and visualize the graphic.

C R I T I C A L   T H I N K I N G

Exercise Overview

This exercise will help you apply what you have learned about the importance of graphics and how to read them.

Exercise Background

Charts, tables, diagrams, and photographs are not just filler. They play an important role in a textbook chapter, illustrating complex ideas in a visual way that makes them easier to remember. A single graphic may summarize and condense concepts or idea relationships that take pages to explain in detail. However, you need to read both the graphic and its explanation in the text to get the full picture.

Exercise Task

Choose a graphic from one of your textbooks. Using PRT (purpose, relationship, text), read the graphic and interpret its meaning by answering the following questions.

1. What is the graphic's title?

2. Is there a caption? If so, summarize its contents.

3. Based on your answers to questions 1 and 2, what is the graphic's purpose?

4. What type of graphic have you chosen?

5. Based on your answer to question 4, what idea relationship does the graphic illustrate?

6. What is the connection between the graphic and the text that accompanies it?

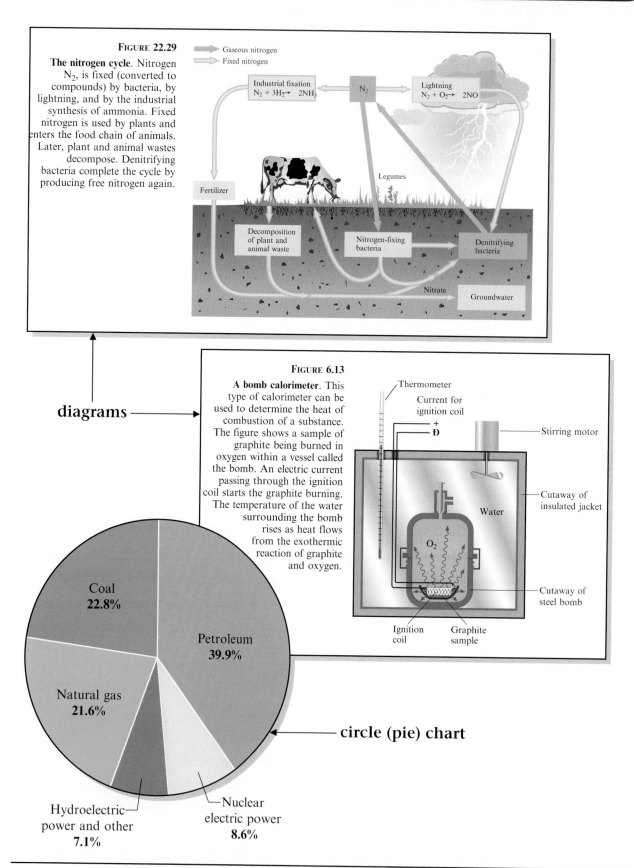

Figure 22.29

The nitrogen cycle. Nitrogen N₂, is fixed (converted to compounds) by bacteria, by lightning, and by the industrial synthesis of ammonia. Fixed nitrogen is used by plants and enters the food chain of animals. Later, plant and animal wastes decompose. Denitrifying bacteria complete the cycle by producing free nitrogen again.

Gaseous nitrogen
Fixed nitrogen

Industrial fixation $N_2 + 3H_2 \rightarrow 2NH_3$

N_2

Lightning $N_2 + O_2 \rightarrow 2NO$

Fertilizer

Legumes

Decomposition of plant and animal waste

Nitrogen-fixing bacteria

Denitrifying bacteria

Nitrate

Groundwater

diagrams

Figure 6.13

A bomb calorimeter. This type of calorimeter can be used to determine the heat of combustion of a substance. The figure shows a sample of graphite being burned in oxygen within a vessel called the bomb. An electric current passing through the ignition coil starts the graphite burning. The temperature of the water surrounding the bomb rises as heat flows from the exothermic reaction of graphite and oxygen.

Thermometer

Current for ignition coil

Stirring motor

Cutaway of insulated jacket

Water

O_2

Cutaway of steel bomb

Ignition coil

Graphite sample

Coal
22.8%

Petroleum
39.9%

Natural gas
21.6%

circle (pie) chart

Hydroelectric power and other
7.1%

Nuclear electric power
8.6%

Source: Figures from Darrell Ebbing, *General Chemistry*, Eighth Edition. Copyright © 2005 by Houghton Mifflin Company. Used with permission.

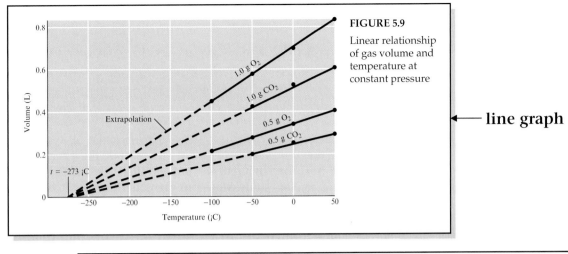

FIGURE 5.9
Linear relationship of gas volume and temperature at constant pressure

← line graph

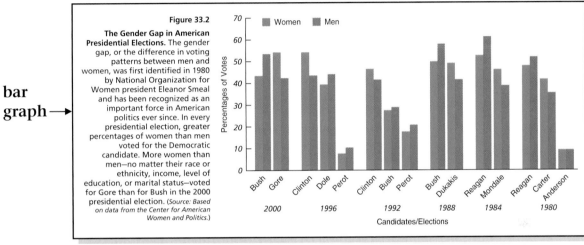

Figure 33.2

The Gender Gap in American Presidential Elections. The gender gap, or the difference in voting patterns between men and women, was first identified in 1980 by National Organization for Women president Eleanor Smeal and has been recognized as an important force in American politics ever since. In every presidential election, greater percentages of women than men voted for the Democratic candidate. More women than men—no matter their race or ethnicity, income, level of education, or marital status—voted for Gore than for Bush in the 2000 presidential election. (*Source: Based on data from the Center for American Women and Politics.*)

bar graph →

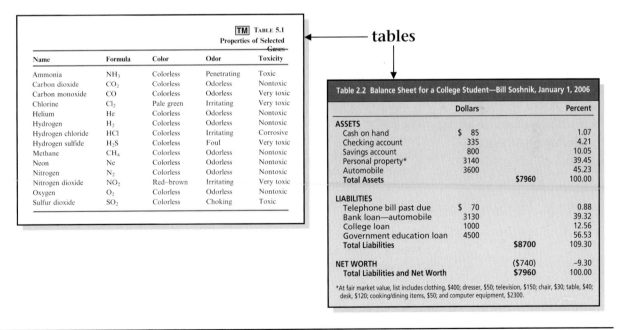

tables

Fig. 5.9 and Table 5.1 from Darrell Ebbing, *General Chemistry*, Eighth Edition. Copyright © 2005 by Houghton Mifflin Company. Used with permission. Figure 33.2 from Norton, *A People and a Nation*, Vol. 2: Since 1895, Seventh Edition, Copyright © 2005 by Houghton Mifflin Company. Used with permission. Table 2.2 from Thomas E. Garman and Raymond E. Forgue, *Personal Finance*, Eighth Edition. Copyright © 2006 by Houghton Mifflin Company. Used with permission.

HOW TO CREATE YOUR STUDY SYSTEM

> *Start with a basic system like SQ3R and adapt it to your learning style. Vary the system's steps to meet the reading and study needs of different courses.*

No one has discovered the best way to learn because no system works best for everyone all the time. Most systems are variations on the basic one, SQ3R. The best system for *you* is one that reflects your learning style and is a good fit for the material that you need to study. Most important, be committed to active learning and use your system consistently. Try SQ3R as is or make slight variations in its steps to create your own best system for studying the material in any course.

Ways to vary SQ3R may take into account whether you prefer to study alone or with someone else and whether you prefer visual, verbal, auditory, or tactile modes of learning. For example, if you prefer to study with someone, do your surveying, questioning, and reading on your own but recite and review with a study partner. If you prefer auditory modes of instruction, tape the material you want to review—a list of vocabulary words and definitions, for example—and then listen to the tape. If you prefer visual modes of learning, make charts, diagrams, and illustrations for review. If taking notes from textbooks and outlining are strategies that work for you, by all means, use them. You will have to resort to these strategies if you are studying from library books or materials your professor has put on reserve.

Connect and reflect is a review process. Connect new information with prior knowledge and reflect on ways to use the information.

As part of your review for any course, **connect and reflect**. Make connections between what you already know and what you have learned. How does the new information add to or change what you already know? Reflect on ways to use new information or apply it in different contexts. For example, use the research and writing skills acquired in a composition class to write papers and compile reports due in other classes. Use the information learned in one course as a source of topics for writing papers in other courses. The interpersonal skills that you learn in a business course may improve your relations with others at work. The skills learned in an accounting course may help you improve the way you keep track of your spending. Through connection and reflection, you can personalize what you have learned, making the information your own so that you are less likely to forget it.

CONCEPT CHECK 8.2

Can you connect and reflect? Think about a skill or process that you have learned recently. How has your new knowledge affected the way that you think or act? How will you use the skill or process? What will it help you accomplish?

Once you have settled on a study system that works, use it consistently. Knowing that you have a study system will make you feel confident that you can learn and remember. Also, if you are like many students and have trouble getting started when you try to study, a study system will provide the starting point you need. Figure 8.4 on page 205 lists ways to vary the SQ3R study system to meet specific course needs. It shows that surveying, questioning, and reading, reciting, and reviewing are essential for studying every subject. Variations in the system can be made in the way you apply the steps or in the addition of a step. As you become more comfortable using a study system, you will think of many more variations. Some of them may be better for you than those suggested in this chapter because they will be based on your learning style.

FIGURE 8.4

VARY THE STEPS OF SQ3R TO MEET SPECIFIC NEEDS

DISCIPLINE	WHAT TO STUDY FROM THE TEXTBOOK	STEPS TO ADD OR EXPAND
Math	• Sample problems and solutions • Mathematical rules and procedures	• Add a **practice** step for solving problems. • Expand the **recite** and **review** steps for making flash cards of rules, terms, and procedures to study.
Science	• Scientific theories and breakthroughs • Scientists and their discoveries • Laws and principles of science • Experiments that illustrate key concepts	• Add a **draw** step for making diagrams of processes that you can use as study guides. • Expand the **recite** and **review** steps by making flash cards of terms, formulas, and principles to study. • Add a **write** step to summarize experiments: who did it, what they found, and why.
Social Science	• Theories of behavior and personality • Names of people who developed the theories • Key experiments that test the theories	• Add a **write** step for summarizing theories: Briefly explain the theory, who developed it, and its significance and limitations. • Expand the **review** step to include experiments: who was involved, what they found, and why it is important.
History	• Important people and events • Important documents and their significance • Laws and policies	• Add a **draw** step for making time lines that help you trace events. • Add a **write** step for summarizing the significance of documents, laws, or policies.
Literature	• Names of authors and their works • Types of fiction: similarities and differences • Literary terms • The elements of fiction: plot, characters, setting, theme, point of view, style and tone	• Expand the **recite** and **review** steps by making flash cards of literary terms to study. • Add a **draw** step for making plot time lines to review. • Add a **write** step for explaining themes and their significance.
Languages	• Words and meanings • Pronunciation • Verb conjugations • Spelling and grammar rules	• Add a **draw** step for making conjugation charts. • Add a **write** step to practice translating from one language to another. • Expand **recite** and **review** to include flash cards of words and meanings, spelling, and grammar rules to study.

EXERCISE 8.4 LEARNING STYLE

READ THE NEXT ASSIGNED CHAPTER in one of your textbooks and try out the SQ3R study system. When you have finished, answer *yes* or *no* to questions 1–7; then write your answers to questions 8–10.

YES NO

☐ ☐ 1. Did surveying the chapter before reading it give you an idea of what the chapter would cover?

☐ ☐ 2. Were you able to formulate questions from the headings to guide your reading?

☐ ☐ 3. Did you find answers to most of your questions as you read each section?

☐ ☐ 4. After doing the reading, did you know what to underline?

☐ ☐ 5. Did you make any marginal notes?

☐ ☐ 6. Did you find any material that would be easier to understand if you were to diagram it to make it more visual?

☐ ☐ 7. After reciting and reviewing, did you have a thorough understanding of the information contained in the chapter?

8. Did you vary the SQ3R system? If so, how and why?

_____

_____

9. Given your learning style, is SQ3R an effective system for you? Why or why not?

_____

_____

10. How can you adapt SQ3R to fit your learning style?

_____

_____

Thinking ahead about Career

Purpose and Instructions

A workplace focus in Chapter 8 is on acquiring information. Use the knowledge you have gained from this chapter to solve work-related problems such as the one explained in the following case study. Read the case study on your own or with a partner and then answer the case questions.

Case Study

To support himself while attending college, Samuel works as a research assistant at a local newspaper. His job is to research a topic, read relevant articles and reports, and then summarize them for his boss. Samuel has good library and Internet skills, so he has no trouble finding the information he needs. However, reading the articles is difficult for him. Samuel loses interest in some of the topics, and he always has trouble remembering what he has read. He spends a lot of time rereading material, so it takes him forever to get his work done. He is worried that his college assignments may suffer as a result. "You need a reading system," said a friend of his. "Why?" asked Samuel. "Reading is reading."

Case Questions

1. **What is Samuel's problem?**

   _____

   _____

2. **What are Samuel's strengths and weaknesses?**

   _____

   _____

3. **What strategies would you suggest that Samuel try, and why?**

   _____

   _____

4. **Access the Career Resource Center and read the article entitled "When Reading is Tough" in the** *Building Learning Strategies* **section of** *The Bridge*. **Based on this article, what additional advice can you give Samuel?**

   _____

   _____

Your *Reflections*

Reflect on what you have learned from this chapter about study systems and how you can use them to acquire information and enhance learning. Use the following questions to stimulate your thinking; then write your reflections. Include in your writing specific information from the chapter.

- Describe the way that you study now. Does your system work? What can you do to improve it?
- What course gives you the most trouble? What have you learned from this chapter that will improve the way you study for that course?
- Are you taking a course in a discipline that is not listed in Figure 8.4? If so, how can you adapt SQ3R to improve the way you study?
- What is one skill or attitude explained in this chapter that you would like to develop, and what can you begin doing today to make that happen?

_____

_____

_____

_____

_____

_____

_____

_____

_____

_____

_____

_____

_____

_____

_____

Chapter review

To review the chapter, reflect on the following confidence-building attitudes and skills. Complete **Concepts to Understand** by filling in the blanks with words or terms from the list provided. Then practice your new skills at every opportunity.

ATTITUDES TO DEVELOP
- commitment to learning
- consistency of effort
- willingness to persist

SKILLS TO PRACTICE
- using textbook and chapter study aids
- using the SQ3R system
- creating your own system

CONCEPTS TO UNDERSTAND

learning style	survey	index	summary	reflect
headings	SQ3R	connect	graphic aids	system

Is your textbook an indispensable tool or dead weight in your backpack? To get the most out of a textbook chapter, read and study with a system such as (1) _____, the classic system. Always (2) _____ a chapter before you read it. To read actively, turn (3) _____ into questions; then look for the answers as you read.

Your textbooks contain many helpful aids. Looking up an item in the (4) _____ saves time. A chapter (5) _____ is useful for either prereading or review because it focuses your attention on the chapter's key ideas. Students often overlook (6) _____, which condense and summarize complex ideas in visual formats. Familiarize yourself with the common parts of textbooks and chapters and use them to enhance learning.

Studying with a (7) _____ enhances memory and is an efficient way to acquire information. You can use a proven system or create a variation that reflects your (8) _____ and is tailored to the material. Whatever system you use, remember to (9) _____ and (10) _____ as part of your review process.

To access additional review exercises, go to **college.hmco.com/pic/KanarTCS6e.**

Online Study Center
Review Exercise
ACE Self-Test

Online Study Center

Prepare for Class, Improve Your Grade, and ACE the Test. This chapter's *Student Achievement* resources include

Chapter exercises/forms   Review exercise   Confidence Builder Web search
ACE Self-Test

To access these learning and study tools, go to **college.hmco.com/pic/KanarTCS6e.**

9 Organizing information for study

Chart your course to better grades.

Show the relationship between general and specific ideas in a visual format.

Organize information by categories to compare their similarities and differences.

Trace a sequence of events or stages of development through time.

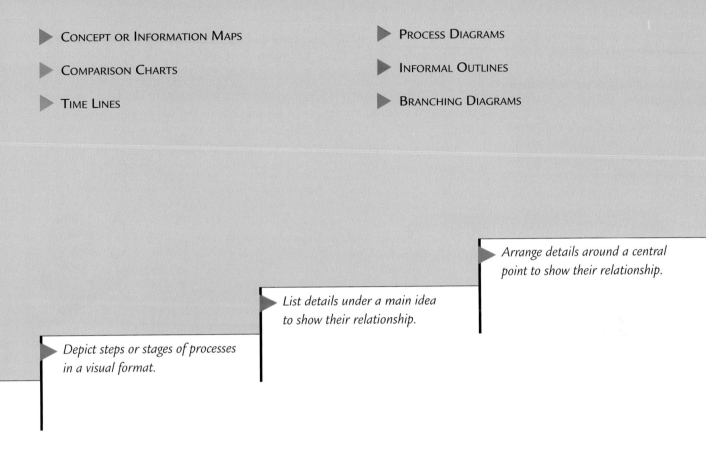

CONCEPT OR INFORMATION MAPS

COMPARISON CHARTS

TIME LINES

PROCESS DIAGRAMS

INFORMAL OUTLINES

BRANCHING DIAGRAMS

Arrange details around a central point to show their relationship.

List details under a main idea to show their relationship.

Depict steps or stages of processes in a visual format.

Memorizing lists of facts, concepts, and other important information may not be the most effective way to study. For example, you could memorize the definitions of the terms *id, ego,* and *superego,* but would that help you understand Freud's theory of personality and how the id, ego, and superego interact to affect human behavior? Would learning only the definitions of Freud's terms help you to explain how Freud's theory compares with other personality theories or what the limitations of his theory are? Probably not.

One good way to study Freud's theory is to make a chart that lists his components of personality, a brief explanation of each, and an example showing how each affects behavior. In making such a chart, what have you done? You have restructured the information in a format that gives it meaning. Your chart is called a **graphic organizer,** of which there are many types.

Diagrams, charts, and other organizers have three advantages. First, they condense information into smaller, meaningful chunks that are easier to

Graphic organizer refers to any type of chart, table, diagram, or other format for grouping ideas to show their relationship.

KEY TERMS

graphic organizer, *p. 211*
linear, *p. 214*
spatial, *p. 214*
hierarchy, *p. 215*

SCANS TERMS

organizational skill, *p. 212*
decision making, *p. 212*

Organizational skill as an information competency refers to your ability to find and organize data in meaningful ways both for your own use and for communication to others.

Decision making is a critical thinking skill you will use for solving problems and for other tasks where choosing among alternatives is involved.

remember than an author's exact words. Second, they help you visualize relationships among ideas. Third, the process of deciding what is important and choosing the best organizer for your purpose builds **organizational skill,** an information competency, and provides experience in **decision making,** a thinking skill. Both are essential for success in the workplace as well as in college.

This chapter explains how to make six types of organizers for efficient and productive study.

AWARENESS CHECK 15

How Well Do You Organize Information for Study?

The following Awareness Check will help you determine whether you are getting all the information you can out of your textbooks and using it effectively for studying, remembering, and recalling what you have learned. Check the statements that apply to you.

1. ☐ Part of my textbook study includes making some type of study guide to help me remember important information.

2. ☐ I rarely, if ever, outline chapters or make study guides.

3. ☐ When I make notes from textbooks, I don't copy the information directly; I put it into my own words.

4. ☐ If I make notes, I usually copy directly from the text.

5. ☐ I have tried or heard about information maps and other ways of organizing information.

6. ☐ I am not aware of ways to organize information. I study by rereading textbook chapters or reviewing my lecture notes.

7. ☐ I can usually decide what is important in a chapter, and that is what I study.

8. ☐ I have difficulty deciding what is important in a chapter, so I try to study all of it.

9. ☐ Overall, I would say that my method of studying from textbooks is effective.

10. ☐ Overall, I think that my method of studying from textbooks needs improvement.

If you checked mostly odd-numbered statements, you are probably already using an effective method of organizing information from textbooks. If you checked mostly even-numbered statements, you may want to try some of the helpful organizers suggested in this chapter. Although no one of them is necessarily better than the others, you may discover one that works best for you.

CONFIDENCE BUILDER

Attitudes for Study

Reading and studying take time; there are no shortcuts, only efficient study techniques. To make the most of your study time, use proven strategies and develop the confidence-building attitudes of commitment and persistence. What are these attitudes, and what do they have to do with studying?

Commitment. A commitment is a pledge. For example, in marriage, a couple pledge to love one another. Similarly, people who pledge their money and time to support a cause are committed. In academic terms an *attitude of commitment* means a willingness to pledge your time and effort to reach your goals. For example, if you are committed to success, then you will adopt the behaviors that promote success such as regular attendance, sufficient preparation, and studying. Commitment also involves desire. Therefore, if you know what you want and how to get it, and you are willing to set goals, then you have the attitude of commitment.

Persistence. Persistence is *the willingness to sustain effort over time, even in the face of difficulty*. Remember when you learned to ride a bicycle or drive a car? These skills took time to master. But no matter how many times you fell off the bike or how many times you had to practice parking and backing up the car, finally you learned to ride or drive. Finally, you got your license. That took persistence. Moreover, you were committed to learn because you *desired* having those skills and the freedom they would give you. In academic terms, an attitude of persistence means a willingness to try out new strategies and to practice new skills as often as necessary until you achieve mastery. Persistence means not giving up in the face of failure but instead analyzing your mistakes to see what went wrong, then trying again. Through commitment and persistence, you can take control of your learning. Here are seven suggestions:

1. Choose success. Commit yourself to the idea that you will succeed.

2. Be self-motivated. Think about why you are in college. Look to the future. Where do you want to be in five years? What is your dream job or career? Let your desires be your motivators.

3. Set goals. Dreams don't come true without planning and effort. Set long-term goals (complete requirements for my major), set short-term goals (attain a 3.0 GPA this semester; earn an A on the next assignment), and make action plans to reach them. Commit yourself to the plans and then follow through.

4. Remember that each day, each assignment or each test brings you closer to achieving your goals. Make them all count. Put forth your best effort.

5. Try out the strategies that you are learning. They won't do you any good if you read about them and then forget about them. For SQ3R or any study system to work, you have to use it consistently so that it becomes second nature. When surveying before you read becomes a habit, when you read with a pencil or other marker in your hand, and when you take time to review after *every* time you read, you will see your understanding grow and your memory increase. Like SQ3R, making organizers is an *active* process that involves you in learning. The value of both of these methods is that they involve all your concentration, making it less likely that a part of your brain will be on vacation while you are attempting to study.

6. Don't give up. Suppose you have made a bad grade, or you think you aren't making progress. Perhaps more practice is needed, or perhaps you need to try a new strategy. Seek help and be persistent.

7. Turn to your learning community. You are not alone. Other students are experiencing the same successes and failures that you are. Form a study group. Find out from others what works and doesn't work for them. Then revise your plans or methods as needed. Remember, *you* are in control.

The attitudes of commitment and persistence also have a workplace connection. Being committed to a company's goals and being persistent in your efforts to reach them make you a valued employee. To pursue the topic of attitudes and how they affect your academic, personal, and career goals, do an online search using these keywords as a starting point: *interpersonal skills, Character Counts Coalition, positive thinking, self-efficacy.*

Online Study Center
Confidence Builder
Web Search

Linear means sequential, or following in order, one after another.

Spatial means organized visually, by position in space.

CONCEPT OR INFORMATION MAPS

> *Show the relationship between general and specific ideas in a visual format.*

Unlike an outline, which is a **linear,** or sequential, listing of main ideas and supporting details, a *concept or information map* is a **spatial,** or visual, breakdown of a topic that may not be sequential. But like an outline, a map breaks down the information from general to specific concepts or ideas. If your learning style is visual, you may prefer information maps to outlines. To construct an information map, first identify the topic and write it in a box. Identify the ideas that relate to the topic and write them in connecting boxes to show their relationship to the topic.

Read the following paragraph. Then study the concept map shown in Figure 9.1.

*Television advertisers use five common fallacies, among others, to manipulate viewers' attitudes toward their products and to get them to buy. **Glittering generalities** are words and phrases that make viewers respond favorably to a product. Phrases such as "no preservatives," "low fat and cholesterol," or "97% fat free" associated with food products make people believe they're getting something that is healthful. **Transfer** is a fallacious type of reasoning whereby a product is related to an idea or activity with which the viewer is likely to identify. Restaurant*

CONCEPT MAP

FIGURE 9.1

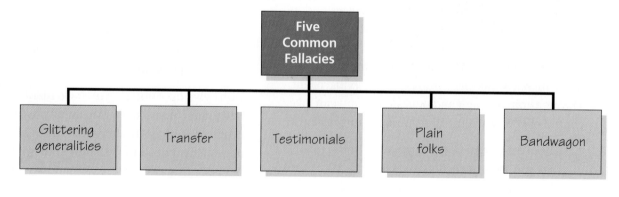

*commercials are a good example of transfer. Families are shown having a good time in a restaurant, or a young couple is depicted in a romantic cafe. Viewers are supposed to get the idea that if they eat at these restaurants, they will become like the happy families and couples in these ads. Many advertisers use **testimonials** of famous people to endorse their products. A film star advocates the use of one brand of shampoo. A sports celebrity endorses a company's athletic shoes. Some advertisers use **plain folks,** people the audience can identify with, to sell products; others encourage viewers to jump on the **bandwagon** and buy a product because "everybody does it." Viewers need to pay attention to ads and sift the hype from the facts. Of course, they can always press the mute button on their remote control unit.*

The map shown in Figure 9.1 is very simple. It breaks down the topic *Five Common Fallacies* into its five supporting details, providing the key term for each one. For a more detailed map, you could attach two more boxes to each of the five detail boxes. In one you could write a definition of the term; in the other you could write an example of your own that is similar to one given in the paragraph. Concept maps can break down ideas as far as you need to in order to show how they relate.

In some material, an order of importance, or **hierarchy,** is stated or implied. When that is the case, your map must show that one concept is more important than another or that one stage precedes another.

Read the next paragraph. Then look at Figure 9.2 for two ways to map the information.

*Abraham Maslow was a psychologist who believed that five basic needs motivate human behavior. In Maslow's view, low-level needs have to be at least partially satisfied before higher-level needs can be met. At the bottom of Maslow's hierarchy are **biological** needs for food, oxygen, water, and sleep. At the next level are **safety** needs: the need for shelter and clothing and the need to protect oneself from harm. Working to satisfy safety needs consumes the energy of many people. When safety needs are met, the need for **belongingness and love**—the desire for affection and the need to feel part of a group or society—asserts itself. At the next-to-highest*

Hierarchy means an arrangement by order of importance or rank.

CONCEPT CHECK 9.1

Hierarchy within organizations refers to the ranking of jobs or positions. Your college administration is a hierarchy with the board of trustees at the top, followed by your college president, and so on. What other hierarchies can you describe?

TWO WAYS TO MAP MASLOW'S HIERARCHY OF NEEDS

FIGURE 9.2

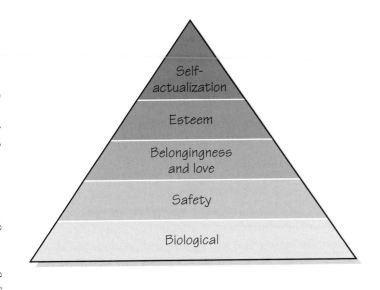

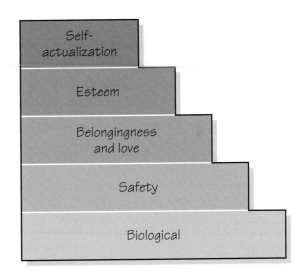

EXERCISE 9.1

FROM ONE OF YOUR TEXTBOOKS, select some material that is hierarchically arranged—that is, arranged in a certain order from lowest to highest or most important to least important. Map this information to clearly show the hierarchy. Use the pyramid or staircase pattern illustrated in Figure 9.2 or devise a pattern of your own. Then share your map with the rest of the class.

*level is the need for **esteem,** or recognition by others of one's self-worth and achievements. At the top of Maslow's hierarchy is **self-actualization,** the need to achieve one's fullest potential as a human being. Maslow believed that only a few people, such as Jesus or Gandhi, have ever achieved self-actualization, though everyone has the potential to do so.*

Notice how the pyramid and the staircase shown in Figure 9.2 on page 215 effectively illustrate the hierarchy of needs that Maslow described. The staircase and pyramid are common patterns that you can use to represent any hierarchical arrangement of ideas.

To study from an information map, look it over a few times. Read the information you have diagrammed. Then close your eyes and try to picture the diagram. If you were studying the staircase of Maslow's needs, for example, you would picture the staircase and visualize each need falling into place on the appropriate stair. During a test, you would visualize your map to recall the information.

COMPARISON CHARTS

> *Organize information by categories to compare their similarities and differences.*

Comparison charts organize facts and other information into categories according to similarities and differences or group characteristics. A comparison chart enables you to take information out of context and reorganize it in a way that makes sense to you. Furthermore, a comparison chart arranges information visually, allowing you to *see* relationships among categories and to compare information that is sorted into each category. If your learning style is visual, you may enjoy making and using comparison charts as study guides. Read the following annotated paragraph and examine the comparison chart shown in Figure 9.3. The annotations show how one student thought through the information explained in the paragraph before making a comparison chart.

Main idea: 3 purposes for writing	*An author may have one of three major purposes for writing. Authors who want to* (inform) *the reader present facts in an objective way and cover all sides of a topic. Their language is usually formal, and their goal is to explain or*

Main idea:
3 purposes for writing

1st: inform
2nd: entertain

3rd: persuade

Purpose determines language, goals, type of material.

An author may have one of three major purposes for writing. Authors who want to (inform) *the reader present facts in an objective way and cover all sides of a topic. Their language is usually formal, and their goal is to explain or instruct. Informational writing is characteristic of textbooks, periodicals, and scholarly journals. Authors whose purpose is to* (entertain) *are, primarily, storytellers. Their language may be formal or informal, but it is always descriptive. To amuse, delight, and engage the reader's imagination are goals of writers who want to entertain. They write short stories, novels, essays, and poems. Authors whose purpose is to* (persuade) *have taken a stand on an issue of importance to their readers. These authors may attempt to inflame their readers with emotional language. Their prose is a mix of fact and opinion, and they may slant evidence in their favor. Their goal is to change readers' minds; they speak out from books, from the editorial pages of newspapers, and from popular magazines. Authors' purposes may determine what they write, how they write, and for whom they write.*

Figure 9.3 shows the relationship among three purposes for writing and compares their similarities and differences in three categories: the language, goals, and type of material best suited to each purpose. Read down the chart for purposes; read across for a comparison of similarities and differences.

A comparison chart lets you organize a lot of information into a relatively small and compact format that you can put in a notebook for frequent review. You may be able to draw comparison charts on 5" × 7" note cards, which are even easier to carry with you.

COMPARISON CHART

FIGURE 9.3

An Author's Three Purposes

	Inform	Entertain	Persuade
Language	Usually formal	Formal or informal; descriptive	May be emotional, slanted
Goals	To explain or instruct	To amuse, delight, engage imagination	To change reader's mind
Type of Material	Textbooks, periodicals, journals	Short stories, novels, poems, essays	Books, editorials, magazine articles

EXERCISE 9.2

READ THE PASSAGE THAT FOLLOWS. Then organize the important information on the comparison chart, which is partially filled in. Give the chart a title that indicates what the paragraph is about.

Several types of social groups play important roles in our lives. Sociologists study two major types of social groups.

Primary groups *are small, and people's relationships within these groups are intimate and personal. Examples of primary groups include families, teams, friends, and lovers. The function of these groups is to act as a buffer against the larger society. You can always come back to a primary group and find security and acceptance.*

Secondary groups *may be either small or large. They are usually organized around a task or a goal, and relationships within them are usually impersonal. Examples of secondary groups include the military, businesses, colleges, and universities. The purpose of these groups is to help you reach a goal or accomplish some type of work. These groups remain fairly impersonal in order to get their work done, but it is possible to develop close relationships with members of your secondary group.*

Title: _____

Type	Size	Relationships		
Primary groups				Families, teams
		Usually impersonal		

TIME LINES

> *Trace a sequence of events or stages of development through time.*

Time lines are effective organizers for material that is presented chronologically. They are especially useful for visualizing a historical development or a sequence of events. Review a time line by looking at it and reciting the events in order. Then close your eyes and try to visualize the events as positions on the line.

To make a time line, draw a vertical or horizontal line. Divide the line into sections. On one side of the line, write dates; on the other side, write events that correspond to the dates. Give your time line a title that summarizes what it covers, as shown in Figure 9.4.

TIME LINE

FIGURE 9.4

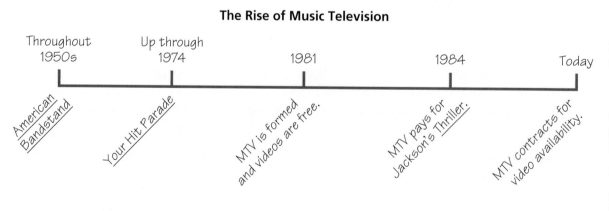

The Rise of Music Television

Throughout 1950s — American Bandstand
Up through 1974 — Your Hit Parade
1981 — MTV is formed and videos are free.
1984 — MTV pays for Jackson's Thriller.
Today — MTV contracts for video availability.

Graphic organizers not only make good study guides; they are also useful for supplementing oral presentations.

PROCESS DIAGRAMS

▶ *Depict steps or stages of processes in a visual format.*

Processes are methods, steps, and stages that describe how events occur. They are an essential part of most courses. In a biology class, you learn how diseases are transmitted or how food is processed in the human body. In a political science class, you learn how a bill becomes a law. In an economics class, you learn how periods of inflation and recession develop. In a social science or psychology class, you read about experiments that explain certain aspects of human behavior. A chart that visually represents a complicated process may make it easier for you to learn and remember each step or stage. The process diagram shown in Figure 9.5, page 221, illustrates the natural movement of water from the ocean to fresh-water sources and back to the ocean.

EXERCISE 9.3   COLLABORATIVE ACTIVITY

WORK WITH GROUP MEMBERS TO identify and read a process diagram. Follow the guidelines for group discussion that appear on the inside back cover. Search through your textbooks to find a good example of a process diagram. These diagrams are typical of science and social science textbooks but may also appear in other texts.

Process diagrams are easy to recognize. Look for drawings connected by arrows showing the direction of the process. Look for stages illustrated by connected boxes or circles, as in the diagram of the water cycle (Figure 9.5). When you have found a process diagram, examine it carefully and read the textbook explanation that accompanies it. Use the following questions to guide your discussion. Record the group's answers to the questions and the group's evaluation.

1. **What process does the diagram illustrate?**

    _____

    _____

    _____

2. **How many stages or steps are in the process, and what are they?**

    _____

    _____

3. **Which seems easier to understand, the textbook explanation or the process diagram? Why?**

    _____

    _____

    _____

4. **Does the answer to question 3 depend on your learning style? How?**

    _____

    _____

    _____

Group Evaluation:

How will you use what you learned about process diagrams? Did your group complete its tasks successfully? What improvements can you suggest? What additional questions do you have about process diagrams? How will you find answers to your questions? Write the evaluation on your own paper, or go to the Online Study Center at college.hmco.com/pic/KanarTCS6e to download the form.

Online Study Center
Chapter Exercises/
Forms

PROCESS DIAGRAM

FIGURE 9.5

The Water Cycle

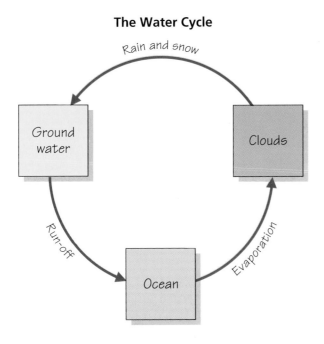

INFORMAL OUTLINES

▶ *List details under a main idea to show their relationship.*

Like many students, you probably use some form of outlining to take notes during lectures, to organize your ideas before writing, or to plan a speech. You can also use outlining to organize information for study. An *informal outline* illustrating essential concepts and the details that explain them can be a convenient study guide.

Suppose that you are taking a psychology course. You have just finished reading a chapter on motivation and listening to a lecture in class on theories of motivation. During the lecture, your instructor listed some theories on the board and said, "This is important." You have a test in a few days, and you know what you should study: theories of motivation. Your study guide for Maslow's theory might look like the outline shown in Figure 9.6 on page 222. The outline has four major details indicated by the numbers *1, 2, 3,* and *4.* Stars and indentations signal material that supports or explains each of the four major details.

You could write the outline on a 5" × 7" note card. You could make outlines on note cards for all of the theories and cover the same four points: the name of the originator, the gist of the theory, a weakness, and what makes the theory useful. How would you study from your guides? You could read and recite the information written on your cards. You could mentally try to fill in details. For example, can you explain each level of need in Maslow's hierarchy without looking back at the chapter? Suppose you get to esteem needs and draw a blank. Suppose you can't even remember Maslow's definition of *esteem.* The value of your study guide becomes clear: It tells you what information you need to review or reread.

STUDY GUIDE FOR MASLOW'S HIERARCHY OF NEEDS

FIGURE 9.6

Concept Check 9.2

One advantage of using graphic organizers is that they condense information into smaller, meaningful chunks. Can you think of two more advantages?

Maslow's Hierarchy

1. Originator: Abraham Maslow

2. Theory: Five basic needs motivate human behavior and form a hierarchy from lowest to highest. Lower-level needs have to be met first.
   * Biological, physiological needs (lowest level)
   * Safety
   * Belongingness and love
   * Esteem
   * Self-actualization (highest level)

3. Weakness of theory: People don't always act according to the hierarchy.
   * A higher-level need might be satisfied before a lower-level need.

4. Researchers agree theory useful because it describes motivation in general.

An outline serves the same purpose as any other type of organizer. It shows how ideas relate to one another and to the topic, and it indicates the relative importance of the ideas. Outlines use a listing and indentation system that makes clear which ideas support one another.

A study guide that is easy to make is an outline of a chapter's title and headings. For example, see Figure 9.7. By making the guide, you not only reveal the writer's outline, but you also condense the chapter's most important ideas into one review sheet. Instead of re-reading a chapter before a test or flipping through

OUTLINE OF A CHAPTER'S TITLE AND HEADINGS

FIGURE 9.7

Public Opinion

What Is Public Opinion?
* How Polling Works
* How Opinions Differ

Political Socialization: The Family
* Religion
* The Gender Gap
* Schooling and Information

Cleavages in Public Opinion
* Social Class
* Race and Ethnicity
* Region

Political Ideology
* Consistent Attitudes
* What do Liberalism and Conservatism Mean?
* Various Categories
* Analyzing Consistency
* Political Elites

Adapted from James Q. Wilson and John J. DiLulio Jr., *American Government*, Tenth Edition, p.154. Copyright © 2006 by Houghton Mifflin Company. Used with permission.

all the pages to read the headings, simply read the outline on your review sheet. As you read a heading, try to recite the main idea and a few details covered in that section. If you can recall the important ideas, then you know the material. If you cannot remember some of the information under a certain heading, then you know exactly which section of the chapter you should study some more. If you like to study with a partner, take turns quizzing each other from your review sheets.

BRANCHING DIAGRAMS

▶ *Arrange details around a central point to show their relationship.*

Branching is a less formal, less structured technique than outlining or other techniques for creating study guides. In a *branching diagram*, ideas radiate outward from a central point instead of following a sequence. To branch out from a topic, draw a circle in the middle of your page. Inside the circle, write a key word or phrase that summarizes the author's main idea. Draw lines from the circle like the spokes of a wheel, but don't put them too close together. On these lines write the major details that support the main idea. Draw more lines coming off these lines and write in additional examples that support each of the details. Figure 9.8 shows a branching diagram of the five organizational techniques described in this chapter.

BRANCHING DIAGRAM   FIGURE 9.8

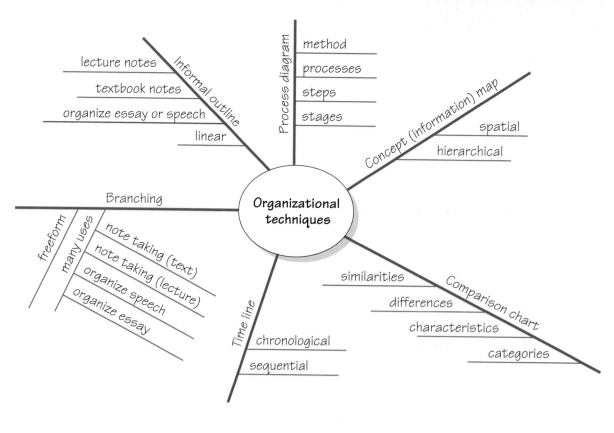

EXERCISE 9.4　　COMPUTER APPLICATION

READ THE FOLLOWING PASSAGE ABOUT the five objectives of financial planning. Using a computer, make a study guide for the passage. As explained in this chapter's Computer Confidence, for example, you could make an informal outline or experiment with different fonts to make important ideas stand out. Share your study guide with the rest of the class and discuss any advantages or disadvantages of making study guides on a computer that you may have discovered during the process of making your guide.

> For most people, effective financial planning takes into account five lifetime objectives.
>
> **Making money** is a goal that can be reached either through employment or investments.
>
> **Managing money** so that there is some left over for savings after spending is a goal people can reach by becoming effective consumers. Preparing and following a budget, using credit wisely, choosing good investments, buying economical insurance, establishing inexpensive bank accounts, and keeping accurate records of all transactions are all part of being an effective consumer.
>
> **Living well** is a goal many people strive for, in part, by trying to achieve financial success. Personal achievement, a challenging career, good health, satisfying relationships, community service, and material comforts are among some of the factors most people equate with living well. The decisions a person makes about all these factors determine the level of income and savings needed to achieve the quality of life he or she desires.
>
> **Becoming financially secure** is a goal best achieved through effective money management. People who are financially secure are free from debt and concerns about money. They have enough to buy the things they need plus occasional luxuries. They have savings, investments, and insurance to maintain their quality of life in the future.
>
> **Planning for the future** is a primary reason for saving money and making investments. It is a goal of many people who want to save money for their children's education, to live well in retirement, and to leave an estate for their heirs. This objective, like the other four, is a lifetime one.
>
> Making money, managing money, living well, becoming financially secure, and planning for the future are related goals in the sense that achieving one usually requires achieving the others.

Like outlining, branching can also be used as an organizational method for writing, speaking, and taking notes. But unlike outlining, which creates a linear organizer, branching creates a visual organizer. To brainstorm a topic for writing, draw a circle in the center of your paper around your topic. Add branches to the circle as ideas occur to you. Unlike outlining, branching does not require that you list your ideas in order. You can branch all over your paper, leaving one branch when you think of an idea to connect to another branch. You can also use branching to diagram the major points of a speech. Transfer your diagram to a 5" × 7" note card for easy reference during your speech. Finally, branching is a good note-taking method to use when listening to a speaker who does not explain ideas sequentially. Add a new branch whenever the speaker makes another point. If the speaker returns to a previous point that you have already branched, add another line to that branch.

To study from your branching diagrams, read them over several times. Make sure that you understand how the ideas relate. Then turn your diagram over and, on a clean sheet of paper, try to recreate it. When you've finished, check your new diagram against the original, filling in any details you might have missed.

Using a Computer to Make Study Guides

Once you become comfortable using your computer to organize notes, you can use it to create study guides as well. If you like concept or information maps, experiment with ways to arrange your notes onscreen. Some software programs allow you to place boxes and circles around type. You can also use your tabs and margins to set off words or blocks of type in an ordered way. Then pencil in boxes or circles on the hard copy.

If you want a map that shows a hierarchy, your program may allow you to use various type sizes to represent levels. Start with the largest type for the most important concept and reduce the type size for each step, ending with the least important stage in the smallest type. You can also use type style functions to diagram differences. Use capitals, boldface, italics, underlines, double underlines, and plain text to make up your own hierarchy, selecting a different style for each idea on your map. Write a key to remember your choices. For example, ALL CAPS = most important idea; **boldface** = secondary idea; *italics* = supporting detail.

If you already use the computer to make informal outlines from class notes, you can begin constructing a study guide by inputting chapter titles and headings from your textbook in outline form. Then, using the "Copy" and "Move" functions on your computer, pick up portions of your class notes and insert them in appropriate places in the chapter outline.

Try using numbers for main ideas and asterisks (stars) for details. Or make up your own symbols to set off main and supporting ideas. You can also use different spacing, type styles, or type sizes to make distinctions. Some programs give you a choice of typeface or font so that you can even change the look of the letters. Have fun experimenting with different treatments for important ideas until you find one that helps you visualize your outline at test time.

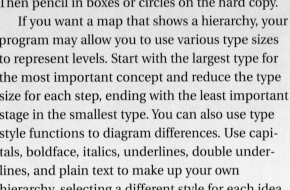

CRITICAL THINKING

Exercise Overview

This exercise will help you think critically about graphic organizers and apply what you have learned.

Exercise Background

Graphic organizers such as charts, tables, diagrams, and outlines have many uses.

As study guides, they condense a lot of information into a format that is easy to review. As illustrations for speeches and presentations, they provide the audience with a visual example. As examples in reports and research papers, they help explain complex ideas.

Exercise Task

Working with a partner or small group, follow these instructions to plan, rehearse, and present an oral presentation on the use of a graphic organizer.

1. Choose one type of organizer explained in this chapter. If possible, choose an organizer that one or more of you have used successfully so that your presentation will have practical value.

2. Define your type of organizer. Review the textbook explanation, but state the definition in your own words.

3. Explain the purpose of the organizer: the kind of information it organizes and how to use it as a study guide.

4. Illustrate your presentation with graphics and be creative.

EXERCISE 9.5   LEARNING STYLE

READ THIS EXCERPT FROM A psychology textbook; then underline and mark it to make the important ideas stand out. Using an organizer that best supports your learning style, make a study guide.

The Structure of Personality

Freud believed that people are born with basic needs or instincts—not only for food and water, but also for sex and aggression. He believed that needs for love, knowledge, security, and the like arise from these more fundamental desires. Each person faces the task of figuring out how to meet his or her needs in a world that often frustrates these efforts. According to Freud, personality develops out of each person's struggle with this task and is reflected in how the person carries it out.

Id, Ego, and Superego   *Freud described the personality as having three major components: the id, the ego, and the superego (Allen, 2003; see Figure 11.1). The **id** represents the inborn, unconscious portion of the personality where life and death instincts reside. The life instincts promote positive, constructive behavior; the death instincts are responsible for human aggression and destructiveness. The id operates on the **pleasure principle,** seeking immediate satisfaction of both kinds of instincts, regardless of society's rules or the rights and feelings of others. The hungry person who pushes to the front of the line at Burger King would be satisfying an id-driven impulse.*

*As parents, teachers, and others place greater restrictions on the expression of id impulses, a second part of the personality, called the ego (or "self"), evolves from the id. The **ego** is responsible for organizing ways to get what a person wants in the real world, as opposed to the fantasy world of the id. Operating on the **reality principle,** the ego makes compromises between the id's unreasoning demands for immediate satisfaction and the restrictions of the social world. The ego would influence that hungry person at Burger King to wait in line and think about what to order rather than risk punishment by pushing ahead.*

*As children gain experience with the rules and values of society, they tend to adopt them. This process of internalizing parental and societal values creates the third component of personality, the **superego,** which tells us what we should and should not do. The superego represents our sense of morality and is just as relentless and unreasonable as the id in its demands to be obeyed. It would make the pushy person at Burger King feel guilty for even thinking about violating culturally approved rules about standing in line and taking turns.*

Douglas A. Bernstein and Peggy W. Nash, *Essentials of Psychology*, Third Edition, pp. 402–403. Copyright © 2005 by Houghton Mifflin Company. Used with permission.

Thinking ahead about Career

Purpose and Instructions

A workplace focus in Chapter 9 is on organizing information, a skill that is enhanced by knowing how to determine what is important and by using graphic organizers to condense ideas. Use the knowledge that you have gained from this chapter to solve work-related problems such as the one explained in the following case study. Read the case study on your own or with a partner and then answer the case questions.

Case Study

Qualifying exams for the RN (Registered Nurse) certification are only two weeks away, and Miranda is worried. Nurses are in high demand, and Miranda has a job waiting for her if she qualifies. Passing the exam is an essential first step to achieving success in her chosen field. Although Miranda has an impressive transcript and high recommendations from the director of her practicum and the nurses with whom she interned, she is overwhelmed with the amount of material she has to review from her textbooks, research, and notes. How can she determine what is important? How can she select and organize information for study? Miranda doesn't know where to begin.

Case Questions

1. **What is Miranda's problem?**

   _____

   _____

2. **What do you think is the best strategy that Miranda could use to prepare for the exam?**

   _____

   _____

3. **Write a plan that would help Miranda use her study time productively.**

   _____

   _____

4. **Access the Career Resource Center and read the article entitled "Survival Tips for Taking Tests" in the *Building Learning Strategies* section of *The Bridge*. Based on this article, what additional advice can you give Miranda?**

   _____

   _____

Your *Reflections*

Reflect on what you have learned from this chapter about graphic organizers and how you can use them as study guides. Use the following questions to stimulate your thinking; then write your reflections. Include in your writing specific information from the chapter.

- Do you currently use graphic organizers to make study guides?

- Of the graphic organizers presented in this chapter, which one appeals to you most? Why?

- How can you incorporate study guides with the SQ3R system?

- What is one skill or attitude explained in this chapter that you would like to develop, and what can you begin doing today to make that happen?

_____

_____

_____

_____

_____

_____

_____

_____

_____

_____

_____

_____

_____

_____

_____

_____

_____

_____

_____

_____

Chapter review

ATTITUDES TO DEVELOP
- commitment to a goal
- persistence of effort
- openness to new strategies

SKILLS TO PRACTICE
- deciding what is important
- deciding what to study
- organizing information

To review the chapter, reflect on the following confidence-building attitudes and skills. Complete **Concepts to Understand** by filling in the blanks with words or terms from the list provided. Then practice your new skills at every opportunity.

CONCEPTS TO UNDERSTAND

comparison chart	branching	spatial	process	time line
relationship	hierarchy	graphic	linear	format

This chapter explains how to make a type of study guide called a (1) _____ organizer, which takes many forms. A concept or information map is a (2) _____, or visual, breakdown of a topic. Some maps arrange information in a (3) _____, or order of importance. A (4) _____ organizes facts and other ideas into categories based on similarities and differences. A (5) _____ presents dates and events chronologically. A (6) _____ diagram illustrates steps or stages leading to an outcome. An outline is a (7) _____ rather than spatial presentation of ideas. (8) _____ diagrams serve the same purpose as outlines but are less structured. These organizers share one thing in common: They help you visualize the (9) _____ among ideas.

Making organizers is a good idea for several reasons. For one thing, the process of deciding what is important and how to organize it forces you to think about ideas and how they relate to each other. Also, arranging the information in a (10) _____ that appeals to you makes it easier to remember.

To access additional review exercises, go to **college.hmco.com/pic/KanarTCS6e**.

Online Study Center
Review Exercise
ACE Self-Test

Online Study Center

Prepare for Class, Improve Your Grade, and ACE the Test. This chapter's *Student Achievement* resources include

Chapter exercises/forms	Review exercise	Confidence Builder Web search
ACE Self-Test		

To access these learning and study tools, go to **college.hmco.com/pic/KanarTCS6e**.

10 Controlling concentration and memory

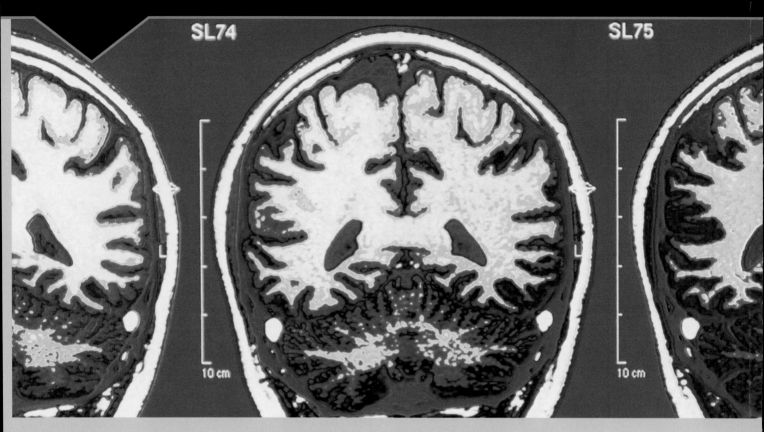

SL74　　　　　SL75

10 cm　　　　10 cm

Exercising your memory is a workout for your brain that strengthens neural connections and improves your performance.

▶ *Identify the causes of poor concentration. Eliminate internal and external distractions. Learn how to create a favorable environment for study. Practice active learning to control concentration and improve memory.*

▶ *Understand the stages and functions of memory and how they work to process information. Learn why you forget and how you can minimize forgetting.*

232

▶ CONTROL YOUR CONCENTRATION

Eliminate Distractions
Find Your Best Study Environment
Use Active Learning Strategies

▶ MANAGE YOUR MEMORY

Understand How Your Memory Works
Combat Forgetting

▶ INCREASE YOUR MEMORY POWER

*Identify and try common memory techniques
to focus your study and enhance learning.*

Up to this point we have emphasized the importance of active learning. Now let's expand upon that concept. If you sit in class only half aware of what is going on, letting yourself be distracted by noise, students talking, or random thoughts unrelated to the subject, you will not learn anything. Because you are not involved, you will easily become bored, and you will leave class feeling that it has been a waste of time. Chances are good that your grades will be less than exceptional. "But I can't help the way I feel," you say. "I can't control what goes on around me," you say. Active learning isn't about controlling what goes on around you. It is about controlling what goes on inside your mind, and, yes, you can control your feelings, your thoughts, and even the way you learn.

The key to taking control is in **knowing how to learn.** This means being able to think critically and having at your command various learning strategies that you can apply in different situations. Simply put, your brain is an information-processing system. Your five senses are the pathways into your

Knowing how to learn is a competency valued in the workplace, where you are presented with new information almost daily and are required to upgrade your knowledge and skills.

KEY TERMS

concentration, *p. 235*
internal distractions, *p. 235*
external distractions, *p. 235*
memory, *p. 245*
reception, *p. 245*
retention, *p. 246*
recollection, *p. 247*
memory cues, *p. 247*
sensory memory, *p. 248*
selective attention, *p. 248*
short-term memory, *p. 248*
long-term memory, *p. 250*
acronym, *p. 253*
association, *p. 253*

SCANS TERM

knowing how to learn, *p. 233*

brain. If you listen to a lecture, take notes, and observe the speaker's gestures, your active use of these strategies has opened three pathways for the information to travel: visual, aural, and tactile/kinesthetic. Obviously, the more active you are, the more you are likely to learn. By reviewing your notes immediately following a lecture, you deepen the inroads that the information has made.

This chapter is about becoming more actively involved in learning through controlling your concentration and by making the most of your memory.

AWARENESS CHECK 16

How Well Do You Control Concentration and Memory?

Choose one of the following as your response to each statement: *always* **(4 points),** *usually* **(3 points),** *occasionally* **(2 points),** *rarely* **(1 point). Write your number of points in the box beside each statement. When you are finished, add your score.**

Points

1. When studying, I am able to avoid distractions.

2. It is easy to maintain my interest in reading.

3. I am able to listen and take notes at the same time.

4. Even if an assignment is difficult, I am able to maintain concentration.

5. I may not like the instructor or the class, but I can still keep my interest going.

6. Generally speaking, I have a good memory for factual material.

7. I know several common memory techniques, and I use them regularly.

8. I know that memory is a process, and I understand how it works.

9. I understand the differences among sensory, short-term, and long-term memory.

10. I use a study system consistently for reading and studying for tests.

Total

Add your score. If your total is 35–40, you may already have control of your concentration and memory. If your total is 29–34, you have some control but could strengthen concentration and memory. If your total is 10–28, you have much to gain by developing concentration and memory skills. Whatever your level of skill, this chapter's strategies will help you improve the way you process information.

CONTROL YOUR CONCENTRATION

▶ *Identify the causes of poor concentration. Eliminate internal and external distractions. Learn how to create a favorable environment for study. Practice active learning to control concentration and improve memory.*

Concentration does not happen automatically and without your intervention. **Concentration** is an active process you initiate by deciding that you *will* concentrate and by focusing your attention on whatever it is that you want to learn or do. This may not be as easy as it sounds. We are all prone to distractions that can keep us from concentrating if we let them. To take control, we must learn how to monitor our thoughts and feelings when we are in the act of trying to pay attention. For example, suppose you are reading an assigned textbook chapter. You are concentrating on every word when suddenly you become aware of noise outside, or you feel a draft, or a passage you have just read triggers an emotion that takes your mind away from your reading and onto something else. You have allowed a distraction to take over, but you can regain control by ignoring or eliminating the distraction and by refocusing your attention. You may have to practice this process many times before you can concentrate without becoming distracted. Each time you feel yourself drifting off or losing control, refocus and try to maintain concentration for longer and longer periods of time.

Concentration is the active process of focused attention.

Many factors affect concentration, including the way you study, the environment in which you study, the things that distract you, and how you deal with your distractions. The first step toward improving concentration is to identify the causes of poor concentration.

Eliminate Distractions

Distractions can have internal or external causes. **Internal distractions** originate within you. They include feelings of hunger, tiredness, and discomfort that you can control. **External distractions** originate outside you. They include noise, temperature, and interruptions. You may not be able to eliminate all external distractions, but you can change the way you respond to them so that they don't keep you from concentrating.

Internal distractions originate inside you; hunger and feelings of stress are two examples.

External distractions originate outside you; noise and faulty lighting are two examples.

EXERCISE 10.1

Purpose and Instructions

Do you often feel distracted and lose concentration when you study? Are your distractions internal or external? To find out, read the following lists of common distractions and check all those that trouble you. Then write a paragraph in which you answer these questions: (1) What is your most common and troubling distraction? (2) What can you do to ignore or eliminate the distraction?

INTERNAL DISTRACTIONS

- ☐ Hunger
- ☐ Tiredness
- ☐ Illness
- ☐ Thinking about work or personal problems
- ☐ Worrying about grades, personal matters, etc.
- ☐ Stress
- ☐ Physical discomfort
- ☐ Not knowing how to do an assignment
- ☐ Negative feelings about courses or instructors
- ☐ Lack of interest or motivation
- ☐ Other internal distraction? _____

_____

_____

EXTERNAL DISTRACTIONS

- ☐ People talking to each other
- ☐ Telephones ringing
- ☐ Music or television playing
- ☐ Noise or activity going on outside
- ☐ Lighting too bright or too dim
- ☐ Temperature too high or too low
- ☐ Lack of proper materials
- ☐ Party or other activity that you want to take part in
- ☐ Family members asking you to do something
- ☐ Friends wanting to talk
- ☐ Other external distraction? _____

_____

_____

Online Study Center
**"Internal/External
Distractions" (Article)**

You can eliminate some internal distractions if you anticipate your needs. For example, study when you have eaten and are rested. Study in a comfortable place. Make sure you understand how to do an assignment before you begin. If you are not feeling well, postpone studying until you feel better. Worrying about grades, dwelling on job-related or personal problems, and having negative feelings about courses and instructors cause stress and distracting thoughts. When you have distracting or negative thoughts, stop studying for a moment and remind yourself of what you are trying to accomplish. Focus your attention on completing the task. If you lack interest in what you are studying, or if you don't have the motivation to do the work, studying with a partner might help. Choose someone who *is* interested and motivated. Studying will be more enjoyable, and the time will seem to pass quickly.

You can eliminate most external distractions by creating a study place where *you* may be able to control the lighting, temperature, noise level, and the availability of materials needed for study. Say *no* to friends who distract you from studying by tempting you with invitations to go out and have fun. If you save the fun as a reward for studying, you'll have a better time.

EXERCISE 10.2 COLLABORATIVE ACTIVITY

THE PURPOSE OF THIS EXERCISE is for you and the members of your group to gain experience identifying internal and external distractions and ways to eliminate them. Follow the guidelines for group discussion that appear on the inside back cover. Your tasks are as follows: Read and discuss the following scenario about a student who has trouble concentrating. Then answer the questions on the lines provided. Write your evaluation on your own paper or go to the Online Study Center at college.hmco.com/pic/KanarTCS6e to download the evaluation form.

> *Yesterday afternoon I had some time between classes, so I went to the library, found a comfortable couch in the reading section, and began reading a chapter in my psychology book. Two students came in, sat on the couch next to me, and began talking about their dates from the night before. Their evenings sounded pretty funny. I didn't mean to eavesdrop, but I was sitting right there! Suddenly I realized I was shivering. Why had I forgotten to bring a sweater? I knew the library's temperature was kept at energy-efficient levels. Not only was I cold, but the light also cast a glare on my book. I moved to a warm spot near the window where the sun was coming in and decided to take notes for the upcoming test. I looked all through my backpack for the pen I was sure I had packed. By the time I had borrowed a pen and sat down to take notes, it was time for my next class. I like psychology. Why was I unable to complete my reading assignment? I felt as though I was struggling with an unknown language.*

1. **What is the first distraction the student encounters? Is it an internal or external distraction?**

   _____

   _____

2. **What should the student have done immediately?**

   _____

   _____

3. **What are the student's other distractions? Are they internal or external?**

   _____

   _____

4. **Why is the student unable to complete the reading assignment?**

   _____

   _____

5. **What behavioral changes would help the student eliminate distractions?**

   _____

   _____

Group Evaluation:

What have you learned about internal and external distractions? Do you think some distractions cannot be eliminated? Why or why not? Did your group complete its tasks successfully? What improvements can you suggest? What additional questions do you have about concentration? How will you find answers to your questions?

Online Study Center
**Chapter Exercises/
Forms**

Find Your Best Study Environment

Do you do most of your studying at home, in the library, or in some other place? Where you study is not as important as whether you are able to concentrate on studying when you are there. If you have a lot of distractions at home—small children who need attention, other family members who make demands on your time, or noise from the television or ringing phones—you may find it more pleasant and productive to study on campus. But many students find they can't concentrate in the library or other places on campus, so they set aside a place to study at home.

If you prefer to do most of your studying at home, use your learning style to help you create a home study place that meets your needs. Manage your time so that you do most of your studying when your concentration is greatest. To adapt your study place to your learning style, try these suggestions:

▼ **Visual learners.** Make your place visually appealing. Display calendars, lists, and study aids where you can see and use them.

▼ **Auditory learners.** Record lectures and class discussion if there is no prohibition against doing so. Listen to these recordings at home and take notes from them. You may be able to check out recorded lectures from your college library for use at home. You can also record your own notes and other material to use for recitation and review.

▼ **Tactile learners.** If you have a personal computer, use a word-processing program to make your own study guides. Get a program that lets you create a calendar on which you can record important dates and assignments. Using a computer will also activate your visual sense.

You don't have to spend a lot of money to set up an efficient and convenient workplace in your house, apartment, or residence hall. Consider the following six factors when you plan your study environment: location, lighting, temperature, furniture, supplies, and motivational aids.

Location. You need a study place where you feel comfortable and where you are likely to have few distractions. Ideally, you should do all your studying in the same place, and you should not use your study place for anything but studying. For example, if you get sleepy while studying, don't nap at your desk. Leave your study area and return after you have rested. If you get hungry, don't eat at your desk. Take a break, have something to eat, and then return to finish studying. Then studying will become a habitual response triggered by your study place, and you will be able to maintain concentration.

A spare room in your house can become a workplace where you can close the door and shut out distractions. If space is limited, use a corner of your bedroom as a study area. If you share space with someone—in a residence hall, for example—arrange your desks on opposite sides of the room to create the illusion of privacy. Plan your time so that each of you can study when you are most alert, in a room free of noise and distracting activity.

Lighting. Too much studying in too little light causes eyestrain. Keeping your eyes focused for too long on the pages of your textbook or on a computer screen, especially in poor light, can make you feel tired and tense. Study in a well-lighted place and look up from your work occasionally. Rest your eyes by closing them or by looking off in the distance without focusing on anything.

Overhead lighting should illuminate your whole study area without casting glare or creating shadows. Or use a lamp that can handle a 250-watt bulb and position it close to your work so that you are not reading or writing in glare or shadows. Two lamps, one on each side of your desk, will achieve the same effect if you put a 150-watt bulb in each. Make the best use of whatever lamps are available by placing them properly and by choosing the right bulbs.

Temperature. Your body is a gauge that registers changes in climate and temperature. Extreme changes affect your ability to concentrate because they cause you to focus your attention on your body's discomfort. Optimum temperatures for most people are between 68 and 70 degrees Fahrenheit. In your study area, you may be able to control the temperature and keep it at the level at which you feel most energetic.

Temperatures in public buildings may vary greatly from room to room, and they are usually controlled automatically. If one of your classrooms stays uncomfortably cold, take a sweater or light jacket to that class. You are probably aware of the hot and cold spots on your campus, so if you prefer to study there, find a comfortable place.

Furniture. You'll need a desk or sturdy table big enough to hold a computer (if you have one), with space left over for reading a book, writing a paper, or studying from notes. If you can afford to buy a new desk, get one with drawers for storing paper, pens, and other supplies.

Choose a comfortable chair that provides adequate support for your back and is neither too low nor too high for the table or desk you are using. Studies have shown that many employees who work at computers all day suffer from chronic pain in their necks, arms, and backs. Such discomfort is the result of sitting in one position for long periods of time in a chair that doesn't provide enough support. Your arms or neck may become sore if your elbows and wrists are not supported as you type or if your computer screen is not at eye level. If you cannot buy or do not own a chair that provides enough back support, experiment with placing a pillow behind your lower back and adjusting it for comfort. Figure 10.1 on page 240 illustrates an ergonomically correct seating posture: one that provides proper back support and distance from keyboard and computer screen.

Whenever you have been sitting at your desk for a while and are beginning to feel tired or uncomfortable, try this exercise. Look up from your writing or away from your computer screen. Look to the right or left without focusing your eyes on anything in particular. Lower your shoulders and let your arms hang limp at your sides. Shake your hands. Push back from your desk and stretch your legs. If you still feel tired or stiff, take a short walk before returning to work.

Supplies. Keep your supplies handy and replenished. Whatever you need, including textbooks, make sure your supplies are available so that you don't have to interrupt your studying to look for them.

A cardboard file box provides convenient and inexpensive storage for your papers, returned tests, and materials from previous courses that you want to keep for future reference. You can buy a file box at your campus bookstore or office supply store.

Motivational Aids. Personalize your study environment. Be creative. Make it *your* place. Tack a calendar on a bulletin board or the wall above your desk. Check off the days as you progress through the term. Keep a record of your grades. This will help you see whether your studying is paying off, and it will signal when you need to make an extra effort. Tack up papers and tests on which you earned good grades. When you are feeling discouraged, look at the evidence of your success.

CONCEPT CHECK 10.1

Where do you do most of your studying? Does your study place meet the requirements of a good study environment as explained in this chapter? How would you describe your ideal study place?

Sitting Comfortably

Figure 10.1

The science of ergonomics studies the conditions under which people work most comfortably and efficiently. The design of some office furniture is based on information about the way the human body is structured and best supported.

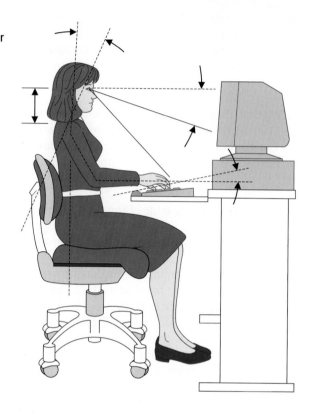

If studying away from home or the residence hall is a better option for you, your college library may be a good choice. Find a quiet area that meets your lighting and temperature requirements. Also, visit the library at different times of the day to find a time when it is most distraction-free.

Make studying in your place a habit so that it becomes your trigger for concentrated effort. Research has shown that studying at the same time every day reinforces the habit. Although your present schedule may not permit a set study time, this is a goal you can work toward.

An added advantage of finding or creating your best study environment is that you can transfer what you have learned in the process to your workplace environment. The same conditions will apply: location, lighting, temperature, furniture, supplies within reach, and motivational aids. You might not have control of all these conditions, but you may be able to make some changes in the environment that help you increase your productivity.

EXERCISE 10.3   LEARNING STYLE

YOUR BODY'S REACTIONS AND YOUR preferred learning environment are aspects of your learning style that affect both concentration and your choice of a study place. To review these aspects of learning style, complete the following items.

1. Based on the items you checked in Exercise 10.1 on page 236, are your distractions mostly internal or external?

   _____

2. What seems to be your greatest distraction, and why?

   _____

   _____

3. What relationship do you see between your locus of control and the distractions you checked in Exercise 10.1? Remember that *locus of control*, as explained in Chapter 2, means "source of motivation." The more internal your locus of control is, the more self-motivated you are. The more external your locus of control is, the more you need others to motivate you.

   _____

   _____

4. What is your preferred learning environment? Do you prefer working alone or with others, and why?

   _____

   _____

5. Taking into consideration your learning environment preference and your body's reactions to hunger, tiredness, temperature, and lighting, describe your ideal study place and explain what you will do to achieve it.

   _____

   _____

Use Active Learning Strategies

Remember that concentration and memory are linked by your active involvement in both processes. Using a study system such as SQ3R, which has specific steps to follow, is an active learning strategy. Here are some others to try:

▼ **Use the RMO system.** RMO stands for *read, mark, organize.* Read one section at a time and underline important ideas. When you are finished, review your underlining and make a graphic organizer you can use as a study guide for additional review.

▼ **Read with a pen in hand.** Make marginal notes: Write definitions, brief examples, or two-line summaries. Then review your notes.

▼ **Read with a dictionary.** Don't skip over words whose meanings you don't understand. First re-read the sentence and the ones just above and below it. You may be able to figure out the meaning based on the context in which the word appears. If that fails, turn to your dictionary.

▼ **Monitor your thinking while studying.** You may find yourself disagreeing with something you read. Instead of giving in to these thoughts, remember that your first priority is to *understand* the author's ideas and the evidence on which they are based. You can disagree later.

▼ **Study with a partner or group.** Compare notes. Quiz each other. Restate concepts in your own words.

Most people cannot concentrate for more than an hour without becoming distracted. Take short breaks away from your study area to refresh your mind and body. In addition, try these tips for improving concentration and memory function: Break lengthy assignments into smaller units that you can complete in one sitting. Instead of reading a sixty-page chapter all at once, read twenty pages in three separate sessions. Study difficult subjects first, before you get tired. If you can afford to buy your own new textbooks, do so. Although buying used books will save you money, someone else's underlining is distracting and may not accurately identify the most important ideas. If you start with a clean page, you will have to do your own thinking, which is always a good idea.

To prevent eyestrain during long study sessions, rest your eyes by periodically looking off into the distance.

CONFIDENCE BUILDER

A Desktop Relaxation Technique

When you are taking a test and your mind goes blank because you are nervous, this simple technique will calm you down so that you can finish the test.

1. Relax your shoulders and sit comfortably with both feet on the floor.

2. Place your elbows on the desktop, lower your head, close your eyes, and gently cup the palms of your hands over your eyes. Your fingers should be curled over the top of your head, and you should see no light coming in around your hands.

3. In this position, slowly count to ten while you breathe deeply.

4. Empty your mind of all negative thoughts by concentrating on feeling calm and relaxed.

5. When you are feeling calm, lower your hands and open your eyes.

6. You should feel relaxed enough to continue taking the test.

This technique works because you can't feel relaxed and anxious at the same time. As you concentrate on becoming calm, you forget about your test anxiety. When you return to the test calmly, the information you had blanked out because of nervousness will come back to you. You need not be self-conscious because other students will not know what you are doing. They may think you are just resting your eyes.

To pursue this topic further, do an online search using these keywords as a starting point: *relaxation techniques, relaxation response, stress relief.*

EXERCISE 10.4

ATTITUDE AND BEHAVIOR AFFECT CONCENTRATION. Your attitude and behavior in a class are related to the degree of responsibility you take for your performance in a course. Select as a target a course in which you would like to do better. Complete the analysis that follows; then decide what you can do to become a more internally controlled student.

1. **What is the name of the course in which you would like to improve your grades?** _____

_____

2. **Is there anything about the course that you don't like or that you think is difficult?** _____

_____

_____

3. **What are your distractions in this class?** _____

_____

_____

4. **Are the distractions internal or external?** _____

_____

_____

5. **What is your attitude toward this class? Check** *yes* **or** *no* **for the following statements.**

	YES	NO
I enjoy coming to this class.	☐	☐
I like the instructor's teaching style.	☐	☐
I feel confident in this class.	☐	☐
I am not afraid to ask questions in this class.	☐	☐
I am learning something in this course.	☐	☐
I see a relationship between this course and my goals.	☐	☐
I am interested in the subject taught in this course.	☐	☐

6. **On your own paper, write an action plan to improve your concentration in the course. Select a behavior or attitude that you want to change; then explain what you will do. Try out your plan long enough to receive at least two test or assignment grades. If you are satisfied with the results, continue with your plan. If not, evaluate your plan and make whatever changes are needed.**

EXERCISE 10.5 COMPUTER APPLICATION

SURFING THE WEB CAN BE a distraction if you don't remain focused on your topic. On the other hand, if you do remain focused, online researching can help you find information quickly, leaving you more time for study. Discuss with class members other ways in which using a computer can both help and hinder studying. Come up with a list of guidelines for avoiding distractions and remaining focused while researching, writing, or doing other learning activities online.

MANAGE YOUR MEMORY

Understand the stages and functions of memory and how they work to process information. Learn why you forget and how you can minimize forgetting.

Becoming aware of and taking control of the way you process information can ensure lifelong learning. A college degree does not represent knowledge gained or skills learned once and for all. Instead, a degree merely represents where you stand academically at a given time. Throughout life you will face tasks, problems, and decisions that require you to apply your knowledge in new ways and to develop new skills.

The next few sections of the chapter will help you understand the stages and functions of memory so that you can improve the way you learn. As you read, keep in mind three simple truths about memory: It is normal to forget. You can remember more and retain information longer than you think. By using a few proven memory aids, you can increase your memory power.

Understand How Your Memory Works

When you were a child, your teacher explained the multiplication tables and wrote them on the chalkboard. While you were listening to the teacher and looking at the board, you were *receiving* information about the tables through your senses of sight and sound. Then, to help you learn them, your teacher asked you to write them out on paper, and that activity engaged your sense of touch. You also recited the tables aloud. Those practices in the classroom helped you to *retain* the tables in memory. Finally, the teacher told you to practice your tables at home because you would be tested on them. You would have to *recall* them. If your practice and memory techniques have served you well, then you have retained the tables and can recall them even now.

Memory is a three-stage process by which your mind receives information and either discards it or stores it for later use. Memory involves *reception* of information, *retention* of information that has been received, and *recollection* of information that has been retained. (Researchers also refer to these activities as *encoding*, *storage*, and *retrieval*.) Figure 10.2 suggests a convenient way to remember the stages.

Memory is a process by which information from the senses is taken into the brain and then either discarded or stored.

Reception. Your mind receives, or processes, information through your five senses of sight, hearing, taste, touch, and smell. This stage of memory is called **reception.** Understanding is the key to effective reception because you can't learn what you don't understand. To aid understanding, relate new ideas or concepts to your prior knowledge. Placing new information in a familiar context not only makes it easier to remember but also establishes a mental network that you can expand with related concepts as you learn.

Reception is the stage of memory that processes information from your five senses.

THE THREE RS OF MEMORY

FIGURE 10.2

Reception

Retention

Recollection

Suppose you have been assigned a chapter on stress in your psychology text. Before reading, assess your prior knowledge. Ask yourself what stress means to you. Imagine yourself in stressful situations, and recall what you have done to overcome stress. If you have not successfully managed stress in the past, the chapter may suggest a new method to try. Read to find out whether the author's ideas about stress confirm what you already know or give you new information.

Here are some more tips to improve your reception:

▼ **Become more attentive and observant.** If you stay alert in class and keep your attention focused, you will be a better receiver.

▼ **Engage as many of your senses as possible when receiving information.** During a lecture, *look* at the speaker. *Listen* attentively to what he or she says. *Take notes* to help you remember. These strategies make full use of your visual, auditory, and tactile senses.

▼ **Ask questions, as needed, to aid understanding.** Remember: *You can't recall what you don't understand.* Make sure that you understand the information you receive.

▼ **Before you read a textbook chapter, survey it** to get an overview of its content and to establish a purpose for reading. This step is especially helpful when the chapter covers a topic that is new to you. As explained in Chapter 8, surveying is the first step in the SQ3R study system: *survey, question, read, recite,* and *review.*

Retention. Your mind stores and retains, for varying lengths of time, the information it receives. This stage of memory is called **retention.** Some information—your name, your birthplace, your birthday—you remember for life. Such information is part of you, although you may not remember when you first learned it. You retain other information—the multiplication tables, how to ride a bicycle—through use or practice. Was it difficult for you to learn to drive a car? You probably had trouble at first, but eventually you were able to get into a car and drive without mentally reviewing each step. When you reached that point, you had *internalized* the process of driving. You do not easily forget information you have internalized. Like your name, it has become part of you.

Anything you really want to learn is going to stay with you because you are motivated to remember it. The key to retaining academic information is to *make a conscious effort to remember.* Here are some ways to make retention an active and effective process:

▼ **Motivate yourself.** *Why* you study is as important as *what* you study. You will be more attentive, more receptive to learning, if you have a goal—even if it's simply a desire for a better grade. Try to get beyond the immediate reward of a good grade. Think about what you are studying and how the skills you are learning will bring you closer to your goals.

▼ **Listen and read actively.** Before a lecture and before reading, assess your prior knowledge about the topic as an aid to comprehension. During a lecture or reading, concentrate, ignore distractions, take notes, and think critically about the ideas and their meaning. During your review, reflect on what you have learned and try to think of practical ways to apply it.

▼ **Recite and review.** Reciting aloud during review activates your aural sense and opens another pathway into your brain. The more senses you involve, the greater will be your retention. Review immediately after studying and frequently thereafter. Schedule daily and weekly reviews so that you don't have to cram before an exam. Cramming isn't learning. Although you may pick up a few points on a test by cramming the night before, you will quickly forget the information.

Retention is the storage stage of memory. Review and practice ensure long-term storage of new information.

▼ **Do all assigned work and then some.** The more you use new information and practice new skills, the more you will retain. Frequent practice helps you internalize rules and procedures.

Recollection. What happens when you try to remember a date, a name, a concept, or a procedure for working an algebra problem? This is the **recollection** stage of memory by which you retrieve stored information. For some information, recall is immediate: Frequently dialed numbers and your zip code are two examples. If you've ever had trouble remembering a name or one of the steps required to solve a math problem, then you have experienced recollection in action. Your brain is searching for the information much as a computer searches through files.

Why are essay questions more difficult to answer than multiple-choice questions? The essay question requires you to construct your answer from memory without any help. The multiple-choice question lists several answer choices, some of which will contain **memory cues**—certain words, phrases, or ideas—that act as triggers to help you recognize the correct answer. To improve recollection, try these suggestions:

▼ **Prepare for tests.** Study and review to ensure understanding. Do not memorize your notes. Instead, recite from your notes in your own words or discuss concepts with a study partner or group. This may help you to recognize concepts when you see them in different contexts.

▼ **Choose your memory cues.** Use key words to recall concepts. For example, can you describe the characteristics of a reachable goal as explained in Chapter 4? Two key words are *realistic* and *flexible*. Do you remember any others? A diagram can also serve as a memory cue. Study the diagram; then picture it in your mind to recall the process it illustrates.

▼ **Study similar subjects separately.** When two subjects are similar, you may confuse their concepts, and doing this can cause problems at both the storage and retrieval stages of memory. Because your understanding is incomplete, your recall will be sketchy as well. To avoid this problem, do not study for two similar courses back to back. In other words, put a little mental distance between the two similar courses so that you don't confuse their concepts.

▼ **Make and take practice tests.** Practice is the key to long-term retention. Anticipate test questions and quiz yourself. Better yet, study with a partner and quiz each other.

Combat Forgetting

Forgetting is not only normal; it's also necessary. If you never forgot anything, your mind would be so crammed with useless information that you wouldn't be able to think. Do you remember what your phone number was in every place you have lived? You probably don't. Information that you cease to use soon passes out of your memory unless it has special significance. *Your mind stores only what you need and discards the rest.* In fact, when you learn something new, forgetting starts within an hour. After several days, you remember very little of the new information unless you take action to combat forgetting.

The stages of memory—reception, retention, and recollection—work because of three functions. Your *sensory memory, short-term memory,* and *long-term memory* determine what you remember and for how long. You have some control over each of these functions. Together, the stages and functions of memory make it possible for you to process information. Figure 10.3 on page 248 illustrates the process.

Recollection is the retrieval stage of memory whereby you attempt to recall or recognize stored information.

Memory cues are triggers that aid your recall.

Sensory memory takes in data from the senses and registers it fleetingly.

Selective attention is a process that focuses attention on certain things, ignoring others.

Sensory Memory. Your five senses—sight, hearing, taste, smell, and touch—are the media through which you experience the world. Your **sensory memory** translates information from the senses into mental images or impressions. Everything that is happening around you is conveyed to you by your senses. Your mind takes in all this information and, through a process called **selective attention,** sorts the important from the insignificant.

You've felt this process at work whenever you've been so caught up in watching a television program that you didn't hear someone speak to you. Your mind screened out the interfering sound of the person's voice. Had you lost interest in the show, your attention would have shifted to something else.

In class, when you are listening to a lecture, your task is to concentrate on the speaker's words and take notes on the important ideas. Although everything the speaker says registers on your sensory memory, you may have to work at maintaining concentration and ignoring external stimuli such as a conversation between two students who are sitting next to you.

Everything registers on your sensory memory—but only for a few seconds. By concentrating on a certain idea, image, or piece of information, you transfer it to your short-term memory, where you can retain it for a while longer.

Short-term memory has a limited capacity and retains information, such as the name of someone you just met, for less than a minute.

Short-Term Memory. You can hold information in your **short-term memory** for a little under a minute. For example, you meet someone at a party. He tells you his name, and you strike up a conversation. A few minutes later you see a friend you want to introduce to the person whom you just met, but you can't remember his name. Or you're in a phone booth, and you look up a telephone number. You close

HOW YOU PROCESS INFORMATION

FIGURE 10.3

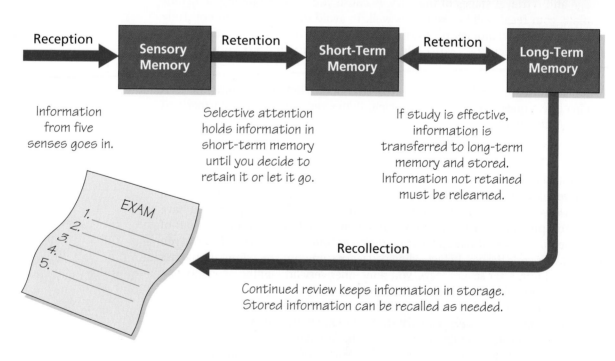

the directory and start to dial; you reach in your pocket for some change, and you realize you've forgotten the number. You probably have had such experiences, but you can do something about them. You will remember names, phone numbers, and other bits of information longer if you recite them. Reciting activates your short-term memory by engaging another of your senses. Every time you look up a phone number, repeat it to yourself; you may soon be able to dial it from memory.

Research has shown that short-term memory has a limited capacity. You can hold only about five to nine numbers at a time in your short-term memory. Seven is average for most people. Most phone numbers have seven digits; most zip codes have five digits. You might have difficulty remembering your nine-digit driver's license number or a sixteen-digit credit card number unless you make a point of transferring it into your long-term memory. You won't remember the important ideas from lectures or textbook chapters either—unless you review them enough to transfer them into long-term memory. Using a study system aids the transfer of information from short-term memory to long-term memory.

EXERCISE 10.6

HOW GOOD IS YOUR SHORT-TERM memory? Imagine that you are at a party full of strangers. By the end of the evening, you have met many people and have learned a great deal about them. How much can you remember? Study the facts about these people for three or four minutes. Then cover up the facts and try to answer the questions.

Name:	Matt	Claudia	Bill
Age:	34	29	23
Eye color:	Brown	Blue	Brown
Favorite book:	War and Peace	The Wind in the Willows	The Terminal Man
Favorite place:	Disney World	The Grand Canyon	The Wind River
Favorite film:	The Quiet Man	Casablanca	The Matrix
Favorite activity:	Traveling	Hiking	Web surfing
Favorite color:	Purple	Red	Sky blue

1. **Whose favorite activity is hiking?** _____

2. **How old is Matt?** _____

3. **Who has blue eyes?** _____

4. **Who loves to travel?** _____

5. **Who would love to hike in the Grand Canyon?** _____

6. **Who is the youngest?** _____

Now uncover the facts and check your answers. How accurate was your short-term memory? If you got fewer than three answers right, you probably did not use a memory aid such as recitation or grouping of similar items. For example, did you notice that Claudia's favorite activity, hiking, could be done at her favorite place, the Grand Canyon? Bill's favorite book, film, and activity are all related, too.

Long-term memory has a vast capacity, is more or less permanent, and retains information such as learned skills and personal experiences.

Long-Term Memory. Your **long-term memory** is more or less permanent and can hold a vast amount of information—everything from names, dates, facts, and images to learned skills and personal experiences. Stored information falls into three categories. *Verbal information* comes from books and other printed sources. Verbal information that is oral, such as music or a lecture, is transmitted through your auditory sense. To improve retention of verbal information, become an active reader and listener. *Visual information* includes everything you see—paintings and other artwork, photographs, dance, the world around you. To improve retention of visual information, become more observant, attentive, and involved in what you are learning. *Physical and motor information* includes things you learn by doing: writing, drawing, participating in sports, and operating machines, for example. To improve retention of physical and motor information, practice new skills or activities until they become automatic.

Do you see a relationship between the categories of stored information and learning style? Which kind of information is easiest for you to remember? Which is the hardest? For example, some visual learners may find it easier to remember visual information than physical or motor information. Imagine a person who is learning to drive a vehicle with a standard transmission. Whereas a strongly tactile/kinesthetic learner would be able to feel or sense where the gears are, a strongly visual learner would do better with a diagram that illustrates the positions of the gears. You can see in this example that the diagram enables the visual learner to adapt to a physical learning task. Similarly, you can find effective ways to learn any kind of information, no matter what your learning style is.

In conclusion, getting and keeping information in your long-term memory requires your active involvement, a desire to remember, and regular practice. Actions such as using study systems, reciting and reviewing, and making study guides all aid retention.

Try Awareness Check 17 to see more examples of the information stored in your long-term memory.

AWARENESS CHECK 17

Write your answers on the lines provided.

1. What is your zip code? _____

2. Does the Statue of Liberty hold the torch in her right or left hand? _____

3. What are the steps to follow when pumping gas? _____

   _____

   _____

4. What is five times nine? _____

5. What is the capital of your home state? _____

6. On a vertically hanging traffic signal, which is on top: the red or green light?

   _____

7. In an electrical outlet, which slot is longer, the right or left? _____

   _____

8. How do you parallel park a car? _____

   _____

   _____

9. What are the names of three U.S. Presidents? _____

   _____

   _____

10. How do you perform an exercise such as a sit-up or bicep curl? _____

    _____

Items 1, 4, 5, and 9 call for verbal information. Items 2, 6, and 7 call for visual information. Items 3, 8, and 10 call for physical or motor information.

INCREASE YOUR MEMORY POWER

▶ *Identify and try common memory techniques to focus your study and enhance learning.*

The strategies that follow have worked for many students. Perhaps you already use some of them, or maybe you'll discover a new technique to try.

▶ **Decide to remember.** Resist passivity. Become an active learner by making a conscious, deliberate decision to remember. Follow through on this decision. This is the most important step you can take. Unless you *decide* to remember, none of the other techniques will work.

▶ **Try relaxed review.** Don't wait until the last minute before a test to do your reviewing. Review regularly and do it in a relaxed way. When you are tense, you cannot concentrate. Try the chair-seat relaxation technique described next and shown in Figure 10.4 on page 252.

1. **Start off in a positive frame of mind. Believe that you can and will remember.**

2. **Sit in a straight-backed chair with your feet together, flat on the floor.**

3. **Close your eyes; grasp the chair seat with both hands.**

4. **Pull up on the chair seat as hard as you can.**

5. **While you are pulling up with your hands, press your feet firmly to the floor.**

6. **Hold that position and count slowly to ten. Feel how tense all the muscles of your body are becoming.**

CONCEPT CHECK 10.2

How does stress affect your ability to study? If you are feeling anxious, does your classroom performance suffer? What ways have you found to reduce stress that is associated with being in an academic setting where you are expected to achieve?

THE CHAIR-SEAT RELAXATION METHOD

FIGURE 10.4

Steps 1 and 2   Steps 3–6   Steps 7 and 8   Step 9

7. **Now relax completely, letting your arms hang loosely at your sides. Settle down into the chair and feel how calm you've become.**

8. **With your eyes still closed, visualize yourself being successful. Experience how success feels.**

9. **Slowly open your eyes and, in this calm state, begin to review your study material.**

10. **If you feel yourself becoming tense again, repeat steps 1–9.**

This relaxation technique is a variation of anxiety-reduction techniques used by professionals in fields such as psychology, medicine, education, and sports.

▶ **Combine review with a physical activity.** Each sense that you use while reviewing provides another pathway for information to reach your brain. Recite, either silently or aloud, while riding a bicycle, while doing aerobics or calisthenics (floor exercises like sit-ups and jumping jacks), and while walking and running. Feel good about yourself for keeping fit *and* for exercising your mind. This technique works well for anyone but is especially good for student athletes.

▼ **Use mnemonics.** *Mnemonics* are tricks, games, or rhymes that aid memory. You may know the rhyme that begins with "Thirty days hath September" to help you remember the number of days in each month. Here is one that you probably haven't heard: "Tyranny nixed in '76." This rhyme recalls the year the Declaration of Independence was signed.

▼ **Use acronyms.** An **acronym** is a word formed by the first letters of other words. COPE, a problem-solving method, and GRAB, a time management technique, are just two examples of acronyms used in *The Confident Student*. You probably know many others such as ASAP, a business acronym that means *as soon as possible*, and HUD, a government acronym that stands for the Department of Housing and Urban Development. An acronym may help you remember the steps in a process. Choose a key word to remind you of each step. Then, using the first letter of each key word, create your acronym.

Acronym refers to a pronounceable word that is made up from the first letters of a group of words that stand for something. ASAP is a business acronym that means "as soon as possible."

▼ **Associate to remember.** **Association** is the process of connecting new information that you want to remember to something that you already know. An association is often personal. For example, a student who wanted to remember these particles of the atom—proton, electron, and neutron—associated the names of the particles with the names of her brothers—Paul, Eric, and Norman. Her brothers' names and the particle names begin with the same letters, and they form the acronym *PEN*.

Association is a memory aid whereby you connect a familiar idea with a new idea.

To recall the three stages of memory, you could associate the mind with a computer and associate memory's three stages (reception, retention, and recollection) with three computer processes (input, storage, and output). If your instructor asks you to describe the three stages of memory, think of how a computer works, and you should be able to recall the three stages.

▼ **Visualize.** Form an image, or picture, in your mind of something that you want to remember. Visualization is an especially good way to link names with places or parts with locations. In geography, visualize places on a map. In physical science, draw an idealized continent that could stand for any continent and fill in climate zones. When reviewing this information or recalling it during a test, picture the continent and visualize the zones. In anatomy, label the bones on a drawing of a human skeleton. When reviewing or recalling, close your eyes and see the skeleton with your labels.

▼ **Use an organizational technique.** Organize information in a meaningful pattern that shows how each item relates to the others. List steps in a process. Outline complex material. Make charts, diagrams, and information maps that show the relationship of parts to a whole or one part to another. Figure 10.5 on page 254 is a comparison chart showing the memory functions and stages discussed in this chapter. The chart condenses the information for quick reference. Read the chart across the rows *and* down the columns. As you can see, the stages and functions are related: Your sensory, short-term, and long-term memory functions process information throughout the three stages.

▼ **Sleep on it.** Reviewing before sleep helps you retain information. Because you are relaxed, your concentration is focused. The information stays in your mind while you are sleeping, and interference from conflicting sounds, images, or ideas is minimal. When you wake, try to recall what you reviewed the night before. Chances are good that you will remember.

▼ **Remember key words.** Sometimes you have to remember a series of connected ideas and explanations, such as the chair-seat relaxation technique described on pages 251–252. To recall items stated in phrases or sentences, select one or

FIGURE 10.5

FUNCTIONS AND STAGES OF MEMORY

FUNCTIONS OF MEMORY	STAGES OF MEMORY		
	RECEPTION: GETTING INFORMATION	**RETENTION: STORING INFORMATION**	**RECOLLECTION: RECALLING INFORMATION**
Sensory Memory	Registers perceptions	Quickly lost without selective attention	Automatic from second to second
Short-Term Memory	Focuses on facts and details	Quickly lost unless recited or reviewed	Possible for short time only until information is lost
Long-Term Memory	Forms general ideas, images, and meanings	Integrates information transferred from short-term memory for storage	Possible for long periods of time or for a lifetime

more key words in each item that sum up the phrase or sentence. Recalling key words will help you recall the whole item.

▼ **Memorize.** Some educators have reservations about memorization. They say memorization is not learning because it is usually done out of context. Students may not be able to recall items memorized in a certain order if the instructor puts them in a different order on a test. Critics also say that memorization is an inefficient technique and that memorized items are difficult to recall. Yet memorization does work. What is 9 times 9? You probably know the answer.

Memorization can be a useful technique for recalling certain kinds of information, especially if it is combined with another memory strategy and is not the only technique you know how to use. Of course, you cannot expect to remember anything that you do not understand. First, make sure you comprehend any new information well enough to link it to knowledge you have already acquired. Memorization works best on information such as the spelling and definition of words, math and chemical formulas, poetry, and facts that belong in a certain order, such as historical events, life cycles, or food chains.

C R I T I C A L

T H I N K I N G

Exercise Overview

This exercise will help you practice selecting appropriate memory strategies and memory aids.

Exercise Background

As explained in this chapter, memory is a three-stage process by which the brain takes in information through the senses and sorts it either for discarding or storage. You can manage this process by deciding to remember, by concentrating, and by using a study system and various techniques, strategies, or aids that enhance memory function. What this means is that learning and remembering are not random acts. You have the power to improve the way you learn.

Exercise Task

Listed next are some typical learning activities required of college students. Choose one that you think may be difficult for you. Then review the memory strategies explained in this chapter. Using the questions that follow the list, decide which strategy would best help you complete the activity. Write your answers on your own paper and then share them in a class discussion.

- Reading a chapter from a biology textbook
- Listening to a lecture
- Taking notes from a lecture
- Learning the names of the bones of the human body
- Matching the names of artists with examples of their work
- Solving an equation that has two unknowns

1. Which activity did you choose, and why do you think it may be difficult for you?
2. Does the activity require you to process verbal, visual, or physical/motor information?
3. What memory strategy will improve your *reception* of the information, and how?
4. What memory strategy would improve your *retention* of the information, and how?
5. What memory strategy would improve your *recollection* of the information, and how?

Thinking ahead about Career

Purpose and Instructions

A workplace focus in Chapter 10 is on knowing how to learn**. You demonstrate this thinking skill when you choose an appropriate learning strategy for a specific task. Use the knowledge you have gained from this chapter to solve work-related problems such as the one explained in the following case study. Read the case study on your own or with a partner and then answer the questions.**

Case Study

Tracy has landed a summer job at an architect's firm. She is excited about working there because she is majoring in architecture, and this job will give her some firsthand experience. Her duties include various sec-retarial services such as running errands, copying and delivering blueprints, and any other tasks her bosses assign her. This job gives Tracy the opportunity to meet everyone in the firm and acquaints her with the duties and responsibilities of everyone from the chief architect to the maintenance crew. Because Tracy has so many different jobs to do for so many people, she has difficulty remembering who is who and who needs what. Tracy would like to try some of the memory techniques she studied last quarter in her student success class—if only she could remember them!

Case Questions

1. **What is Tracy's problem, and what are its causes?**

   _____

   _____

   _____

2. **What are Tracy's job responsibilities?**

   _____

   _____

   _____

3. **What memory techniques have you tried that might work for Tracy?**

   _____

   _____

   _____

4. **Access the Career Resource Center and read the article entitled "Remembering Names" in the** *Building Learning Strategies* **section of** *The Bridge.* **Based on this article, what additional advice can you give Tracy?**

   _____

   _____

Your *Reflections*

Reflect on what you have learned from this chapter about controlling concentration and managing memory. Use the following questions to stimulate your thinking; then write your reflections. Include in your writing specific information from the chapter.

- How are concentration and memory linked?

- What are your internal and external distractions, and how are you managing them?

- In what class do you make your best grades? What memory techniques or study methods do you use in this class that you could use in other classes to the same advantage?

- What is one skill or attitude explained in this chapter that you would like to develop, and what can you begin doing today to make that happen?

_____

_____

_____

_____

_____

_____

_____

_____

_____

_____

_____

_____

_____

_____

_____

_____

_____

Chapter review

ATTITUDES TO DEVELOP
- self-discipline
- flexibility
- commitment

SKILLS TO PRACTICE
- controlling concentration
- eliminating distractions
- using memory aids and study systems

CONCEPTS TO UNDERSTAND

environment	positive	internal	sensory	active
recollection	long-term	reception	external	verbal

Concentration and memory are linked; both are within your power to control and use to your advantage. To improve concentration, identify and eliminate your (1) _____ and (2) _____ distractions. Maintain a (3) _____ attitude for study, and find or create a study (4) _____ that meets your requirements for location, lighting, temperature, furniture, supplies, and motivational aids.

To improve memory, understand how your memory works to process information. The three stages of memory are (5) _____, retention, and (6) _____. The functions of memory describe how information is taken in, sorted, and stored and for how long. Your (7) _____ memory is the most fleeting. Short-term memory lasts a little longer, but (8) _____ memory is the most permanent and has the greatest capacity. Stored information falls into three categories: (9) _____, visual, and physical/motor, which also correspond to the learning modes explained in Chapter 2.

Choosing memory strategies that reflect your learning style will improve your retention, as will using a study system consistently.

Although there are many tips and techniques for improving concentration and memory, deciding to concentrate and deciding to remember are the most important of all for two reasons: They reflect your commitment to learn and your willingness to become a more (10) _____ learner.

To access additional review exercises, go to **college.hmco.com/pic/KanarTCS6e.**

Online Study Center
Review Exercise
ACE Self-Test

Online Study Center

Prepare for Class, Improve Your Grade, and ACE the Test. This chapter's *Student Achievement* resources include

"Internal/External Distractions" (article)   Chapter exercises/forms   Review exercise
Confidence Builder Web search   ACE Self-Test

To access these learning and study tools, go to **college.hmco.com/pic/KanarTCS6e.**

11 Preparing for tests

When you are well prepared, you can face
any test of your skill with confidence.

> *Schedule sufficient time for review before a test.
> Determine what skills or concepts to study.
> Use your study system to aid retention.*

> *Follow a routine for taking tests: Know what to
> do before, during, and after a test to improve
> your preparation and performance.*

▶ HOW TO PREPARE FOR TESTS: THREE STEPS

Make a Study Schedule
Decide What, When, and How to Study
Use Your Study System

▶ DEVELOP A TEST-TAKING ROUTINE

Arrive on Time
Jot Down Memory Cues
Survey the Test
Plan and Use All Your Time
Read Directions
Do Easy Questions First
Skip and Return to Difficult Questions
Guess (If There Is No Penalty)
Control Your Feelings and Attention
Check Your Work
Learn From Your Mistakes

▶ MASTER OBJECTIVE TESTS

True-False Tests
Multiple-Choice Tests
Fill-in-the-Blank Tests

▶ ANSWER ESSAY QUESTIONS WITH CONFIDENCE

▶ *Identify the instruction words that tell you what kind of information an essay question is seeking. Know how to write an effective answer.*

▶ *Learn how to think through a multiple-choice question to improve your chances of getting it right. Know when to use guessing strategies.*

Personal responsibility is a quality of people who take initiative and accept the consequences of their actions.

Self-management means self-control or self-discipline, and it is one of several personal qualities that are essential to career success.

If you ask college students what their most persistent academic worry is, many will say "Grades." Like most college students, you may be looking for ways to improve your grades and may even wish there were a secret formula or shortcut to success. Although there are no shortcuts, there *is* a key to good grades, and it's no secret: preparation.

Time management, planning, and the use of appropriate study skills are your keys to preparing for tests. **Personal responsibility** and **self-management** keep you motivated and on task. Being responsible means accepting that grades are the direct result of your effort. Being a good self-manager means having the self-discipline to put study first.

As you can see, preparing for tests requires the interaction of several skills and attitudes that not only lead to good grades but also have an added benefit. Planning, managing your time, being responsible, and choosing appropriate strategies are marketable workplace competencies you can carry into the future.

Do you need to improve the way you prepare for tests? Find out by completing Awareness Check 18. The strategies explained in this chapter can help you prepare for tests with confidence.

AWARENESS CHECK 18

How Well Do You Prepare for Tests?

Choose one of the following as your response to each statement: *always* (4 points), *usually* (3 points), *occasionally* (2 points), *rarely* (1 point). Write your number of points in the box beside each statement. When you are finished, add your score.

Points

1. I allow enough time for daily, weekly, and pre-exam reviews.

2. I am good at figuring out what I should study for a test.

3. I use SQ3R or another system for studying.

4. I am satisfied with my grades.

5. When reviewing my mistakes, I can tell what kinds of errors they are.

6. I do not become distracted during a test.

7. I enter a testing situation feeling mentally and physically prepared.

8. I have a test-taking routine: There are certain things I do before, during, and after any test.

9. I am good at taking objective tests (true-false, fill-in, multiple-choice).

10. I know how to plan and write an effective answer for an essay exam.

Total

Add your score. If your total is 35–40, you have developed some strategies that help you prepare for tests. If your total is 29–34, you may be prepared most of the time, but you could do better. If your total is 10–28, you probably are not satisfied with your grades and would benefit by being better prepared for tests. Whatever your level of skill, this chapter's strategies will help you improve the way you prepare for tests.

How to Prepare for Tests: Three Steps

▶ *Schedule sufficient time for review before a test. Determine what skills or concepts to study. Use your study system to aid retention.*

If you walk into a test knowing that you are well prepared, you will feel confident that you can succeed. If you do not prepare sufficiently, you will probably feel a lack of confidence and perhaps even some anxiety that you will not earn a good grade. To ensure that you will be prepared for every test, follow these three essential steps:

1. Make a study schedule.

2. Decide what to study.

3. Use your study system.

These steps are the answers to three common questions students ask about studying for tests: When should I study? What should I study? How should I study?

Make a Study Schedule

The purpose of making a study schedule is to establish fixed times for review so that review becomes a habit and you never have to cram for a test. Allow time in your schedule for daily, weekly, and exam reviews.

Daily Reviews. Take five to ten minutes per day to review each course. Begin by reviewing your notes and assignments for the previous class. Immediately or as soon as possible after class, review new material and try to relate it to what you have learned in the course so far. In doing this, you will make connections among topics and gain a broad perspective on the course.

Weekly Reviews. In addition to the time you spend doing assignments, spend about an hour a week reviewing each subject. Review lecture notes, textbook notes, and your study guides and try to anticipate test questions. A weekly review is an in-depth look at what you have covered in a course during one week. Relate the current week's work to the previous week's work and determine how the new material fits into the course.

Pre-Exam Reviews. About one week before a test, conduct a major review. Exam reviews will take longer than weekly reviews because they may cover several weeks' material. To prepare for exams, review lecture notes, textbook notes, study guides, note cards, instructors' handouts, and previous tests, papers, or graded assignments. Your daily and weekly reviews will make the material seem familiar so that you may see a pattern in the topics you are studying and may think of possible test questions.

Your study schedule should allow five to ten minutes a day per course for daily reviews, an hour per course for weekly reviews, and two hours or more for a specific exam review. Enter times for review on your schedule and make a commitment to follow it.

Exam reviews are the hardest because they take the longest and cover the most material. Try these tips for improving concentration when you have to study for two or more hours:

▶ Review at the time of day when you are most alert.

▶ Study for your hardest exam first.

Relaxing and talking with others for a few moments is a good way to break from an exam review.

> ▼ About once every hour, take a break. Get up and walk around; do something unrelated to studying.

> ▼ Reward yourself for getting the job done. Plan to go out with friends or do something that's fun when you have finished your review.

Decide What, When, and How to Study

Test questions can come from a variety of sources. To study for a major test, review lecture notes, textbook chapters, textbook notes and study guides, previous tests, papers, homework, and instructors' handouts. Don't waste time reviewing information you already know; study material you have not fully grasped. Study the most difficult material first. If you study the easiest topics first, then by the time you get to the hard ones, you will probably be tired and unable to give them your best effort. Study the most complex or technical concepts when you are most alert; be willing to look up definitions and re-read sentences until you grasp their meaning. Later, when you are tired, take a short break and then study less challenging material. Your understanding of the subject will lead to improved confidence and productivity.

Lecture Notes. Lectures often supplement information presented in textbooks. They are usually organized around a major topic in the course outline. If your instructor gives weekly lectures, the lecture topics probably build on weekly assigned chapters and the week's topic listed in your syllabus.

Textbook Chapters. Review your underlining and marginal notes. If you have underlined or annotated the most important ideas, your review will be both efficient and thorough.

MAKE OUT A NEW WEEK'S schedule. Include time for daily reviews and for one weekly review. After you have completed this schedule, update your semester or quarter calendar. Schedule times for major exam reviews one week before each test date. Go to the Online Study Center at college.hmco.com/pic/KanarTCS6e to download extra copies as needed.

	Sunday	Monday	Tuesday	Wednesday	Thursday	Friday	Saturday
6:00 – 7:00							
7:00 – 8:00							
8:00 – 9:00							
9:00 – 10:00							
10:00 – 11:00							
11:00 – 12:00							
12:00 – 1:00							
1:00 – 2:00							
2:00 – 3:00							
3:00 – 4:00							
4:00 – 5:00							
5:00 – 6:00							
6:00 – 7:00							
7:00 – 8:00							
8:00 – 9:00							
9:00 – 10:00							
10:00 – 11:00							
11:00 – 12:00							
12:00 – 1:00							

*Outdoor exercise is a great reward for completing your review. It can help
to relieve pre-exam stress and ensure a good night's rest as well.*

Textbook Notes and Study Guides. Review any additional notes, maps, outlines, note cards, or other study materials you have made. Since your own notes and guides are summaries of textbook material written in your own words, they will be the easiest for you to remember.

Graded Tests, Papers, Homework, and Other Assignments. Your previous tests are useful for two reasons. First, you can determine from these tests the kinds of questions your instructor asks. Second, you can learn from your mistakes. Questions that you missed enable you to spot weak points in your studying—information that you forgot, ignored, or didn't understand. Instructors' comments on papers and other graded assignments may also point out strengths and weaknesses and provide clues about what you should study.

Instructors' Handouts. Anything your instructor hands out is bound to be important. Instructors frequently summarize information on handouts. Don't overlook these important study aids when you review for a major test.

Figure 11.1 is a checklist showing what to study for tests. Make your own checklist. Before a test, check off the items you need to study. Organizing your materials beforehand establishes a framework for studying and builds confidence.

You may benefit from studying with another student. Comparing your notes with someone else's can help both of you. What one of you misses the other may have in his or her notes. Also, students vary in their understanding of lectures and textbooks chapters. A topic that gave you trouble may have been easy for a friend. Talking it over gives you another perspective on the subject.

FIGURE **11.1**

WHAT TO STUDY FOR TESTS: A CHECKLIST

☐ Lecture notes

☐ Underlining, highlighting, marginal notes

☐ Graphic organizers, note cards, and other study aids

☐ Graded tests and exercises

☐ Instructor's comments on papers

☐ Instructor's handouts

☐ Terms and definitions

☐ Formulas and sample problems

☐ Broad concepts and theories

☐ Lab notes

Use Your Study System

Once you have decided *what* to study, *how* you study will determine the effectiveness of your review. Don't study in a hit-or-miss fashion and don't re-read chapters. Instead, use a system. By now you may have tried the suggestions in Chapter 8 for using SQ3R or for adapting a system to your learning style. If your system is working, use it. If you would like to try a different strategy, follow these steps to prepare for a major test in one of your courses:

1. One week before the test, schedule two or more hours of time to review all chapters and topics that the test will cover. Do not attempt to study for two hours straight without taking a break because you will lose interest and concentration. Instead, plan your study time to review specific material in several short sessions, taking a break in between.

2. Organize your materials. Sort lecture notes, textbook notes, study guides, handouts, and previously graded tests and assignments by chapter or topic; then make a list of the important topics, kinds of problems, or other specific information you think will be on a test.

3. If you must review a lot of facts, terms, formulas, steps in a process, or similar material, put the information on 3" × 5" note cards to carry in your pocket or purse. Recite from these cards, silently or aloud, at every opportunity. Look at the sample note cards in Figure 11.2 on page 268 for examples of the kind of information to include and how much to write. Keep your cards simple; write just enough to serve as a memory cue.

4. Map or diagram any information that you think will be difficult to remember. Maps, as explained in Chapter 9, are charts and tables that visually represent the relationship among ideas. Maps are convenient; they summarize a lot of information in a little space. When

NOTE CARDS FOR REVIEW

FIGURE **11.2**

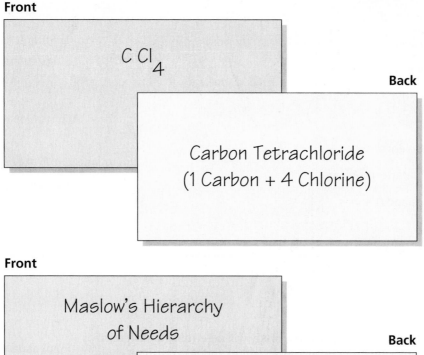

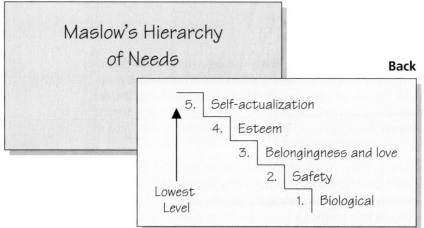

studying for a test, try to redraw your maps from memory. When taking a test, close your eyes and visualize your maps. Reconstruct them in your mind and try to "see" what you have written in each square or circle. Figure 11.3 is an example of a concept map to be used as a study guide.

5. Once a day until you take the test, review your maps and other materials. Review them again the night before the test, just before you go to sleep. Research shows that studying before sleeping improves retention. Then review once more the day of the test.

A CONCEPT MAP FOR REVIEW

FIGURE 11.3

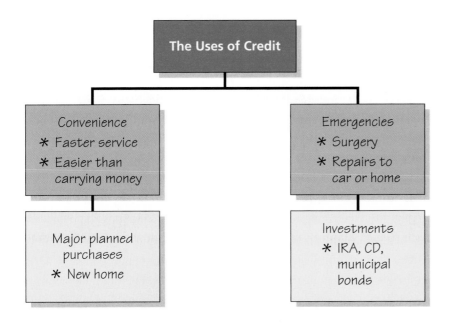

DEVELOP A TEST-TAKING ROUTINE

▶ *Follow a routine for taking tests: Know what to do before, during, and after a test to improve your preparation and performance.*

You can improve your grades on tests by developing a routine to follow that helps you stay calm, avoid distractions, and demonstrate your knowledge. Your test-taking routine should include most or all of the steps discussed in this section (pp. 269–272).

Arrive on Time

If hearing other students discuss the test makes you nervous and distracted, don't arrive early. Arrive on time and try to sit near the front of the room, where you are less likely to be distracted. If you feel a little nervous, close your eyes, take a few deep breaths, and think positive thoughts. If anxiety either before or during tests is a problem for you, see Chapter 12 for an explanation of how to reduce test anxiety.

Jot Down Memory Cues

If you are likely to forget facts, formulas, dates, names, terms, or other items, write them in the margin or on the back of the test as soon as you get it. For

EXERCISE 11.2 LEARNING STYLE

DISCOVER YOUR OWN BEST WAY to prepare for a test by answering the following questions about test preparation and your learning style.

1. **Based on your answers to Awareness Check 18, what are your strengths and weaknesses in preparing for tests?**

   _____

   _____

2. **What relationship do you see between your body's reactions and the way you prepare for tests? For example, when is your best time to study, and how do you accommodate your body's reactions to hunger, tiredness, stress, and so on when preparing for tests?**

   _____

   _____

3. **What is your preferred learning style (visual, auditory, tactile/kinesthetic), and how does it affect the way you prepare for tests?**

   _____

   _____

4. **Are you self-motivated or other-motivated, and how does your locus of control (source of motivation) affect your ability to study for tests?**

   _____

   _____

5. **What changes can you make in the way you prepare for tests that will help you take advantage of your learning style preference?**

   _____

   _____

example, math students tend to get nervous when they are working on a difficult problem or can't remember the next step in a mathematical operation. This anxiety can cause them to forget other concepts and applications. The facts, formulas, and other items that you jot down on your test are memory cues. Knowing that the cues are there will boost your confidence. You won't be worried about forgetting the information, and you will be able to concentrate on taking the test.

Survey the Test

As soon as you receive your test and after you have jotted down your memory cues, survey the test to determine how many questions there are, how many points each is worth, and what kinds of questions you must answer: true-false, multiple-choice, fill-in, or essay. If it's not clear from the test how many points

Exercise Overview

This exercise will help you think critically about the material covered in one of your courses and determine what to study for the next test.

Exercise Background

Many students say they are often not prepared for tests because they do not know what to study. As a result, they may not study at all, or their studying may be hit or miss. The easiest way to determine what a test will cover is to ask the instructor. Most instructors conduct a review before a test anyway, and most are happy to tell you what chapters to review. Some may emphasize specific skills or concepts to practice. Therefore, there is really no excuse for not knowing what to study.

Exercise Task

Choose a study partner who is in one of your other classes, algebra or psychology, for example. Discuss what your class has covered recently and when your next test will be. Look through all of your course materials together and make a checklist similar to the one in Figure 11.1. Beside each item on your checklist, write something specific to study. For example, if "textbook notes" is on your list, write down the chapters that you need to study. Plan a time to study with your partner. When you get your test results, evaluate your checklist to determine whether your study was effective.

each question is worth, ask your instructor. A quick survey of the test will let you know what you must accomplish within the time limit so that you can plan your test-taking time.

Plan and Use All Your Time

Plan to spend the most time answering the questions that are worth the most points. If twenty-five multiple-choice questions are worth one point each, and two essay questions are worth twenty-five points each, and you have fifty minutes to complete the test, answer as many of the multiple-choice questions as you can in ten minutes. That will leave you forty minutes to complete the two essay questions. Spend fifteen minutes answering the first question; then stop and go on to the next one, even if you have not finished. Spend fifteen minutes on the second question. You will now have ten minutes left. Use the ten minutes as needed. You can return to the multiple-choice questions if you have completed the essays, or you can work more on your essays if you finished the multiple-choice questions earlier. Save a few minutes to proofread the whole test and answer any multiple-choice questions that you may have skipped.

Although there are many ways to plan your time, the one suggested here will help you gain some points for each part of the test, even if you are unable to finish all of the questions. If you plan your time and stick to your plan, you will not have to rush. Use all of your time, even if you don't need it. The extra care you take may help you spot mistakes or think of a better way to state an answer.

Read Directions

It may seem obvious that you should read test directions before beginning, but a surprising number of students skip directions. Perhaps they think that reading directions wastes time or that they already know what to do. To avoid needless mistakes, always read directions and ask the instructor to explain anything that you do not understand.

Do Easy Questions First

When you survey the test, you will probably spot questions that will be easy for you to answer. Do those first since you have a good chance of getting the answers right. In addition, doing the easy questions first will raise your confidence in your ability to answer the rest of the questions.

Skip and Return to Difficult Questions

Don't spend too much time on a difficult question. Skip it and return to it later. If something you read or recall as you answer the other questions triggers your memory, you can go back to the one you didn't answer and then resume the test where you left off.

CONCEPT CHECK 11.1

How important is preparing for a test? Think about your most recent test grade in one of your courses. Were you satisfied with the grade? How did you prepare for the test? What did you do well? What could you have done better?

Guess (If There Is No Penalty)

If there is a penalty for wrong answers, the test directions will probably say so. If you are in doubt, ask the instructor. If there is no penalty, guess. Don't leave questions blank; even if you don't think you know the answer, write something anyway. You may pick up a few points. If you guess the answer to a multiple-choice question that has four choices, your chances are one in four that you will get the right answer. If you don't answer, your chances are zero.

Control Your Feelings and Attention

Remain in control of your feelings and attention throughout the test. To avoid becoming distracted, focus your attention on the test. Keep your eyes on the test and don't look up or around. If you don't know what other students are doing, you're not likely to be disturbed by them. You won't notice what page someone else is on or whether someone finishes early.

Maintain a positive attitude. Don't let negative thoughts undermine your work. Counteract them with positive ones. Say to yourself, "I have studied, and I am doing fine." If you become anxious, close your eyes, breathe deeply, and relax. When you feel calm, return to the test and give it your full attention. See Chapter 12 for more suggestions on how to reduce test anxiety.

Check Your Work

Always save time to proofread your test for careless errors and for questions you skipped or forgot to answer. Because first choices are usually correct, change answers only if you're absolutely sure your first answer was wrong.

Learn from Your Mistakes

The next time your instructor returns a graded test, determine what kinds of mistakes you made. Look for a pattern. If you are like many students, you probably make the same mistakes over and over again. If you can prevent these errors, you will improve your test scores.

MASTER OBJECTIVE TESTS

▶ *Learn how to think through a multiple-choice question to improve your*
chances of getting it right. Know when to use guessing strategies.

If you are well prepared for a test, you should be able to answer the questions whether they are true-false, multiple-choice, or fill-in-the-blank. But when confronted with questions you cannot answer, try to gain points by making informed guesses.

True-False Tests

Since a true-false question has only two possible answers, you have a 50 percent chance of choosing the right answer if you guess. Use two strategies for guessing the answer to a true-false question when you are sure that you don't know the answer:

1. **Assume a statement is false if it contains absolute words**.

2. **Assume a statement is false if any part of it is false**.

Mark a statement *false* if it contains **absolute words** such as *always, never, invariably, none, no one, all,* and *everyone*. Absolute words tend to make statements false because they do not allow for exceptions. For example, you should mark the statement "It never gets cold in Florida" *false* because the word *never* means "never in the history of the world." It is highly unlikely that there is a place on Earth where it has never gotten cold even once. Is the next statement true or false? "A statement that contains an absolute word is always false." The statement is false. Remember, absolute words *usually* make statements false, but not always.

Mark a statement *false* if any part of it is false. If part of a statement is untrue, then the whole statement is untrue. For example, the statement "*Hamlet, Macbeth,* and *The Dream Merchant* are three of Shakespeare's most famous tragedies" is false. Although Shakespeare did write *Hamlet* and *Macbeth*, he did not write *The Dream Merchant*. If you don't know whether a statement is true or false, but you're certain that part of it is untrue, mark it *false*.

Absolute words, like *always* and *never*, rule out exceptions.

Multiple-Choice Tests

The part of a multiple-choice item that asks the question is called the **stem**. The answer choices are called **options**. The incorrect options are called **distractors** because they distract your attention away from the correct option. Usually there are four options, though there might be three or five. Your job is to identify the one correct option. You can do this in several ways.

▶ If you know the material, first answer the question mentally and then read all the options and choose the correct one.

▶ If you know the material but cannot answer the question mentally, read the options, eliminate those you know are incorrect, and choose the answer from those remaining. The more options you eliminate, the more likely your choice will be correct.

▶ If you do not know the material, or if you cannot figure out the answer, guess.

Options that contain the phrases "all of the above" or "none of the above" are frequently the correct choices. If two options are similar—for example, "Northern Hemisphere" and "Southern Hemisphere"—one of the options is probably the correct answer. Finally, if one option is more complete or contains more information than the others, it may be the correct one.

Stem refers to the question part of a multiple-choice item.
Options refers to the answer choices in a multiple-choice item.
Distractors are the wrong options in a multiple-choice item.

An option that contains an absolute word such as *all, always,* or *never* is probably a distractor, an incorrect answer. An option that contains an unfamiliar word may also be a distractor. Many students assume that an unfamiliar term is probably the correct answer, but it is more often a wrong answer. When you are guessing, you are more likely to choose the right answer if you choose an option that is familiar to you. Finally, if the list of options is a list of numbers, middle numbers tend to be correct answers, and the highest and lowest numbers in the list tend to be distractors. These strategies are not foolproof, but they may be useful as a last resort if you must guess the answer to a question.

One final word of caution: A well-written multiple-choice test makes guesswork difficult. Thorough preparation is still your best strategy for taking any kind of test.

Fill-in-the-Blank Tests

A fill-in test may require you to recall an answer from memory or choose an answer from a list of options. Choosing an answer from a list is easier than recalling an answer from memory. In either case, the information given in the incomplete statement may provide clues that will help you decide what to write in the blanks. Three strategies can help you fill in the blanks correctly.

EXERCISE 11.3

USE THE GUESSING STRATEGIES YOU just learned to mark the following statements *T* for *true* and *F* for *false*. Work with a partner or complete the exercise on your own.

	T	F
1. The heart contains a left and right ventricle.	☐	☐
2. You can look up the meaning of a word in a glossary, index, or dictionary.	☐	☐
3. All fears are acquired at an early age.	☐	☐
4. Making note cards is the only way to study vocabulary.	☐	☐
5. Whenever there is a fatal accident on the highway, drinking is invariably involved.	☐	☐
6. It is doubtful whether there is human life on other planets.	☐	☐
7. College graduates will always be able to find good jobs.	☐	☐
8. Most violent crime today is drug related.	☐	☐
9. Carl Jung has been called "the father of modern psychology."	☐	☐
10. The numbers *1, 3, 5,* and *9* are prime numbers.	☐	☐

First, decide what kind of answer the statement requires. Read the statement carefully and decide whether you are required to supply a name, a date, a place, or some other kind of information. Knowing what the question asks will help you recall or select the right answer.

Second, the way that a statement is written may help you decide how to complete it. Your answer should complete the statement logically and grammatically. For example, if you are asked to choose options from a list to fill in the blanks, and the statement you are working on requires a verb to complete it, scan the list for verbs and choose the one that best fits the context.

Third, key words in statements may help you determine what topic the question covers. Knowing the topic will help you recall information needed to complete the statement. For example, if a question asks you to briefly describe Piaget's third stage of development, the key words *Piaget* and *third stage of development* let you know that the topic is Piaget's stages. If you can't recall the third stage, mentally reconstructing the other stages in your mind may jog your memory.

EXERCISE 11.4   COLLABORATIVE ACTIVITY

THIS EXERCISE ASKS YOU AND the members of your group to practice the guessing strategies that are appropriate to use when you do not know the answer to a multiple-choice item. Follow the guidelines for group discussion that appear on the inside back cover. Your tasks are as follows: First, each person should answer questions 1–10. Next, discuss your answers and come to a consensus about the best answer choice for each question. Be able to explain why you think your answer is correct and the strategy you used to arrive at it. Review the guessing strategies explained in this chapter as needed. Finally, summarize your answers and explanations on a separate piece of paper to be handed in along with the group evaluation. To download an evaluation form, go to the Online Study Center at college.hmco.com/pic/KanarTCS6e.

1. **A marriage may have a better chance of succeeding if the wife and husband have which characteristic in common?**

   a. **a similar level of education**

   b. **similar social and economic backgrounds**

   c. **shared interests and goals**

   d. **all of the above**

2. **Most of the assignments college students are asked to do require them to use**

   a. **left-brain capacities.**

   b. **right-brain capacities.**

   c. **learning styles.**

   d. **visualization.**

3. **Which of the following are examples of fallacious reasoning?**

   a. **glittering generalities**

   b. **plain folks**

   c. **bandwagon**

   d. **glittering generalities, plain folks, and bandwagon**

4. **A balanced diet should include**

   a. **milk, cheese, and fruit.**

   b. **bread, cereal, and whole grains.**

   c. **milk, fruit, vegetables, meat, and whole grains.**

   d. **vegetables, fruit, and meat.**

5. Most of the world's population is situated

   a. in the Pacific islands.

   b. in the Northern Hemisphere.

   c. in the Southern Hemisphere.

   d. near the equator.

6. Approximately what percentage of immigrants to the United States between 1971 and 1984 came from Asia?

   a. 60 percent

   b. 30 percent

   c. 40 percent

   d. 15 percent

7. Which of the following words is a synonym for *intractable?*

   a. synergistic

   b. acerbic

   c. exacerbating

   d. stubborn

8. Television commercials

   a. always attempt to deceive viewers.

   b. are sometimes interesting to viewers.

   c. are never in the public interest.

   d. influence only people who listen to them.

9. The first quiz programs were televised

   a. in the 1970s.

   b. in the 1950s.

   c. in the 1940s.

   d. before 1920.

10. A smile

    a. may mean different things in different societies.

    b. always signifies happiness.

    c. occurs among the people of only some societies.

    d. never occurs involuntarily.

Group Evaluation:

What advantage do guessing strategies offer? What is the best way to avoid having to guess? Did your group complete its tasks successfully? What improvements can you suggest? What additional questions do you have about taking multiple-choice tests, and how will you find answers to your questions?

Online Study Center
Chapter Exercises/ Forms

ANSWER ESSAY QUESTIONS WITH CONFIDENCE

▶ *Identify the instruction words that tell you what kind of information an essay question is seeking. Know how to write an effective answer.*

You can expect to see two kinds of essay questions—those that require a short answer and those that require a longer, more developed answer. You can often tell how much you are expected to write by the number of points a question is worth or the amount of space left between questions. Sometimes the directions will be specific: "Answer any two of the five questions that follow and devote no more than a page to each." If you are not sure how much you should write or how detailed your instructor expects your answer to be, ask. In general, follow these guidelines for composing answers to essay questions of the short-answer type:

▼ Read the question carefully and make sure you understand what the question asks.

▼ Watch for instruction words. Short-answer questions often ask you to supply definitions, examples, or other specific pieces of information.

▼ Concentrate on answering the question briefly and precisely.

▼ Stay on the topic and avoid stating your opinion or making judgments unless the question asks you to do so.

▼ Restate the question in your answer. Doing this makes it easier for your instructor to read and follow your explanation.

If you do not know the answer to a question, go on to another part of the test and return to it later. Information you read in another question may jog your memory. In any case, don't leave a question unanswered. Try to write something. Essay questions are often worth several points, and you have nothing to lose by attempting to answer. Read the following sample test question and its answer:

Question: Define *memory* and illustrate your definition with examples.

Answer: *Memory is a mental process that occurs in three stages: reception, retention, and recollection. In the reception stage you take in information through your senses. Most of this is information you will forget unless you store it during the retention stage in your short-term or long-term memory. Short-term memory is fleeting. It enables you to remember a phone number you have looked up long enough to dial it, or the name of someone you met at a party long enough to introduce him or her to someone else. Long-term memory can be permanent. For example, you never forget your birthday. In the recollection stage you retrieve information you have stored much as you would retrieve a file from a computer's directory.*

EXERCISE 11.5

THE FOLLOWING FILL-IN-THE-BLANK test covers the preceding section, Master Objective Tests. Review the section; then complete the test for practice without looking back at the book. When you have finished, look back to check your answers. Any questions that you missed indicate material that you need to review.

1. **Three common types of objective tests are** _____, _____, **and** _____.

2. **Words such as** *always, never,* **and** *only* **are called** _____.

3. **These words generally indicate a wrong answer because** _____

   _____.

4. **A statement is false if any part of it is** _____.

5. **The question part of a multiple-choice item is called the** _____.

6. _____ **are the possible answers to a multiple-choice question.**

7. **Incorrect answer choices to a multiple-choice question are called** _____.

8. **Three strategies to use when taking fill-in-the-blank tests are** _____, _____, **and**

   _____.

Instruction words are terms that tell you how to answer a question. *Discuss* and *compare* are two examples of instruction words.

This answer responds to both **instruction words** in the question: *define* and *illustrate*. The student defines memory as a three-stage process, names and explains each stage, and gives examples of each. Figure 11.4 contains a list of instruction words that are frequently used in essay questions and their meanings.

Some essay questions require a longer answer that may cover several points. You will stand a better chance of getting a good grade if your answer is detailed but not rambling, if you stick to facts and information and avoid opinions and judgments, if your answer follows a logical plan of development, and if you state your ideas clearly in error-free sentences. In general, apply the same skills you use for writing essays in your composition class to composing answers to essay questions. Be sure to look for instruction words in each question that will tell you what kind of answer to write.

The following general guidelines will help you compose good answers to longer essay test questions:

▼ Read the question carefully. Watch for instruction words and make sure you understand what the question asks you to do. Ask the instructor for an explanation if necessary.

▼ Think about what you will write. Plan your answer and allow yourself enough time to write thoughtfully.

▼ Jot down a rough outline of the important ideas you will cover so that you don't forget them.

FIGURE 11.4

INSTRUCTION WORDS USED IN ESSAY QUESTIONS

INSTRUCTION WORDS	MEANINGS
Compare	Explain similarities and differences.
Contrast	Explain differences only.
Criticize or evaluate	Make a judgment about strengths and weaknesses, worth or merit, or positive or negative aspects.
Define	Give a precise and accurate meaning.
Describe	Give a mental impression, a detailed account.
Discuss or explain	Give reasons, facts, or details that show you understand.
Enumerate or list	State points one by one and briefly explain.
Illustrate	Explain by using examples.
Interpret	Explain in your own words and discuss significance.
Justify or prove	Construct an argument for or against and support with evidence.
Outline	Describe in general and cover main ideas.
Relate	Show a connection among ideas.
Summarize	Condense main ideas; state them briefly.
Trace	Describe a series of steps, stages, or events.

▼ Incorporate the question into your first sentence and briefly state your answer to the question.

▼ In the rest of your essay, provide enough details to explain your answer and to demonstrate your knowledge of the material.

▼ Save time at the end of the exam to proofread your essay and correct errors.

The following essay question and list show how to plan an effective answer. The instruction word is in bold type and the topic is in italics.

Question	How can a student learn to improve *time management?* **Discuss** the effective use of a semester schedule, a weekly schedule, and a daily list.
Paragraph 1:	Briefly introduce and restate the question, and briefly state your answer.
Paragraph 2:	Discuss semester schedule.
Paragraph 3:	Discuss weekly schedule.
Paragraph 4:	Discuss daily list.
Paragraph 5:	Summarize what you have said.

Time management is the topic, and it is broken down into three types of schedules. The instruction word *discuss* tells you to supply reasons, facts, or details to explain the schedules.

When your test paper is returned to you, read over your answers to the essay questions. Notice how many points you gained, how many you lost, and the reasons for each. Check for these three common mistakes: First, did you read the directions carefully? If not, your answer may be off the topic. Second, did you cover all parts of the question to receive full credit? Third, did you include enough details? If not, you may have lost points. Read your instructor's comments to determine what you need to do to improve your grade on the next test. If you scored poorly on the essay portion of the test, and you do not understand why, make an appointment with your instructor to discuss your grade. Be sure to ask your instructor what you can do to improve.

EXERCISE 11.6 COMPUTER APPLICATION

SEARCH THE INTERNET FOR MORE suggestions on ways to prepare for and take tests. As a starting point, try these search words: *test-wiseness, study skills, test-taking techniques.* If you have trouble, go to the Online Study Center at college.hmco.com/pic/KanarTCS6e to begin your search. Also, visit your college's web site to see what is available. In addition, choose another college or university and check out its web site for information on preparing for tests. Share what you find with the rest of the class.

How to Raise Scores on Standardized Tests

You can't study for a standardized test, but try these ways to prepare yourself for success.

Check your campus or local bookstore to see if you can purchase a study guide for the test you need to take. Find out if your college offers a prep course or review session that will help you get ready for the test. In addition, try these suggestions:

- Know how many sections there are on the test and what each section covers. Find out whether you will be required to write one or more essays.

- Find out whether the test will be timed, how long it will last, and how much time you will have to complete each section. If the test will last longer than two hours, take a snack that you can eat during a break for a quick energy boost.

- If you must write an essay as part of the test, practice writing in a timed situation. Choose a topic, set a timer or alarm clock, and write your essay. If you practice writing within a time limit, you are less likely to become anxious when taking a timed test.

- Find out if you will be allowed to use a dictionary, calculator, or other aids during the test.

- Find out whether the test is administered online or with examination booklets. Then purchase any special materials you will need.

- Get a good night's sleep, eat a nourishing breakfast, and arrive at the testing site on time, rested, and in a positive frame of mind.

- To increase your chances of scoring well, apply the test-taking strategies you have learned from this chapter. Use guessing strategies if there is no penalty for guessing, and you do not know the answer.

- During breaks between sections of the test, stand up and move around to increase your circulation. This little bit of exercise will make you feel more alert when you return to the test.

- Whether working online or on an answer sheet, use any remaining time to proofread and correct your answers.

Don't worry if you are unable to complete a section of the test. On some standardized tests, hardly anyone finishes. Also, you can miss many of the items and still make a passing score. Finally, even if you score below a cutoff on a standardized test, you may be allowed to retake the part of the test on which you scored low.

To learn more about this topic, do an online search using these keywords as a starting point: *testing, standardized tests, preparing for tests*. To find out about a particular test and any prep courses or materials that may be available, use the name of the test such as *GRE, LSAT*, and so on as a search word.

Online Study Center
Confidence Builder
Web Search

Thinking ahead about Career

Purpose and Instructions

A workplace focus in Chapter 11 is on personal responsibility, a personal quality that makes you responsible for deciding what, when, and how to study for tests that relate directly to your career. Use the knowledge you have gained from this chapter to solve work-related problems such as the one explained in the following case study. Read the case study on your own or with a partner and then answer the questions.

Case Study

Dan is a recent law school graduate hired by a large firm. Keeping this job requires that he pass the bar exam, which he is scheduled to take in two weeks. He knows what to study, but he also knows that several questions will require him to write detailed answers. Although Dan had excellent grades in law school, two things have always given him trouble: writing under the pressure of a time limit and deciding what to write. Dan is a good writer when he has time to plan and organize an essay, but in a testing situation, he has trouble getting started. Dan is willing to do whatever will help him increase his chances for success on the exam.

Case Questions

1. **What is Dan's problem in preparing for the bar exam?**

   _____

   _____

2. **With respect to his upcoming exam, what are Dan's strengths and weaknesses?**

   _____

   _____

3. **What specific strategies would help Dan write good responses to the exam questions?**

   _____

   _____

4. **Access the Career Resource Center and read the article entitled "Common Rhetorical Modes in Academic Writing" in the *Building Learning Strategies* section of *The Bridge*. Based on this article, what else have you learned that would help Dan?**

   _____

   _____

Your *Reflections*

Reflect on what you have learned from this chapter about preparing for tests. Use the following questions to stimulate your thinking; then write your reflections. Include in your writing specific information from the chapter.

- What are your grades in your courses so far, and are you satisfied with them? Why or why not?

- To what extent has each of the following affected your grades on tests: anxiety, amount and kind of preparation, attitude, and health?

- Which of the factors affecting your grades can you control? How?

- What is one skill or attitude explained in this chapter that you would like to develop, and what can you begin doing today to make that happen?

Chapter review

To review the chapter, reflect on the following confidence-building attitudes and skills. Complete **Concepts to Understand** by filling in the blanks with words or terms from the list provided. Then practice your new skills at every opportunity.

ATTITUDES TO DEVELOP
- responsibility
- self-management
- positive thinking

SKILLS TO PRACTICE
- making and following schedules
- preparing for tests
- using study systems

CONCEPTS TO UNDERSTAND

| standardized | true-false | guessing | memory | daily |
| distractor | absolute | fill-in | weekly | stem |

To prepare for tests, follow three steps: First, make a study schedule that allows time for (1) _____, (2) _____, and exam review for each course. Second, decide what to study by reviewing your notes, returned tests, and other appropriate materials. Third, study with a system that works for you.

To increase confidence and reduce anxiety during a test, follow a test-taking routine that includes these steps: Arrive on time, jot down (3) _____ cues, survey the test, plan and use all your time, read directions, use (4) _____ strategies if there is no penalty.

Be able to recognize different types of tests and choose appropriate strategies for taking each. Objective tests include (5) _____, multiple-choice, and (6) _____. The parts of a multiple-choice item include the question or (7) _____ and the answer choices or options. A wrong answer choice is called a (8) _____. Wrong answer choices may contain (9) _____ words such as *always* and *never*. Essay tests call for well-developed written answers. Although you cannot study for a (10) _____ test, you can prepare yourself for success by following the suggestions in this chapter.

To access additional review exercises, go to
college.hmco.com/pic/KanarTCS6e.

Online Study Center
Review Exercise
ACE Self-Test

Online Study Center

Prepare for Class, Improve Your Grade, and ACE the Test. This chapter's *Student Achievement* resources include

Chapter exercises/forms   Review exercise   Confidence Builder Web search
ACE Self-test

To access these learning and study tools, go to **college.hmco.com/pic/KanarTCS6e**.

Visualize a peaceful scene to reduce stress and restore calm.

The fear of failure or the fear of success can sabotage your performance. Learn to face your fears and overcome them.

Relaxation is a learned response. Learn relaxation techniques and practice them to reduce stress and anxiety.

Identify the causes of your test anxiety and work to eliminate them.

*Confident students are **assertive**. They have the strength to face challenges and take intellectual risks.*

► WHAT CAUSES TEST ANXIETY?
Expectations
Grades and Self-Esteem
Feelings of Helplessness

► LEARN TO RELAX

► FACE YOUR FEARS

► ENGAGE IN POSITIVE SELF-TALK

► FIND YOUR BEST SOLUTION

► *We all respond differently to stress and anxiety. Choose your best solution from available alternatives.*

► *Your inner thoughts shape your feelings and behavior. Learn how to turn negative thoughts into positive thoughts that promote calmness and success.*

T esting is stressful. Poor test scores may lower your grade average. In some courses, a final exam may determine whether you pass or fail. Scholarships, admittance to graduate school or a profession, entry to some job markets or careers, and even a promotion within a company may, in part, depend on test scores. It is no wonder that you may feel some anxiety when faced with a test. In fact, it would be unusual if you didn't.

Test anxiety is stress that is related to a testing situation, and it may affect students in different ways. Bonnie's test anxiety causes her to have various physical and mental reactions. Before she takes a test, her palms sweat, her head aches, or her stomach may be upset. During the test she tries to calm herself, but her anxiety increases. She reads a question, and her mind goes blank, even though she may have known the answer before the test began. Her inner voice says, "I'm going to fail." Bonnie's reactions are triggered by any test, whether she is prepared for it or not. However, Jerome has reactions like Bonnie's only when he is not well prepared. Although he should be able to

Test anxiety is a learned response. It is test related in origin.

test anxiety, *p. 285*
situational test anxiety, *p. 286*
chronic test anxiety, *p. 286*
perceptions, *p. 288*

SCANS TERM

problem-solving skills, *p. 286*

answer all the questions for which he has studied, he may miss some of them because his anxiety blocks his recall. As soon as the test is over, he remembers what he should have written.

Jerome's test anxiety results from lack of preparation. Effective study skills and a test-taking routine, as explained in Chapter 11, are his keys to anxiety relief. However, Bonnie's anxiety may be the result of causes that are not so easily or quickly resolved. Self-assessment is Bonnie's key to understanding what causes her anxiety. Eliminating the causes will bring relief. Both students can use their **problem-solving skills** not only to find ways to reduce test anxiety but also to relieve work-related stress.

The good thing about test anxiety is that it is a *learned response;* therefore, it can be unlearned. This chapter explains what you can do to reduce test anxiety.

Problem-solving skills involve decision making. Being able to identify problems and find solutions is a valued workplace competency.

WHAT CAUSES TEST ANXIETY?

▶ *Identify the causes of your test anxiety and work to eliminate them.*

Test anxiety is of two types: situational and chronic. **Situational test anxiety** is the most common and may occur only when you are unprepared or when the test has a lot riding on it. Final exams, certification or board exams, and other tests of skill that determine whether you move forward or stay behind are anxiety provoking for most students. Some situational test anxiety is both rational and expected. **Chronic test anxiety** is more severe and less common. Students who have this type of anxiety get nervous at the mere mention of a test. Their fear of testing may be so paralyzing that it affects their performance. Chronic test anxiety that does not respond to relaxation techniques combined with adequate test preparation is best dealt with by professionals who can provide the kind of help needed to overcome the anxiety.

The best way to overcome test anxiety is to understand its causes and to realize that the specific triggers and effects of test anxiety may vary. The most common cause of most test anxiety is lack of preparation. Test anxiety may result from these other common causes as well:

Situational test anxiety commonly results when a person is insufficiently prepared for a test or when the test is an important one.

Chronic test anxiety is less common, but those who have it may become anxious even when they are prepared.

▼ Being afraid that you won't live up to the expectations of important people in your life and worrying that you will lose the affection of people you care about if you don't succeed

▼ Believing grades are a measure of self-worth

▼ Feeling helpless, believing that you have no control over your performance or grades.

To find out whether you have test anxiety, complete Awareness Check 19.

AWARENESS CHECK 19

Do You Have Test Anxiety?

Check the response that seems most characteristic of you.

Never	Sometimes	Usually	
☐	☐	☐	1. I have trouble sleeping the night before a test.
☐	☐	☐	2. During a test, my palms sweat.
☐	☐	☐	3. Before a test, I get a headache.
☐	☐	☐	4. During a test, I become nauseated.
☐	☐	☐	5. Because of panic, I sometimes cut class on a test day.
☐	☐	☐	6. I have pains in my neck, back, or legs during a test.
☐	☐	☐	7. My heart pounds just before or during a test.
☐	☐	☐	8. I feel nervous and jittery when I am taking a test.
☐	☐	☐	9. During a test, I have trouble remembering.
☐	☐	☐	10. I lose my appetite before a test.
☐	☐	☐	11. I make careless errors on tests.
☐	☐	☐	12. My mind goes blank during tests.
☐	☐	☐	13. I worry when other students are finished before I am.
☐	☐	☐	14. I feel pressed for time when I am taking a test.
☐	☐	☐	15. I worry that I may be doing poorly on a test but that everyone else is doing all right.
☐	☐	☐	16. When I am taking a test, I think about my past failures.
☐	☐	☐	17. During a test, I feel as if I have studied all the wrong things.
☐	☐	☐	18. I can't think clearly during tests.
☐	☐	☐	19. I have a hard time understanding and remembering directions when I am taking a test.
☐	☐	☐	20. After a test, I remember answers to questions I either left blank or answered incorrectly.

Items 1–10 refer to physical symptoms of test anxiety, and items 11–20 refer to mental symptoms. If you checked "sometimes" or "usually" ten or more times, you may have some test anxiety. To be sure, you might want to talk to your advisor about how you feel before, during, and after taking tests.

Perceptions involve an awareness or understanding gained through the senses. Perceptions may or may not reflect reality.

Expectations

Many students' **perceptions** of what their parents or important others expect may be inaccurate. If you worry that you may alienate people you care about unless you do well in college, you may become fearful and anxious that you will disappoint them or make them angry. If you believe that you can't live up to the expectations of others, tests may make you especially anxious. Suppose your parents or important others become angry if you earn any grade lower than an A or B. You need to talk this over with them to determine the source of their anger. Perhaps they feel that a grade lower than an A or B means that you aren't trying hard enough or that you aren't committed to getting an education. But there may be other reasons why you are not performing as expected in a course. You may have been unprepared for the level of the course, or illness or other hardships may have affected your level of performance. It is unreasonable to expect a student to achieve someone else's ideal grade, but it is not unreasonable to expect a student to do his or her best. If a C represents a student's best effort, then it is a good grade. Try to separate yourself from others' expectations of you. Focus instead on what *you* expect from yourself and work hard to achieve it.

Grades and Self-Esteem

Test anxiety can result from placing too great an emphasis on grades. A low grade for some students translates into "I don't measure up." The result is a loss of self-esteem. One way to reduce test anxiety is to emphasize *performance* instead of grades. Rather than letting grades control your feelings, take control of your performance.

Turn each testing situation into an opportunity for self-assessment. Use tests to track your performance in a course. Keep a record of the number and type of items you missed, your level of anxiety during the test, your level of preparation, and what you now need to review. Over a period of time, you may see a pattern in your study and testing behavior. For example, if you consistently miss the same type of question or if your level of anxiety goes up when you haven't prepared sufficiently, then you will know what and how much to study for the next test.

When you emphasize performance over grades, a test becomes a personal challenge, a chance for you to apply your knowledge and skill to new problems and tasks, an opportunity for you to discover your strengths and weaknesses. Improved performance is the goal. Grades are not a measure of self-worth. They are merely a way to keep score. To track your performance on tests, make a chart like the one in Figure 12.1 or devise one of your own. The chart is filled in as an example. To download a blank copy of the chart for your own use, go to the Online Study Center at college.hmco.com/pic/KanarTCS6e.

Feelings of Helplessness

Are you self-motivated (internal locus of control) or other-motivated (external locus of control)? Other-motivated students often do not see a connection between studying and grades. They blame their poor grades on the perceived unfairness of the instructor or the difficulty of the test instead of blaming their own lack of preparation. As a result, they feel helpless and out of control and experience test anxiety. The more self-motivated you are, the more likely you are to see a connection between your preparation and your grades. When you are well prepared for a test, you are in control of your emotions and of your reactions to the testing situation. As a result, you enter the classroom feeling calm and confident, ready to do your best.

By identifying the cause of your test anxiety, you can do what is necessary to eliminate it. Figure 12.2 lists common causes of test anxiety and how to eliminate them.

CONCEPT CHECK 12.1

Read again the examples of Bonnie and Jerome in this chapter's opening paragraphs. Which student may have situational test anxiety? Which one may have chronic test anxiety?

Online Study Center
Chapter Exercises/ Forms

FIGURE 12.1

A CHART FOR TRACKING PERFORMANCE ON TESTS

TEST/ COURSE	ITEMS MISSED	TYPE OF ITEM	ANXIETY LEVEL	PREPARATION LEVEL	TO DO
Chemistry chapter quiz	#3	Avogadro's Law	high	low (1 hr.)	1. Review laws.
	#6, #7	ratio of effusion ratio of gasses			2. Do more practice problems.
	#10	partial pressures and mole fractions			

FIGURE 12.2

TEST ANXIETY: CAUSES AND ELIMINATORS

CAUSES	ELIMINATORS
1. Trying to meet others' expectations	Decide whether living up to these expectations is something you want to do for yourself. Set your own goals and live up to your own expectations.
2. Letting grades determine your self-worth	Emphasize performance over grades. Take control by tracking performance to overcome weaknesses.
3. Inadequate preparation and guilt	So you weren't prepared this time. Keep your goal in sight and resolve to do better.
4. Feeling helpless, with no control over what happens	Develop an internal locus of control. Improve your study habits. Prepare for your next test and observe the connection between the amount and quality of your studying and the grade you receive.

LEARN TO RELAX

▶ *Relaxation is a learned response. Learn relaxation techniques and practice them to reduce stress and anxiety.*

A proven way to reduce the physical and mental discomfort caused by test anxiety is to learn how to relax. You can't be relaxed and anxious at the same time. When you feel nervous before or during a test, you need to be able to relax so that you become calm enough to focus your attention on the task of taking the test.

Muscle relaxation exercises can help you control the physical symptoms of test anxiety. Become aware of the sixteen muscle groups of your body (see Figure 12.3) and practice a technique that will help you relax each group. When you are relaxed, you can program yourself for success.

Some people don't even know when they are tense. As you locate each of the sixteen muscle groups in Figure 12.3, try to sense whether you are holding any tension in your own muscles at each site. Try this exercise: Close your eyes and search for the tension in your body. Are you clenching your teeth? If so, open your mouth slightly and relax your jaw. Are your shoulders hunched? Lower your shoulders and feel an immediate sense of relief. Now breathe deeply. Uncross your legs if they are crossed and press your feet flat on the floor. Do not tense your leg muscles. Settle comfortably into your chair and enjoy how good you feel when your muscles are relaxed. Imagine taking a test when you are this calm.

SIXTEEN MUSCLE GROUPS   FIGURE 12.3

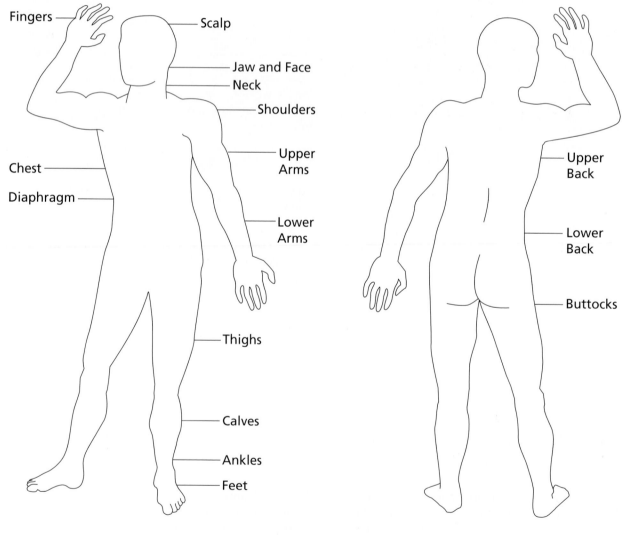

To feel the difference between tension and relaxation even more, try this exercise: Clench your hand into a fist. Squeeze as tightly as you can until you feel your fingers pressing uncomfortably into your palm. Hold that position for a few seconds. Feel your pulse pounding in your fingertips. Very slowly, open your hand. Uncurl your fingers and let go of the tension. When you are experiencing test anxiety, your mind is like your clenched fist. When you relax, your mind is like your hand opening and letting go of the tension.

Here is another relaxation exercise you can do the evening or morning before a test. Either sit or lie down comfortably; close your eyes and breathe deeply for a few seconds. Beginning with your feet, focus on each muscle group, one at a time; tense and then relax the muscles so that there is a sharp difference between tensing and letting go. While you are relaxed, visualize a pleasant scene. For example, imagine yourself lying on a beach in the warm sun. Hear the waves washing up on the shore. Enjoy this scene for a few seconds; then let it fade. Concentrate on relaxing your body even more. Breathe slowly and deeply for a few more minutes; then open your eyes.

To relax yourself in a classroom situation, try these two simple but effective exercises:

1. Take a deep breath and relax your shoulders. Put your hands in your lap and clench your fists to feel the tension. Slowly open your hands and let them drop down at your sides, letting go of the tension.

2. With your elbows on the desk, bow your head over your open book or test paper while resting your forehead on top of your hands. Either close your eyes or leave them open but unfocused. Breathe slowly and deeply until you feel calm.

You can do these exercises without calling attention to yourself. Instead, it will seem as if you are simply concentrating or relaxing.

Your best defense against test anxiety is preparation for tests.

You can relieve test anxiety by focusing all your attention on the test. Avoid thinking about what other students are doing and fight distractions.

FACE YOUR FEARS

> *The fear of failure or the fear of success can sabotage your performance. Learn to face your fears and overcome them.*

Whether your test anxiety is moderate or severe, it may be the result of fears that you have not faced. The fear of failure as well as the fear of success can sabotage your efforts and affect your performance. By bringing your fears out into the open, you can examine them rationally and find ways to overcome them. As Franklin Delano Roosevelt famously said, "We have nothing to fear but fear itself."

What kind of fear can bring on test anxiety? The fear of failure tops the list. For example, if you have had a history of failure in math courses, you may become anxious whenever you take a math test. When a test determines whether you will get a scholarship, or a poor grade in a course may lead to academic probation, then the fear of failure and its consequences can consume you with worry and anxiety.

Less common, but also self-sabotaging, is the fear of success. Some students whose grades have been only average may actually fear making above average grades because this would set a new standard of performance for them to live up to. The higher grades would require more work and study time to maintain, and these students might not be ready to make that commitment.

Identifying and facing your fears, whatever their source, is the first step toward taking control of your test anxiety. Being well-prepared for any test, no matter how important, is your best defense.

ENGAGE IN POSITIVE SELF-TALK

> *Your inner thoughts shape your feelings and behavior. Learn how to turn negative thoughts into positive thoughts that promote calmness and success.*

Although you may sometimes think that your mind is blank, it really is not. A mental dialogue plays like a radio in your mind, no matter what else is going on. While you are listening to a lecture, you are also thinking ahead to what you will do when class is over, or recalling something that happened earlier, or thinking about a problem that has been on your mind. When you have a conversation with someone, while you are listening, you are also thinking about what you will say next. Your inner voice is talking to you, and it is extremely persistent.

Take a few minutes right now to listen to that inner voice. Try this simple exercise: Sit or lie down comfortably; close your eyes and breathe deeply. Concentrate on making your mind go blank. You will probably find it very hard to think about nothing because your inner voice will keep interrupting. What are your thoughts? Are they positive or negative? Do you praise or belittle yourself? Students who have test anxiety are frequently troubled by negative thoughts such as these:

"I'm going to fail this test."

"I hate this class."

"This course is doing nothing for me."

"The instructor doesn't care whether I pass or fail."

"Everybody in this class is doing better than I am."

Examine each negative thought and see how it hurts you. If you think and believe, "I am going to fail this test," then you probably will because you will become more anxious and less able to focus your attention on the test. If you say to yourself, "I hate this class" or "This course is doing nothing for me," you are wasting time indulging thoughts that keep you from concentrating on recalling information you need to answer questions. Saying to yourself, "This instructor doesn't care whether I pass or fail" or "Everybody in this class is doing better than I am" causes you to focus attention on other people instead of on the test. To combat negative thoughts, become task-oriented. Block out all but positive thoughts specifically related to the task of taking and passing the test. Negative thinking can become a habit. To break the habit and program yourself for success, do three things:

1. Become aware of all the negative messages you may be sending yourself.

2. Replace negative thoughts with positive ones such as these:

   "I'll pass this test."

   "I'm learning something in this class."

   "The instructor wants me to succeed."

   "This course is a step toward my goals."

   "I am well prepared, and I will do my best."

3. Change your inner voice into one that is calm and confident.

You may have to apply conscious effort for a long time before you learn to control your inner voice. Chances are good that your negative thoughts about yourself go back to your early childhood; they are probably so automatic that you hardly even notice them when you are involved in an activity such as taking a test. But learning to silence those thoughts and to replace them with positive, supportive ones will have a positive effect on other areas of your life besides test taking. You may find yourself having more fun in your classes and in activities such as sports, hobbies, and work if you aren't so critical of your performance. Studying will become easier, too, and your chances for success in college will improve. Thinking positively about yourself can even change the expression on your face. If you look and feel confident, people will assume that you are.

EXERCISE 12.1

PRACTICE POSITIVE THINKING. LISTEN TO your inner voice. In the first column, list any negative thoughts you are having. Then, in the second column, rewrite them as positive self-directions. For example, the negative thought "I'm going to fail this test" becomes the positive direction "I'm well prepared for this test, so I will earn a good grade."

Negative Thoughts

1. _____

_____

2. _____

_____

3. _____

_____

4. _____

_____

5. _____

_____

Positive Thoughts

1. _____

_____

2. _____

_____

3. _____

_____

4. _____

_____

5. _____

_____

CONFIDENCE BUILDER

Help for the Math-Anxious Student

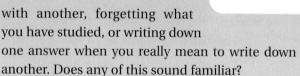

If you ask students what their most difficult subject is, more often than not, they will say "math." Estimates of the percentage of entering college students who are underprepared in math may run as high as 60 percent at some institutions. It is no wonder that many students suffer from math anxiety.

Math anxiety is mental disorganization, fear, or panic associated with math courses and other math-related situations. Are you a math-anxious student? If so, the fear or panic that you feel may produce physical or mental symptoms, or both. Physical symptoms include sweaty palms, nausea, headaches, and jittery feelings. Mental symptoms include the fear of failure and mental disorganization during a test, such as confusing one concept

with another, forgetting what you have studied, or writing down one answer when you really mean to write down another. Does any of this sound familiar?

Like test anxiety, math anxiety is a learned response that you can unlearn, but be patient because it may take some time. As with test anxiety, the best defense against math anxiety is to be prepared. Keep up with assignments and do your daily, weekly, and pre-exam reviews for all tests. In addition, try these tips:

• Remember that you can't be relaxed and anxious at the same time, so practice relaxation techniques before you sit down to study and before a test. The *desk-top* and *chair-seat* relaxation techniques (see Chapter 10) and the visualization technique explained in this chapter are all good ones to try.

- As soon as you receive a test, jot down memory cues—rules and formulas that you will need to use but are likely to forget if you become anxious.

- Learn mathematical terms. Math has its own language. Numbers, symbols, and formulas stand for ideas and relationships. Review these often until you know them; then you will be less likely to forget them on a test.

- Always do all the problems at the end of a textbook chapter even if they have not been assigned. Practice develops skill, and with skill comes confidence.

- Learn from your mistakes. Know the differences among concept errors, application errors, and careless errors. *Concept errors* occur when you haven't learned a rule or principle needed to solve a problem. *Application errors* occur when you do know the concept, but you apply it incorrectly. *Careless errors* are often proofreading errors, such as dropping a plus or minus sign.

- If more than one math course is required for your program, take them in consecutive terms so that there is no loss of skill.

- Above all, attend class regularly and keep up with assignments. A math course develops sequentially and gets more difficult towards the end of the term.

To learn more about this topic, do an online search using *math anxiety* as a keyword.

EXERCISE 12.2   LEARNING STYLE

CANDACE IS OVERWHELMED WITH TEST anxiety when she thinks about her biology midterm. Read about her attempt to overcome this problem; then answer the questions.

Even though the exam is more than three weeks away, Candace is already waking up at night panicked by the thought of her biology midterm. She knows that she is always well prepared for class. She does all the reading. Why does she feel so anxious about the exam? In desperation, she decides to try a visualization technique that her psychology professor explained to her. Here is what she does.

Each day for about twenty minutes, she sits alone in her room. Closing her eyes, she begins to breathe deeply and then, through a process of tensing and relaxing each muscle individually, she relaxes her entire body. When she feels totally relaxed, she imagines herself sinking into the overstuffed pillows of a lovely old chair in a beautiful garden. Feeling the warmth of the sun on her face, she breathes in the fragrances that surround her. She enjoys this imaginary scene for a few long seconds, then lets the scene slowly fade and replaces it with another scene. She is sitting in her biology class, about to begin taking her exam. She feels totally relaxed and prepared for the test. Calmly, she opens the test booklet and begins to write. Again, she imagines how prepared she is, how good she feels at that moment. She knows she can pass the exam. She feels confidence flow through her body. After lingering for a few moments on this image, Candace imagines one last scene. Her professor is handing back the test booklets. Confidently accepting hers, Candace opens the cover and reads the handwritten note at the top of the page: "Great work. You should be proud of your success on this exam." Candace concentrates on her intense feelings of success and then allows the scene to fade. She breathes deeply for a few more moments, then slowly opens her eyes.

1. **How does Candace begin her visualization technique?** _____
    _____

2. **Why does she imagine a beautiful garden?** _____
    _____

3. **What other scenes might she imagine?** _____
    _____

4. **Why do you think she visualizes the garden scene before visualizing the classroom scene?** _____
    _____

5. **What is the final image that Candace visualizes?** _____
    _____

6. **Why is it important for Candace to visualize this final scene?** _____
    _____
    _____

7. **How might this visualization exercise help reduce Candace's test anxiety?** _____
    _____
    _____

8. **Based on your learning style, what changes would you make to Candace's visualization if you were to try this technique yourself?** _____
    _____
    _____
    _____

Once you have learned to focus all of your attention on taking a test, to speak positively to yourself, and to feel confident that you will be able to demonstrate your knowledge, test taking may become an enjoyable intellectual challenge for you.

Find Your Best Solution

We all respond differently to stress and anxiety. Choose your best solution from available alternatives.

Test anxiety is an individual problem. Anxiety differs in degree and kind from student to student. It is important to remember two things. First, a little anxiety won't hurt you and may even be the incentive you need to do your best. Second, even if you have a great deal of anxiety that causes you considerable discomfort, you are not a hopeless case. Furthermore, you have a lot of company. For many students, test anxiety has become a way of life, but it doesn't have to remain so.

The coping strategies discussed in this chapter have worked for many students. Here are six more tips for reducing test anxiety:

▼ Improve the way you prepare for tests by allowing sufficient time for study, by using a study system, and by reviewing frequently. Most test anxiety is the result of irrational fears. The only real cause for fear is insufficient preparation for a test, which almost always *does* result in a poor grade. If you know you are not prepared, then you can expect to have some anxiety. Calm yourself by using the relaxation techniques explained in this chapter; then do your best on the questions you are able to answer.

▼ Your body will tell you when you are becoming anxious during a test. Learn to recognize the signals that may be signs of stress: increased pulse rate, excessive perspiration, shallow breathing, sweaty palms, upset stomach, and headache.

▼ Dress comfortably for tests. Wear loose-fitting clothes and comfortable shoes. Dress in layers so that you can put something on or take something off if the temperature in the room is too cold or too hot.

▼ Arrive at the testing site on time. Don't be too early. If you have time on your hands before the test, waiting may make you nervous. Also, you may get into conversations with other students who will shake your confidence by reminding you of material you haven't studied.

▼ Develop a test-day tradition. Viana wears a pair of "good luck" jeans on test days. For reasons only she knows, these jeans have pleasant associations and make her feel successful. Another student, Nguyen, plays the *1812 Overture* to get himself ready for a test. Maybe you have a lucky pen or some other talisman that can serve as a confidence builder.

▼ See test anxiety for what it is—a learned response that you can unlearn, a habit that you can break.

Online Study Center
Stress: A Common Denominator (Article)

C R I T I C A L

T H I N K I N G

Exercise Overview

This exercise will help you think critically about the relationship between test anxiety and other forms of stress.

Exercise Background

We all experience stress in our lives from many different sources, of which test anxiety may be one. Though some stress is normal and to be expected, stress can become debilitating, making it difficult to perform at our best. To cope with this level of stress, determine its cause. Then you may be able to find a way to reduce or eliminate it.

Exercise Task

What kinds of situations are stress provoking for you? Is test anxiety one of them? Does having to give a speech make you nervous? Do you feel stress when something goes wrong at work? Are relationships a source of stress for you? Write a short essay about a stressful situation in your life and what you did to cope with it. Explain how one of this chapter's strategies could have helped or might help in the future in similar situations.

EXERCISE 12.3 COLLABORATIVE ACTIVITY

APPLY WHAT YOU HAVE LEARNED about test anxiety by completing this exercise with group members. Follow the guidelines for group discussion that appear on the inside back cover. The four steps of the COPE problem-solving method, as explained in Chapter 3, are *challenge, option, plan,* and *evaluation*. Discuss how a student could use COPE to solve a test-anxiety problem. Then work through COPE's steps to illustrate your solution. You can make up a hypothetical student with a problem, or you can use a real test-anxiety problem contributed by one of your group members. Record your answers on the lines provided. Then write your evaluation on your own paper or go to the Online Study Center at college.hmco.com/pic/KanarTCS6e to download the evaluation form.

1. *Challenge:* State the problem, its causes, and the result you want.

   _____

   _____

2. *Options:* List possible options to reduce anxiety and their advantages and disadvantages.

   _____

   _____

3. *Plan:* Choose the best option, write your plan, and set a time limit for reaching your goal.

   _____

   _____

4. *Evaluation:* How will you evaluate your plan? How will you know whether it has worked? What will you do if it hasn't?

   _____

   _____

Group Evaluation:

Evaluate your discussion. Did everyone contribute? Did you accomplish your task successfully? What additional questions do you have about test anxiety, and how will you find answers to your questions?

EXERCISE 12.4 COMPUTER APPLICATION

VISIT THE INTERNET TO FIND out more about test anxiety, its causes, and ways to eliminate it. Search the Web for any information you can find on test anxiety, including any test anxiety surveys students can take. Then discuss your findings with the rest of the class. Some search words to try as starting points are *test anxiety, test anxiety reduction, stress relief* and *anxiety reduction techniques*.

Thinking ahead about Career

Purpose and Instructions

A workplace focus in Chapter 12 is on problem solving, a thinking skill that can help you determine what causes your stress or anxiety and how to reduce it. Use the knowledge you have gained from this chapter to solve work-related problems such as the one explained in the following case study. Read the case study on your own or with a partner and then answer the case questions.

Case Study

Jade is an assistant to the financial manager of a title company that checks public records to determine ownership of real estate. Jade has an important meeting next week in which she must fill in for the financial manager, who is away on a business trip. Jade's task is to present a feasibility study on the company's purchase of a property to the management team. She knows that her facts, figures, and conclusions are right and that her presentation is well organized, but this is the first time she has been asked to fill in for her boss. Also, giving oral presentations always makes her nervous. Jade needs to reduce her stress so that she can do a good job, but she doesn't know how to relax.

Case Questions

1. Why is Jade under stress?

2. What are Jade's strengths concerning the presentation?

3. Based on this chapter, what are some relaxation techniques Jade could try?

4. Access the Career Resource Center and read the article entitled "The Interactive Communication Process" in the *Effective Communication* section of *Skills for Your Future*. Based on this article, what else have you learned about speaking or presenting that could help Jade give an effective presentation?

Your *Reflections*

Reflect on what you have learned from this chapter about preparing for tests. Use the following questions to stimulate your thinking; then write your reflections. Include in your writing specific information from the chapter.

- Do you have physical or mental reactions to tests that are similar to Bonnie's or Jerome's as described at the beginning of the chapter? What are your reactions?

- Do you perform better on some kinds of tests than on others? Which ones, and why?

- What have you learned from this chapter that you can apply to reduce your test anxiety or other types of stress?

- What is one skill or attitude explained in this chapter that you would like to develop, and what can you begin doing today to make that happen?

_____

_____

_____

_____

_____

_____

_____

_____

_____

_____

_____

_____

_____

_____

_____

_____

_____

_____

Chapter review

To review the chapter, reflect on the following confidence-building attitudes and skills. Complete **Concepts to Understand** by filling in the blanks with words or terms from the list provided. Then practice your new skills at every opportunity.

ATTITUDES TO DEVELOP

- positive thinking
- the willingness to take control
- the desire to self-motivate and self-manage

SKILLS TO PRACTICE

- recognizing when you are tense or anxious
- using relaxation techniques
- controlling your inner dialogue

CONCEPTS TO UNDERSTAND

expectations	helplessness	physical	learned	stress
distractions	positive	negative	mental	testing

Test anxiety is (1) _____ that is related to a (2) _____ situation. It may be caused by your inability to cope with the (3) _____ of important people in your life, by a belief that grades are a reflection of your self-worth, or by feelings of (4) _____ resulting from past failures. If you have test anxiety, you may suffer from (5) _____ symptoms such as headaches and nausea and (6) _____ symptoms such as a lack of confidence and negative thoughts and feelings. Because test anxiety is a (7) _____ response, it can be unlearned.

Being prepared for tests and feeling confident about your abilities may reduce some of your anxiety. Or you may need to develop coping strategies such as learning to relax, facing and dealing with your fears, fighting internal and external (8) _____, and programming yourself for success by replacing (9) _____ thoughts with (10) _____ ones. If your anxiety is extremely severe, you might want to talk about your problem with your instructor or advisor.

To access additional review exercises, go to **college.hmco.com/pic/KanarTCS6e**.

Online Study Center
Review Exercise
ACE Self-Test

Online Study Center

Prepare for Class, Improve Your Grade, and ACE the Test. This chapter's *Student Achievement* resources include

"Stress: A Common Denominator" (article)   Chapter exercises/forms   Review exercise
Confidence Builder Web search   ACE Self-Test

To access these learning and study tools, go to **college.hmco.com/pic/KanarTCS6e**.

13 Becoming an active reader

Reading is the exploration of inner space where two minds engage—yours and the author's.

Learn how you can break passive reading habits to become an active reader.

Develop three skills to improve your reading comprehension: Find the main idea; identify supporting details; make inferences from your reading.

*Confident students are **skilled.** They know their strengths and weaknesses, and they work hard to develop new skills.*

▶ *Know what and how to mark in textbooks.*
Write summaries to enhance learning.

Communication skills refers to a set of basic skills that include reading, writing, and listening. Employers in every field most often rate communication skills as essential to success.

Reading is a lifelong skill and a key to success in college and career. Reading for your college courses may include textbook assignments, articles from journals and periodicals, and information gathered from books and web sites. As one of the **communication skills** that employers expect, reading is essential for success in any career where processing information from correspondence, email messages, manuals, and graphics is a daily occurrence. By practicing active reading habits in your personal life, you can improve your understanding of everything from the fine print on contracts and insurance policies to the latest best-selling novel.

Reading is also a necessary part of any study system. You can gain essential information from your textbooks by knowing what to underline, by using a textbook marking system, and by writing summaries.

To find out whether you are an active reader, complete Awareness Check 20.

KEY TERMS

active readers, *p. 305*
passive readers, *p. 305*
interact, *p. 305*
facts, *p. 309*
reasons, *p. 310*
examples, *p. 311*
personal inferences, *p. 312*
textual inferences, *p. 312*

SCANS TERM

communication skills, *p. 303*

AWARENESS CHECK 20

Are You an Active Reader?

To determine how actively you read, check all of the following statements that apply to you.

1. I usually read straight through a textbook chapter from beginning to end without stopping.

2. I stop frequently to re-read difficult parts or to check my comprehension by asking myself questions about what I have read.

3. If I don't understand something I have read, I wait to hear the instructor's explanation in class.

4. When I hit a rough spot, I make a note to remind myself to ask about it in class.

5. I usually have trouble deciding what is important in a chapter; often I'm not sure what the main idea is.

6. I can usually find the author's main idea, and I rarely have trouble determining what is important.

7. I often have a hard time relating textbook information to my life or to the course as a whole.

8. I can often see a connection between something I've read in a chapter and my life or the course.

9. I rarely underline, mark, highlight, or write notes in my textbooks.

10. I usually mark, underline, highlight, or write notes in my textbooks.

11. I have difficulty deciding what to mark or underline.

12. I can usually tell what to mark or underline.

13. I have to be interested in what I am reading to get anything out of it.

14. Even if a subject covered in a textbook doesn't interest me, I can still determine what I should learn and remember from it.

15. I think I should be able to read something once and remember the information covered in it.

16. I know that I may have to read something several times before the information sinks in.

17. When I read documents on the Internet, I can't tell which ones are reliable sources and which ones are not.

18. I am able to evaluate the reliability of Internet documents and sources.

If you checked mostly even-numbered statements, you are probably already an active reader. If you checked mostly odd-numbered statements, you may be a passive reader who would benefit from developing active reading strategies.

ACTIVE VERSUS PASSIVE READING

▶ *Learn how you can break passive reading habits to become an active reader.*

Readers fall into two categories: active readers and passive readers. **Active readers** control their interest level and concentration. They read with a purpose: They know what information to look for and why. Active readers constantly question what they read. They relate the author's ideas to their own experience and prior knowledge. On the other hand, **passive readers** are not in control of their reading. They lose interest easily and give in to distractions. They read the same way that they watch television programs and movies, expecting others to engage them and keep their attention. A common passive reading experience is to "wake up" in the middle of a paragraph, wondering what you have just read. Active readers control the process of reading; passive readers are unaware that reading *is* a process they can control.

The key to active reading is to **interact** with the text, to engage your mind with the author's. Taking notes, marking the text, questioning, thinking about the author's ideas, even talking them over with a friend—these are all ways to interact with the text. Passive readers do none of these things. They open the book to the assigned chapter and read from the first word to the last without really thinking about the author's ideas. As a result, they can't decide what is important, don't know what to review, and soon forget what they have read. Consequently, passive readers often feel "lost" in class. The chart in Figure 13.1 on page 306 compares active and passive readers.

Becoming an active reader takes self-motivation, a commitment to try proven strategies, the desire to succeed, and the persistence to make it happen. To read actively, follow these suggestions:

▼ **Set a realistic reading goal.** Don't try to read sixty pages all at once. Break up the assignment into two or three sessions—for whatever amount of time you think you can maintain optimum concentration. If you feel your concentration slipping before your time is up, stop, take a break, and then refocus your attention.

▼ **Read with a purpose.** Know what you are expected to get out of the assignment. Perhaps you will be tested on the material or asked to summarize the information, or perhaps you have several questions in mind that you expect the assignment to answer. Having specific information to look for may help you keep your attention focused on your reading and should give you a reason to talk yourself out of any boredom or lack of interest.

Active readers are aware of and are in control of their reading process. They use active learning strategies.

Passive readers are not aware of their reading process. They read inattentively and usually do not make use of active learning strategies.

Interact, as applied to the reading process, means to engage your mind with the writer's through questioning and other active strategies.

FIGURE 13.1

ACTIVE AND PASSIVE READERS

ACTIVE READERS:	PASSIVE READERS:
• have a positive attitude toward reading	• have a negative attitude toward reading
• read for ideas	• read only words
• ask questions to guide their reading and thinking	• read without thinking or questioning
• manage their reading process	• are unaware that reading is a process they can manage
• schedule time for reading	• read only if they have time
• have a purpose for reading	• read because "it is assigned"
• know how to keep their interest and motivation high	• expect the author to interest and motivate them
• control their concentration	• are easily distracted
• use study systems and memory strategies	• resist using study systems and memory strategies
• underline and annotate textbooks	• do not use marking systems
• make graphic organizers to use as study guides	• think making graphic organizers is too much work
• relate what they read to prior knowledge and experience	• see no connection between college reading and life or work
• review by reading notes and other materials	• review by re-reading entire chapters
• seek help as needed	• resist asking for help
• know what is going on in class due to active reading	• often feel lost in class due to passive reading

- **Read with a pen or highlighter** so you can mark parts of the chapter that answer your questions, suggest possible test questions, explain concepts, or expand on topics covered in class lectures. If you are reading from a library book or other source that you cannot mark, take notes on note cards or in a notebook, making sure to label them with the source's title, page number, web site address (or URL), or any other identifying information you may need later. For more information on marking textbooks, see pages 317–319 of this chapter.
- **Review and recite from your notes or markings.** Reviewing helps reinforce your learning so that it stays in your memory. Reciting from notes or textbook markings provides another pathway into your memory: the auditory sense. Reciting is especially helpful for those who have an auditory learning preference, but anyone can benefit from it.

The more active you become in taking control of your reading process, the less likely you will be to lapse into passive reading habits. As an active reader, you are *doing something* throughout the process, whether it is marking the text, stopping

EXERCISE 13.1 — LEARNING STYLE

WRITE AN EVALUATION OF YOURSELF as an active or passive reader. Describe your study system for reading a textbook chapter or other assigned reading material. Be specific. What type of learning style is dominant in the way you read? For example, would you rather read on your own, forming your own opinions, or would you prefer to read, then discuss the assignment with others? If possible, describe the study system you used for an assigned reading in one of your classes and any difficulties you had. Also, take into consideration your results from Awareness Check 20 as you complete this exercise.

to think about what you have read, re-reading difficult passages, asking questions and looking for answers, or reciting from your notes and markings. These activities aid in the transfer of information from your short-term memory to your long-term memory. For more on how the memory process works and is enhanced by the way that you study, see Chapter 10.

You can become aware of the times when you are either comprehending well or poorly. To read actively and consciously, you must be able to follow the development of ideas as they occur in a chapter or other source. One way you can do this is by reading for the main idea and details and by making inferences.

IMPROVE YOUR READING COMPREHENSION

▶ *You can develop three skills to improve your reading comprehension: Find the main idea; identify supporting details; make inferences from your reading.*

Ideas develop from words to sentences, to paragraphs, to larger units of meaning such as multiparagraph essays, articles, and textbook chapters. The sentences in a paragraph are related: They all support one main idea. The paragraphs in a longer passage are similarly related: They all support the one central idea of the entire passage. This is why the main idea of a multiparagraph passage such as a textbook chapter or newspaper article is often called the *central idea* to distinguish it from the main idea of each paragraph.

In a textbook chapter, the title and introductory paragraphs usually provide strong clues to the chapter's central idea. In fact, the central idea of a longer passage is often stated near the beginning. Therefore, you can use the title and introduction to create a context for reading. For example, the title of this chapter, *Becoming an Active Reader*, and the introductory paragraphs make clear that the central idea is that several strategies can help you become an active reader. Both the title and the introductory paragraphs should raise two questions in your mind: "What is an active reader?" and "What are the strategies?" Using these as guide questions, you can read the chapter to find the answers. Each paragraph within a chapter provides important information that is essential to your understanding of the entire chapter's central idea.

To improve your reading, begin by learning how to find a paragraph's main idea. A paragraph can be anywhere from one to several sentences long, and it may contain three types of sentences:

1. The *topic sentence* is a direct statement of the author's main idea.

2. The *support sentences* contain major or minor details that develop, or explain, the main idea.

3. The *concluding sentence* may restate the main idea, introduce a new but related idea, make an inference, end the paragraph with another detail, or provide a transition to the next paragraph.

For examples of these three kinds of sentences, read the next paragraph and the explanation that follows it.

Topic sentence: Main idea

Adjusting to college can be difficult for students because of the pressures they face from family, instructors, and friends. *Family members, for example, may expect a student to add studying and attending classes to his or her other responsibilities. They may resent being asked to take on more chores or spending time alone while the student studies. A student who faces this kind of pressure from family may have difficulty reaching desired goals. Another pressure students face is from instructors. From the student's point of view, each instructor acts as if the student has no other courses to take. Add to this the need to get to every class on time, to attend class regularly, and to keep up with all assignments. Friends can also make a student's adjustment difficult. For one thing, they may pressure a student to put off studying to engage in leisure-time activities. Friends who are not attending college feel threatened and, without meaning to, may do or say things that can make a student wonder if college is worth it.* **To overcome these pressures, a college student must have a strong desire to succeed.**

Support sentences: Details

Concluding sentence

The first sentence of this paragraph is the *topic sentence*, which states the author's main idea: Pressures from family, instructors, and friends can make students' adjustment to college difficult. The last sentence of the paragraph is the *concluding sentence*. In between are the *support sentences*, which give examples of three kinds of pressures and explain how these pressures can make it difficult for a student to adjust to college. The concluding sentence then introduces a new but related idea: Students can overcome these pressures.

Find the Main Idea

In a paragraph, an author may express the main idea in one of two ways: (1) by stating it directly in a topic sentence, as in the example paragraph about pressures students face, or (2) by implying it through the choice of details and use of key words.

Now read another paragraph about students' pressures:

Some parents insist that a student carry a full-time load and maintain an A or B average while also working part-time and sharing household tasks. A student who has too many things to do may not be able to do any one of them very well. Another pressure students face is from instructors' expectations. Instructors expect students to arrive on time, to attend class regularly, and to keep up with all assignments. They also expect students to participate in class, ask questions, and do extra work or get help outside of class if they are having trouble meeting course objectives. Friends, too, can make a student's adjustment difficult. For one thing, they may pressure a student to put off studying in order to party or to engage in some other leisure-time activity. Friends who choose not to attend college may try to make a student feel guilty for leaving them behind. To overcome these pressures, a college student must have a strong desire to succeed.

This paragraph has no topic sentence, but several clues can help you infer the author's main idea. From the third sentence, which begins with "Another pressure," you can infer that the first two sentences explain one kind of pressure and that now you are reading about another kind. The sixth sentence, which begins with "Friends, too," introduces a third pressure students face. In the last sentence, the phrase "these pressures" is the strongest clue that the paragraph is about the effects of the three kinds of pressure.

When a paragraph has no topic sentence, the author's main idea is implied by the details in the supporting sentences. Once you identify the idea or topic that all the details support, you should be able to state the author's main idea in your own words.

To find the author's main idea, read a paragraph carefully and then follow these steps:

1. Look for the topic sentence. It can be anywhere in the paragraph, but it is often the first sentence. The topic sentence is the most general sentence in the paragraph. It combines the author's topic and opinion, and it summarizes *all* the information presented in the support sentences. The topic sentence expresses the author's main idea.

2. If the main idea is not stated in a topic sentence, identify the topic by inferring it from the details. Ask yourself, "What subject do all the sentences in the paragraph support?" Look for signal words— such as *for one thing, another,* and *for example*—that introduce major details.

3. Determine the author's opinion about the topic. In general, what does the author say to expand your knowledge about the topic? Does the author *explain how* to do something? Does the author *compare two things?* Does the author *explain why* something exists or *give reasons* as to why something happens in a certain way? Does the author *argue for or against* one point of view? By identifying the author's opinion, you may be able to infer the main idea.

CONCEPT CHECK 13.1

You may get more out of your reading by discussing the author's ideas with members of a study group.

Identify Supporting Details

By itself, the main idea is only a statement of fact or opinion that means little without evidence to support it. An author's evidence may include three types of details.

▼ Facts

▼ Reasons

▼ Examples

Facts. A **fact** is a direct observation, quotation, statistic, date, number, report of an event, or expert testimony that can be verified. For example, if a movie critic says there are twelve shootings within the first seven minutes of a new action film, you can verify this information by seeing the movie and counting the shootings that occur within the first seven minutes.

The author of the following paragraph supports the main idea with facts:

Facts can be verified. They include such things as dates, names, places, and events.

Robert B. Parker is one of America's most prolific writers of popular fiction. His genre is mystery, and his most popular character is Spenser, a hard-boiled detective with a soft spot for women and dogs. Spenser, also the hero of a hit television series in the 1980s, Spenser for Hire, *appears in thirty-four of Parker's novels. Parker introduced readers to two new detectives in the 1990s: Jesse Stone, who appears in five novels, and Sunny Randall, whose fifth appearance in a Parker mystery was released in August 2006. Parker is also the author of two more mysteries based on the work of Raymond Chandler, and several other fiction and nonfiction works.*

The author's main idea, stated in the first sentence, is that Parker is a prolific writer. The supporting evidence includes how many novels and nonfiction books he has published, the names of his characters, and the name of a television series based on one of his characters. Book titles, characters' names, and an author's number of works can all be determined by checking your library's reference works on books and authors. To research an author on the Internet, simply type the author's name as a keyword.

EXERCISE 13.2

FIND THE MAIN IDEA IN each paragraph. If the main idea is stated, underline it. If the main idea is implied, write a sentence that expresses it.

1. During the 1960s, several prominent African American authors wrote fiction and nonfiction works about lives of poverty and disenfranchisement. One of these, Claude Brown, died in February 2002. While still a student at Howard University, Brown wrote his novel, Manchild in the Promised Land, *about growing up in the streets of Harlem. Brown, once a gang member himself, became an advocate for those trapped in the cycle of poverty, drugs, violence, and death.*

_____

_____

2. Binge drinking is defined as having five or more drinks in quick succession. According to Harvard University's Public Health College Alcohol Study conducted in 1999, 44 percent of the students surveyed at 119 colleges had engaged in binge drinking two weeks prior to the survey. One in four of this group said they were frequent binge drinkers. The survey's purpose was to determine who binges, why, and what the effects of binge drinking are. Among the causes of binge drinking cited were drinking to get drunk, drinking to fit in with the campus alcohol culture, and drinking to reduce academic stress. The study concluded that binge drinking is a widespread problem that interferes with students' education and puts their health and lives at risk. In 2006, binge drinking remain a serious problem on college campuses.

_____

_____

3. In the United States, 276,000 men and 142,000 women die of smoking-related causes each year. The highest number of cancer deaths among women is from lung cancer, 90 percent of which is related to smoking. In 1990, one in five adult women smoked. Although the total number of women who smoked declined somewhat during the 1990s, smoking increased among teenage girls during that same period. Female smokers, like their male counterparts, suffer an increased risk of incurring heart disease, lung cancer, or another smoking-related illness. Surgeon General David Satcher issued these disturbing findings in Women and Smoking: A Report of the Surgeon General, 2001.

_____

_____

Reasons are details that answer the question "Why?" Either facts or opinions can be given as reasons.

Reasons. Authors use **reasons** to support a main idea when their purpose is to explain *why* something happens, *why* something is important, *why* one thing is better than another, or *why* they feel or think as they do. Think of reasons as the *causes* that are responsible for producing certain effects, results, or outcomes. For example, a sportswriter may use reasons to explain why a basketball team lost an important game that it was favored to win. Or a political commentator might write an article explaining reasons for a presidential candidate's popularity among a certain group of voters.

In the following paragraph, reasons support the author's main idea:

One of the most important goals that a college student can aim for is an expanded vocabulary. One reason this goal is so important is that an expanded vocabulary can improve students' writing. With sufficient words and definitions at their command, students will have less difficulty writing what they mean. Also, increased reading improves vocabulary, which leads to greater comprehension. A third reason for improving vocabulary is the confidence students feel when they use words accurately. Students are less afraid to speak out in class discussions or to give reports and speeches when they know they are not going to mispronounce or misuse words. Increasing the vocabulary is a worthwhile goal for students who also want to improve their speaking, reading, and writing.

The main idea of this paragraph is that an expanded vocabulary is an important goal that students should try to reach. The main idea is stated in a topic sentence, which is the first sentence of the paragraph. The author supports the main idea with reasons that explain why students should increase their vocabularies.

1. An expanded vocabulary improves writing.

2. An increased vocabulary improves reading comprehension.

3. An improved vocabulary results in confidence.

The *signal phrases* "one reason" and "third reason" help you locate the major details. The second reason follows the signal word *also.*

Examples. **Examples** are situations, instances, or even people that authors use to illustrate, support, or clarify a main idea. Authors may use one extended example or several short ones. Or they may support a main idea with an example, then use facts or reasons as additional evidence. Some use examples as minor details to explain and clarify major details.

Notice how the authors of the next paragraph use examples:

Many legends were based on bizarre possibilities of matings between individuals of different species. The wife of Minos, according to Greek mythology, mated with a bull and produced the Minotaur. Folk heroes of Russia and Scandinavia were traditionally the sons of women who had been captured by bears, from which these men derived their great strength and so enriched the national stock. The camel and the leopard also mated from time to time, according to the early naturalists, who were otherwise unable—and it is hard to blame them—to explain an animal as improbable as the giraffe (the common giraffe still bears the scientific name of Giraffa camelopardalis*). Thus folklore reflected early and imperfect glimpses into the nature of hereditary relationships.* (From Helena Curtis and N. Sue Barnes, *Biology,* 5/e, Worth, 1989.)

In the first sentence of this paragraph, the authors state the idea that many legends are based on strange matings between members of different species. Examples of three legends support this main idea:

1. The Minotaur was a legendary being born of Minos's wife, who mated with a bull.

2. Russian and Scandinavian folk heroes were believed to have great strength because they were the sons of women who had mated with bears.

3. Because the giraffe was such an odd-looking creature, a legend developed that giraffes were the offspring of camels and leopards.

These examples, or major details, are easy to understand. The authors also add a minor detail that makes the giraffe example even more interesting: The animal's scientific name reflects earlier scientists' beliefs about its heredity.

Examples are illustrations used to describe or explain. Red is one *example* of a color.

▬ CONCEPT CHECK 13.2

Can you distinguish among facts, reasons, and examples? Select a newspaper article that interests you. As you read it, try to find one or two examples of each of the three types of details.

EXERCISE 13.3

READ EACH PASSAGE AND DETERMINE whether the details are mainly facts, reasons, or examples. Then check the appropriate box.

---

*1. A balance sheet consists of three parts: assets, liabilities, and net worth. Your **assets** include everything you own that has monetary value. Your **liabilities** are your debts—what you owe to others. Your **net worth** is the dollar amount left when what is owed is subtracted from the dollar value of what is owned—that is, when liabilities are subtracted from assets.*

(From Thomas E. Garman and Raymond E. Forgue, *Personal Finance*, Eighth Edition, p. 36. Copyright © 2006 by Houghton Mifflin Company. Used with permission.)

☐ **Facts**   ☐ **Reasons**   ☐ **Examples**

---

2. Memo to All Employees
From J. Todd, Manager

It is with deep regret that I inform you of the passing of one whose life has been an example to all of us. Spot was the mainstay of Curtis Nursery and Landscaping. The first to arrive and the last to leave, he greeted everyone warmly. He was a friend to all and discriminated against none. Who among us has not sought Spot's company when in need of a little cheering up? Spot has never been one to miss a day at work. This morning, we knew something was wrong when he was not waiting for us in the back of the truck. Instead, we found him in his favorite place under the house, where he had died peacefully during the night. A gentleman among dalmatians, he will be missed.

☐ **Facts**   ☐ **Reasons**   ☐ **Examples**

---

3. A job with the United States Government provides security, a stable income, and a sense of purpose. Moreover, career opportunities have never been better according to the U.S. Department of Labor, which predicts that 53 percent of federal employees will reach retirement age over the next few years. What this means is that about 900,000 new job openings will be available for those seeking government jobs.

☐ **Facts**   ☐ **Reasons**   ☐ **Examples**

Make Inferences

As explained in Chapter 3, an *inference* is an idea that is implied, not stated. When the author's main idea is unstated, try to infer it from the details that are given. You might make many inferences from an author's main idea and details, but most can be classified into one of two categories. **Personal inferences** are those you can make by relating ideas you have read to what you know or have experienced. **Textual inferences** are educated guesses or conclusions drawn about an author's meaning based on stated details. The ability to make inferences is a critical thinking skill.

Personal inferences are educated guesses based on personal experience or common knowledge.

Textual inferences are conclusions drawn from stated information.

Personal Inferences. You probably make personal inferences about every day's events because your experience tells you what to expect or what seems likely. Suppose you are absent from several classes, and the next time you attend, the classroom is empty. You wait ten minutes, and still no one shows up. You conclude that class must not be meeting for some reason that was announced during your absence.

When you log on to your favorite web site, you know the information will be accurate and up-to-date because every time you have visited the site in the past, the information you have gained has proven to be reliable.

The manager of the company where you are employed needs someone to work overtime. You assume she will ask you because she knows you need the extra money and because you have helped out before.

Earlier in this chapter you found the main idea and details in a paragraph about the pressures students face from instructors, family, and friends. Now read a paragraph about another common source of pressure:

Stress is one pressure you bring on yourself when you go to class unprepared or when you don't manage your time effectively. Poor preparation results in inattention and that "lost" feeling. When you haven't read the assignment, you can't enter into the class discussion. If you haven't studied for a test, you are not likely to do well. In either situation, knowing your performance is not at its best creates stress. Being unprepared is almost always the result of poor time management. If you are like many students, you have more to do than you can possibly get done unless you schedule your time. Time management also involves setting priorities. You have to decide which is more important, seeing that new movie with a friend tonight or getting those algebra problems done for tomorrow's class. If you consistently put off doing things you need to do so that you can do what you want to do, the stress will eventually catch up with you. Make a decision now to improve your time management and to become better prepared for class, and you will have taken the first step toward reducing some of your stress.

One student who read this paragraph said, "Boy, that's me; I can always find something else to do besides algebra." This student related a detail from the paragraph to his own experience: "It's not that I don't want to do the work or that I don't realize I'm undermining my chances for success in the course. It's just that algebra is so hard. I know I'm going to get frustrated, so I dread getting started. As a result, I wait until the last minute, and doing that stresses me out." Relating the idea that stress can be self-induced to what she had read about locus of control (source of internal or external motivation), another student said, "Since this kind of stress is the result of your own behavior, you can get rid of it by changing your behavior. In a way, this is easier to deal with than the stress that comes from the pressures you get from family, instructors, and friends. Those pressures are outside you, so they're harder to control."

Textual Inferences. What you read in your college textbooks will be more meaningful for you if you relate it to your experience with and your knowledge of the author's subject. Just as you can make personal inferences about what you read, you can make textual inferences about what an author writes. A valid inference is one that can be supported by an author's main idea and details.

Read the following paragraph:

*Styles in cars, dress, furniture, and architecture come and go. Some styles become outdated or may disappear. Others never really go away but reassert themselves, with some changes, over many years. A **fad** is a style of short duration. A **fashion** is a more lasting style. Both fads and fashions are engaged in by large groups of people. Fads of the past forty years include the hula hoop, hot pants, love beads, disco dancing, automobile "tail fins," and Klick-Klack Blocks. You may be thinking, "I've never heard of some of these fads" and for good reason: They have come and gone. Fashions stay with us. Miniskirts—once considered a fad—have enjoyed several* *revivals. Columns, a feature of ancient Greek architecture, have never gone out of style. You see them on public buildings and private homes—wherever a "classic" look is desired. Because fashions are more lasting than fads, they tend to be more socially acceptable. What is the difference between a fashionable person and a faddist? One is selective about which trends and behaviors to embrace, developing his or her own personal style. The other is swept along by each new fad that enjoys a brief popularity and seems to have no recognizable style.*

According to this paragraph, both fads and fashions are forms of collective behavior, but they differ in duration. You can use this information to make inferences about other behaviors. For example, if you are in your twenties, your parents can probably remember when tattoos were considered vulgar. In the nineties, tattoos became a fad among the young, probably as a result of their prevalence among rock musicians. Now tattoos have gone mainstream with everyone from soccer moms to celebrities sporting them. At this point, tattoos may be more fashion than fad.

Vanity plates and smiley faces also began as fads but lasted long enough to become fashions. The "Baby on Board" car sign that mothers posted in the eighties was a fad that faded. The American flag, an enduring symbol, is always in fashion: on clothing, on bumper stickers, as a lapel pin. What fads or fashions do you embrace?

EXERCISE 13.4 COLLABORATIVE ACTIVITY

APPLY WHAT YOU HAVE LEARNED about main idea, details, and inferences by completing this exercise with group members. Follow the guidelines for group discussion that appear on the inside back cover. Read each paragraph. Then discuss the main idea, identify the details, and read the inferences that are listed. If you think most readers would make these inferences, check *yes*. If not, check *no*. In either case, explain your answer. Record your conclusions on the lines provided. Next, evaluate your work. Then write your evaluation on your own paper, or go to college.hmco.com/pic/KanarTCS6e to download the group evaluation form.

If you want to expand your vocabulary, there are two methods you might want to try. The first method involves making note cards and using them for recitation and review of words that you want to learn. Prepare each note card by writing the word on one side of the card and its definition on the other side. Recite to learn by pronouncing the word and saying its definition. Then turn the card over and check yourself. Do this with each card until you can recite all the definitions from memory. Review the words by repeating these steps once a week, or as often as needed, to keep the words in your memory. The second method for learning words involves keeping a word list as you read. As you are reading an assigned chapter in one of your textbooks, jot down in a notebook any unfamiliar words you encounter. Look at these words and write the definitions that fit the contexts in which the words appear. The next time you read a chapter from the same textbook, keep your word list handy. You can add to the list or use it to review definitions of your words when they appear in new contexts. These two methods have worked for many students.

Main Idea: If you want to expand your vocabulary, there are two methods you might want to try.

Details:

a. _____

_____

_____

b. _____

_____

_____

Inferences:

	Yes	No

a. **These vocabulary-building methods may work for you.** ☐ ☐

   Explain your answer: _____

   _____

   _____

	Yes	No

b. **Using one of these two methods is the only way to expand your vocabulary.** ☐ ☐

   Explain your answer: _____

   _____

   _____

Group Evaluation:

Evaluate your discussion. Did everyone contribute? Did you accomplish your task successfully? What additional questions do you have about the main idea, details, and inferences? How will you find answers to your questions?

CONFIDENCE BUILDER

Calculate Your Reading Rate

Does Speed Reading Really Work?

You may have read accounts of people who can "read" 1,700 words per minute, and you may have wished you could read that fast. Speed reading is a controversial issue. Although you may want to increase your reading rate in order to save time or improve your chances of answering all the items on a timed reading test, you may lose comprehension as you gain reading speed if you try to read *too* fast.

Let *efficient reading*, not speed reading, be your goal. To read efficiently, vary your reading rate with the *type of material* and your *purpose* for reading. For example, you can skim a news or magazine article that you read for personal interest, but when you read textbooks and other materials to gain and retain knowledge, you must read slowly and carefully for maximum comprehension.

Do you read everything at the same rate? If you do, then you are not reading as efficiently as you could. Use this formula to calculate your reading rate; then experiment with adjusting your rate to the type of material and your purpose for reading it.

$$\frac{\text{No. of words in passage}}{\text{Reading time}} = \frac{\text{Reading rate in words}}{\text{per minute (wpm)}}$$

To estimate the number of words in a passage, find the average number of words per line and multiply that number by the number of lines in the whole passage (if the passage is less than one page) or by the number of lines on one page (if the passage is several pages). Then use a stopwatch, digital watch, or clock with a second hand to time yourself, in minutes and seconds, as you read. Finally, round off to the nearest minute to use the formula.

Knowing that your reading rate for difficult or unfamiliar material is naturally going to be slower than your rate for less complex kinds of information can help you plan your study time. Suppose you are taking a biology course and have been assigned a 60-page chapter to read for the next class meeting. First, time yourself to determine how many minutes it will take you to read one page. Then multiply your time by 60 (the number of pages in your assignment) to get your total time in minutes. Divide this total by 60 to determine how many hours and minutes you will need to schedule for reading the assigned chapter. If it will take you three hours to read 60 pages, then you may want to break up the time into three one-hour segments so that you stay focused. To read efficiently, adjust your reading rate and schedule your reading time to meet the demands of any reading task.

To learn more about this topic, do an online search using these keywords as a starting point: *reading speed, reading rate, reading efficiency, reading retention.*

Online Study Center
Confidence Builder
Web Search

USE A TEXTBOOK MARKING SYSTEM

▶ *Know what and how to mark in textbooks. Write summaries to enhance learning.*

Marking your textbooks by *underlining* or *highlighting* and by *annotating* (making notes) improves your concentration for two reasons: It focuses your attention on the task of reading, and it provides a tactile/kinesthetic pathway to the brain. You must think critically about what you read so that you can make decisions about what to underline, highlight, or annotate. When done well, marking your textbook saves time by providing you with specific information to review so that you do not have to re-read a whole chapter in order to study for a test. Whether you underline or highlight is a matter of personal preference. Highlighting pens come in a variety of colors, and the type of ink they contain may vary. Experiment with highlighters to find one that won't bleed through your pages. Underlining is best done with a fine-line ballpoint pen or felt-tip marker. Again, choose one that doesn't bleed through. A pencil may not be as good a choice for underlining. A sharp point may tear the paper; also, pencil smudges and fades and doesn't show up nearly as well as ink.

Marking your textbook is an essential part of any study system because it improves your reception and retention of information. In the next paragraph a student, Alex, describes the system he worked out for underlining and marking his textbook:

I read one section at a time. After I read the section, I draw a bracket, [ ], around the main idea and put a star beside it in the margin. I underline the major details, and I put a number in a circle next to each detail. That way I can see how many details there are when I review the section for a test. If a word I don't know is defined in a section, I underline it and write "def." in the margin. If I have to look up a word that is not defined, I circle it and write my definition in the margin. Also, I don't underline everything in a sentence. I just underline key words. Before I did this, I used to underline too much; then I would end up having to re-read almost the whole chapter when I reviewed instead of studying just the important parts.

Alex makes a good point: Underlining too much is not useful (nor is underlining too little). The purpose of marking textbooks is to make the important ideas stand out and to provide memory cues. Then you can determine what you need to study in depth and what you can skip when you review. Here is what one of Alex's underlined passages looks like. Notice how he has annotated the passage in the margins.

DRESSING FOR SUCCESS

The most effective strategy for <u>making a good impression</u> is to <u>pay careful attention to your dress, grooming, and posture.</u> Dress in a manner that flatters your appearance while conforming to the office norm. The employment interview is not the place for a fashion statement. You want the interviewer to remember what you had to say and not what you wore. Although different positions, different companies, different industries, and different parts of the country and world have different norms, in general [they] <u>prefer well-tailored, clean, conservative clothing for the interview.</u>

Dress conservatively for an interview.

For most business interviews, <u>men</u> should dress in a <u>blue or gray suit and a white or pale blue shirt with a subtle tie, dark socks, and black shoes.</u> <u>Women</u> should dress in a <u>blue or gray tailored suit with a light-colored blouse</u> and <u>medium-height heels.</u> Avoid excessive or distracting jewelry, heavy perfumes or after-shave lotions, and elaborate hairstyles. <u>Impeccable grooming</u> is <u>a must,</u> including clothing clean and free of wrinkles, shoes shined, teeth brushed, and hair neatly styled and combed. <u>Blend in;</u> you will have plenty of opportunity to express your individual style once you've been hired.

Be well-groomed; blend in.

Avoid anything excessive: perfume, elaborate hairstyles.

From Scot Ober, *Contemporary Business Communication*, Sixth Edition. Copyright © 2006 by Houghton Mifflin Company. Used with permission.

Marking your textbooks focuses your attention on the task of reading and helps you think critically about what you read.

Try these guidelines for effective textbook marking. Then, like Alex, develop a system that works for you and use it consistently.

What to Mark in Textbooks

Deciding what to mark is the same as deciding what is important. *Definitions of terms* are important. Even if they are already italicized or printed in boldface, mark them anyway if you do not already know them. *Examples* used to illustrate theories are important; so are *experiments*, including who conducted them, what happened, and what they proved. *Names, dates,* and *historical events* are important. *Principles, rules,* and *characteristics* are additional examples of the kinds of information that may be important within the context of what you are reading.

How to Mark Your Textbooks

1. It is usually better to read before you underline and to read one section at a time. You may not be able to tell what is important until you have read a whole section to see how the ideas relate to each other.

2. In the margin, write key words or symbols that will serve as memory cues to call your attention to special terms, names, dates, and other important information.

3. Use your own words when you make notes in your textbook. Putting the author's ideas into your own words will help you test your understanding, and you will be more likely to retain them.

EXERCISE 13.5

TARGET A COURSE IN WHICH you would like to improve your grade. Read an assigned chapter in the textbook for that course. Underline and annotate the chapter. Then make an appointment to discuss your work with your student success instructor, who can suggest ways to improve your marking system.

4. Decide on some symbols to indicate certain kinds of information and use your symbols consistently. Here are some common symbols students use. You probably already use some of them.

   def. = definition

   ex. = example

   T = possible test item

   * = an important point

   1., 2., 3., etc. = used when sequence matters

5. Underline or highlight keywords and phrases.

Review for a test or prepare for class by reciting from what you have marked or annotated in the margin. Use your underlining and marking to identify processes or concepts you can illustrate, using charts or diagrams for easy review and recall.

Summarize Information from Textbooks

Most textbook chapters have a summary at the end that condenses the chapter's main ideas. Reading the summary before you read the entire chapter builds background for the reading by focusing your attention on the ideas that the author thinks are important. Also, reading the summary is part of the survey step of the SQ3R reading system, as explained in Chapter 8. Just as reading a summary is a helpful study strategy, so is writing your own summary.

By now, you know that writing engages your tactile/kinesthetic sense. Also, writing a summary tests both your comprehension and your critical thinking. Summarizing information requires that you understand it well enough to explain it in your own words, in a condensed version. Your summaries make good study guides that you can review along with your other study materials as part of your preparation for a test.

A summary of a passage, or body of information, includes three things:

▼ The main idea

▼ The major supporting details

▼ Why the information is significant

Although the summary should be stated in your own words, it should maintain the author's meaning. A good summary will be shorter than the original but no less complex. The following paragraph summarizes "Dressing for Success" on page 317.

To make a good impression in an interview, be well groomed and wear an appropriate outfit. Clean, conservative clothes are best. For both men and women, this means a well-tailored blue or gray suit. The idea is to blend in, not stand out.

EXERCISE 13.6   COLLABORATIVE ACTIVITY

WORKING WITH A PARTNER, SELECT some information to summarize from this chapter or from another chapter of *The Confident Student*. For example, you could summarize types of schedules from Chapter 6, the SQ3R system from Chapter 8, or the types of tests from Chapter 11. Discuss the information, decide what is important, and then write your summary. Share your finished product with the class.

C R I T I C A L

T H I N K I N G

Exercise Overview

This exercise will help you think critically about what and how to underline and annotate in textbooks.

Exercise Background

Deciding what or how much to underline is difficult for many students. Basically, you should underline only as much as necessary to clearly identify the important ideas. Look for the same three things that you would include in a summary: the main idea, the major details, and the information's significance. Special terms and definitions should also be marked or annotated in the margin.

Exercise Task

Examples A and B show the same passage as marked by two different students. Evaluate each student's markings for their usefulness. Determine which student has successfully applied the suggestions for marking textbooks as explained in this chapter. Briefly explain in writing which summary does the best job.

Example A

Behavioral Stress Responses. <u>Clues about people's physical and emotional stress reactions come from changes in how they look, act, or talk.</u> Strained facial expressions, a shaky voice, tremors, and jumpiness are common behavioral stress responses. Posture can also convey information about stress, a fact well known to skilled interviewers.

Stress shows in your face, voice, actions, posture.

Even <u>more obvious behavioral stress responses</u> appear as people attempt to escape or avoid stressors. Some people <u>quit their jobs,</u> <u>drop out</u> of school, turn to <u>alcohol,</u> } *avoidance* or even attempt <u>suicide.</u> Unfortunately, as discussed in Chapter 5, learning escape } *tactics* and avoidance tactics deprive people of the opportunity to learn more adaptive ways of coping with stressful environments, including college (<u>M. L. Cooper et al.,</u> 1992). <u>Aggression is another common behavioral response to stressors.</u> All too often, this response is directed at members of one's own <u>family</u> (<u>Polusny & Follette, 1995</u>). For instance, in the wake of hurricanes and other <u>natural disasters,</u> it is not

Cooper et al.: avoidance tactics keep you from dealing with stress. Aggression often directed at family.

uncommon to see dramatic increases in the rate of domestic-violence reports in the devastated area (Rotton, 1990).

Example B

Behavioral Stress Responses. Clues about people's physical and emotional stress reactions come from changes in how they look, act, or talk. Strained facial expressions, a shaky voice, tremors, and jumpiness are common behavioral stress responses. Posture can also convey information about stress, a fact well known to skilled interviewers.

Avoidance tactics

Even more obvious behavioral stress responses appear as people attempt to escape or avoid stressors. Some people quit their jobs, drop out of school, turn to alcohol, or even attempt suicide. Unfortunately, as discussed in Chapter 5, learning escape and avoidance tactics deprive people of the opportunity to learn more adaptive ways of coping with stressful environments, including college (M. L. Cooper et al., 1992). Aggression is another common behavioral response to stressors. All too often, this response is directed at members of one's own family (Polusny & Follette,

Polusny, Follette, Rotton

1995). For instance, in the wake of hurricanes and other natural disasters, it is not uncommon to see dramatic increases in the rate of domestic-violence reports in the devastated area (Rotton, 1990).

Thinking ahead about Career

Purpose and Instructions

A workplace focus in Chapter 13 is on reading, a basic communication skill essential for keeping up with research and development in your field. Use the knowledge that you have gained from this chapter to solve work-related problems such as the one explained in the following case study. Read the case study on your own or with a partner and then answer the case questions.

Case Study

After graduating from high school, Hector went to work as a delivery worker for a company that supplies gum, candy, tobacco products, and other assorted goods to stores and restaurants. He drives a company truck and has an excellent driving record. Although Hector enjoys driving a truck, making his rounds, and interacting with the customers on his route, he knows that his job offers no opportunities for advancement. Recently he applied for a job with a postal delivery company that would net him a salary increase, a benefits package better than the one he has now, and a chance for advancement to a management level.

Although his qualifications were good in every other aspect, Hector was denied the job because of his poor reading skills. "Reading is important," the personnel manager told Hector, "because our employees have to keep accurate records of deliveries, make sure packages get to the right addresses, and be able to use maps and directories. Moreover, employees on a management track must have superior communication skills and those include reading." Because she liked Hector and was impressed with his driving record and interpersonal skills, the personnel manager advised him to enroll at a community college to upgrade his reading skills. "Come back to see me," she said, "when you have your associate of arts degree." Hector has taken her advice and will soon be starting classes. Looking at the books he has just purchased for his courses, Hector is wondering how he will ever get through them. But he is determined to succeed because he really wants a better job.

Case Questions

1. **What is Hector's goal?**

   _____

   _____

2. **What are Hector's strengths and weaknesses concerning the job he wants?**

   _____

   _____

3. **What active reading strategies can you suggest that will help Hector succeed in his courses?**

   _____

   _____

4. **Access the Career Resource Center and read the article entitled "Improve Your Reading Study Strategies with PQ4R" in the *Building Learning Strategies* section of *The Bridge*. Based on this article, what additional advice can you give Hector about his reading?**

   _____

Your *Reflections*

R **eflect on what you have learned from this chapter about preparing for tests.** Use the following questions to stimulate your thinking; then write your reflections. Include in your writing specific information from the chapter.

- What role does reading play in your life? What kinds of reading do you do?

- Review the traits of active and passive readers listed in Figure 13.1 near the beginning of this chapter. Which traits of active readers do you have? Which ones do you need to develop?

- Has the way that you mark textbooks changed as a result of reading this chapter? Explain your answer.

- What is one skill or attitude explained in this chapter that you would like to develop, and what can you begin doing today to make that happen?

_____

_____

_____

_____

_____

_____

_____

_____

_____

_____

_____

_____

_____

_____

_____

_____

_____

_____

Chapter review

To review the chapter, reflect on the following confidence-building attitudes and skills. Complete **Concepts to Understand** by filling in the blanks with words or terms from the list provided. Then practice your new skills at every opportunity.

ATTITUDES TO DEVELOP
- self-motivation
- commitment to learn
- desire to succeed
- persistence

SKILLS TO PRACTICE
- reading actively
- making inferences
- using reading and marking systems
- writing summaries

CONCEPTS TO UNDERSTAND

annotate	main idea	details	facts	cues
personal	examples	textual	topic	key

Active reading is an essential part of any study system. Two basic reading and marking strategies will help you read actively. First, read for (1) _____, (2) _____, and implications. Second, underline or highlight and (3) _____ in the margin.

To find a stated main idea, look for a (4) _____ sentence in a paragraph. If the main idea is implied, try to infer it from the details, which may consist of (5) _____, reasons, or (6) _____.

Inferences may be of two types: (7) _____ inferences are those you make by relating the author's ideas to your own experience. (8) _____ inferences are based on an author's stated main idea and details.

Marking your text helps you concentrate and encourages you to think critically about what you read. The value of marking is that it makes important ideas stand out. To mark effectively, underline or highlight (9) _____ ideas and make marginal notes that will serve as memory (10) _____ to aid your review. To reinforce what you have read, summarize important ideas.

To access additional review exercises, go to **college.hmco.com/pic/KanarTCS6e.**

Online Study Center
Review Exercise
ACE Self-Test

Online Study Center

Prepare for Class, Improve Your Grade, and ACE the Test. This chapter's *Student Achievement* resources include

Chapter exercises/forms   Review exercise   Confidence Builder Web search
ACE Self-Test

To access these learning and study tools, go to **college.hmco.com/pic/KanarTCS6e.**

14 Building career skills

Graduation from college is an intersection on the road of life. Where will you go from here?

To make wise choices of a major and career, inform yourself about the job market you will enter.

Take control of your future by replacing false career assumptions with career realities, choosing a major or course of study, and writing your action plan.

Prepare yourself for working in an economy that is increasingly global, technology-driven, and reactive to change.

*Confident students are **future-oriented**. They set goals, make action plans, and follow through on their plans.*

▶ WORKING IN THE NEW ECONOMY

▶ WHERE THE JOBS WILL BE

▶ CHOOSING YOUR FUTURE
Your Career Assumptions
Your Major or Course of Study
Your Action Plan

▶ WHAT EMPLOYERS WANT
Career Skills to Develop
Workplace Ethics

▶ FROM COLLEGE TO WORK
Your Résumé and Cover Letter
The Interview

▶ *Make a smooth transition from college to work by knowing how to present yourself to employers and by using the resources that will help you prepare for a successful future.*

▶ *Identify the SCANS essential skills and find ways to apply them in both academic and workplace environments.*

Adult learner refers to an older college student who may or may not have attended college in the past.

"**W**hat do you want to be when you grow up?" You probably remember being asked this question as a child. What was your answer then, and do you still have the same career goal now? Whether you are a first-time college student or a returning student who has already had some success in the workplace, what are your hopes for the future? Keep in mind that a career is much more than a job. For many people, a career defines who they are and embodies not only what they want to achieve in life but also what they value most. In addition, most people change careers as their values and needs evolve over time.

If you are a recent high-school graduate, your skills may be untried and your values uncertain. You may not have yet decided what your life's work will be. As mentioned in previous chapters, choosing a major will get you started on a career path. If you are an **adult learner** (one who has either postponed college until now or who is returning to college after having left to pursue other goals), you too may need some direction in planning for your future. Are you a highly motivated student who has already selected a major and a career? Then remember that plans change, and that life is uncertain at best. Do not

KEY TERMS

adult learner, *p. 327*
technology-driven, *p. 329*
technologically literate, *p. 329*
global economy, *p. 329*
reactive to change, *p. 330*
job fair, *p. 346*
résumé, *p. 347*
cover letter, *p. 347*

SCANS TERM

SCANS skills, *p. 328*

SCANS skills are the essential skills that employers expect job applicants to have, based on a Department of Labor report. Figure 14.3 lists the skills.

pass up an interesting elective because it isn't required for your major or doesn't relate to your chosen career. College provides many opportunities and resources that can help all students make good choices.

Whatever your age or your current plans, using this chapter's career-readiness strategies and developing the **SCANS skills** can help you prepare for your future with enthusiasm and confidence.

AWARENESS CHECK 21

Are You Ready for Tomorrow's Workforce?

Choose one of the following as your response to each statement: *always* (4 points), *usually* (3 points), *occasionally* (2 points), *rarely* (1 point). Write your number of points in the box beside each statement. When you are finished, add your score.

Points

1. I know what the new economy is like and understand its implications for me.

2. I have heard of the SCANS Report, and I know what its findings are.

3. I know what my strengths and weaknesses are in the skills that employers value.

4. I have selected a major or program of study.

5. I have researched careers and job opportunities in my chosen field.

6. I have a career mentor or advisor.

7. I have work or volunteer experience in my chosen field.

8. I consider myself Internet wise and technologically competent.

9. I have thought about my values and how they will affect my career choice.

10. I have set academic, career, and personal goals and am working to achieve them.

Total

Add your score. If your total is 35–40, the skills you already possess should help you make a smooth transition from college to work. If your total is 30–34, you have some workplace knowledge on which to build strong career skills. If your total is 25–29, practicing this chapter's strategies will relieve some of the uncertainty about your career readiness that you may be feeling. If your score is 10–24, supplement this chapter with a visit to a career counselor or career center. Whatever your level of skill, this chapter will help you think critically about your academic and career goals and how they intersect.

WORKING IN THE NEW ECONOMY

▶ *Prepare yourself for working in an economy that is increasingly global, technology-driven, and reactive to change.*

Tomorrow's workplace is already here. For some time now, we have been living in a new economy, one that is increasingly *technology-driven, global*, and *reactive to change*. These characteristics will have serious implications for you. First of all, you will enter a **technology-driven** workplace. Networked computers, cell phones, wireless technology, and other developments have made it possible to conduct business at any time, anywhere. Employers will expect you to be Internet wise, computer savvy, and technologically literate to enter and advance in most careers and especially in the highest-paying ones. Although you may already feel comfortable with technology and have some computing skills, the level of skill expected in the workplace is generally much higher than that required of college students. To be **technologically literate** means more than knowing how to use the Internet. It also means that you are aware of developments in such fields as biotechnology. For example, the use of biologically engineered cells and tissues has led to important scientific and medical breakthroughs such as lab-grown blood vessels for kidney dialysis patients. Most newspapers and newsmagazines have a technology section where you can keep up with new trends and developments such as this one.

Second, you will be working in a **global economy** in which many American corporations have facilities overseas. Willingness to travel and fluency in another language may improve your career options with some companies. Also, changing demographics due to immigration and globalization have made the American workforce more diverse. Highly skilled international workers compete for American jobs, especially in fields like engineering and health care. Information services provided by credit card companies, title companies, and others are often outsourced to countries such as China and India. With the pool of applicants for

Technology-driven refers to an economy in which businesses are increasingly dependent on technology and its developments to thrive.

Technologically literate means having an awareness of the new discoveries and developments that technology is making possible every day.

Global economy refers to the reality that companies have become borderless, establishing businesses and contacts in all parts of the world.

Through classroom interaction, you can develop interpersonal skills essential to success in the workplace.

many jobs reaching across borders, it is clear that U.S. graduates will need increasingly higher levels of skill to remain competitive. You are in the right place at the right time to develop marketable skills. College also provides opportunities for you to work cooperatively with others whose cultural, ethnic, and religious backgrounds and nationalities differ from your own.

Third, today's economy is **reactive to change** for several reasons: instability of foreign governments and currencies, political unrest, natural disasters, and rapid social and technological change. These factors take a toll on investors, employers, and workers alike. To meet the challenge of finding work in a changing economy, keep your options open. Choose some of your electives in fields other than your major to broaden your experience and ensure your flexibility. Also remember that learning is a lifelong process. The critical thinking skills and learning strategies you are developing now will prepare you to gain new knowledge and develop new skills after graduation.

Reactive to change refers to the ups and downs our economy experiences in response to national and global events.

EXERCISE 14.1

HAVE YOU THOUGHT ABOUT WHAT you want to do for the rest of your life? One of the first steps toward choosing a major or career is to assess your career readiness, using six self-image keys. As explained in Chapter 4, career satisfaction depends on finding work that you enjoy doing, that fulfills one or more of your life's goals, and that integrates well with the life you want to lead. Complete the following survey one category at a time. First, read statements 1 through 4. Second, write a statement of your own in the blank provided. Third, rank the statements from one (most important) to five (least important) in each category. Based on your highest-ranked statements (1 and 2) in each category, write a paragraph or short essay describing your readiness for a career you have chosen or one that you would consider choosing.

INTERESTS: WHAT DO I LIKE TO DO?

_____ 1.   **I enjoy quiet activities like reading, drawing, or writing.**

_____ 2.   **I like to do things with my hands like building something or making handcrafts.**

_____ 3.   **I am an outdoors person who enjoys physical activities.**

_____ 4.   **I enjoy doing research on the Internet.**

_____ 5.   **Write your own statement:** _____

STRENGTHS: WHAT COMES NATURALLY TO ME?

_____ 1.   **I am very good at reading people's motives and feelings.**

_____ 2.   **I have a natural feel for mechanical things and how they work.**

_____ 3.   **I am talented in one or more of the creative or artistic fields.**

_____ 4.   **I am an idea person with an aptitude for logical thinking and problem solving.**

_____ 5.   **Write your own statement:** _____

VALUES: WHAT IS IMPORTANT TO ME?

_____ 1. I like money and the things it buys such as a beautiful home and good clothes.

_____ 2. I'd like to be powerful and influential—someone people look up to.

_____ 3. I'm concerned about the quality of life today and want to make a difference.

_____ 4. I value my family and my relationships with friends.

_____ 5. Write your own statement: _____

CAREER GOALS: WHAT DO I WANT TO ACHIEVE?

_____ 1. I want job security, a comfortable income, and good employee benefits.

_____ 2. I want wealth and a chance for advancement.

_____ 3. I want to travel and get to know other cultures.

_____ 4. I want a career that allows me to work at doing what I enjoy most.

_____ 5. Write your own statement: _____

PERSONALITY: HOW DO I RANK MY PERSONALITY TRAITS?

_____ 1. I am well organized.

_____ 2. I am responsible.

_____ 3. I am sociable.

_____ 4. I am self-disciplined.

_____ 5. Write your own statement: _____

EXPERIENCE: HOW DO I RANK MY WORK EXPERIENCE AS IT APPLIES TO MY CAREER?

_____ 1. I have full- or part-time work experience in the private sector.

_____ 2. I have on-campus work experience.

_____ 3. I have either worked as a volunteer or participated in service learning.

_____ 4. I have had an internship, fellowship, or other work experience.

_____ 5. Write your own statement: _____

This informal survey is meant simply as a guide. For example, if a big-money career is what you want most, then you will probably need to include postgraduate work in your planning. High-paying careers such as physician, attorney, accountant with CPA license, and many others require advanced degrees. If job security is more important to you, then a service career such as teaching or working in a government agency may be a good choice because of its employee benefits such as health care and retirement plans. If family and relationships are your most important value, then your career choice may take into account factors such as family or maternity leave, vacations and holidays that coincide with school holidays, investment opportunities to provide for children's education, and the amount and frequency of job-related travel that can restrict time spent with family. All of the personal qualities listed are among those employers desire most, so all your rankings in the personality section would mean a plus for you in the job market. Your highest ranking in this category may serve as a clue to your best career choice. For example, sociability is a desired trait in any career, but it is especially desirable in sales, teaching, and other careers where dealing face to face with customers or clients is an important part of your work.

For a formal interest inventory, visit your academic advisor or career center. For more help on evaluating your interests and skills, review Gardner's intelligences and your answers to Awareness Check 2 in Chapter 2, pages 35–37.

WHERE THE JOBS WILL BE

> *To make wise choices of a major and career, inform yourself about the job market you will enter.*

Online Study Center
Remembering Cultural Diversity

Not surprisingly, the U.S. Department of Labor predicts that from now until 2014, the fastest-growing, highest-paying jobs will go to those who earn college degrees. Occupations requiring associate and postgraduate degrees are all expected to increase by 20 to 30 percent. Most of the new jobs will be in business and professional services, health-related services, and computer and data-processing services. Massive retirement of employees from the teaching profession, postal service, and other careers in federal, state, and local government will provide many opportunities for employment. Students who major in the sciences or mathematics will have access to some of the highest-paying careers in biomedical research, engineering, and computer systems technology. Students earning business degrees in accounting and marketing, English degrees that emphasize technical writing, and degrees in the social sciences will have transferable skills that will give them an edge in an economy in which career change is commonplace. Also, students who have fluency in more than one language will have an advantage in our increasingly diverse workplace.

If you are like many students, a high-paying career may be your first priority. As competition for these occupations will be great, you need to focus on building the essential workplace skills that will make you a valued employee. Although you may not land the career of your dreams at first, the experience you gain in related jobs or fields will bring you closer to that goal.

However, money may not be your first priority. In a recent Higher Education Research Institute (HERI) report, entering freshmen showed an increased interest in helping others and a greater incidence of civic concern and social responsibility than respondents of previous studies had shown. Like these students, you may prefer to work in one of the service industries or professions such as teaching or health care technology. Although these occupations offer comparatively lower pay than some others, a secure income, a benefits package, and personal rewards make them attractive. For a growing number of students, as reported in national polls and surveys conducted since September 11, 2001, job satisfaction, meaningful work, and opportunities for service to the community are more important than a big salary.

Like many students on today's college campuses, you may already have extensive job, career, or military experience. You may desire a career change or need some retraining to upgrade your employability after a job layoff or company closing. The following chart, based on U.S. Department of Labor employment projections for the period of 2004–2014, may interest you. Figure 14.1 lists seven of the nation's fastest-growing careers in which jobs are expected to remain plentiful for the next eight years. However, remember that our economy reacts to change, and no one can predict the future with absolute certainty.

As you consider career options, do not overlook working for the federal government. According to the U.S. Office of Personnel Management, federal government jobs are expected to increase over the next few years as baby boomers retire from these positions, leaving widespread vacancies. The government employs workers in many fields including nurses, engineers, criminal investigators, accountants, attorneys, and aircraft mechanics. Though many jobs with the government do not pay as well as their counterparts in the private sector, some workers in these positions think that the benefits of job security, pensions, good health care, and personal satisfaction outweigh the reduction in salary.

FIGURE 14.1

HOT CAREERS

CAREERS	MEDIAN ANNUAL EARNINGS (SOME MAKE MORE, SOME LESS.)	EDUCATION/TRAINING
Registered Nurse Treats patients, educates people about medical conditions and therapies	$52,330	Bachelor's degree, associate degree, diploma from an approved nursing program
Physical Therapist Helps restore function and movement to disabled patients and those recovering from surgery	$60,000	Graduation from an accredited physical therapy education program followed by obtaining a state license
Diagnostic Medical Sonographer Uses x-ray, MRI, and sonograph technology to diagnose illness	$52,490	Associate or bachelor's degree; some training offered by hospitals or vocational technical institutions
Paralegal and Legal Assistant Except for fee setting, legal advising, and making court presentations, performs many of the tasks that a lawyer does	$39,130	Associate degree or certification in paralegal studies
Pharmacist Distributes drugs and information about medications	$84,000	Graduation from an accredited college of pharmacy, followed by obtaining a state license
Computer and Information Systems Manager Plans, oversees, and directs Internet operations and network security	$92,570	Master's degree and computer-related work experience
Computer Systems Analyst Solves computer problems and applies computer technology to meet a company's various needs	$66,460	Bachelor's degree in computer science, information science, or management information systems (MIS)

EXERCISE 14.2   COMPUTER APPLICATION

Would you be interested in a career with your federal, state, or local government? Find out if working for the government is right for you. Visit one of the following web sites. Select a career to research; take notes on the job description, requirements, salary and benefits; and be prepared to share your findings in a class discussion:

www.USAJobs.gov.net
www.federaljobs.net
www.careersingovernment.com
www.Jobweb.com

See also college.hmco.com/pic/KanarTCS6e for more up-to-date URLs.

CHOOSING YOUR FUTURE

> *Take control of your future by replacing false career assumptions with career realities, choosing a major or course of study, and writing your action plan.*

It is *your* future. Choosing a major or career or seeking a change of career is a personal decision because it is so closely linked with your future happiness and success. What do you want to do? What do you want to have? What do you want to accomplish? Seeking the advice of a career counselor or advisor is helpful, but only you can answer these questions. Knowing what the workplace of the future will be like, what kinds of jobs will be available, and what your interests and values are will help you begin to narrow down your career choices. The next steps are to examine your career assumptions, choose a course of study (major or certificate program), and then write an action plan for achieving your goal.

Your Career Assumptions

As explained in Chapter 3, examining your assumptions is a key component of critical thinking. Assumptions are long-held beliefs or opinions that shape the way we view the world and that influence our decision making. If your assumptions are based on false evidence, untested theories, or unexamined emotions, then your choices and decisions will not operate in your best interests. They may even hold you back, preventing you from achieving the success you deserve. False assumptions about careers are based on commonly held beliefs that don't measure up to reality. Figure 14.2 contrasts each assumption with a reality check. To think critically about choosing a major or course of study, examine your career assumptions and ask yourself, "Am I being realistic?"

Your Major or Course of Study

If you are attending a community college, you may be planning to transfer to a four-year college, or you may be enrolled in a certificate program. As explained in Chapter 1, before transferring to a four-year college or university, you will earn either an AA or AS degree. These degrees both require general education courses, additional courses in one of the academic disciplines, and elective courses. The AS degree requires more courses in the sciences. *Certificate programs* are career programs that do not prepare you for transfer to a four-year college; instead, they focus on job skills needed for a specific career such as nursing, fire technology, hospitality services, ornamental horticulture, building and contracting, and electrical engineering.

If you are attending a four-year college or university, you will be earning a bachelor's degree in a major discipline such as biology, English, or psychology. If you have chosen to pursue a career in one of the professions such as law or medicine, then your major will prepare you for additional work at the master or doctorate level. Some careers require a specific degree; others may not. The four-year degree requires general education courses that set a foundation for all future courses plus required courses and electives based on your major.

The following guidelines may help you choose an appropriate major. If you are still not sure what career you want to pursue, choosing a major will narrow the field.

▼ **Look at your grades.** In what subject area have you consistently done your best? For example, if science courses have been very difficult for you, then you may not want to major in biology.

▼ **Be honest about your skills.** Does math come easy for you? Do you read and write well? Choose a major that will allow you to use your strengths.

CONCEPT CHECK 14.1

Think about a job you have held. What is one skill you learned at that job that will be a career asset for you in the future?

Figure 14.2

WHAT ARE YOUR CAREER ASSUMPTIONS?

FALSE ASSUMPTION:	REALITY CHECK:
Only one career is just right for me.	You possess a range of skills, interests, and abilities that would make you well suited to a variety of jobs and careers.
All the good jobs go to people with experience.	Good communication skills, interpersonal skills, enthusiasm, and a positive attitude make up for a lack of experience, especially in entry-level jobs. You can gain experience through volunteer work, service learning, apprenticeships, fellowships, and part-time employment.
I won't be able to overcome the negative effect of poor grades.	Your transcript is only one part of your résumé, and as you gain experience, it will become less and less important.
I have a spotty work history that will hold me back.	Employers look at the most recent job you held and your reason for leaving. They are more interested in how you deal with setbacks and whether you are persistent in trying to get ahead.
My major or course of study will dictate my career choice.	Majors are not as directly related to specific careers as you might think. A major in psychology or English, for example, is a good background for a career in law. Technical skills are useful in many jobs, and your real education will begin after you are hired through on-the-job training and work-related seminars.
I cannot waste my time taking courses that do not relate to my major.	Employers like well-rounded people who are conversant on a variety of subjects. No course is a waste of time if it broadens your perspective, makes you a more interesting person, or teaches you a new skill that you may use later on.

- **Consider your interests.** Choose a major (and a career) based on your interests, the things you enjoy doing most. You are more likely to enjoy your work if you like what you are doing.
- **Talk to people.** Get advice or information from your advisor, from students who are majoring in the field you are considering, and from family or others who know you well and who know what your skills and interests are. Make your own choice, but listen to their suggestions. Also, review the sections on *mentors* and *academic support groups* in Chapter 1.

Your Action Plan

Once you have selected a program or major based on a tentative career choice, deciding what courses to take is only one step in good planning. Continue to explore careers until you settle on what you want to do. Build work experience by taking a part-time job on or off campus. If you take summers off, use them wisely: Study overseas, work or intern in your chosen field, do volunteer work, or engage in other activities to build your résumé. During the semester or quarter, make time for clubs and organizations that relate to your major or career and try to work yourself into a leadership position. In addition, follow these steps to fulfill the requirements of your course of study.

Use your catalog to determine your degree or program requirements and deadlines. For example, what courses are required? Are your electives restricted to additional courses within your major, or are they free? When must you apply for a degree or transfer credit? Does your program include an internship? Does your program lead to certification in a field? These answers and other important information are contained in your college catalog or on your college web site.

List all the courses you will need. Map out a tentative guide for each semester or quarter from now until the completion of your program.

Work with an advisor to determine which courses you should take first and how best to arrange each term's schedule. Complete required courses as soon as you can to avoid any delays in graduation. For example, some courses may be offered only in alternate semesters or quarters. You might have to retake a course because of a poor grade or other unfortunate circumstance. Some courses, like math courses, are better taken consecutively to avoid skill gaps. Also, you will do better if you do not try to take too many heavy reading courses in one term.

If you will be transferring from a two-year college to a four-year institution, find out which courses will transfer and plan your program accordingly.

Check with your advisor regularly to monitor your progress, to make sure you haven't overlooked anything, and to troubleshoot if you decide to change majors, programs, or degrees.

The key to success is to write out your action plan. List your long-term goal and explain how it meets the six characteristics of reachable goals as explained in Chapter 4. List the short-term goals you will have to meet as you pursue the long-term goal. Finally, explain how you will evaluate whether your plan is working. Your action plan is your commitment to do the work that will impel you toward your goal. Also, when things go wrong, as they probably will, having your plan in writing makes it easy for you to see what you have accomplished, what still needs to be done, and where any problems lie. A good plan is flexible and will accommodate changing circumstances.

EXERCISE 14.3 LEARNING STYLE

WHAT IS YOUR WORK STYLE? Your work style is simply your learning style applied in a workplace context. For example, if you are a morning person, do your hardest tasks early in the day when you are most alert. If you like working with others as opposed to working alone, volunteer for team projects and committees. If you like to manage your time and schedule tasks without interference, consider a career that allows you to work from home. To refresh your memory about learning styles, review Chapter 2, especially your answers to the Awareness Checks. Then complete Parts I and II, which follow.

Part I: Read each question and check each statement that applies to you.

_____ 1. **My energy level is at its highest in the morning.**

_____ 2. **I feel most energetic at night.**

_____ 3. **I work best when I am physically involved, doing hands-on tasks.**

_____ 4. **I am at my best when mentally challenged.**

_____ 5. **I prefer tasks that require me to interact with others.**

_____ 6. **I would rather do most of my work on my own.**

_____ 7. **I enjoy researching online, sending and receiving email, and word processing.**

_____ 8. **The less time I spend online the better.**

_____ 9. **I think of myself as a people person.**

_____10. **I think of myself as an idea person.**

_____11. **I want a career that will take me outdoors.**

_____12. **I would be most comfortable working in an office.**

_____13. **I would be happiest in a career that requires frequent travel.**

_____14. **Ideally, I would like to do most of my work from home.**

_____15. **I'm a worker bee; just tell me what to do.**

_____16. **I like to take the lead; throw out an idea and let me run with it.**

_____17. **I work best when tasks and responsibilities are clearly defined.**

_____18. **I work best when given the freedom to define my own tasks.**

_____19. **I like routine tasks that are pretty much the same every day.**

_____20. **I need challenges and opportunities to innovate or create.**

_____21. **I am best at teaching, leading, or managing others.**

_____22. **I am best at being a team member or filling a niche.**

_____23. **I am well organized, a detail person.**

_____24. **I tend to look at the big picture, leaving the details to others.**

_____25. **I am good at gathering, compiling, and interpreting information.**

_____26. **I am best at applying the information others have gathered.**

_____27. **Most people would describe me as practical and reality-oriented.**

_____28. **Most people would describe me as idealistic and future-oriented.**

Part II: Based on the items you checked in Part I, what is your work style? Write a paragraph or short essay describing your work style. If you have already chosen a career, explain how your work style makes this career a good fit for you. If you are still undecided, then explain how you will use the checklist results as part of your decision-making process.

CONFIDENCE BUILDER

College *Is* the Real World

How many times have you heard remarks like these or made them yourself?

- "Why do I need this course? It won't help me in my career."

- "I'm just marking time until I graduate."

- "Professors are so out of touch with the real world."

College *is* the real world. Professors are not teaching theory alone. They are helping you lay the foundation for lifelong learning and skill development. Much of what you learn in college is a thought process—a way of approaching problems and making decisions. Any course you take, whether in your major field or not, is the vehicle through which skills such as thinking critically and communicating effectively are conveyed. An equation you solved on a test or a speech you gave in class may seem unimportant. However, the logical problem-solving process you learn by working equations and the communication skills you learn by writing and making speeches are transferable skills that employers value.

What are you learning in college, and how does it relate to the skills you will need for career success? What skills do you already possess that will enhance your career readiness? Your courses, assignments, and extracurricular activities have a workplace application, as you can see from the following list. Read the list and determine which skills you already possess and which ones you need to develop.

- **Algebra** teaches critical thinking within the context of mathematical terms, operations, and procedures. Algebra helps you develop three transferable thinking skills that employers value: *logical reasoning, decision making,* and *problem-solving* skills. Do you make decisions primarily on the basis of feeling or thinking? Can you determine the causes of a

problem and find ways to solve it? Do you see logical connections between events and outcomes?

- **Psychology** deals with human motivation and behavior. The knowledge you gain from a psychology course may lead to self-understanding and acceptance of others whose values and motivations differ from yours. Psychology also explores the workings of your mind and memory—knowledge that can help you learn *how* to learn. Employers seek applicants who are flexible and able to quickly pick up new skills as the job requires. Moreover, the personal qualities employers value such as *self-management, self-esteem,* and *personal responsibility* are a direct outgrowth of self-knowledge. What personal qualities do you prize in yourself, and how will they help you in your career? What personal qualities do you need to develop?

- **Composition** helps you develop the writing skills of selecting and organizing details to support a central idea, writing clear and error-free sentences, and expressing ideas that are concrete and concise. Writing is an essential *communication skill* that employers value. They expect employees to write reports that are readable, meaningful, and useful. How are your writing skills?

- **Speech** courses teach you the fundamentals of public speaking and active listening, and they provide plenty of opportunities for you to practice these *communication skills*. Good speaking and listening skills are essential for careers in which you will be required to make presentations; attend meetings, conferences, and seminars; or conduct tours or training programs. Do you know how to plan a purposeful, well-organized speech? How are your listening skills?

- **Researching** print and online resources for reports or term papers teaches you to *acquire, evaluate, organize, interpret*, and *synthesize information*. Just as these skills demonstrate to an instructor that you understand and can apply what you have learned, they also demonstrate to employers that you know how to find and manage information relevant to a specific need or work assignment. Do you need to develop your research skills? Do you have good computer skills?

- **Extracurricular activities** such as playing a sport, joining an organization, volunteering your service to the community, and holding a student government office help you build *interpersonal skills* such as teamwork, leadership, and working with others from diverse backgrounds. Service learning, an instructional method used on many campuses, provides opportunities for you to gain skills that

can be applied in the workplace. These skills are essential in any job or career, especially those that require you to interact directly with coworkers, clients, or customers. How would you rate your interpersonal skills?

Do not underestimate the value of your courses. By identifying a skill or concept that has a direct application to your major or career for each course you are taking this semester, you will find the motivation for doing your best. Think of college as a training ground or an apprenticeship in learning how to learn. If you are marking time until you graduate, you are missing the point. College is not the end of learning. At graduation you are just beginning.

To pursue this topic further, extend the career research you began in Exercise 14.2 by determining the skills your career choice requires. Which skills do you already possess? Which ones do you need to develop? To help you in your online search, go to www.facts.org or type *careers* followed by a comma and a field that interests you such as engineering, technical writing, or marketing.

Online Study Center
Confidence Builder
Web Search

WHAT EMPLOYERS WANT

▶ *Identify the SCANS essential skills and find ways to apply them in both academic and workplace environments.*

The acronym SCANS stands for the *Secretary's Commission of Achieving Necessary Skills*. The Commission, led by then-Secretary of Labor Elizabeth Dole and including members from industry, labor, education, and government, published *What Work Requires of Schools: A SCANS Report for America 2000*. Completed in the early 1990s, the SCANS report identified the skills essential for success in the workplace. Today, the Commission's recommendations continue to be a valuable source of information for educators and others involved in developing a strong workforce. *The Confident Student* acknowledges SCANS at the beginning of each chapter and in the workplace case studies near the end of each chapter. Figure 14.3 on page 340 summarizes the skills.

Workplace know-how consists of having good foundational skills and competencies as well as mastery of the specific skills and training that qualify you for your chosen career. Let's compare three different careers. Michael works for a company that provides food and products to supermarkets. Michael's job is to keep track of the company's inventory, using a computerized system. To do this job effectively requires the systems and technology competencies, the basic skills of reading and mathematics, and the thinking skills of problem solving and decision making.

FIGURE 14.3

SCANS ESSENTIAL CAREER SKILLS

THE FOUNDATION

Basic Skills	Mathematics and the communication skills of reading, writing, speaking, and listening.
Thinking Skills	Thinking critically and creatively, making decisions, solving problems, reasoning, knowing how to learn, and seeing things in the mind's eye (visualizing, looking ahead, predicting outcomes)
Personal Qualities	Personal responsibility, self-esteem, sociability, self-management, and integrity

THE COMPETENCIES

Resources	Allocating time, money, materials, space, and staff
Interpersonal Skills	Working on teams, teaching others, serving customers, leading, negotiating, working with others from culturally diverse backgrounds
Information	Acquiring and evaluating data, organizing and maintaining files, interpreting and communicating, using computers
Systems	Understanding social, organizational, and technological systems, monitoring and correcting performance, and designing or improving systems
Technology	Selecting equipment and tools, applying technology to specific tasks, and maintaining and troubleshooting technologies

Isabel is a high-school English teacher. For this job she needs good interpersonal skills to help her work with students from diverse backgrounds; the communication skills of reading, writing, speaking, and listening on which the content of her course is based; and thinking skills that will help her solve problems in the classroom, make decisions about grades, and teach students how to learn. Because Isabel's school has a computer lab and because all students in English classes are required to use computers for researching and writing, Isabel has been taking a course to upgrade her computer skills.

Ping manages a landscape nursery. She spends part of her time in the office monitoring employees, assigning work tasks, and troubleshooting with customers. She also spends time out of the office investigating new sources for plants and other products the company uses. To manage the company's resources and employees, Ping must have good personal and interpersonal skills, the ability to make decisions and solve problems, and the mathematical skills needed to spend the company's money wisely. These examples illustrate several ways employees in different workplace settings can apply the SCANS foundation skills and competencies listed in Figure 14.3.

Career Skills to Develop

What SCANS skills are essential to your career? No matter what you decide to do, the foundational skills will be essential as well as some experience in the use of

AWARENESS CHECK 22

How Are Your Communication Skills?

Choose one of the following as your response to each statement:
always **(4 points),** *usually* **(3 points),** *occasionally* **(2 points),** *rarely*
**(1 point). Write your number of points in the box beside each statement.
When you are finished, add your score.**

Points

1. I know how to plan and organize an effective oral presentation.

2. I am nervous when speaking in front of a large group.

3. When working with a team or in a small group, I do not hesitate to share my ideas or ask questions.

4. I do an excellent job of expressing my thoughts in writing.

5. I am able to read information from printed and online sources with understanding.

6. When interacting with others, I spend more time listening than talking.

7. I can easily determine which ideas in an oral presentation are the most important.

8. I am able to express my ideas without offending anyone.

9. The contributions that I make to group projects, whether in speaking or in writing, are helpful and to the point.

10. I try to dress and conduct myself in ways that communicate my respect for others and for myself.

Total

Add your score. If your total is 35–40, your communication skills are a valuable career asset. Practice them at every opportunity. If your total is 30–34, the communication skills that you have are a good foundation for developing new ones. If your total is 25–29, seek out opportunities to work with others so that you can build your communication and interpersonal skills. If your score is 10–24, supplement this chapter with a review of the speaking, listening, and teamwork skills explained in Chapter 5. The communication skills, personal qualities, and interpersonal skills that ensure success in class also ensure success at work.

computers and other technology. Good interpersonal skills and the ability to find information are essential competencies for any career. No doubt, whatever you decide to do will require some understanding of how systems work and how to manage resources. For example, can you think of many jobs that would *not* require you to manage your time (resource) or to understand the organizational framework or relationship among supervisors, managers, employees, and others within a company (organizational system)? In other words, all the SCANS skills are essential to a successful career. However, your communication skills are probably the ones employees value most for these reasons:

▼ Reading, whether from printed or online sources, is one of the primary means of gathering information and keeping up with new research and trends in a field. Being able to read and understand ideas communicated to you through printed and online sources is an essential skill. Evaluating these sources and challenging and reporting the information may be part of your duties at work.

▼ The ability to clearly and concisely express your ideas in an email, letter, report, or other written form is the mark of an educated person—a good point to keep in mind when writing a résumé.

▼ Whether brainstorming ideas in a meeting, giving a formal speech at a conference, or making an oral presentation to coworkers, the ability to state your ideas in a clear, well-organized manner is an asset.

▼ Everyone loves a good listener, and this is true in the workplace, where time is scarce and people don't want to repeat themselves. Listening and hearing are two different things. Listening is an active process; hearing is a passive behavior. To listen actively, focus your attention on the speaker, listen for ideas, and think critically about their meaning. Ask clarifying questions and make appropriate comments. Active listening is a vital communication skill.

Workplace Ethics

Following September 11, 2001, many Americans began to question the meaning of their lives and work. Some left secure jobs and gave up stable incomes to pursue less lucrative but more purposeful careers. The selfless actions of those who risked their lives to save others sparked a renewed emphasis on character and personal responsibility, which has fueled the drive for accountability and workplace ethics.

What this means to you is that employers are taking a closer look than ever before at the personal qualities and interpersonal skills you bring to the workplace. What are these qualities and skills? SCANS defines personal qualities as *personal responsibility, self-esteem, sociability, self-management,* and *integrity.* The SCANS interpersonal skills listed in Figure 14.3 spell out the ways people work cooperatively and interact with others from culturally diverse backgrounds: through *teamwork* and by *teaching, serving, leading,* and *negotiating.* In other words, your personal qualities determine how effective your interpersonal relationships will be. See also the discussion on interpersonal skills for college and career, pages 122–123. Following is a list of the SCANS personal qualities and what they mean.

▼ **Personal responsibility.** People who take personal responsibility do not blame others for their own mistakes and do not expect others to do their work. For example, a personally responsible student accepts a bad grade as the result of his or her own misunderstanding or lack of effort. Similarly, a personally responsible manager accepts that his or her subordinates need direction and supervision. If they fail at their tasks, then the manager must accept his or her share of the accountability. To develop personal responsibility, do not make excuses for lateness, bad grades, poorly done assignments, unkind words, or bad behavior. Take the initiative to improve your performance.

► **Self-esteem.** Self-esteem means *self-respect*. Students and employees who have self-esteem regard themselves favorably. They think of themselves as essentially good people even when they make mistakes, and they work honestly to correct mistakes. People who have self-esteem have a positive attitude toward themselves and others. To develop your self-esteem, think positively. Focus on the things you do well; be honest with yourself about skills, attitudes, and behaviors that need improving; and make whatever changes are needed.

► **Sociability.** You don't have to be outgoing to be sociable. Many introverts are sociable people. Being sociable means being friendly, pleasant, and agreeable. If you are a sociable student or coworker, then you enjoy the company of others and they enjoy being with you. To become more sociable, listen to others, be encouraging, and make an effort to befriend others—especially those who are culturally diverse.

► **Self-management.** Self-management means *self-discipline*. In many ways, you are your own boss. It is up to you to determine when, what, and how to study. It is up to you to manage your time, control your concentration, and say no to invitations that interfere with something important that you need to do. It is also up to you to determine what is and is not important. In other words, a self-managed student or employee has an *internal locus of control*, as explained in Chapter 2. Daniel Goleman, author of *Emotional Intelligence*, explains several qualities of the self-managed person such as *persistence, hopefulness*, and the *ability to regulate moods*. For more on this topic, see page 177. To become more internally controlled or self-managed, find ways to motivate yourself, and do not expect others to motivate you. Set goals and find incentives such as a higher grade in one of your courses or a promotion at work, and let those provide your motivation. Employers value employees who are self-starters: people who don't have to be told what to do. Be a self-starter.

► **Integrity.** Integrity means following a moral or ethical code. Moral codes are often based on religious beliefs. Ethical codes are often based on what is socially acceptable. In either case, such codes provide guidelines for personal and corporate behavior. A person or company that has integrity has these qualities: *trustworthiness, fairness, honesty, respect*, and *obedience to the law*. As a student, you show integrity when you do not cheat on exams or plagiarize others' work. As an employee, you show integrity in little ways when you do not pilfer from the supply cabinet and when you do not make personal calls at work. You show integrity in big ways when you do not attempt to undermine others' work in order to advance yourself and when you do not engage in illegal or unethical business practices such as falsifying records or accounts. To develop integrity, use the Golden Rule and the physicians' Hippocratic Oath as guidelines. The Rule says to treat others as you would like them to treat you. The Oath says, "First, do no harm."

CONCEPT CHECK 14.2

Which one of the SCANS skills is your strongest? How do you apply this skill, either at work or in your classes?

In addition to ethical behavior, and the other personal qualities listed previously, employers also value flexibility and a positive attitude. These qualities make people pleasant and easy to work with. Flexibility enables you to adjust to the changing circumstances and needs of the workplace. A positive attitude makes you open to new ideas and accepting of others' differences. For more information on the ideas discussed in this section, review the following pages: flexibility, page 15; values and ethics, pages 86–89 and Figure 4.1; positive attitude, pages 95–96.

COMPUTER CONFIDENCE

Researching Careers on the Internet

Traditional ways to find out about careers include interviewing someone you know who has a job that interests you, going to job fairs, and taking a part-time job in a company you admire. In addition to these methods, which are time-consuming but worth the effort, the Internet provides quick and easy access to hundreds of careers and to career-related information. The Internet can be a powerful research tool if you know what to look for and how to avoid the pitfalls. Here are some guidelines:

- **Research an industry.** Look up industry web sites or periodicals for a particular field in which you are interested. You can find an industry's main web site by using a search engine such as Yahoo! or Google. Discussion groups may list articles and other information about the industry.

- **Research a company.** To find out everything you can about a company, visit its web site. Start with the company name followed by *.com*, or try another keyword search if that method doesn't work. Company ads may also list the web site, or you can call the company and ask. Research the company to learn about its products, services, background, and job openings.

- **Join an online career discussion group.** Visit a major career site such as those listed to find a chat room where you can talk about careers with others who share your interests.

- **Check electronic bulletin boards.** Users can post and read notices and post résumés. Most are free and include job listings. Bulletin boards can be found on major career sites.

- **Seek career guidance.** You can find sites that will help you with your career search and allow you to take interest tests, develop résumés, read articles, and participate in discussion forums. At www.acinet.org, for example, you can access a list of free online assessment tests.

Two pitfalls to watch out for are the rapidity with which web sites appear and disappear and the fact that anyone can put anything on the Internet. Go to familiar sites, especially those for which you have a trusted recommendation. If you have trouble finding a site, check the URL for errors in spelling first. Then if you still have trouble, check to determine whether the site still exists. Your college librarian has references that list current web sites. Finally, evaluate sites using the criteria explained in Chapter 3. Now try out your research skills on the following six web sites:

- America's CareerInfoNet www.acinet.org

- America's Job Bank www.ajb.dni.us

- Careerbuilder www.careerbuilder.com

- Careers OnLine www.careersonline.com

- Hotjobs www.hotjobs.com

- Monster.com www.monster.com

EXERCISE 14.4   COMPUTER APPLICATION

CAN YOU DETERMINE HOW YOU would apply a skill learned in one of your courses to a work-related task? Complete the following comparison chart by filling in the blank spaces. When you get to item 10, you will fill in all the spaces, starting with a course of your choice. You may use a course more than once. Use the Confidence Builder on pages 338–339 and Figure 14.3 on page 340 as references, and look for clues in the blanks that are filled in. To download an exercise form, go to www.college.hmco.com/pic/KanarTCS6e.

APPLYING COLLEGE SKILLS IN THE WORKPLACE

College Course	Skill Learned/Applied	Workplace Application
1. Freshman Composition	Write a well-organized essay.	Prepare a report.
2. College Study Skills	_____	Take notes in a meeting.
3. _____	Make a speech in class.	Make a presentation at work.
4. Biology	Work with group members to design and run a lab experiment.	_____
5. Personal Finance	_____	Manage a departmental budget.
6. _____	Compare wedding rituals and ceremonies across cultures.	Working with others from diverse backgrounds.
7. Introduction to Psychology	_____	_____
8. _____	Build a working model of an electrical circuit.	_____
9. _____	_____	Prepare a résumé and cover letter for a position you seek.
10. _____	_____	_____

FROM COLLEGE TO WORK

▶ *Make a smooth transition from college to work by knowing how to present yourself to employers and by using the resources that will help you prepare for a successful future.*

Your college has many resources that you can draw on as you prepare yourself for the future. Your courses provide the knowledge and skills you will need to succeed in life and work. The organizations you choose to support, be a member of, or take a leadership role in prepare you for involvement in your professional and community life. Living in a dorm and having roommates afford opportunities for you to build people skills as you interact with others from diverse backgrounds. For example, a residence hall, a sorority or fraternity, or an apartment you share with roommates places you in close quarters with others—some of whom you may not know well or even like. Your adjustment depends on the effort *you* make to cooperate with your roommates and resolve conflicts. Your college can help you gain work experience through part-time campus jobs, internships, fellowships, and teaching assistantships, and may put you in touch with prospective employers through job fairs and placement services. No matter how much or how little work experience you have had, your college has resources that can help you prepare for the life you want.

Your college career center or other department that dispenses career information can tell you where and when a job fair is being held in your area. A **job fair** is an event where companies set up booths and send representatives to collect résumés and screen potential candidates for positions they need to fill. A job fair is a great place to learn about a company you are interested in, check leads on positions for which you may qualify, or learn about a company with which you are unfamiliar or may not have considered. Representatives bring literature about their companies that you can take away, and many set up equipment for viewing videos or visiting their web sites, which are also excellent sources of information. Good preparation is the key to getting the most you can out of a job fair. Figure 14.4 is a checklist to help you prepare for the next job fair in your area.

Although you may not get the career of your dreams at first, every job you take is a step in that direction. Another key to success is knowing how to present yourself to employers through a résumé, cover letter, and personal interview.

Job fair refers to an event at which companies gather in one place to attract applicants and fill positions.

A job fair is an excellent resource for researching careers and networking.

FIGURE 14.4

JOB FAIR CHECKLIST

☑ **Target companies.** Since many companies will have booths at a job fair, and you can't visit them all, target several that interest you most. Research them ahead of time so that you appear knowledgeable. The Internet, career center, and library are good places to begin your research.

☑ **Be professional.** Dress conservatively, as you would for a job interview. Carry a nice-looking tote bag, briefcase, zippered notebook, or pocket folder for storing copies of your résumé, representatives' business cards, and company literature. This will send the message that you are well organized.

☑ **Make an impression.** Shake hands, make eye contact, state your name and introduce yourself, but keep your comments brief. Think of your introduction as a brief presentation, covering several points: your major or career choice, why you're interested in the company, and your desire for an interview.

☑ **Ask questions.** Questioning representatives about their companies shows interest. Keep your questions brief. Your goal is to find out more about the company and the name of a contact person to whom you can write personally if you decide to make a formal application. Be sure to ask for a representative's business card so that you have a contact to mention in a cover letter.

☑ **Take notes.** You will not remember names, specific information about a company, or helpful tips unless you jot them down. Carry a note pad for this purpose, or write the information on a representative's business card or on a company flyer or brochure.

☑ **Hand out résumés.** Representatives expect to collect résumés from potential applicants, so do not hesitate to hand yours out. Bring plenty of copies. Consider preparing a cover letter that introduces your qualifications and provides the company with a sample of your writing.

☑ **Collect company literature.** The booths at a job fair are usually well stocked with materials such as leaflets, pamphlets, and brochures that contain valuable information about the company's policies and operations. Take whatever literature is available.

☑ **Follow through.** Send thank you notes to the company representatives who expressed interest in you. Following up with a thank you leaves a favorable impression the representative may recall should you decide to formally apply for a position with the company.

Your Résumé and Cover Letter

A **résumé** is a document that summarizes your qualifications and work experience. A **cover letter** accompanies the résumé and introduces you to the employer. Both documents create a potential employer's first impression of you, so they should honestly and concisely state the appropriate information and also make you look good. Grammar and typing errors do not make a good impression. Employers in a national poll listed these errors among the most common mistakes that they see on résumés. Before sending your résumé and cover letter, proofread them to find and correct errors. Get a second opinion from an advisor or instructor who can spot additional errors that you may have missed.

Opinions differ concerning what kind of information to include on a résumé and what format to use. An employer is more likely to read your résumé and cover letter if they are limited to one page each. If you have extensive work experience or additional qualifications that are impressive, you can attach a second page.

Résumé refers to a summary of work experience and qualifications as part of a job application.

Cover letter refers to a document that introduces you to a potential employer.

Many companies ask for online submissions of the résumé through a web site or by email. If you are submitting a résumé online, the font (typeface) that you use and the way that you set up the information on the page should be kept simple. Some companies specify the format that they require. Use your career center for submitting a résumé online; someone there can help you navigate the system. Listed next are some general guidelines for preparing résumés, followed by Figure 14.5, which contains special tips for submitting résumés online. For examples of a printed résumé and cover letter, see Figure 14.6 on page 349.

Heading. Head your résumé with your name, address, phone number, and email address. If you have a temporary address, include it along with your permanent address. Make your name stand out by using a larger font, all caps, bold type, or a combination of these features.

FIGURE 14.5

SPECIAL TIPS FOR ONLINE SUBMISSION OF RÉSUMÉS

TIP	EXPLANATION
Follow Directions	Pay attention to what you are asked to write. Enter the correct information in the right field. Fill in all fields, required or not.
Keep It Simple	As with print résumés, your online résumé should be direct and to the point. Use a font that is uncluttered and easy to read.
Sharpen Your Focus	Market your skills. Focus on what you can offer the company rather than what the job will do for you.
Be Specific	Include complete work history, school time, and any gaps in employment. Keep these entries brief and to the point.
Use Key Words and Phrases	Employers use key words, buzz words, and industry shorthand when searching through résumés for applicants to fill a job. Browse the company's ads and other information on their web site to find key words and phrases that you can include in your job experience descriptions.
Be Professional	Avoid using a cute or clever email address. Just your last name preceded or followed by a first initial is both professional and efficient.
Use the Comments Section	If there is a comments section, use it to list your special skills or to demonstrate what you know about the company. For example, you might comment on some new product or research that has been reported in the news.
Follow Up	After sending your résumé, write a follow-up email addressed to the person to whom you submitted the résumé.

SAMPLE RÉSUMÉ AND COVER LETTER

FIGURE **14.6**

Résumé

225 West 70 Street
New York, NY 10023
Phone: 212-555-3821
Email: agomez@nyu.edu

Aurelia Gomez

Objective	Entry-level staff accounting position with a public accounting firm	
Experience	Summer 2002	***Accounting Intern:*** Coopers & Lybrand, NYC • Assisted in preparing corporate tax returns • Attended meetings with clients • Conducted research in corporate tax library and wrote research reports
	Nov. 1998 – Aug. 2000	***Payroll Specialist:*** City of New York • Worked in a full-time civil service position in the Department of Administration • Used payroll and other accounting software on both DEC 1034 minicomputer and Pentium III • Represented 28-person work unit on the department's management–labor committee • Left job to pursue college degree full-time
Education	Jan. 1996 – Present	Pursuing a 5-year bachelor of business administration degree (major in accounting) from NYU • Expected graduation date: June 2003 • Attended part-time from 1996 until 2001 while holding down a full-time job • Have financed 100% of all college expenses through savings, work, and student loans • Plan to sit for the CPA exam in May 2004
Personal Data		• Helped start the Minority Business Student Association at NYU and served as program director for two years; secured the publisher of *Black Enterprise* magazine as a banquet speaker • Have traveled extensively throughout South America • Am a member of the Accounting Society • Am willing to relocate
References	Available upon request	

Cover Letter

March 13, 20—

Mr. David Norman, Partner
Ross, Russell & Weston
452 Fifth Avenue
New York, NY 10018

Dear Mr. Norman:

Subject: EDP Specialist Position (Reference No. 103-G)

My varied work experience in accounting and payroll services, coupled with my accounting degree, has prepared me for the position of EDP specialist that you advertised in the March 9 *New York Times.*

In addition to taking required courses in accounting and management information systems as part of my accounting major at New York University, I took an elective course in EDP auditing and control. The training I received in this course in applications, software, systems, and service-center records would enable me to immediately become a productive member of your EDP consulting staff.

My college training has been supplemented by an internship in a large accounting firm. In addition, my two and one-half years of experience as a payroll specialist for the city of New York have given me firsthand knowledge of the operation and needs of nonprofit agencies. This experience should help me to contribute to your large consulting practice with governmental agencies.

After you have reviewed my enclosed résumé, I would appreciate having the opportunity to discuss with you why I believe I have the right qualifications and personality to serve you and your clients. I can be reached by phone after 3 p.m. daily.

Sincerely,

Aurelia Gomez

Aurelia Gomez
225 West 70 Street
New York, NY 10023
Phone: 212-555-3821
Email: agomez@nyu.edu

Enclosure

Scott Ober, *Contemporary Business Communication*, Sixth Edition. Copyright © 2006 by Houghton Mifflin Company. Reprinted with permission.

Objective. In one sentence, state the position for which you are applying. Use the job title if you know what it is, or summarize the type of job (skills and duties) that you are seeking.

Education. List degrees, month and year of graduation or anticipated graduation date, schools and locations, and your GPA, if it's exceptional.

Work experience. List jobs related to your major or career choice separately from other work experience. List them chronologically, starting with the most recent. Include job titles, businesses or organizations, military service, locations, and dates of employment. Include accomplishments, honors, and awards, if relevant. If you have very little work experience, focus on your accomplishments and other experience, and relate both to general career skills (communication, money handling, leadership), other SCANS skills, or specific skills required of the job for which you are applying.

Skills. If you want to emphasize special skills such as "fluent in ASL (American Sign Language)," "fluent in Spanish," or "thorough knowledge of MS Word" or other computing skills, describe them in a short paragraph or bulleted list.

Interests. List activities and hobbies, memberships in organizations, volunteer work, service learning projects—anything that reflects your work experience and career preference. This section of the résumé is optional. If you do list interests and activities, be sure not to include anything that might prejudice the employer against you.

References. A *reference* is someone who knows the kind of person you are and is familiar with your work habits. List one to four employers or instructors as references along with their titles and where they can be reached. Proper etiquette requires that you contact your references first, asking their permission to be listed on your résumé. It is also accepted practice to type the words *references available upon request.*

Send a cover letter with your résumé; but first, do your homework. The title of the person or department that handles résumés differs according to the company or employer. For example, if you were seeking a high-school teaching position, you would write to the superintendent of schools. In some companies, you might send your letter to the director of human resources or to the personnel director. In any case, your inquiries are more likely to lead to a job if you have taken the time to learn the name and title of the appropriate contact person. A career counselor or job placement specialist can help you find the information you need, or you can ask your academic advisor to direct you to the appropriate campus resource. Most companies list this information on their web site.

Address your letter to the appropriate person, and use a standard business letter format as shown in Figure 14.6. The body of your letter should consist of several paragraphs containing the following information: In the first paragraph, explain your purpose for writing by stating the position you want and how you learned about it. Follow with one or more paragraphs in which you very briefly summarize the experience or qualifications that make you the right person for the job. End your letter with a paragraph requesting a meeting and stating when you will be available. Give the employer a time range that allows for flexibility in scheduling.

The Interview

When you are called for an interview, you are being considered for the position. An interview serves several purposes. It allows the employer to observe how you handle yourself in a stressful situation. The employer can tell from the way you dress, the way you speak, and the way you respond to questions whether you are serious about working in the company and how you would fit into the workplace. The interview provides you with an opportunity to find out more about the company and what your responsibilities would be. To shine in an interview, follow these guidelines:

- Familiarize yourself with the company, its goals, and the duties of the position you are seeking. Do your research at the library or online by reading industry reports or company documents. Ask questions about the job that show you have researched it and know something about the company. When you are asked questions about your experience and qualifications, frame your answers to show how you would be an asset to the company.

C R I T I C A L

T H I N K I N G

Exercise Overview

Self-knowledge is an indispensable tool for preparing a résumé that reflects who you are. This exercise will help you think critically about your assets and accomplishments.

Exercise Background

Many students have difficulty talking or writing about themselves. They may devalue their interests and experience, or they may not be aware of the marketable skills they have developed through working. Now is the time to get over any misgivings you may have and to think confidently about who you are and what you know.

Exercise Task

Make a list of your assets and accomplishments. These might include a skill you mastered quickly, a talent you have developed, an obstacle you have overcome, or an award or special recognition you have received. Your list might also include a new skill or ability you developed at work—something you thought you couldn't do but were able to accomplish. Do you have a personal skill for which you are well known? Are you a good listener or someone who helps others resolve conflicts? Do people enjoy working with you? Keep your list and add to it over time. Use your accomplishments list to remind yourself of your personal qualities and skills when it comes time to prepare a résumé.

▻ Dress appropriately. The key to making a good impression is to be neither overdressed nor underdressed. One way to determine what is appropriate is to visit the company or place of employment before your interview and observe what people in the type of position you are seeking are wearing. A book or article on the topic of dressing for success may also provide some useful tips.

▻ Be prepared for both positive and negative questions. For example, an interviewer might ask you why you left your previous place of employment, or what special skill or quality you would bring to the company. An employer wants to know how confident you are and how you react under pressure.

▻ Do not ask about pay unless the employer brings it up. When you are offered the job, it is appropriate to discuss pay and benefits. Do ask intelligent questions that will help you get the information you need to determine whether the career is right for you. For example, questions about the specific duties, responsibilities, special training required, travel requirements, and promotion possibilities show that you are interested in the job. Questions about the company's customers or clients, products, and plans for the future show that you are interested in the company's success.

It is not likely that you will be offered a job at the interview. Send a follow-up letter, thanking the employer for the interview and expressing your desire to meet

EXERCISE 14.5

PART I: FOLLOWING IS A LIST of typical questions an applicant might ask in an interview. Read the questions and decide which ones would make a positive impression on the interviewer and which ones would make a negative impression. Write *P* for positive or *N* for negative in the blank beside each question.

_____ 1. **What are the demographics of your customers?**

_____ 2. **Is this a 9-to-5 job?**

_____ 3. **Do you have a printed job description?**

_____ 4. **What opportunities for advancement does the company offer?**

_____ 5. **What would my benefits be?**

_____ 6. **How much paid vacation would I get?**

_____ 7. **Will you tell me about some additional products you sell?**

_____ 8. **Do you have any plans to produce new products?**

_____ 9. **Most companies provide for maternity leave or family leave. Do you?**

_____10. **Do you offer any special training for new employees?**

Part II: Read the classified section of your local newspaper. Find a job that interests you. Imagine that you have been invited to interview for this position. Write three questions that you think would be appropriate to ask about this job in an interview.

1. _____

2. _____

3. _____

again to discuss the job further. The purpose of this letter is to make a lasting impression, yet it is a final step that many job seekers forget. For example, if several applicants were interviewed, your thank you letter could earn you a callback for another interview. Keep your letter brief. Include these important points, which the sample letter in Figure 14.7 covers in under 100 words:

1. Your thanks for the interviewer's time

2. A positive statement about the company

3. Your interest in the job

4. Your potential value to the company or contribution you could make

5. Your desire for continued consideration

SAMPLE THANK YOU LETTER

FIGURE 14.7

1504 Lemon Tree Lane
Banyon, FL 32653
April 22, 2006

Ms. Dorsey Gray, Sales Director
Rayburn Chemicals, Inc.
866 Mercury Ave.
Banyon, FL 32653

Dear Ms. Gray:

I appreciate your taking time to interview me on Tuesday afternoon.
It was a pleasure to tour Rayburn Chemicals and learn about the
company's operations both in the United States and overseas.

As I said on Tuesday, I am seeking the position of regional sales
manager. What I would bring to Rayburn Chemicals is my marketing
background, sales experience, and enthusiasm for this work. Thank
you again for your consideration, and I hope to hear from you again.

Sincerely,

Leslie Duvall

Leslie Duvall

Thinking ahead about Career

Purpose and Instructions

A workplace focus in Chapter 14 is on building interpersonal skills. Use the knowledge you have gained from this chapter to solve work-related problems such as the one explained in the following case study. Read the case study on your own or with a partner and then answer the case questions.

Case Study

Roxanne is an adult learner who has returned to college now that her children are in high school. She has recently begun working part-time at a large company where she shares responsibilities with members of her work team. Whether in class or at work, Roxanne has difficulty expressing herself. She is intelligent and a good listener, but she hesitates to voice her opinion during discussions. Often she has a question that goes unanswered either because she will not ask it or because no one else raises it. Part of the problem is that her classmates are younger, and her team members are more experienced at their jobs. In both situations, she lacks confidence because she sees herself as "different." To succeed in college and at work, Roxanne knows that she needs to improve her interpersonal skills and would welcome advice.

Case Questions

1. What are Roxanne's strengths and weaknesses both in class and at work?

   _____

   _____

2. Based on what you have learned from *The Confident Student,* explain one strategy that would help Roxanne be more effective in situations that call for group participation or teamwork.

   _____

   _____

3. What action plan would you suggest that Roxanne follow to develop her interpersonal skills?

   _____

   _____

4. Access the Career Resource Center and select an article in the *Teamwork* section of *Skills for Your Future.* Identify the article you have selected and, based on the article, provide a suggestion you would give Roxanne for working through her problem.

   _____

   _____

Your *Reflections*

Reflect on what you have learned either from this chapter or from previous chapters that has helped you become a more confident student. Use the following questions to stimulate your thinking; then write your reflections. Include in your writing specific information from one or more chapters.

- In your opinion, what does the term "confident student" mean?

- What attitude, value, or skill makes you feel most confident about your future?

- Would you describe yourself as career-confident? Why or why not?

- What is one skill or attitude explained in this chapter, or any other chapter, that you would like to develop, and what can you begin doing today to make that happen?

_____

_____

_____

_____

_____

_____

_____

_____

_____

_____

_____

_____

_____

_____

_____

_____

_____

_____

_____

Chapter review

To review the chapter, reflect on the following confidence-building attitudes and skills. Complete **Concepts to Understand** by filling in the blanks with words or terms from the list provided. Then practice your new skills at every opportunity.

ATTITUDES TO DEVELOP
- flexibility
- optimism
- cooperation

SKILLS TO PRACTICE
- Researching and choosing a career
- Writing a résumé and cover letter
- Preparing for an interview

CONCEPTS TO UNDERSTAND

communication	cover letter	major	global	SCANS
interpersonal	interview	personal	résumé	ethics

To develop your career readiness, use the strategies explained in this chapter. Understand that today's new economy is technology-driven, (1) _____, and reactive to change. Attending college is one of the best things you can do to prepare yourself for work in the new economy because the highest-paying, fastest-growing jobs will go to college graduates.

To make the most of your college years, examine your career assumptions, and choose a (2) _____ or course of study. Select courses wisely, seek the help of an advisor or mentor, and follow a plan to reach your career goal. In addition, become proficient in the skills employers value most. According to (3) _____, a government report that identified essential workplace skills, the foundation on which all of the skills rest includes basic skills, thinking skills, and (4) _____ qualities. (5) _____ skills (reading, writing, listening, and speaking) are valued in almost any career. Workplace (6) _____ are also of great concern to employers.

Another important workplace competency is your ability to get along with others. For this you need strong (7) _____ skills, such as teamwork and leadership skills. Because most employers require you to apply technology to specific tasks, make use of your college years to develop or upgrade your computer skills.

As you move from college to the workplace, four career tools can help you get the position you seek. A (8) _____ introduces you to the employer. A (9) _____ lists your work experience and accomplishments. If an employer is impressed with your qualifications, you may get a call to schedule a visit. The (10) _____ allows the employer to meet you and observe how you handle yourself in person. Remember to follow up on the interview with a thank you letter.

Finally, be aware of the relationship between the academic skills you are learning now and the skills demanded of you in the workplace. From course work to extracurricular activities, everything you do in college can help you to develop transferable skills that will improve your life and career opportunities.

To access additional review exercises, go to
college.hmco.com/pic/KanarTCS6e.

Online Study Center
Review Exercise
ACE Self-Test

Online Study Center

Prepare for Class, Improve Your Grade, and ACE the Test. This chapter's *Student Achievement* resources include

Remembering Cultural Differences   Confidence Builder Web search   ACE Self-Test

To access these learning and study tools, go to **college.hmco.com/pic/KanarTCS6e.**

Photo Credits

Index